# Doctor WHO

## A History of the Universe

# Doctor WHO

# A History of the Universe

### Lance Parkin

Doctor WHO

First published in 1996 by
Doctor Who Books
an imprint of Virgin Publishing Ltd
332 Ladbroke Grove
London W10 5AH

Cover illustration by Alister Pearson

Designed & Typeset by Mark Stammers Design, London

Printed and bound in Great Britain by Cox & Wyman Ltd, Reading Berks

ISBN 0 426 20471 9

# Contents

'I loathe and detest people who produce these elaborate histories. As a writer you have to memorise this but it's gobbledygook.'

[Gerry Davis, story editor (1966–67), writer and co-creator of the Cybermen]

# Acknowledgements

Three people have been with this project since the start, offering wide-ranging advice and encouragement: Mark Jones, Cassandra May and Andrew Pixley. In return, I offer my special thanks – without them, this book would be very different, and not terribly good.

Thanks to the many other people who have offered information, comments, help, material, corrections or just said nice things. In alphabetical order, these are: Ben Aaronovitch, Nadir Ahmed, Keith Ansell, Richard Bignall, John Binns, Jon Blum, David Brunt, Andy Campbell, Andrew Cartmel, Shaun Chmara, Mark Clapham, Finn Clark, Paul Cornell, Jeremy Daw, Martin Day, Zoltan Dery, Jonathan Evans, Michael Evans, Martin Foster, Gary Gillatt, Donald and Patricia Gillikin, Craig Hinton, David Howe, Edward Hutchinson, Alison Jacobs, William Keith, Andy Lane, Paul Lee, Daniel O'Mahony, April McKennar, Adrian Middleton, John Molyneux, Kate Orman, David Pitcher, Marc Platt, Jon Preddle, Gareth Roberts, Trevor Ruppe, Gary Russell, Shannon Sullivan, Richard Thacker, Steve Traylen, Stephen James Walker, Peter Ware, Martin Wiggins, Gareth Wigmore and Guy Wigmore. I'm genuinely sorry if I missed anyone.

And to everyone on rec.arts.drwho, at Virgin Publishing, in Seventh Door, and members of the University of York Multimedia Society.

Thanks most of all to the innumerable people involved with the production of *Doctor Who*, in any and every form – past, present and future.

# Introduction

A total adherence to continuity has always been rather less important to the successive *Doctor Who* production teams than the main order of business: writing exciting stories, telling good jokes and scaring small children with big monsters. This, most people will tell you, is just how it should be.

It is, in any case, impossible to come up with a consistent view of history according to *Doctor Who*. Strictly speaking, the Brigadier retires three years before the first UNIT story is set. The Daleks and Atlantis are both utterly destroyed, once and for all, three times that we know about. Characters 'remember' scenes, sometimes entire stories, that they weren't present to witness.

'Continuity' has always been flexible, even on the fundamentals of the show's mythology: *The Dalek Invasion of Earth*, *The War Games*, *Genesis of the Daleks* and *The Deadly Assassin* all shamelessly threw out the show's established history in the name of a good story – and their version of events (the Daleks are galactic conquerors; the Doctor is a Time Lord who stole his TARDIS and fled his home planet; the Daleks were created by the Kaled scientist, Davros; Gallifreyan society is far from perfect and Time Lords are limited to twelve regenerations) is now taken to be the 'truth'. The previous versions (the Daleks are confined to one city; the Doctor invented the 'ship' and his granddaughter named it before their exile; the Daleks are descendants of the squat humanoid Dals, mutated by radiation; the Time Lords are godlike and immortal) have quietly been forgotten.

Many fans, though, like to think that *Doctor Who* stories fit into a consistent framework. They draw links between the separate stories and try to explain away the discrepancies that emerge. It is a process that, at its best, can spark the imaginations of other fans, shed a new perspective on a story and provide a fascinating insight into the show's attempts to chart the past and future.

Anyone attempting to fit together all the pieces of information we are given has to lay some ground rules and prioritise the information. If a line of dialogue from a story broadcast in 1983 flatly contradicts what was said in one from 1968 which is 'right'? Some people would suggest that the newer story 'got it wrong', that the later production team didn't pay enough attention to what came before. Others might argue that the new information 'corrects' what we were told before. In practice, most fans are inconsistent, choosing the facts that best support their arguments or preferences. *The Discontinuity Guide* has some very healthy advice regarding continuity: 'Take what you want and ignore what you don't. Future continuity cops will just have to adapt to your version'.

This is 'A History of the Universe', not the 'definitive' or 'official' version. *Doctor Who* has had hundreds of creators, all pulling in slightly different directions, all with their own vision of what *Doctor Who* was about. Without that diversity, the *Doctor Who* universe would no doubt be more internally consistent, but it would certainly be a much smaller and less interesting place. Nowadays, fans are writing the New and Missing Adventures, contributing to and editing Marvel's *Doctor Who Magazine*, and compiling reference books for Virgin. *Doctor Who* fans have become part of the creative process. Ultimately, we control the heritage of the show that we love. I hope people will enjoy this book, and I know that they will challenge it.

## Basic Principles

For the purposes of this book I work from the following assumptions:

● Every *Doctor Who* story takes place in the same universe, unless explicitly stated, and nothing (short of a being with godlike powers) can significantly change the course of history within that universe. The Mars attacked by the Fendahl is the Mars of the Ice Warriors.

● I have noted where each date I have assigned comes from: usually it is from dialogue (in which case I quote it), but often it comes from behind-the-scenes sources, such as scripts, publicity material and the like. It is up to the individual reader whether a date from a BBC press release or draft script is as 'valid' as one given on-screen.

● In many cases, no date was ever given for a story – here, I pick a year and explain my reasons. Often I will assign a date that is consistent with information given in other stories. (So, I suggest that the Cyber-War mentioned in *Revenge Of The Cybermen* must take place after *The Tomb of the Cybermen*, and probably after *Earthshock* because of what is said in those other stories.) These dates are marked as arbitrary and the reasoning behind them is explained in the footnotes.

● Where a date isn't established on-screen I have also included the dates suggested by others who have compiled timelines or listed dates given in the series (principally David Banks, Malcolm Hulke and Terrance Dicks, Richard Landen, Jean-Marc Lofficier, and John Peel). Several similar works to this have been attempted, and I have listed the most important in the bibliography at the end of this section.

● I have assumed that historical events take place at the same time and for the same reasons as they did in 'real history', unless specifically contradicted by the television series.

● I assume that the Doctor is telling the truth about meeting historical figures, and that his historical analysis is correct. It has, however, been established that the Doctor is fallible and/or an incorrigible name-dropper.

● My version of Earth's future history is generally one of steady progress, and as such I tend to lump together stories featuring similar themes and concepts, say, intergalactic travel, isolated colonies, humanoid robots and so on. If the technology, transportation or weaponry seen in story A is more advanced than in story B, then I suggest that story A is set in the future of story B. I also assume that throughout the centuries humans age at the same rate, their life spans don't alter too dramatically, etc. – a 'lifetime' in the year 4000 is still about 100 years.

● All dates, again unless specifically stated otherwise, work from our Gregorian calendar, and all are 'AD'. It is assumed that the system of Leap Years will remain the same in the future. For convenience, all documents use our system of dating, even those of alien civilisations. The 'present' of the narrative is now, the late twentieth century, so if an event happened 'two hundred years ago' it happened in the late eighteenth century. On a number of occasions we are told that a specific date takes place on the wrong day: in *The War Machines*, July 16th 1966 is a Monday, really it was a Saturday.

● I assume that a 'year' is an Earth year of 365 days, even when an alien is speaking, unless this is specifically contradicted. This also applies to terms such as 'Space Year' (*Genesis of the Daleks*), 'light year' (which is used as a unit of time in *The Savages* and possibly *Terror of the Autons*) and 'cycle' (e.g. *Zamper*).

● If an event is said to take place 'fifty years ago' I take it to mean exactly fifty years ago, unless a more precise date is given elsewhere or it refers to a known historical event. If an event occurs in the distant past or the far future, I tend to round up: 'Image of the Fendahl' is set in about 1977; the Fifth Planet was destroyed 'twelve million years' before. I say this happened in 12,000,000 BC, not 11,998,023 BC. When an event takes place an undefined number of 'centuries', 'millennia' or 'millions of years' before or after a story, I arbitrarily set a date. A 'generation', as per the Doctor's definition in *Four to Doomsday* is assumed to be twenty-five years. A 'couple' of years is always two years, a 'few' is generally three to five, 'several' six to nine, 'many' more than ten, with 'some' taken to be an arbitrary or unknown number. A 'billion' is generally the American and modern British unit (a thousand million) rather than the old British definition (a million million).

● If a story takes place in a given century or era, I arbitrarily choose a date, usually the anniversary of the story's transmission (e.g. *The Sensorites* takes place in the 'twenty-eighth century' – I choose 2764 because the story was first shown in *1964*).

# The Stories

This book restricts itself to events described in the BBC television series *Doctor Who* and Virgin's New and Missing Adventures. This is not an attempt to enter the debate about the *Doctor Who* 'canon', it is simply an attempt to limit the length and scale of this book. Any text which is a direct quotation from a book or TV episode is placed in double rather than single quotation marks. There are three types of information in this book, and these are distinguished by three different typefaces:

**1: The Television Series** Included are the episodes and on-screen credits of the BBC television series *Doctor Who* as first broadcast; *K9 and Company*; and extended or unbroadcast versions that have since been commercially released or broadcast anywhere in the world – there are few cases of 'extended' material contradicting what was said in the original.

Priority is given to sources closest to the finished product or the production team of the time the story was made. In descending order of authority are the following: the programme as broadcast; the *Radio Times* and other contemporary BBC publicity material (which was often written by the producer or script editor); the camera script; the novelisation of a story by the original author or an author working closely from the camera script; contemporary interviews with members of the production team; televised trailers; rehearsal and draft scripts; novelisations by people other than the original author; storylines and writers' guides (which often contradict on-screen information); interviews with members of the production team after the story was broadcast; and finally any other material, such as fan speculation.

I have not included information from unreleased material that exists (for example extended footage from *The Claws of Axos, Invasion of the Dinosaurs, Kinda, Vengeance on Varos, Ghost Light*) or that no longer exists (for example *Terror of the Autons, Terror of the Zygons, The Hand of Fear*); neither is the first version of *An Unearthly Child* to be filmed (the so-called 'pilot episode') or 'in-character' appearances by the Doctor on other programmes (e.g. on *Animal Magic, Children in Need, Blue Peter* etc.).

**2: The New and Missing Adventures** This book encompasses the New and Missing Adventures that have been released to date, up to and including *Happy Endings* and *The Sands of Time*. I have tried not to contradict anything in the upcoming books that have been commissioned at time of going to press. The golden rule is that the television series takes priority over what is said in the NA/MAs, and where a detail or reference given in one of the books appears to contradict what was established on television, I have noted as much and attempted to rationalise the 'mistake' away.

The New and Missing Adventures have built up a broadly consistent 'future history' of the universe. This was, in part, based on the 'History of Mankind' in Jean-Marc Lofficier's *The Terrestrial Index*, which mixes information from the series with facts from the novelisations and the author's own speculation. Many authors, though, have contradicted or ignored Lofficier's version of events. For the purposes of this book, *The Terrestrial Index* is non-canonical.

Useful information appears in Writers' Guides, Discussion Documents and the authors' original submissions and storylines. Where possible, I have referred to this material.

I haven't included information from the Decalogs, *Who Killed Kennedy* or the 'Preludes' to the New Adventures that appeared in *Doctor Who Magazine*.

**3: Speculation** *Inevitably, I have had to include some of my own theories to try and explain away continuity clashes or historical details. I have attempted to keep speculation to a minimum, though, and it is clearly marked as such.*

In the text of the book, the following marker appears to indicate when the action of specific stories take place:

## c 1996 – THE ADJECTIVE OF NOUN

The title is exactly as it appeared on-screen or on the cover of the novel. For the Hartnell stories without an overall title given on-screen, I have used the names that were used by the production team at the time the story was broadcast.

The letter before the date, the 'code', indicates how accurately we know the date. If there is no code, then precisely that date is established in the story itself (e.g. *The Daleks' Master Plan* is set in "4000"). 'c' means that the story is set circa that year (e.g. *The Dalek Invasion of Earth* is set "c 2167"). '?' indicates a guess, and my reasons are given in the footnotes (e.g. we don't know what year *Destiny of the Daleks* is set, but it must be "centuries" after *The Dalek Master Plan*, so I set it '? 4500'. '&' means that the story is dated relative to another (e.g. we know that *Resurrection of the Daleks* is set "ninety years" after *Destiny of the Daleks*, so I set *Resurrection of the Daleks* in '& 4590'). 'u' means that the story featured UNIT – [see also Appendix One 'UNIT Dating']. '=' indicates that we are told that the action takes place in a parallel universe or divergent timestream.

# Bibliography

*The Making of Doctor Who* (Malcolm Hulke and Terrance Dicks: first edition Piccolo/Pan Books, April 1972; second edition Target/Tandem Books, November 1976):
The earliest source of dates, often direct from BBC material.

*Doctor Who Radio Times Special* (ed. David Driver, Jack Lundin: BBC, November 1973):
The tenth anniversary *Radio Times* special, including many previously unpublished story details – this magazine perpetuated the 'incorrect' story titles, used by many fans.

*The Doctor Who Programme Guide* (Jean-Marc Lofficier: first edition [2 vols] WH Allen, May 1981; second edition [2 Vols] Target/WH Allen, October 1981 – second edition has separate volume titles 'The Programmes' and 'What's What and Who's Who'); *Doctor Who – The Programme Guide* (Jean-Marc Lofficier: third edition Target/WH Allen, December 1989); *Doctor Who – The Terrestrial Index* (Jean-Marc Lofficier: Target/Virgin Publishing, November 1991); *Doctor Who – The Universal Databank* (Jean-Marc Lofficier: Doctor Who Books/Virgin Publishing, November 1992); *Doctor Who Programme Guide* (Jean-Marc Lofficier: fourth edition Doctor Who Books/Virgin Publishing, June 1994)
The standard reference work, with most fans owning a copy of at least one of these books. A good starting point.

*Doctor Who Monthly* (Marvel Comics Ltd.)
Richard Landen wrote a series of pseudohistories in the twentieth anniversary year: Issues 75–83 (April 1983 – December 1983) featured 'The TARDIS Logs', a list of TARDIS landings riddled with annoying little errors; Issue 77 had a more concise list, 'Travels with the Doctor', and a good attempt at 'A History of the Daleks'; 'A History of the Cybermen' (Issue 83, with Michael Daniels) and 'Shades of Piccolo' (UNIT history, Issue 80) were both sensible, simple treatments of potential minefields.

*The Doctor Who Role-Playing Game* (FASA Corporation [US], 1985; Supplements published 1985–6)
Various dates, including many invented for the purposes of the game.

*Doctor Who* (Marvel Comics Group [US])
A series of pseudohistories written by Patrick Daniel O'Neill, covering 'A Probable History of the Daleks' (Issue 9, June 1985), 'A Probable History of the Cybermen' (Issue 10, July 1985) and 'The Master Log' Parts I and II (Issues 14 and 15, November and December 1985): enthu-

siastic but ill-researched.

*The Doctor Who File* (Peter Haining: WH Allen, September 1986) – Pages 223 to 228 contain a table listing the Doctor's adventures and where and when they took place.

*The Official Doctor Who & the Daleks Book* (John Peel & Terry Nation: St Martin's Press [US], April 1989)
Dalek History, including various other sources (comic strips etc). Approved by Terry Nation.

*In-Vision 11: UNIT Special* (CMS, December 1988)
Includes 'Down to Earth', a history of UNIT by Garry Bradbury. Each issue of *In-Vision* is a comprehensive analysis of an individual story, and the magazine is an indispensable reference work.

*Doctor Who – Cybermen* (David Banks, with Andrew Skilleter, Adrian Rigelsford and Jan Vincent-Rudzki: Who Dares, November 1988; Virgin Publishing, September 1990)
Comprehensive, if elaborate, history of the Cybermen. The first, and still best, reference book of its kind.

*Doctor Who Magazine* (Marvel Comics Ltd)
Issue 174, *The TARDIS Special* (12 June 1991) features 'Journeys' by Andrew Pixley, a superbly researched list of every landing made by the TARDIS. Issue 176 (7 August 1991) contains an addendum.

*The Gallifrey Chronicles* (John Peel: Doctor Who Books/Virgin Publishing, October 1991)
Gallifreyan history and other information.

*Doctor Who Magazine Winter Special 1991 – UNIT Exposed* (Marvel Comics Ltd, 28 November 1991)
Includes an excellent UNIT chronology by John Freeman and Gary Russell, as well as 'UNIT Exposed' by Andrew Dylan.

*The Doctor Who Writers' Guide* (Peter Darvill-Evans, Rebecca Levene & Andy Bodle: Virgin Publishing, 1991–date)
The guidelines for prospective authors of New and Missing Adventures. Includes notes on Gallifreyan history.

*Apocrypha* (Adrian Middleton: 1993–95). Fan-published chronology drawing together everything the author can get his hands on: comic strips, novelisations, role-playing scenarios and so on.

*The Discontinuity Guide* (Paul Cornell, Martin Day and Keith Topping: Virgin Publishing, May 1994)
Survey of the series' continuity and continuity mistakes. Many interesting fan theories, all marked as such.

Section One
Prehistory

## TIMELINE: Event One to 2000 BC

1 [see also 'THE GREAT OLD ONES' page 13]. The Doctor claims at the end of *Ghost Light* that Light is "an evil older than time itself". From the context of the story this would seem to mean that Light arrived on Earth before human history started, and not that he existed before the creation of the universe but perhaps he is also a Great Old One.

2 The Doctor reads *The Origins of the Universe* in *Destiny of the Daleks*, and remarks that the author "got it wrong on the first line. Why didn't he ask someone who saw it happen?" The author in question is 'Oolon Caluphid', whose works were also cited in *The Hitch-Hikers' Guide to the Galaxy* (where his surname was spelt 'Coluphid'), written by then-*Doctor Who* script editor Douglas Adams. The term "Event One" is first used in *Castrovalva* to mean the creation of "the galaxy", but in *Terminus* the Doctor talks of "the biggest explosion in history: Event One", which he confirms is "the Big Bang" that "created the universe".

3 This appears on the console screen in *Castrovalva*.

4 THE AGE OF THE UNIVERSE – The date of the creation of the universe is not clearly established on-screen, although we are told it took place "billions of years" before *Terminus*. Modern scientific consensus is that the universe is fifteen billion years old, and a couple of the New Adventures,

Before our universe, another existed, with different physical laws. This universe had its own Time Lords, and as their universe reached the point of collapse, they shunted themselves into a parallel universe and discovered that they now possessed almost infinite power. [1]

> 'The universe was created fifteen billion years ago, in a huge explosion known as the Big Bang. As this was the very first thing to happen, scientists sometimes call it "Event One".'
> [*The Origins of the Universe*, Oolon Caluphid] [2]

> "Among the adherents of Scientific Mythology [q.v.] the element (Hydrogen) is widely believed to be the basic constituent out of which the Galaxy was first formed [see EVENT ONE] and evidence in support of this hypothesis includes its supposed appearance in spectroscopic analysis of massive star bodies"
> [The TARDIS Information File] [3]

**The Time Lords of Gallifrey have monitored the Big Bang, and have precisely determined the date of Event One as 13,500,017,903 BC. [4]**

One Time Lord claims to have been an eye-witness at the origins of the universe:

> "The dawn of time. The beginning of all beginnings. Two forces only: Good and Evil. Then chaos. Time is born: matter, space. The universe cries out like a newborn. The forces shatter as the Universe explodes outwards. Only echoes remain, and yet somehow, somehow the evil force survives. An intelligence. Pure evil."

The evil force retained its sentience and its influence spread throughout time and space becoming the entity that the Vikings would call Fenric. The fate of the good force is a mystery. [5]

The Urbankan Monarch believed that if his ship could travel faster than light then it would move backwards in time to the Big Bang and beyond. He was obsessed with solving "the riddle of the universe". Monarch believed that he was God and that he would meet himself at the creation of the universe. [6]

One ship managed to travel to the dawn of creation, albeit by accident. Terminus was a vast spaceship built by an infinitely advanced ancient race capable of time travel. It developed a fault, and the pilot was forced to eject some of its unstable fuel into the void, before making a timejump. The explosion that resulted was the Big Bang, and Terminus was thrown billions of years into the future, where it came to settle in the exact centre of the universe. [7]

The first few chaotic microseconds of the universe saw extreme temperatures and the forging of bizarre elements that would not be able to exist later. This was the Leptonic Era, and one of the bizarre elements was Helium 2, which the Rani would later attempt to recreate on Lakertya. *Time and Space as we understand them began as these bizarre elements reacted with each other and cooled.* [8]

A fraction of a second after Event One, the explosion became a vast outrush of simple hydrogen, the basic building block of the universe. The Master attempted to kill the newly-regenerated Fifth Doctor by sending him backwards in time to this point. Travelling backwards it appeared to be a Hydrogen Inrush. [9]

*Matter coalesced, elements formed.*

**The Time Lords from the pre-universe entered our universe, and discovered that they had undreamt of powers. They became the Great Old Ones: Hastur the Unspeakable became Fenric; Yog-Sothoth, also known as the Intelligence, began billennia of conquests; The Lloigor, or Animus, dominated Vortis; Shub-Niggurath conquered Polymos and colonised it with her offspring, the Nestene Consciousness; Dagon was worshipped by the Sea Devils. Other Great Old Ones included Cthulu, Nyarlathotep and the Gods of Ragnarok. Across the universe, the earliest civilisations worshipped the Great Old Ones. [10]**

Forces such as the Guardians, the Mandragora Helix and the grey man's race sprang into being. The Black Guardian placed the Shadow at the beginning of eternity, waiting for the Key to Time. **Over the first few billions of years, the first stars were born. Planets and galaxies formed.** On many of these worlds, sugars, proteins and amino acids combined to become primor-

*Timewyrm: Apocalypse* (p1) and *Falls the Shadow* (p251), concur with this date. In *Transit* (set c. 2109), the Doctor drunkenly celebrates the universe's 13,500,020,012th birthday.

5 This is the Doctor's speech from *The Curse of Fenric*. It perhaps supports his claim in *Destiny of the Daleks* that he was present to witness the origins of the universe.

6 *Four to Doomsday.*

7 *Terminus.*

8 *Time and the Rani.*

9 *Castrovalva.*

10 THE GREAT OLD ONES – The novels *All-Consuming Fire* and *Millennial Rites* suggest that many of the godlike beings seen in *Doctor Who* have a common origin. The Great Old Ones were a pantheon of ancient, incomprehensible forces created by horror writer H P Lovecraft. The first appearance of the Great Old Ones in the books is the New adventure *White Darkness*, where we learn that there are legends of them on many planets, and that they influence their followers mentally from afar rather than conquering physically. In *All-Consuming Fire* we learn that the Old One fought in that book was Cthulu, perhaps Lovecraft's best known creation.

Other entities we have seen that are explicitly referred to as Great Old Ones are Fenric (*The Curse of Fenric*), the

Intelligence (*The Abominable Snowmen, The Web of Fear*, and the novels *Millennial Rites* and *Downtime*), the Animus (*The Web Planet*), the Nestene Consciousness (*Spearhead from Space*, and *Terror of the Autons*) and the Gods of Ragnarok (*The Greatest Show in the Galaxy*). In *All-Consuming Fire* the Doctor and Sherlock Holmes come up against an entity pretending to be another of Lovecraft's creations, Azathoth.

The Doctor knows a great deal about the Great Old Ones and their origins...

11 The Guardians were first seen in *The Ribos Operation*. In *The Armageddon Factor*, the Shadow claims to have "waited since eternity began" for the Key to Time. The Mandragora Helix appears in *The Masque of Mandragora*, and the grey man in *Falls the Shadow*. The prologue to *Timewyrm: Apocalypse* is a brief history of the formation of the universe. Primordial soup appears in *City of Death* and *Ghost Light* and the quotation comes from the second of those stories.

12 *Falls the Shadow*.

13 The Dæmons appear in the story of that name. The Great Vampires feature in *State of Decay* (in which it is revealed that the folklore sections of K9's databank contain vampire legends from seventeen worlds) as well as its two sequels, the novels *Blood Harvest* and *Goth Opera*. Light is the force behind *Ghost Light*.

dial soup, "the most precious substance in the Universe, from which all life springs". Hundreds of millions of years later, the first civilisations began to rise and fall. [11]

Thirty thousand million light years from our solar system, the first civilisation came into being. They were humanoid, and developed for ten thousand years, before wiping themselves out in a bacteriological war. The grey man and his race saw all this, and he constructed the Cathedral, a machine "designed to alter the structure of reality". It formed ambiguities and chaotic forces that ran throughout the universe, breaking down certainty. Its interface with physical reality was the Metahedron, a device that moved from world to world every eighty thousand years, remaining hidden. [12]

'What remains of the ancient races suggests awesome power; many had great psychic ability and powers to transmute matter that were almost indistinguishable from magic. Immortal beings such as the Dæmons of Damos, the Great Vampires and Light were worshipped as gods by more primitive races, and all considered it their right to intervene in the development of whole planets – and to destroy these worlds if they failed to match up to their expectations. The legends and race memories of many planets contain traces of these ancient civilisations. Seventeen known worlds, including Earth, have stories of vampires. On Earth, since man began, horns have been a symbol of power, and beings of light have been worshipped.'

[*Extinct Civilisations*, Woris Bossard][13]

Nothing lasts forever, though, and these great races gradually disappeared from the universe. New societies sprang up to replace them, and soon the universe was teeming with life. In the late twentieth century, the Institute of Space Studies at Baltimore estimated that there were over five hundred planets capable of supporting life in Earth's section of the galaxy alone. [14]

We know of millions of other civilisations in the universe that never had any contact with Earth: the planet Marinus – a planet of acid seas – the inhabitants of which built a machine Conscience that kept the planet in peace for seven hundred

years, before the warlike Voord managed to break its influence
– thirteen hundred years after that, the Voord's power was
finally broken; the once-mighty Morok Empire, with a space
museum on Xeros demonstrating their past glories, including
an attack on Skaro; the planet Aridius, formerly a world of oceans,
now a desert; the planets of Galaxy 4, with the planets of the
Rills and the Drahvins; the planet Dulkis, a peaceful world invaded by the Dominators, that had abandoned nuclear weapons 172 years before in the time of Olin; the planet of the
Gonds, ruled for thousands of years by the Krotons; the planet
Inter Minor in the Acteon Group, which became insular and
xenophobic for thousands of years following a space plague; the
twin planets Atrios and Zeos in the Helical Galaxy, which fought
a nuclear war for five years; the planet Chloris, rich in vegetation, but with no mineral wealth; for fifteen years the evil Lady
Adrastra kept the Tythonian Erato prisoner; the Skonnan Empire, which stretched over one hundred star systems, including
that of Aneth, until a civil war on the planet wiped out everyone
on Skonnos except the military; the planet Manussa, for three
hundred years the home of the Sumaran Empire, until the Mara
was banished for five hundred years; and Lakertya, the home of
an indolent race of lizard people who were invaded by the Rani
and her army of Tetraps. The Psychic Circus, billed as "The Greatest Show in the Galaxy" probably travelled through the Milky
Way. The Circus visited Marpesia, Othrys, the Grand Pagoda
on Cinethon, and the Boriatic Wastes. It ended up on Segonax
in the Southern Nebula. **Mightiest of all is the People, trillions
of people living on a Dyson Sphere, so advanced that they
have signed a non-aggression pact with the Time Lords themselves.** [15]

[Voldek's Theory: 'Life in the universe is infinitely variable.'
*The Encyclopaedia of Cosmic Science*]

'While, as Voldek suggested, there is a great diversity of
life throughout the cosmos, a great many races closely resemble humans, and as one scientist has noted "it is strange
how the same life patterns occur throughout the universe".

**14** *Spearhead from Space.*

**15** Some stories, or parts of
stories, are impossible to place
within this chronology as they
contain no reference point to
Earth history: *Inside the
Spaceship* (which is based
entirely within the TARDIS); *The
Keys of Marinus*; *The Space
Museum*; *The Chase* (the
sequence set on Aridius);
*Galaxy 4*; *The Daleks' Master
Plan* (the sequences set on
Tigus and the Ice Planet); *The
Celestial Toymaker* (which is set
in a timeless dimension); *The
Dominators*; *The Mind Robber*
(which is set in a timeless
dimension); *The Krotons*;
*Carnival of Monsters*; *The
Ribos Operation* (The sequence
with the Guardian takes place
in a timeless void. In a
document dated 30 November
1976, Graham Williams
suggested that the Guardians
lived in 'The Centre of Time',
and this scene may take place
there); *The Armageddon Factor*;
*The Creature from the Pit*; *The
Horns of Nimon*; *Full Circle*,
*State of Decay*, *Warriors' Gate*
(all of which take place in the
universe of E-Space);
*Castrovalva*; Snakedance;
*Enlightenment* (which does
take place in our solar system,
at an unspecified point); *The
Five Doctors* (the sequences in
which the first Doctor is
kidnapped and the fifth Doctor
is on the Eye of Orion are
impossible to date clearly);
*Time and the Rani* (as the Rani
wants to take Earth "back" to
the Cretaceous Era it is
reasonable to assume that the

story takes place after that time); *The Greatest Show in the Galaxy* and the New Adventures *Sky Pirates!* and *The Also People*.

16 *Carnival of Monsters*. The Lurman Vorg refers to Voldek and points out that humans (or "Tellurians", as we are called here and in *The Two Doctors*) resemble the people of Inter Minor.

17 The Doctor states that Gallifrey is the oldest civilisation in the universe in *The Trial of a Time Lord*. In *Genesis of the Daleks* the Time Lord messenger reminds the Doctor of their race's mastery of transmat technology. Gallifrey's impact on the evolutionary development of the universe is revealed in *Lucifer Rising* (p320-1).

18 THE ETERNAL WAR – [see also 'The Great Old Ones' page 13] On-screen, we learn that the Time Lords fought campaigns against the Great Vampires (*State of Decay*) and that they protected other races from invaders (*The Hand of Fear*). In the New Adventures, particularly *Cat's Cradle: Time's Crucible* and *The Pit*, this was the Eternal War in which the forces of superstition and magic were defeated by the forces of rationality and science.

Scientists in the Acteon Group noticed the basic similarity between Tellurians, Lurmans and the people of Inter Minor, and the inhabitants of hundreds of worlds from Aneth to Zanak. In many cases, this similarity is purely superficial: the internal structure of a Kaled bears no resemblance to a Terran human, while the inhabitants of Dulkis have three hearts.

The bipedal, binocular humanoid form, however, has evolved in isolation throughout the universe. Nothing links the Kraals and the Voord, the Mandrels and the Kastrians, or the Draconians and the Sea Devils except their basic size and form. Of course there are many races who do not fit this template, such as the Tythonians, the Rills and the Macra, but it is still an intriguing mystery that so many thousands of races have evolved into such a similar form.'

[*Flora and Fauna of the Universe*, Professor Thripstead][16]

The first humanoid civilisation in the universe evolved on Gallifrey, mastering the principles of transmat technology while the universe was half its present size, and becoming the first race to master Time. **As the Gallifreyans were the first sentient race to evolve, they established a morphic field for humanoids, making it more probable that races evolving later would also be bipedal and binocular. Non-humanoid races only evolved in environments that would be hostile to humanoids.** The Time Lords explored space and time, making contact with many worlds and becoming legends on many others. Crucially, though, the Time Lords recognised the dangers of intervention, and withdrew from the universe. They remained content to observe, but monitored the universe to try to prevent other, less principled races from discovering the secrets of time travel. *Because they can travel throughout time and space, it is difficult to place events on Gallifrey relative to the rest of the universe.* There are legends that the Time Lords existed far in the past; there is some evidence that they live in the present; some say they come from the future. [17]

The origins of the Time Lords are obscure, but in the distant past they fought the Eternal War against the Great Old Ones and other invaders from other universes, beating them back. Magic and chaos were supplanted by science and order. [18]

The Key to Time was created by the Guardians to maintain the balance between order and chaos. It was composed of six segments that were scattered throughout time and space to prevent it falling into the wrong hands. [19]

While the Earth was still forming, the Time Lords were in negotiations with the Tranmetgurans, trying to organise a planetary government and end the war that was ravaging the planet. The Hoothi – a fungoid group-mind that lived off dead matter and farmed entire sentient species – attacked Tranmetgura, introducing their dead soldiers into the battle. Full-scale war broke out, and two-thirds of the population were killed. The Hoothi harvested the dead, taking them aboard their silent gas dirigibles. When the Time Lords sent an ambassador to the Hoothi worlds, the Hoothi used him as a host and attempted to conquer Gallifrey. The Time Lords launched a counterattack, forcing the Hoothi to flee into hyperspace. The Hoothi vanished from the universe. [20]

## c 3,000,000,000 BC – VENUSIAN LULLABY [21]

'The Venusians were an advanced race – surprisingly so since all metals were poisonous to them with the exception of gold, platinum and titanium. Their cities were crude, the buildings in cities such as Cracdhalltar and Bikugih resembling soap-bubbles made from mud and crude stone, but the civilisation lasted for three million years. From measuring the day, which got steadily longer, the Venusians calculated that their planet was dying, and for tens of thousands of years most were resigned to their fate. Most of the Venusian animal species had become extinct: the shanghorn, the klak-kluk and the pattifangs. Death Inspectors killed Venusians who had outlived their useful lives to conserve resources. Anti-Acceptancer factions such as the Rocketeers, the Below the Sun Believers, the Magnetologists, the Water-Breathers, the Volcano People and the Cave-Makers believed that they could escape their fate, but they were seen as cranks by the majority. They were visited by the Sou(ou)shi, a race that offered the Venusians a place within their spacecraft. The Sou(ou)shi were vampires, and

19 *The Ribos Operation*.

20 *Love and War*. The Hoothi are first mentioned in *The Brain of Morbius*.

21 Dating *Venusian Lullaby* – The Doctor tells Ian and Barbara that they have travelled back "oh, about three billion years I should think" (p18).

22 "A thousand million years" before *Spearhead from Space*. "A billion years" before *The Caves of Androzani*.

23 Dating *City of Death* – Scaroth states that his ship came to Earth "four hundred million years ago". *The Terrestrial Index* points out that life on Earth really began three and a half billion years ago.

24 SCAROTH OF THE JAGAROTH – All twelve splinters of Scaroth are accounted for in *City of Death*, assuming that none of them live for more than a century: one demonstrates "the true use of fire", a second gives mankind the wheel, a third "caused the pyramids to be built" as an Egyptian pharoah or god, a fourth "the heavens to be mapped", the fifth is an Ancient Greek, the sixth is an unnamed Roman emperor, the seventh is a crusader, the eighth possibly gives mankind the printing press, the ninth is Tancredi, the tenth is an Elizabethan nobleman, the eleventh lives at the time of Louis XV, and the twelfth is Carlos Scarlioni.

merely wanted to consume the entire Venusian race as they had the Aveletians and the Signortiyu. The Venusians discovered this, and destroyed the Sou(ou)shi craft. The debris from the ship entered the Venusian atmosphere, blocking some of the sun's rays, lowering the temperature of the planet. This prolonged the Venusians' existence for another one hundred generations.'

[*Extinct Civilisations*, Woris Bossard]

The consciousness of the Sou(ou)shi survived and travelled to primeval Earth.

The Nestene, a race of pure energy, began their conquests a thousand million years ago. Around this time, the last seas dried up on Androzani Minor in the Sirius system. [22]

## c 400,000,000 BC – CITY OF DEATH [23]

Four hundred million years ago, one advanced humanoid race, the callous Jagaroth, wiped themselves out in a huge war. The last of the Jagaroth limped to primeval Earth in an advanced spaceship. The pilot of the ship, Scaroth, attempted to take his ship to power three – warp thrust – too close to the Earth's surface and the spacecraft detonated over what would later become the Atlantic Ocean. Scaroth was splintered into twelve fragments and materialised at various points in human history. He would influence humanity's development for tens of thousands of years, culminating in the building of a time machine in the late twentieth century. [24]

Earth at this time was a barren volcanic world, but it had already produced Primordial Soup, and the anti-matter explosion acted as a catalyst. Life on Earth began.

*Life evolved much as palaeontologists and geologists think that it did.*

In the 1970s, Dr Quinn discovered a colony of reptile people living below Wenley Moor in Derbyshire. They were the remnants of an advanced lost civilisation, and they had spent many millions of years in hibernation. Quinn believed that they came from the Silurian Period, and had a globe showing Earth as it was two hundred million years ago. *Quinn was mistaken: in the Silurian Period life on Earth was limited to coral reefs, early land plants and jawless fish. He assumed that the Reptile People came from the same period that the Derbyshire limestone was formed.* It would be another thirty-five million years before even the most primitive dinosaurs evolved, and in actuality the Reptile People came from the Eocene Period, over a hundred and fifty million years after Quinn believed. [25]

## c 150,000,000 BC – THE HAND OF FEAR [26]

'KASTRIA – A cold, inhospitable planet, dead for one hundred and fifty million years. The Kastrian scientist Eldrad built spacial barriers to keep out the solar winds that ravaged the planet; he devised a crystalline silicone form for the race and built machines to replenish the earth and the atmosphere. Once this was done he threatened to usurp the King, Rokon. The Kastrians did not share Eldrad's dreams of galactic conquest, and so Eldrad destroyed the barriers. The Kastrians sentenced Eldrad to death. As killing a silicon lifeform is almost impossible, they constructed an obliteration module and sent it out into space, beyond all solar systems.'

[*Bartholomew's Planetary Gazetteer*, Volume XI]

The module was detonated early at nineteen spans, while there was still a one in three million chance that Eldrad might survive. King Rokon left a recording for Eldrad, should he return:

"Traitor! You think you have victory in your grasp, but I, Rokon, tell you that you have won nothing but defeat. After the premature detonation of the module, we knew there was a remote possibility that one day you would return. But let me tell you, after you destroyed the barriers, after we knew for certain that life on the surface was finished and

**25** *Doctor Who and the Silurians*. It is repeatedly stated that the Reptile People come from the Silurian Period. The production team received a number of letters pointing out that this contradicts the fossil evidence. In *The Sea Devils*, the Doctor has an opportunity to correct the mistake [see also A COMPLETE MISNOMER page 22]. In *Earthshock*, the Doctor states that the dinosaurs existed for "a hundred million years or so" and died out "sixty-five million years ago". The Silurian Period really took place between 436 and 408 million years ago, which according to *City of Death* was before life on Earth began.

**26** Dating *The Hand of Fear* – The Doctor identifies the rock in which Eldrad's hand was discovered, and twice tells Eldrad that he has been away from Kastria for "a hundred and fifty million years".

27 *Invasion of the Dinosaurs.*

28 Dating *Time-Flight* – The Doctor informs the flight crew of the second Concorde that they have landed at Heathrow "one hundred and forty million years ago". He states, correctly, that this is the "Jurassic" Era, but then suggests that they "can't be far off from the Pleistocene Era", which actually took place a mere 1.8 million to ten thousand years ago.

29 These may or may not be the same Vardans (or Vardons) seen in *The Invasion of Time* and the New Adventure *No Future.* In *Planet of Fire*, Turlough reveals that there is a Trion agent posing as an "agrarian commissioner on Verdon".

the alternative was a miserable subterranean existence, the Kastrian race chose final oblivion. And because they feared you might return to wage eternal war throughout the galaxy, they elected also to destroy the race banks. So now you are king, as was your wish. I salute you from the dead. Hail Eldrad – King of Nothing!"

Eldrad's hand eventually reached Earth in the Jurassic Period, where it became buried in a stratum of Blackstone Dolomite.

Whitaker kidnapped various dinosaurs from this time using his Timescoop. [27]

## 140,000,000 BC – TIME-FLIGHT [28]

Around one hundred and forty million years ago, the planet Xeraphas, the home of the Xeraphin, a legendary race with immense mental powers, was rendered uninhabitable when it was caught in the Vardon–Kosnax War. [29] The surviving Xeraphin came to Earth, hoping to colonise the planet, but they suffered from radiation sickness. They abandoned their physical forms, and became a psychic gestalt of bioplasmic energy until they were able to regenerate. The Master became trapped on Earth at this point when his TARDIS malfunctioned. He attempted to harness the power of the Xeraphin Consciousness. Building a Time-Contour Generator, the Master kidnapped a Concorde from the 1980s, and used the passengers as slaves to try to penetrate the Xeraphin citadel. He was defeated when the Doctor followed him back through time and broke their conditioning.

About one hundred and thirty million years ago, the Plesiosaurus became extinct. Before this, an example of the species had been kidnapped by the owner of a Miniscope. Miniscopes were built from molecular-bonded disillion by the Eternity Perpetual Company, and would literally last forever – as a result, the company went bankrupt, because everyone who wanted a Miniscope soon had one that would never need replacing. Concerned that many Miniscopes contained sentient specimens, the Doctor successfully lobbied the High Council of the Time Lords and had Miniscopes banned. Many years later, though, the Lurman showman Vorg travelled the Acteon Group with one of the few surviving Miniscopes, which he had won at the Great Wallarian Exhibition in a game of chance. [30]

One hundred million years ago, the Cretaceous Era was "a very good time for dinosaurs". The Rani visited this period, collecting Tyrannosaur embryos, one of which almost killed her later. She also expressed an interest in reviving the era with the Time Manipulator. More dinosaurs were taken from this era by Whitaker's Timescoop. [31]

## c 65,000,000 BC – EARTHSHOCK [32]

Sixty-five million years ago the dinosaurs became extinct when the anti-matter engines of a space freighter that had spiralled back through time from 2526 AD exploded in Earth's atmosphere.

Some dinosaur species survived until the Eocene Era, around forty five million years ago. By now, some had evolved into intelligent bipeds, the Reptile People. There were two distinct species, a land-based race, the Silurians, who built a great civilisation in areas of extreme heat, and their amphibious cousins, the Sea Devils.

The Silurians domesticated dinosaurs, using a Tyrannosaur species as watchdogs, **Brontosaurs to lift heavy loads, and Dilophosaurs as mounts.** They also genetically engineered creatures such as the Myrka, a ferocious armoured sea creature.

Silurians had advanced psychic powers, apparently concentrated through their third 'eye'. They had telekinetic and hypnotic ability, and could project lethal blasts of energy and establish invisible force fields. **They communicated using a sophisticated language that was a combination of telepathy, speech and gesture.** Much of their equipment was operated by mental commands, although the Silurians were also known to use an almost musical summoning device. Much Silurian technology appears to have been organic. Their science was more advanced than human technology of the late twenty-first century, with particle suppressors and advanced genetic engineering. They also

30 *Carnival of Monsters*. The Doctor states that the Plesiosaurus "has been extinct for one hundred and thirty million years". The Miniscope presumably captures its specimens in a timescoop like those seen in *Invasion of the Dinosaurs* and *The Five Doctors* – Vorg's Scope contains both a Plesiosaurus and humans from 1926, specimens taken from eras over a hundred and thirty million years apart. Presumably the Doctor's campaign to have Miniscopes banned took place before he left Gallifrey.

31 *Invasion of the Dinosaurs*.

32 Dating *Earthshock* – The Doctor dates the extinction of the dinosaurs and confirms that the freighter has travelled to that era, back "sixty-five million years". The pattern of prehistoric Earth's continents are those of modern-day Earth.

**33 A COMPLETE MISNOMER –** The name "Silurian" is coined by Dr Quinn in *Doctor Who and the Silurians*. Although the name is scientifically inaccurate, everyone at Wenley Moor uses the term, including the Doctor. We don't learn what the Reptile People call themselves, but the Doctor calls them "Silurians" to their face and they don't correct him. The on-screen credits also use the term. The description "Sea Devil" is coined by a terrified Clark in *The Sea Devils*, and the term appears in the on-screen credits for all six episodes. In this second story, when Jo calls the Reptile People "Silurians", the Doctor replies: "That's a complete misnomer. The chap that discovered them must have got the period wrong. Properly speaking they should have been called the Eocenes". The Doctor never uses the term in practice, though, and seems to tell Captain Hart that they are called "Sea Devils". For the rest of the story the humans tend to call them "creatures", while the Doctor and the Master refer to them as "the people". In *Warriors of the Deep* and the New Adventure *Blood Heat*, however, the Reptile People have adopted the inaccurate human terms for their people. The novelisation of *Doctor Who and the Silurians* (called *The Cave Monsters* on its first release) called them "Reptile People", and the word "Silurian" only appears as a UNIT password. In *Love and War* we learn that the Silurians

constructed the Disperser, a device capable of dispersing the Van Allen Belt, and had Gravitron technology which allowed a sophisticated degree of weather control.

Silurian Law prevented all but defensive wars, but the Sea Devils had elite army units and hand-held weaponry, and the Silurians built submarine battlecruisers.

The first semi-intelligent primates evolved around this time. The Silurians used a virus to prevent these apes from raiding their crops. [33] [34]

**The Silurians worshipped the Great Old Ones, as did the gargantuan creatures that ruled the Earth one hundred thousand years before their time. The Silurians wrote the Necronomicon, the tome that set down much about the Old Ones.** [35]

On Earth's twin planet Mondas, a species of monkey had evolved into a race almost identical to modern humanity. *In many ways, Silurian and Mondasian civilisations paralleled one another: the Mondasians and Reptile People had similar planet-wide technocratic governments, and both had reached a level of technical achievement that was more advanced than that of the human race in the late twenty-first century. There is no evidence of contact between the two races; it is odd that both were advanced in so many ways, yet neither developed sophisticated space flight at this time. Both races were known to the Time Lords* [36]

At the end of this period, the planets' astronomers observed a rogue planet entering the solar system. The governments of both Mondas and Earth calculated that as the planetoid passed by there would be catastrophic climatic change, but both had time to prepare. The Reptile People spent their time building subterranean hibernation chambers, whereas the Mondasians, lacking such technology, built a giant "propulsion unit" – *perhaps a device similar to those built by the Daleks, utilising the magnetic field of the planet – to shift the planet slightly out of its orbit and so dodge the planetoid.* However, the propulsion unit misfired, hurling Mondas out of the solar system *at near lightspeed.* The rogue planet became Earth's moon.

Vague race memories of Mondas and its inhabitants survived in the Terran humans, *suggesting that some Mondasian refugees reached Earth.* [37]

*'Mondas, travelling at the velocities it did, was subject to time dilation. While forty five million years passed on Earth, only around one thousand passed on Mondas. The disaster had massive repercussions. Most Mondasians survived in underground shelters, but soon realised that return to the solar system would be a long and difficult process. They had to adapt rapidly to the severe changes that followed from leaving the Sun's orbit. After a few decades of chaotic weather, the planet settled into long, dark winter. Starvation, disease, civil unrest and numerous other problems that the Mondasians had conquered in the past had to be overcome once more. Many Mondasians died, but after a few decades they had become fully adapted to life in huge subterranean cities. It soon became clear that the Mondasian race was becoming more sickly. Their life spans were shortening dramatically and the only way they could survive was to replace diseased organs and wasted limbs with metal and plastic substitutes. These primitive Cybermen gradually evolved to incorporate breathing apparatus that allowed them to return to the surface of Mondas, easing the pressures on the underground cities. Fewer and fewer children were being born, and it gradually became apparent that only Cybertisation could possibly save the race. It was several more centuries before they bowed to the inevitable and the Mondasians became full Cybermen. A new race was born.'*

[From the Archive of the Brotherhood of Logicians]

*'While some have suggested that Mondas was affected by "time dilation", they merely betray their lack of understanding of FTL physics. Besides, the continents of Mondas had clearly been affected by just as many millions of years of continental drift as Earth. There is also evidence that the Mondasians had become Cybermen long before Mondas*

of the future "liked to be called Earth Reptiles now", and the term is also used in a number of other New Adventures. In *Blood Heat* the Doctor uses the scientific name "psionsauropodomorpha" (p29). For the purposes of this book, politically incorrect although it may be, I will use the terms "Silurian" and "Sea Devil".

34 THE SILURIAN CIVILISATION – The Silurians appear in *Doctor Who and the Silurians, The Sea Devils* and *Warriors of the Deep*. The New Adventure *Blood Heat* takes place on a parallel Earth in which the Doctor died during the first of the television stories and the Silurians went on to conquer Earth. The Silurians are mentioned in a number of the New and Missing Adventures, notably *Love and War, Transit, The Crystal Bucephalus* and *Original Sin*. It does appear that the Silurians and Sea Devils were contemporaries, as Sauvix appears to recognise Ichtar (or at least his rank) in *Warriors of the Deep*.

While most fans have assumed that the Silurians come from the same time as the dinosaurs, on-screen there is no evidence that the Silurians were contemporaries of any known dinosaur species. Indeed, in *The Sea Devils*, the age of the Silurian civilisation is established as the Eocene Period, around twenty million years after fossil records of dinosaurs end. In *Doctor Who and the Silurians* it is established that the Silurians use a mutant, five-fingered species of Tyrannosaur that the Doctor can't identify, as a guard-dog, and in *Warriors of the Deep* we see the Myrka.

35 [see also THE GREAT OLD ONES page 13]. *All Consuming Fire* (p220), *White Darkness* (p89).

36 In *The Tenth Planet* the Doctor states that "millions of years ago there was a twin planet to Earth". The Doctor already knows of the Cybermen in that story, although he doesn't appear to recognise them in *The Five Doctors*; it is clear though that Susan does. Over the years, a number of fans have speculated that the Mondasians and the Silurians were contemporaries.

In a story outline for a proposed sixth Doctor story, *Genesis of the Cybermen*, Gerry Davis set the date of the creation of the Cybermen at 'several hundred years BC'. *Cybermen* and *The Terrestrial Index* agreed that the Mondasian civilisation developed around '10,000 BC'.

37 We learn of the arrival of Earth's Moon in *Doctor Who and the Silurians*. I speculate that this is also the catastrophe that forces Mondas to leave the solar system. In *Attack of the Cybermen*, the Doctor says that "Mondas had a propulsion unit – a tribute to Cyber-engineering – though why they should want to push a planet through space I've no idea". We learn that the

*left its orbit. Many races across the galaxy: such as the Sontarans and the Ice Warriors suffer from just the same lack of development. Clearly, all such warlike races face massive setbacks from time to time that limit their development.'*

*[From the Archive of the Brotherhood of Logicians]* [38]

On Earth, although the Reptile People preserved some dinosaurs in their shelters, all those in the wild were wiped out. In the late nineteenth century there was a single account of a pocket of dinosaurs surviving on one plateau in Central Africa, but most scientists and reporters, including a young Arthur Conan Doyle, dismissed it as the ravings of a madman:

> "The pygmies from the Oluti Forest led me blindfold for three whole days through uncharted jungle. They took me to a swamp full of giant lizards, like giant dinosaurs."
> [*An Account of My Travels in Africa*, Redvers Fenn-Cooper] [39]

After the Moon's arrival, the Van Allen Belt developed around Earth, filtering out much of the Sun's radiation, cooling the planet. Earth's climate quickly stabilised at a lower temperature than the Reptile People had predicted, and so they were not revived as planned. The monkeys slowly began to evolve a greater degree of intelligence. Before long, the only trace remaining of the Reptile People, dinosaurs, Mondas and the Cybermen were the race memories of these first hominids, the ancestors of mankind. [40]

During the Miocene Era, around twenty-five million years ago, the rocks on which Atlantis would later be built were formed. [41]

The evolution of mankind was slow. It received a boost when the Fendahl skull arrived on Earth. [42]

"Twelve million years ago, on a nameless planet which no longer exists, evolution went up a blind alley. Natural selection turned back on itself, and a creature evolved which prospered by absorbing the energy wavelengths of life itself. It ate life, all life, including that of its own kind. Then the Time Lords decided to destroy the entire planet, and hid the fact from posterity. But when the Time Lords acted it was too late, the Fendahl had already reached Earth, probably taking in Mars on its way through. The Fendahl was buried, not killed. How do you kill death? The energy amassed by the Fendahl was stored in the skull, and dissipated slowly as a biological transmutation field. Any appropriate lifeform that came within the field was altered so that it ultimately evolved into something suitable for the Fendahl to use. The skull did not create man, but it may have affected his evolution. That would explain the dark side of man's nature. Alternatively, the Fendahl fed into the RNA of certain individuals the instincts and compulsions necessary to recreate itself. These were fed through the generations."

[Apocrypha to *The Record of Rassilon*] [43]

'There is evidence of a frightful Martian catastrophe twelve million years ago in which all life was wiped out by the Fendahl and the planet was left desolate. This is obviously problematical, and at first it is difficult to see how the Ice Warriors could ever live on the same planet. Archaeologists have been vexed by the question for centuries, but the consensus nowadays boils down to two possible explanations. Firstly, the Ice Warriors could have originated somewhere other than Mars and came to colonise the Red Planet. However, no one has yet found their planet of origin. One possible candidate is Earth itself. The Ice Warriors could be a branch of homo reptilia: the Arctic equivalent of the Silurians or Sea Devils. They could have fled Earth for Mars when threatened with the arrival of the Moon, and perhaps they continued to evolve. Again, there is absolutely no evidence for this, not even in the Earth Reptiles' records, and the Silurian's need for extreme heat perhaps rules it out. Therefore, I rather prefer the other solution: that pockets of the Ice Warrior civilisation somehow lived through the ravages of the Fendahl. The Ice Warriors can hibernate for hundreds of thousands of years: maybe some survived the Fendahl in the same way, and in the

Daleks have similar technology in *The Dalek Invasion of Earth*. We are told in *The Tenth Planet* that Mondas "is an old name for Earth".

38 Here are two possible explanations why the Cybermen have been around for millions of years yet are still reliant on rather crude mechanical technology.

39 *Ghost Light*. It is unclear from the story whether the plateau really existed or was merely Fenn-Cooper's rationalisation of his adventures in Gabriel Chase. Possibly Fenn-Cooper is delirious: subsequent events in *Ghost Light* suggest that he did not recover Light from Africa – Light was always dormant in the stone spaceship in England. Conan Doyle would later set *The Lost World* in the Amazon.

40 As humanity has race memories of Mondas, it was presumably on the same side of the Sun as Earth.

41 *The Underwater Menace*.

42 THE ORIGINS OF MAN – We know that semi-intelligent primates existed during the Eocene (in *Doctor Who and the Silurians* they resemble orangutans). According to *Image of the Fendahl*, Eustace arrived on Earth twelve million years ago, just as the first humanoid bipeds evolved – this is eight million years before Fendelman had thought.

43 *Image of the Fendahl*. Originally this was a dialogue

between Colby and the Doctor. The Doctor goes on to say "on the other hand, it could all be just a coincidence". The Time Lords presumably acted after they had officially renounced intervention, which is why they kept their actions secret.

**44** The Doctor says in *The Seeds of Death* that the Ice Warriors "adapted" to the Martian climate. The theory that the Martians colonised Mars was first given in the FASA role-playing game, but there is no real evidence for it on-screen and it makes a bit of a mockery of a Martian nationalism. In *The War Games* the Doctor confirms that they are "natives of the planet Mars". It should be noted that the Doctor only speculates that the Fendahl attacked Mars.

**45** *The Seeds of Doom.*

**46** *Love and War.*

**47** *The Daleks.* The Doctor says that the Thal records "must go back nearly a half a million years".

**48** *The War Games.*

**49** THE FIRST ICE AGE – According to *Doctor Who* the Ice Age was a single event around one hundred thousand years ago, whereas in reality it lasted for hundreds of thousands of years as the ice advanced and retreated. *100,000 BC* seems to take place at the end of the Ice Age: Za speaks of "the great cold" – although this might simply mean a particularly harsh

*same limited numbers as the Silurians on Earth survived the coming of the Moon. The Ice Warriors must have reached only a primitive state by the time of the attack, which rules out the theory that Martian astronauts return to find their world destroyed.'*

*[Down Among the Dead Men, Professor B S Summerfield]*[44]

Five million years ago on Earth, the climate of Antarctica was tropical. [45]

A million years ago, the Hoothi made the first moves in their plan to conquer Gallifrey. They enslaved the Heavenites, keeping them as a slave race and turning their planet into a beautiful garden world. [46]

Half a million years ago on Skaro the Thal civilisation had begun, and writings survive from this time. [47]

Two hundred thousand years ago, homo sapiens, "the most vicious species of all", evolved and immediately began killing one another. [48]

One hundred thousand years ago on Earth, the First Ice Age began. By this time, two rival groups of primates had developed: Neanderthals and homo sapiens. [49]

'The Neanderthals were very similar in appearance to homo sapiens, and both species were capable of speech and reasoning, and possessed a highly developed degree of social organisation. The Neanderthals had a religion; they worshipped "the Burning One", whom they contacted using "hunting magic". They also had simple agriculture based on the herding of crops. The First Ice Age was a crucial event in the history of Earth, and there is evidence that the planet was visited by many alien races at that time, virtually all of whom helped homo sapiens at the expense of the Neanderthals.'

*[Extinct Civilisations, Woris Bossard]*[50]

The earliest splinter of Scaroth gave mankind the secret of fire in his efforts to accelerate human development. [51]

Light surveyed Earth at the beginning of the First Ice Age. Ichthyosaurs survived until at least this initial survey, *longer than palaeontologists would have us believe,* and they were included in Light's catalogue of all organic life, as were the Neanderthals. Around this time, the Doctor visited a Neanderthal tribe, and acquired the fang of a cave bear. The Dæmon Azal wiped out almost all the Neanderthals shortly afterwards. Light had preserved the single specimen Nimrod **and a few individual examples of the race survived for tens of thousands of years.** Race memories of beings with horns and their science survive in human rituals. [52]

'When the First Ice Age hit Earth, our planet's new, colder climate made it very attractive to the Martians. A hundred thousand years ago, Martian civilisation bore all the hallmarks of today. Mars was already a dying planet, and Martian technology was already familiar: they had built sonic cannons, augmented their armour with electronic radio equipment and discovered atomic fission. There is no evidence that the Ice Lord caste had developed by this time. At least one spacecraft was built, an atomic powered vessel with a small crew under the command of Varga. They "crashed at the foot of the ice mountain", a glacier, and were buried in an avalanche when they attempted to leave. Trapped in the ice, they went into hibernation.'

[*Down Among the Dead Men Again*, Professor B S Summerfield (unpublished)] [53]

## c 100,000 BC – 100,000 BC [54]

'Early man worshipped the Sun, which they called "Orb". They believed that Orb might provide them with fire, and the "firemaker" was always the leader of any given group. The secret of fire making was passed down from generation to generation.'

[*Religions of the Galaxy*]

'The cave paintings are about one hundred thousand years old, and they tell a simple, clearly mythological story. One interpretation might be: "Za could not make fire. The Old Woman said that Kal would make a better leader. Kal brought meat to the tribe. Horg said he would give his daughter Hur

winter. Similarly, Nimrod talks of "ice floods" and "mammoths" in *Ghost Light*. Nimrod is one of the last generation of Neanderthals. In *The Dæmons* the Doctor says that Azal arrived on Earth "to help homo sapiens take out Neanderthal man", and Miss Hawthorne immediately states that this was "one hundred thousand years" ago. In *The Ice Warriors* Arden judges that Varga was buried before the first Ice Age.

50 In reality, Neanderthals only evolved about one hundred thousand years ago and survived for about sixty thousand years, until the Cro-Magnon Period. Scientists know that Neanderthals had smaller brain cavities than early humans, and don't think that they had larynxes.

51 *City of Death*.

52 *Ghost Light. The Dæmons.* In *Timewyrm: Genesys*, Enkidu is one of the last Neanderthals.

53 *The Ice Warriors*. Arden states that Varga comes from ice dating from "prehistoric times, before the first Ice Age". His team have discovered the remains of mastadons and fossils in the ice before this time. In the New Adventure *Legacy* the Doctor states that Varga "crashed on Earth millions of years ago" (p90).

**54 Dating** *100,000 BC* – Now that we know that the production team called the first televised story *100,000 BC* at the time it was made (the title appears on a press release dated 1 November 1963), the dating of the story has become a lot less problematical. Anthony Coburn's original synopsis of the story also gives the date as '100,000 BC'.

The first edition of *The Making of Doctor Who* placed the story in '33,000 BC' (which is more historically accurate), but the second edition corrected this to '100,000 BC'. *The Programme Guide* claimed a date of '500,000 BC', *The Terrestrial Index* settled on 'c 100,000 BC'. *The Doctor Who File* suggested '200,000 BC'. The TARDIS Special claimed a date of '50,000 BC', *The Discontinuity Guide* '500,000 BC – 30,000 BC'.

**55 MONARCH'S JOURNEY** – There is a great deal of confusion about the dates of Monarch's visits to Earth, as recorded in *Four to Doomsday*. The story is set in 1981. Bigon says that he was abducted "one hundred generations ago" [c 500 BC], and this is confirmed by Enlightenment – she goes on to say that the visit to ancient Greece was the last time the Urbankans had visited Earth. Bigon says that the ship last left Urbanka "1250 years ago", that the initial journey to Earth took "20,000 years", and that "Monarch has doubled the speed of the ship on every subsequent visit".

to Kal, not Za. Kal saw an old man emerge from a blue tree. The old man was a healer. The healer made fire from his fingers. The healer was a messenger of Orb. Kal captured the healer and placed him in the cave of skulls. The Old Woman freed the healer. The Old Woman was killed by a knife. The healer escaped and fled through the forest of fear. Za was attacked by a beast. The healer rescued Za. The healer showed the tribe the knife of Kal. It was covered in blood. Kal had killed the Old Woman. Za was made leader. Za was the firemaker. The healer escaped the cave of skulls, fled through the forest of fear, and returned to his blue tree." '

[*Palaeolithic Art*, Professor Howard Foster]

Scaroth, the Fendahl and the Dæmons all continued to influence human development until the late twentieth century. *As a result of this alien activity, homo sapiens emerged from the Ice Age as the dominant lifeform of the planet for the first time.*

'URBANKA – A planet in the Inokshi solar system in Galaxy RE1489 the home of the technologically advanced, froglike Urbankans. The ozone layer of Urbanka collapsed around 55,500 BC. The Monarch of the planet stored the memories of his population, some three billion, on computer chips, which when necessary could be housed in android bodies. Monarch built a vast spacecraft, which set out for Earth. The ship doubled its speed on each round trip, and the Urbankans landed and took human specimens.'

[*Bartholomew's Planetary Gazetteer*, Volume XXI] [55]

Cave paintings on Lanzarote date from the Cro-Magnon Period, forty thousand years ago, demonstrating that a primitive human culture had developed by this time. [56]

Around 35,500 BC the Australian aboriginal Kurkurtji and other members of his race were kidnapped by the Urbankans. [57]

Two Krynoid pods landed in Antarctica in the late Pleistocene Period, between twenty and thirty thousand years ago. They remained dormant in the Antarctic permafrost until the twentieth century. [58]

Twenty-five thousand years ago the Tzun, a warrior race from S'Arl, the sixth planet of Hadar, began to venture out into space. S'Arl is about one hundred and twenty parsecs from Earth (it is known as Beta Centaurus to human astronomers, and is in the same galactic sector.) At this time, the sector was dominated by the Darklings, fungoids from Yuggoth. The Tzun beat them back to 61 Cygni, but were left with corrupted DNA. As the Tzun continued to travel in space they developed three distinct sub-species: the purebloods (resembling Asiatic humans), the S'Raph pilots (grey-skinned with bulbous black eyes) and the Ph'Sor, fusions of Tzun and the native races of planets they occupy. [59]

Around 15,500 BC, the Urbankans returned to Earth. The Princess Villagra was kidnapped by the Urbankans. [60]

Around ten thousand years ago humanity developed the wheel – with a helping hand from Scaroth. [61]

Around the same time, in the Prion planetary system, the xenophyte Zolfa-Thurans developed a powerful weapon: when the power-source of the Dodecahedron was aligned with the giant Screens of Zolfa-Thura, an energy beam, "a power many magnitudes greater than any intelligence has ever controlled", was formed, which was capable of obliterating any point in the galaxy. Zolfa-Thura fell into bloody civil war, and everything on the planet's surface, except the Screens, was devastated. The Dodecahedron transferred to Zolfa-Thura's sister-planet, Tigella, where it was worshipped by the Deons. [62]

Around 5500 BC, the Urbankans visited Earth for the third time. At this time, the Futu dynasty was flourishing in China. The Urbankans kidnapped the mandarin Lin Futu, along with a number of dancers. [63]

Seven thousand years ago in the Nile delta, the Egyptian civilisation was flourishing. Many extra-terrestrials visited Egypt around this time, and they were seen as gods: Khnum was either one of the Dæmons or a race memory of them, and Scaroth posed as an Egyptian god and Pharaoh around this time, building the earliest Pyramids. *Around this time, the Egyptians discovered copper, hieroglyphics and sea-going ships.* The Osirians fought a war in our solar system. Sutekh, the Typhonian

This is complicated, but the maths does work – the speed only doubles every time the ship arrives at Earth, perhaps because of some kind of slingshot effect. Monarch's ship left Urbanka for the first time in 55,519 BC, it arrived at Earth twenty thousand years later (35,519 BC), the speed doubled so the ship arrived back at Urbanka ten thousand years later (25,519 BC), it returned to Earth (15,519) BC, the speed doubled and the ship travelled back to Urbanka (arriving 10,519 BC). Monarch returned to Earth (in 5519 BC), the speed doubled once again and the ship arrived back at Urbanka (in 3019 BC). The ship made its final visit to Earth around 519 BC, and now the trip back to Urbanka only took 1250 years. The ship left Urbanka (731 AD) and reached Earth in 1981.

This solution leaves a number of historical problems – see the individual entries.

56  Peri has just turned down an opportunity to visit the caves with her mother at the beginning of *Planet of Fire.*

57  [see also MONARCH'S JOURNEY page 28]. Bigon states that Kurkurtji was taken "thirty thousand years" ago. Examples of Australian Aboriginal art at least twenty-five thousand years old survive, so it is possible that Kurkurtji comes from this period.

58  *The Seeds of Doom.*

59  *First Frontier.*

60 [see also MONARCH'S JOURNEY page 28]. Bigon claims that Villagra is a "Mayan". Although the Doctor boasts of his historical knowledge, he then suggests that the Mayans flourished "eight thousand years ago"; the civilisation really dated from c 300 AD – c 900 AD. The Urbankans, though, don't visit Earth after 500 BC. It would appear that Villagra must come from an ancient pre-Mayan civilisation.

61 In *City of Death*, Scaroth says that he "turned the first wheel". Archaeologists think that mankind discovered the wheel around 8000 BC.

62 "Ten thousand years" before *Meglos*.

63 [see also MONARCH'S JOURNEY page 28]. There is no "Futu dynasty" in recorded Chinese history. The Doctor has heard of it, however, and claims it flourished "four thousand years ago". The date does not tie in with the details of Monarch's journey as described in the rest of the story. Archaeologists have discovered a piece of tortoiseshell with a character from the Chinese alphabet on it that is seven thousand years old, so it seems that an early Chinese civilisation was established by that time – this does tie in with the dates established by Bigon.

64 We learn of alien visits to ancient Egypt in *The Dæmons* and *City of Death*. In *Pyramids*

Beast, and his sister Nephthys captured Osiris and sent him into space in a capsule without life support. Sutekh took control of Phaester Osiris, destroying it and leaving a trail of destruction across half the galaxy. Sutekh became known by many names, including Set, Sadok and Satan. Sutekh and Nephthys tracked the body of Osiris to Egypt and totally destroyed it. Horus and seven hundred and forty fellow Osirians located Sutekh on Earth, trapping and sealing him in a pyramid. Nephthys was imprisoned in a human body and mummified. Her mind was fragmented, the evil side placed in a canopic jar. The Pyramid of Mars was built to house the Eye of Horus, and the Osirians set up a beacon that broadcast a warning message. Horus and the other Osirians were worshipped by the Egyptians. Even Sutekh was worshipped by many on Earth, and the Cult of Sutekh survived for many thousands of years. The influence of the Osirians brought on the unification of the Egyptian kingdoms, and the local humans were genetically enhanced, becoming taller and with increased mental capacity. [64]

## c 4000 BC – GENESIS OF THE DALEKS [65]

On Skaro, an even greater force for evil was being created:

> 'Many thousands of years ago, although Skaro was a beautiful world, the Thals and the Kaleds went to war. During the first century of the conflict, foul chemical weapons were used, and monstrous mutations developed in the Thal and Kaled gene pool. To keep their races pure, all Mutos were cast out into the wastelands that now covered the planet. As the war dragged on, resources became more and more scarce – plastic and rifles gave way to animal skins and clubs. The war lasted for a thousand years, until there were only two cities left.'

[Thal Oral Records]

'Fifty years before the end of the war, the Kaleds set up an Elite group, based in a secret bunker below the Wasteland. It was ruled by chief scientist Davros, the greatest scientific mind Skaro had ever seen. Davros had been crippled in an horrific accident, but he survived by designing a life-support system for himself. Davros created energy weapons, artificial hearts and a new material that reinforced the Kaled Dome. Davros had realised that Skaro was dying, but didn't believe that intelligent life could exist on the other planets in the seven galaxies that had been observed by Skaroine electroscopes. Davros did the only logical thing, and succeeded in selectively breeding an intelligent creature that could survive in the radiation-soaked, environmentally desolate world of Skaro. Using the Mark III Travel Machines, the Daleks could survive in virtually any environment, even the dead planet.'

[*The Children of Davros*, Njeri Ngugi]

---

**CELESTIAL INTERVENTION AGENCY SPECIAL REPORT**

LOCATION: Skaro, D5-Gamma-Z-Alpha, Seventh Galaxy

We foresee a time when the Daleks will have exterminated all other lifeforms and have became the supreme power in the universe. The Daleks have threatened us at least twice in the future. The Doctor and his companions are to be sent to Skaro at the time of the Daleks' origin. The Doctor is to be given three options: (1) to avert their creation (destroying them after their creation, of course, will have violated Article Seven of Gallifreyan Law); (2) to affect their genetic development so that they might evolve in a less aggressive fashion; (3) to discover some inherent weakness that may be used against them. The Doctor will fail in his mission, but will set the development of the Daleks back by one thousand years. Our analysis indicates that this 'delay' has always been part of the Web of Time – the Dalek Invasion of Earth will still have occurred on schedule in the twenty-second century.'

'When the Daleks emerged from the Kaled Bunker, the first factionalisation of the race took place: one group of Daleks wanted to remain on Skaro, while the second group planned

---

of Mars* we are introduced to the Osirians (whose name is also sometimes spelt, and always pronounced, "Osirans"). The Cult of Sutekh appears in the New Adventure *Set Piece*. Nephthys appears in the Missing Adventure *The Sands of Time*.

**65  Dating GENESIS OF THE DALEKS** – The date of the Daleks' creation is unknown, although it is at least "many centuries" before *Destiny of the Daleks*. The Daleks have interstellar travel at least two hundred years before *The Power of the Daleks* (1820). My figure is arbitrarily chosen, but tries to take into account that the Doctor sets Dalek development back by a thousand years at the end of this story.

**66 THE TWO DALEK HISTORIES** – There are a number of discrepancies between the accounts of the Daleks' origins in *The Daleks* and *Genesis of the Daleks*. In the first story, the Original Daleks (or Dals) were humanoid, and it is implied that they only mutated after the Neutronic War, whereas in *Genesis of the Daleks* we see Davros deliberately accelerate the mutations that have begun to affect the Kaled race.

Does the Doctor change history? Obviously the Daleks are not destroyed, but this is a good thing, as it leads to many races uniting to fight the Daleks rather than each other. As *The Discontinuity Guide* suggested, it does look as though the Doctor changes established history: on every subsequent appearance, the Daleks are nowhere near as unified a force as they had been before, and Davros plays a major part in Dalek politics, whereas before he wasn't even mentioned. It looks as though the origins of the Daleks have been altered to some extent. Looking closely, though, the Doctor hasn't made much of a difference. According to the Doctor in *Remembrance of the Daleks*, the Daleks still invade Earth on schedule in "the twenty-second century": 2157 and not 3157. I suggest that the Doctor always did set the Daleks back a thousand years and the Time Lords sent the Doctor to Skaro so he could play his part in history. The discrepancy between the accounts can

to abandon the dead planet and embark on galactic conquest. The two groups (which some historians term the Exterminators and the Expansionists) were almost certainly antagonistic: Daleks tend to be intolerant of other views, even the views of other Daleks. The Expansionists, then, left Skaro as soon as they could, not returning for millennia. The group remaining on Skaro became known as the original Daleks, or Dals.

The Dals became locked into the reverse evolution affecting Skaro. *Gradually they lost the secrets of space travel and other advanced technologies.* Surviving Thal records and oral history speak of peaceful co-existence between the Thals and the Original Daleks – the Thals being warriors, the Daleks scientists and teachers. *Later in their history, the Daleks often relied on humanoid workers, such as the Robomen, Ogrons, Exxilons and human slaves, so perhaps the original Daleks needed to keep the Thals alive. Probably though, Thal historians were confusing the Dals and the original Kaled humanoids.'*

[The Children of Davros, Njeri Ngugi] 66

## c 2700 BC – TIMEWYRM: GENESYS 67

By the third millennium before Christ, man had developed irrigation, and the human race was developing from hunters into city-dwellers. In the Middle East, walled cities were built and a warrior aristocracy developed. The earliest surviving human literature was written at this time, and commerce had begun between cities. The deeds of one warrior-king, and his contact with extra-terrestrials, became legend:

'As Gilgamesh returned to Uruk, he saw an antelope in a grove. "Come to me, Gilgamesh," it called to him. He stalked the beast of the forest, and threw his spear, which passed through the flank of the animal. The antelope vanished and in its place stood a vision of the goddess Ishtar. "I have fallen from the heavens in my vast ziggurat," she told him, "I wish to embrace the King". But Gilgamesh refused, saying, "I know that the goddess Ishtar consumes her lovers". Angry with his refusal, Ishtar went to her temple in Kish, and took on the form of a snake-woman, a living statue of silver. No thought of those priests who felt the Touch of Ishtar was secret from the goddess. Ishtar commanded the building of a mighty temple, inlaid with magic bronze that did not tarnish in the rain. And through this temple she hoped to command all men, or else to destroy them in a mighty fire. So she might rule all the kingdoms of the world, Ishtar sent out a party of men, telling them, "Kill Gilgamesh and Enkidu". Ea, god of wisdom and Aya, goddess of the dawn, descended from the heavens to help Gilgamesh, and warded off the attack. Ea, through his wisdom, knew that Ishtar was a false goddess, a demon fallen from the heavens. The gods could destroy her instantly, but what would man learn from that? Aya and Gilgamesh travelled to the mountains of Mashu, to seek an audience with Utnapishtim. The entrance to his domain is guarded by two giant Scorpion-Men. Seeing Gilgamesh and Aya they called, "Why have you come on such a journey, across the lion-filled plains and dangerous waters?". Gilgamesh answered by showing them an item from Ishtar's temple. "See, this was made by the gods, not by a man." Utnapishtim granted Gilgamesh an audience in his heavenly city. Hearing of the false goddess, Utnapishtim was angry, saying, "This demon woman sought immortality, and destroyed my homeland, called Anu, in her quest. Using magic, this city survived and fell to the earth. With my flying magic I shall take you, King Gilgamesh, and your companions Enkidu and Aya across the sky to Kish." Together, the heroes destroyed the temple of Ishtar, and the false Ishtar was banished from the Earth for five thousand years'.

[*The Epic of Gilgamesh* (lost fragment)]

## c 2650 BC – THE DALEKS' MASTER PLAN [68]

The Doctor was pursued to the time of the construction of the Great Pyramids by both the Daleks in their time machine, and the Monk in his TARDIS. The Doctor made his escape during a pitched battle between the Daleks and Egyptian soldiers.

'Five hundred and thirty-seven years before the fall of Atlantis, the priests of that land captured the god Kronos. At this time, a young man called Dalios was King. Kronos transformed a man, one of the friends of the King, into a fearsome man-beast, the Minotaur. After this, the King forbade

perhaps be put down to inaccurate Thal historical records - they would not know every detail of the Kaled experiments and are writing from a biased viewpoint.

67 Dating *Timewyrm: Genesys* – The Doctor's statement that the TARDIS is heading for "Mesopotamia, 2700 BC" (p46) concurs with historical evidence suggesting that a king called Gilgamesh ruled Uruk in the early part of the third millennium BC. Although many names, places and characters in *Timewyrm: Genesys* come from the books of *The Epic of Gilgamesh*, such as Enkidu, the Man-Scorpions and Ishtar herself, the events of the book bear only a slight resemblance to the legends recounted in the Gilgamesh stories, which were written down many centuries after the period they describe.

68 Dating *The Daleks' Master Plan* – The three time machines land at the base of a "Great Pyramid" that has nearly been completed. This might well be the Great Pyramid of King Khufu, built around 2650 BC. *The Terrestrial Index* pins the date at '2620 BC' whereas *The Discontinuity Guide* offers a wider range of '2613 BC – 2494 BC'.

69 *The Time Monster*.

70 *Colony in Space*. This is when scientists believe that the Crab Nebula was formed.

71 *City of Death*. Scaroth says that he caused "the heavens to be mapped". Historically it

appears that mankind's first astronomical measurements were made in China around 2300 BC.

72 Dating *The Sands of Time* – "The Valley of the Kings – 2000 BC" (p57).

73 THE FALL OF ATLANTIS – In three stories we hear of the destruction of Atlantis: *The Underwater Menace, The Dæmons* and *The Time Monster*. In *The Underwater Menace*, the island was in the Atlantic; in *The Time Monster* it is another name for the Minoan civilisation in the Mediterranean. In *The Dæmons*, Azal warns the Master that "My race destroys its failures. Remember Atlantis!". *The Terrestrial Index* suggests that the Dæmons supplied the Minoan civilisation with the Kronos Crystal. This might be true, but there is no hint of it on-screen.

74 Dating *The Time Monster* – *The Terrestrial Index* and *The Discontinuity Guide* both suggested the traditional date of '1500 BC' for the fall of Atlantis, but this is contradicted by dialogue, with the Doctor stating that it was "four thousand years" before the UNIT era. The FASA role-playing game claimed a date of '10,000 BC'. 'The TARDIS Logs' implausibly suggested '1520 AD'.

75 *The Stones of Blood*. The *Terrestrial Index* dated Cessair's arrival on Earth at '3000 BC', but this contradicts

the use of the Crystal of Kronos, for fear of destroying the city.'

[*Critias*, Plato (lost fragment)] **69**

Around 2350 BC, the inhabitants of Uxarieus had used genetic engineering to become a psychic super-race, known to the Time Lords. They built a Doomsday Weapon, a device capable of making stars go supernova. The Crab Nebula was formed as a result of testing the device. Soon, though, radiation began leaking from the weapon's power source; it poisoned the soil and the race began to degenerate into primitives. **70**

Around four thousand three hundred years ago, the Chinese were making the first astronomical measurements, with the help of Scaroth.**71**

## c 2000 BC – THE SANDS OF TIME **72**

Tomb robbers entered the pyramid of Nephthys, breaking the canopic jar that contained her evil impulses. Seeking a pure vessel to contain them, the Egyptian priests chose the Doctor's companion Nyssa, sealing her in a sarcophagus.

## c 2000 BC – THE TIME MONSTER **73 74**

'A man came to Atlantis at this time, claiming to be an emissary of the gods. King Dalios did not believe the stranger, who seduced his wife, Queen Galleia. Together they plotted to steal the Crystal of Kronos. King Dalios died of a broken heart, and the stranger seized power, proclaiming himself to be King. Queen Galleia, filled with remorse, ordered his arrest. The stranger released great Kronos, and that is how the land of Atlantis sank beneath the waves.'

[*Critias*, Plato (lost fragment)]

Some Atlanteans survived beneath the ocean, off the Azores. The Dæmons would later claim to have destroyed Atlantis.

At around the same time as the Fall of Atlantis, Cessair of Diplos, a criminal accused of murder and stealing the Great Seal of Diplos, arrived on Earth. Over the millennia she posed as a succession of powerful women, while her ship remained in hyperspace above Boscombe Moor in Damnonium, England. Around this time, the Nine Travellers, a stone circle, was set up. Subsequent attempts to survey the circle would prove hazardous... [75]

the Doctor and Megara, both of whom claim that only "four thousand" years have elapsed since Cessair came to Earth.

# Section Two
## Known History

## TIMELINE: 2000 BC to 1962 AD

*continued overleaf*

| 1873 | | **STRANGE ENGLAND** |
|------|---|---------------------|
| 1880 | | **EVOLUTION** |
| 1881 | | THE GUNFIGHTERS |
| 1883 | | GHOST LIGHT |
| 1885 | | TIMELASH |
| 1887 | | **ALL-CONSUMING FIRE** |
| 1888 | | **THE PIT** |
| 1889 | c | THE TALONS OF WENG-CHIANG |
| 1895 | | **THE SANDS OF TIME** |
| 1900 | c | HORROR OF FANG ROCK |
| 1909 | | **BIRTHRIGHT** |
| 1911 | | PYRAMIDS OF MARS |
| 1912 | | **THE LEFT-HANDED HUMMINGBIRD** |
| 1914 | | **HUMAN NATURE** |
| 1915 | | **WHITE DARKNESS** |
| 1918 | | **TOY SOLDIERS** |
| 1921 | | THE DALEKS' MASTER PLAN |
| 1923 | | **TIMEWYRM: EXODUS** |
| 1925 | | BLACK ORCHID |
| 1929 | | **BLOOD HARVEST** |
| 1930 | | **THE ENGLISH WAY OF DEATH** |
| 1934 | | **THE EYE OF THE GIANT** |
| 1935 | | THE ABOMINABLE SNOWMEN |
| 1939 | | **TIMEWYRM: EXODUS** |
| 1941 | | **JUST WAR** |
| 1943 | | THE CURSE OF FENRIC |
| 1951 | = | **TIMEWYRM: EXODUS** |
| 1951 | | **TIMEWYRM: EXODUS** |
| 1957 | | **FIRST FRONTIER** |
| 1959 | | DELTA AND THE BANNERMEN |

According to Clent's calculation, human history started around two thousand years before the birth of Christ. [1]

## 1366 BC – SET PIECE [2]

Fleeing from the Ants, Ace spent some time in Egypt at the time of the Pharaoh Akhenaten.

The Monk helped to build Stonehenge using anti-gravity lifts. [3] The Doctor claims to have met Theseus. [4]

## c 1184 BC – THE MYTH MAKERS [5]

Captured by the Greeks, the Doctor was given two days to come up with a scheme to end the ten-year siege. Rejecting the idea of using catapults to propel the Greeks over the walls of Troy (if only after Agamemnon insisted that the Doctor would be the first to try such a contrivance) he came up with the idea of using a wooden horse containing Greek troops.

Vicki left the Doctor, changing her name to Cressida, but Katarina, the handmaiden to the prophetess Cassandra, joined him.

The Rani had been present at the Trojan War, extracting a chemical from human brains. [6]

Elsewhere, advanced races explored the universe and developed incredible technologies. Many of these races visited Earth throughout its history, often influencing humanity and affecting its scientific progress.

Thousands of years ago, the Exxilons, were "the supreme beings of the universe…Exxilon had grown old before life began on other planets". **"There are half a dozen worlds where the native languages develop up to a point, and then are suddenly replaced by one of the Exxilon ones"** (Summerfield). Worlds visited by the Exxilons include **Yemaya and Earth**, where they helped to build temples in Peru. At some point after this date the Doctor visited one of these temples, and examined the carvings there. On their home planet, the Exxilons created one of the Seven Hundred Wonders of the Universe: their City, a vast complex that was designed to last for all eternity. It was

1 *The Ice Warriors* – Clent says that "Five thousand years of civilisation" will be wiped out by the ice.

2 Dating *Set Piece* – It is "1366 BCE" (p31).

3 *The Time Meddler* – The earliest parts of Stonehenge were built around 2800 BC, but the final building activity occurred between 1600 and 1400 BC.

4 *The Horns of Nimon* – Theseus ascended to the throne of Athens around 1235 BC.

5 Dating *The Myth Makers* – The traditional date for the Fall of Troy is 1184 BC, although this date is not given on-screen.

6 *The Mark of the Rani*.

7 *Death to the Daleks* – The Peruvian temples are around three thousand years old. The quote is that of Bellal. The Doctor thinks that the city "must be one of the Seven Hundred Wonders of the Universe". In *Sleepy* Benny detects Exxilon influence in the Yemayan pyramid, dating from around "1500 BCE" (p102).

8 *Mawdryn Undead* – The ship has been operational for "three thousand years" according to the Doctor.

9 "Thousands of years" before *The Sorcerer's Apprentice*.

10 *The Dæmons*.

11 *The Dæmons, City of Death*. Bigon was abducted "one hundred generations" before *Four to Doomsday*. *The War Games*. In *Enlightenment*, the Doctor says that the Greek ship originates in "the time of Pericles", who died at the age of 70 in 429 BC. *Robot* – Alexander lived 356-323 BC. *The Keys of Marinus* – Pyrrho lived c 360-270 BC.

12 *Horror of Fang Rock, Logopolis. The Two Doctors* – Archimedes lived c 287-212 BC. *Set Piece* – during the "fourth century BCE" (p146). "A thousand years" before *Marco Polo. Enlightenment* – the Ch'in dynasty ruled from 221-206 BC.

given a brain to protect, repair and maintain itself, and so it no longer needed the Exxilons, who were driven from the City, and degenerated into primitives. The City needed power, and began to absorb electrical energy directly from the atmosphere of the planet. The City set an intelligence test that allowed access to the City to those who might have some knowledge to offer it. Over the centuries few Exxilons attempted the test, and none returned. [7]

At around the same time, Mawdryn and seven of his companions stole a metamorphic symbiosis generator from the Time Lords, hoping to become immortal. Instead they became horrific, undying mutations, and the Elders exiled them from their home planet. Their ship entered a warp ellipse. Every seventy years it would reach an inhabited planet and one of the crew would transmat down to seek help. [8]

On the planet Avalon, a technologically advanced race discovered a means to focus solar energy to deflect the abnormally large number of asteroids in their system away from their planet. They also built thought-operated nanobots that allowed them to affect matter and energy on their planet. This discovery prolonged their existence but made their lives futile. They drained the machines of energy, but it was too late, and their civilisation fell. [9]

Professor Horner discovered evidence of pagan rituals at Devil's Hump dating from around 800 BC. [10]

Both the Dæmons and Scaroth were present in Greece, overseeing a period of progress in human history. The Athenian philosopher Bigon lived in Greece around two thousand five hundred years ago. In his fifty-sixth year he was kidnapped by the Urbankans. For the first time, the Urbankans encountered resistance on this visit. The Aliens lifted a Grecian battlefield, and the Eternals kidnapped a trireme of Athenian sailors from the time of Pericles. The Doctor has met Alexander the Great and Pyrrho, possibly on the same visit. [11]

The Doctor visited one of the Seven Wonders of the Ancient World, the Pharos lighthouse. A generation or so later he met Archimedes and acquired his business card. **The Doctor replaced Sun Tzu as the Chinese emperor's military advisor but wasn't terribly effective, as he kept holding conflict resolution seminars rather than fighting.** The Great Wall of China was built around 300 BC. The Ch'in dynasty ruled in China at the time, and the Eternals kidnapped a crew of Chinese sailors. [12]

At the height of the Roman Empire, the aliens lifted a Roman battlefield. One of the splinters of Scaroth posed as a Roman Emperor, although which one is unclear. In the fifth century before Christ, the Cult of Demnos sprang up in Italy. The Doctor met Hannibal, and Cleopatra, and was very impressed by the swordsmanship of her bodyguard. [13]

## = 10 BC - STATE OF CHANGE [14]

The entity that called itself Iam copied a section of Earth around 32 BC, creating a flat disc-shaped world. After watching Cleopatra's barge on the Nile in 41 BC, the Doctor and Peri had decided to travel a little way into the future to follow the history of Rome. Caught in the duplication process, the TARDIS console was copied, and came to Earth where it was regarded as an Oracle.

With information from this Oracle, the Roman Empire developed steamships, electric lighting, airships and explosives. The culmination of this technology was "Ultimus", the Roman Empire's atomic bomb programme. Capable of kiloton yields, Ultimus could destroy any known city. History had been changed, and Cleopatra's three children – Cleopatra Selene, Alexander and Ptolemy – ruled as a triumvirate.

The Rani also ended up in this version of Rome. The Doctor defeated her plans, and ensured that "Terra Nova" continued to exist.

## 64 (June/July) - THE ROMANS [15]

The Doctor, Ian, Barbara and Vicki spent nearly a month at a deserted villa just outside Rome. Becoming bored by the lack of adventure, the Doctor and Vicki travelled to the capital. Captured by slave traders, Ian and Barbara were sold at auction. Ian's ship was wrecked, and he ended up as a gladiator in Rome. Barbara became the servant of the Emperor Nero's wife, Poppea, and the object of the Emperor's attentions. The Doctor, meanwhile, was posing as the musician Maximus Pettulian (despite a complete lack of musical ability). When he accidentally set fire to Nero's plans to rebuild Rome, the Emperor was inspired. As Rome began to burn, the four time travellers returned to the TARDIS.

13 *The War Games*. We see the Roman emperor splinter of Scaroth in *City of Death*. "Two thousand years" before *The Masque of Mandragora*, according to Hieronymous. *Robot* – Hannibal lived 247-182 BC, crossing the Alps in 219 BC. The Doctor has already visited Rome on his travels before *The Romans*. *The Masque of Mandragora* – Cleopatra lived 68-30 BC.

14 Dating *State of Change* – The Doctor thinks that it is "the year 10 BC, approximately" (p41). In this reality, Cleopatra died around 15 BC (p45).

15 Dating *The Romans* – The story culminates in the Great Fire of Rome. The TARDIS crew have spent "a month" at the villa.

16 "Seventeen centuries" before *The Curse of Fenric*, according to Fenric.

17 *Marco Polo*. The Cult of Demnos was "supposed to have died out in the third century" according to the Doctor in *The Masque of Mandragora*.

18 [see also THE TIME BRAINS page 42]. *Time and the Rani* – Hypatia lived 370-415.

19 THE TIME BRAINS – Before *Time And The Rani* the Rani kidnaps eleven geniuses. In the televised version only three of these are named: Hypatia, Pasteur and Einstein. In the rehearsal script and novelisation, three more are named: Darwin, Za Panato and Ari Centos. The novelisation also states that Nils Bohr is kidnapped.

20 *Terror of the Zygons* – Broton tells Harry that they crashed "centuries ago by your timescale", and disguised as the Duke he later tells the Doctor that there have been sightings of the Loch Ness Monster "since the Middle Ages", the implication being that the Zygons and Skarasen have been on Earth since then (although in *Timelash* we learn that the Borad is also swimming around Loch Ness from 1179 onwards). *The Programme Guide* claimed that the Zygon ship crashed in '50,000 BC', *The Terrestrial Index* preferred 'c 1676'. *The Talons of Weng-Chiang* – Bede lived c 673–735, although he

In the middle of the third century AD, the Doctor challenged Fenric to solve a chess puzzle in Constantinople. When Fenric failed, the Doctor imprisoned him in a flask, banishing him to the Shadow Dimensions. [16]

By the end of the third century, the Old Silk Road to and from Cathay had been opened. The Cult of Demnos had apparently died out by this century. [17] The Rani kidnapped Hypatia to become part of her Time Brain. [18] [19]

A Zygon spacecraft crashed in Loch Ness. While awaiting a rescue party, they fed on the milk of the Skarasen, an armoured cyborg creature that was often mistaken by the locals for a "monster". The Doctor caught a huge salmon in Fleet and shared it with the Venerable Bede (who "adored fish"). Around this time, Monarch left Urbanka for the last time. The Rani visited Earth during the so-called "Dark Ages". **The Doctor defeated the Tzun at Mimosa II in 733 AD.** [20]

"Sideways in time" on an Earth where the truth about King Arthur was closer to the myths of our world, a future incarnation of the Doctor was known as Merlin. During the eighth century, Arthur and Morgaine fought against one another, despite their childhood together at Selladon. The Doctor, who regenerated at least once during this time, cast down Morgaine at Badon with his mighty arts.

Eventually, though, Morgaine was victorious, and Arthur was killed. The Doctor placed Arthur's body and Excalibur in a semi-organic spaceship, and transferred it to the bottom of Lake Vortigern in our dimension. Morgaine imprisoned the Doctor forever in the Ice Caves and went on to become Empress of the solar system.

Twelve hundred years later, Deathless Morgaine was Battle Queen of the S'Rax, ruler of thirteen worlds. This dimension was scientifically advanced with energy weapons and ornithopters, but the people weren't reliant on technology and still knew the magic arts. There was still resistance against her rule, as Merlin had promised that Arthur would return in the hour of greatest need. Morgaine's son Mordred led her troops to victory at Camlaan, forcing Ancelyn to flee the field. [21]

The Catholic Church founded the Library of St John the Beheaded, which by the nineteenth century was located in the St Giles Rookery, a notorious area of Holborn, London. The library contained unique, suppressed and pagan texts, including information on "alternative zoology and phantasmagorical anthropology". [22]

Fenric still had influence over Earth and the ability to manipulate the timelines: he summoned the Ancient One from half a million years in the future. Over the centuries the Haemovore followed the flask. The flask containing Fenric was stolen from Constantinople and taken to Northumbria by Viking pirates. Slowly the Ancient One followed it to Maiden's Bay. By the tenth century, a nine-letter Viking alphabet was in use, although the later Vikings used a sixteen-letter version; carvings in the earlier alphabet claimed that the Vikings were cursed, and they buried the flask in a burial site under St Jude's church. [23]

The Doctor met Alfred the Great (and his cook Ethelburg, "a dab hand at bear rissoles"). A thousand years ago, the penultimate Keeper of Traken was inaugurated. The Union of Traken in Mettula Orionsis had enjoyed many thousands of years of peace before this time. In 1033, Clancy's Comet was mistaken for the Star of the West, sent to commemorate the millennium of the crucifixion. The first monastery was established on the site of Forgill Castle in the eleventh century. [24]

## c 900 – INVASION OF THE CAT-PEOPLE

The Doctor, Ben and the Cat-People travelled to Baghdad at the time of the Arabian Nights using the RTC.

## 1066 (Late Summer) – THE TIME MEDDLER [25]

Landing on a beach in Northumbria, the Doctor learnt that a renegade from his own people, the Monk, was planning to destroy a Viking invasion with futuristic weapons. Harold's army would then be fresh for the Battle of Hastings, and, after defeating the Norman's invasion, Harold would usher in a new period of peace for Europe. The Monk had arrived several weeks ago and occupied a monastery overlooking the coast.

The Doctor removed the dimensional control from the

never went to London, only leaving Jarrow once to visit Canterbury. *Four to Doomsday* [see also MONARCH'S JOURNEY page 28]. *The Mark of the Rani.* "Twelve hundred and twenty four Terran years" before *First Frontier* (p114, p123).

21 *Battlefield* – Warmsley thinks that Excalibur's scabbard dates "from the eighth century".

22 The Library of St John the Beheaded was mentioned in *Theatre of War*, and made its first appearance in the following New Adventure *All-Consuming Fire*. In that book we learn much about it, including the fact that it has been established for a "thousand years" (p15). The library still exists at the time of *Millennial Rites*. In *The Empire of Glass*, Irving Braxiatel acquires manuscripts for the library (p245).

23 *The Curse of Fenric* – The Ancient Haemovore arrived in "ninth century Constantinople" according to the Doctor. Ace says the inscriptions are "a thousand years old".

24 *The Ghosts of N-Space* (p164) – Alfred reigned 871 – c 900. *The Keeper of Traken. The Ghosts of N-Space* (p220). According to Broton (disguised as the Duke of Forgill) in *Terror of the Zygons.*

25 Dating *The Time Meddler* – The story takes place shortly before the Battle of Hastings (14 October 1066), the Doctor judging it to be "late summer".

The Doctor discovers a horned Viking helmet, although the Vikings never wore such helmets.

26 *The Daleks' Master Plan*

27 *The Stones of Blood. Timelash. The Left-Handed Hummingbird.*

28 Dating *The Crusade* – A document written for Donald Tosh and John Wiles in April/ May 1965 (apparently by Dennis Spooner), 'The History of Doctor Who', stated that the story is set between the Second and Third Crusades, with the Third Crusade starting when Richard's plan fails. Richard is already in Palestine at the start of the story, indicating a date of around 1190. Ian claims in *The Space Museum* that *The Crusade* took place in the 'thirteenth century', but this seems to be an error on his part. The *Radio Times* and *The Making of Doctor Who* both set the story in the 'twelfth century'. *The Programme Guide* gives a date of '1190' *The Terrestrial Index* '1192'.

29 *Invasion of the Dinosaurs. City of Death* – although Julian Glover plays both Richard the Lionheart in *The Crusade* and Scaroth in *City of Death*, I don't think Scaroth posed as King Richard. "Ten years" before The *King's Demons. The Dæmons, Tragedy Day* (p115) – Genghis Khan lived c 1167–1227.

30 Dating *The King's Demons* – The Doctor says it is "March the fourth, twelve hundred and fifteen".

Monk's TARDIS. It "took a bit of time" to fix, but the Monk soon resumed his travels. [26]

During the twelfth century, the Convent of the Little Sisters of St Gudula was founded and Cessair of Diplos posed as the Mother Superior. The other end of the time corridor formed by the Timelash was in 1179 AD. Around 1168, the Aztecs left their original home of Aztlan and became nomads. They took a holy relic, the Xiuhcoatl with them. [27]

## c 1190 – THE CRUSADE [28]

'Richard the Lionheart planned to marry his sister Joanna to Saphadin, the brother of his enemy Saladin. This, he hoped, would bring the endless crusades to a conclusion. But in the end, the cruelty of men on both sides, such as El Akir and the Earl of Leicester led to continued conflict.'

[*The Third Crusade*, B Wright]

A peasant from this time was accidentally kidnapped by Whitaker's Time Scoop. Scaroth posed as a crusader. Around 1205 a man was boiled in oil for the entertainment of King John. The Doctor claimed to have heard Genghis Khan speak, and even to have delivered him. [29]

## 1215 (4 and 5 March) – THE KING'S DEMONS [30]

The Master attempted to pervert the course of constitutional progress on Earth by trying to prevent the signing of Magna Carta. On 3 March 1215, an android controlled by the Master, Kamelion, arrived at Fitzwilliam Castle posing as the King. He was accompanied by the Master, disguised as Sir Giles Estram, a French swordsman. For many years before this time the Fitzwilliams had served the King, giving him their entire fortune to help the war against the abhorrent Saracens; now the King appeared to demand even more of them. "King John" began to challenge the loyalty of even the King's most devoted subjects. The Master's plan was exposed by the Doctor.

## 1242 – SANCTUARY [31]

'The Cathares were based at a fortress, the Rocc near Beziers in modern-day France. The Cathares believed that the world had been created by an evil God, Rex Mundi, whereas people's souls were aspects of the good Amor. All material things were evil to them, and they valued only the spiritual. These beliefs meant that they were declared heretics by the Catholic Church, and much of the information we have about the Cathares comes from the Inquisition. One document exists that speaks of the sect's legendary collection of artefacts, including: a manuscript proving that Homer was a woman; King Arthur's crown; and the skull of Jesus Christ – proof positive that the Crucifixion didn't occur. The sect was destroyed in 1242 by the knights of the Albigensian crusades and the secrets of the sects were lost.'

[*Secrets of the Templar Sects*, Mysteria Press]

Marco Polo was born in Venice in 1252. When he was twelve, English crusaders occupied the African port of Accra. In 1271, Marco Polo left Venice to explore China. The Forgill family served the nation from the late thirteenth century. [32]

During the Middle Ages, Stangmoor was a fortress. The Master used TOM-TIT to kidnap a medieval knight. In 1270 a mysterious doctor, who tended King Alexander, sent his stable boy Tom away. The legends of Kebiria say that the Caliph at Giltat was visited by mysterious demons, the "Al Harwaz", who promised him anything he wanted – gold, spices, slave women – if his people learnt a dance, "dancing the code". For a while the arrangement continued, until the Caliph decided to break the agreement and his city was destroyed by flying monsters. [33]

## c 1273 – THE TIME WARRIOR [34]

(Scholastic note: the verse is one of the few surviving examples of the archaic "three-fingered verse" form)

'Earth to HQ! I'm starting to fall
Crashing to Earth in my spacegoing ball.
Heading for woodland near Irongron's hall.

So spake the short and fat warrior clone

---

31 Dating *Sanctuary* – Benny "persuaded someone to tell her that the year was 1242" (p88).

32 *Marco Polo* – Barbara states that Marco Polo was born in "1252", although actually it was two years later. "Seven centuries" before *Terror of the Zygons* according to Broton (disguised as the Duke of Forgill).

33 *The Mind of Evil. The Time Monster. Birthright.* "Seven hundred years" before *Dancing the Code* (p16).

34 Dating *The Time Warrior* – The story seems to be set either during the Crusades, as Edward talks of "interminable wars" abroad, or quite soon after the Conquest, as Irongron refers to "Normans". The Doctor tells Rubeish that they are in "the early middle ages". However, in *The Sontaran Experiment*, Sarah says that Linx died "in the thirteenth century". *The Programme Guide* set a date of 'c 800', but *The Terrestrial Index* offered 'c 1190'. 'The TARDIS Logs' said '1191 AD'. According to *The Paradise of Death* this was "eight hundred years back" (p12).

35 Dating *Marco Polo* –
Barbara calculates the year as
"1289". *The Programme Guide*
gave the date as '1300'.
Recently, some doubt has been
cast over Marco Polo's reports
– some Chinese historians
have suggested that he didn't
get very far into China, and
might not have met anyone
more important than a
provincial governor.

With hairy dumb fighters he soon felt at home.
Irongron spoke thus to the stunted space-gnome:

"My last sheep has died – are you poisoning me?
The year, I suspect, is twelve seventy-three
And mutton is scarce – but that's history."

Linx kidnapped help with his Osmic Projector
But seventies scientists had found their protector:
A Doctor who carries a Delta Detector.

A towering tin soldier tormented the locals
Linx said he'd build one obedient to vocals,
Silly old Rubeish just made some bifocals.

Two visitors came to the castle in time
One was the Doctor; and he felt just fine.
But Sarah Jane Smith was not quite so benign:

"I'm young and I'm bright and I'm quite a reporter
Lavinia Smith? – She's my grandmother's daughter,
I won't make the tea like you think women oughta."

The Doctor replied "I'm the one with the brains
Linx needs electrified blood in his veins.
Sontarans are weak where they plug in the mains."

A nice Norman nobleman's narrow-hipped vixen
Sent Hal the Archer along on the mission
An arrow slew Linx: this caused nuclear fission!

The Doctor had foiled the Sontaran's vile plotting
Linx had changed time, but this ceased when Hal shot him.
His guns and potatoes were quickly forgotten.'

[Fragments from *The Ballad of Irongron*, trans.
William Keith]

## 1289 – MARCO POLO [35]

In 1274 Marco Polo arrived in Cathay, and the same year Ping-

Cho was born. Three years later, Polo entered the service of Kublai Khan. In 1287, the Khan refused permission for Marco Polo to return to Venice.

> 'In 1289 I led a caravan across the Roof of the World, to the court of the Khan. I took with me Tegana, the emissary of the Mongol warlord Noghai, and Ping-Cho, a beautiful maiden, destined to marry a seventy-five year old noble-man. We discovered Western travellers and a blue cabinet. I decided to present them to the Khan. We traversed Cathay and the Gobi desert, and arrived at Shang-Tu. At the palace, I learnt that Tegana planned to kill the Khan, and I defeated him at swordplay. In gratitude, the cabinet was returned to the travellers.'
>
> [*The Travels of Marco Polo*]

**Jared Khan narrowly missed acquiring the TARDIS at this time.** [36]

The Doctor met Dante and acquired his business card. The Doctor has also met William Tell. [37]

The Monk calculated that if his plan to prevent the Norman Conquest had worked, then mankind would have developed aircraft by 1320. The Malus, a psychic probe from Hakol, arrived in Little Hodcombe "centuries" before the village was destroyed in the English Civil War. **The Doctor met Chaucer in 1388 and was given a copy of his "The Doctour of Science's Tale". Around this time, the Doctor acquired his ticket to the Library of St John the Beheaded.** [38]

The Dæmons inspired the Renaissance. By the end of the fourteenth century, wire-drawing machinery had been developed. **Constantinople was renamed Istanbul.** The Doctor was present at the Battle of Agincourt. [39]

## c 1430 – THE AZTECS [40]

The Aztec chief Yetaxa died and was entombed around 1430. When the TARDIS crew emerged from his sealed tomb they were taken as gods. Barbara, desperate to save the Aztec civili-sation from the Spanish, attempted to use her divine power to end the practice of human sacrifice that so horrified the Euro-

36 *Birthright* (p41).

37 *The Two Doctors* – Dante lived 1265–1321. The *Divinia Commedia* may have been started as early as 1307 and was completed just before his death. *The Face of Evil* – William Tell lived in the early fourteenth century.

38 *The Time Meddler. The Awakening. Cat's Cradle: Time's Crucible* (p43). *All-Consuming Fire* (p30).

39 *The Dæmons.* "A century" before *The Masque of Mandragora. Shadowmind* (p32). *The Talons of Weng-Chiang, Shada* – Agincourt was fought on 25 October 1415.

40 Dating *The Aztecs* – Yetaxa was buried in 1430, according to Barbara. *The Programme Guide* dated the story 'c 1200 AD'. *The Terrestrial Index* suggested '1480', claiming that fifty years elapsed between Yetaxa being buried and the TARDIS landing inside the tomb. This is not supported (or contradicted) by the story itself, although John Lucarotti's novel is set in '1507'. Both editions of *The Making of Doctor Who* placed the story in '1430'.

41 *City of Death* – Movable type was developed in China during the ninth century, and Scaroth possessed a number of Gutenberg Bibles (printed 1453–5).

42 Dating *The Left-Handed Hummingbird* – The year is first given on p39.

43 THE NEUTRONIC WAR – The Neutronic War referred to in *The Daleks* is clearly a different conflict from the Thal–Kaled War seen in *Genesis of the Daleks*: the war in *The Daleks* lasted just "one day", whereas the Thal–Kaled War lasted "nearly a thousand years". In the first story, a Dalek tells the Doctor that "We, the Daleks, and the Thals" fought the Neutronic War, implying that this was after the Daleks were created. Alydon speaks of this as the "final war", maybe suggesting that there was more than one. The Neutronic War took place "five hundred years" before the events of *The Daleks*.

pean conquerors. Her attempts failed.

In the mid-fifteenth century Scaroth aquired a number of Gutenberg Bibles. Possibly it was this splinter that also acquired a Ming vase. [41]

## 1487 – THE LEFT-HANDED HUMMINGBIRD [42]

In the Aztec city of Tenochtitlan, the god Huitzilopochtli's taste for blood grew every year. By 1487 his priests demanded twenty thousand sacrifices. These fed the psychic Huitzilin, a human mutated by the Xiuhcoatl, an Exxilon device that leaked radiation. Huitzilin used his powers to remain alive, and the Xiuhcoatl to make his people worship him. For centuries he would visit the most violent places in human history, amplifying the violence and hatred and feeding from them. He would become known as the Blue.

'There were two races on the planet Skaro: the Original Daleks, or Dals, and we Thals. The Daleks were teachers and philosophers; the Thals were a famous warrior race, and Skaro was a world full of ideas, art and invention. However, there were old rivalries between the two races, and this led to a final war. In one day Skaro was destroyed, when the Daleks detonated a huge neutronic bomb. The radiation from the weapon killed nearly all life on the planet, and petrified the vegetation. The only animals that survived were bizarre mutations: the metallic Magnadons, with bodies held together by a magnetic field; the Varga plants, originally created in Dalek laboratories, with poisonous thorns; the maneating Slyther; and monsters swarming in the Lake of Mutations.

After the Neutronic War, the Daleks retired into a huge city of magical architecture built as a shelter, where they were protected from the radiation. They became dependent on their machines, radiation and static electricity. Most of the Thals perished during the final war, but a handful survived on a plateau a great distance from the Dalek City, where they managed to cultivate small plots of land. We Thals mutated, evolving full circle in the space of five centuries, reaching physical perfection.' [43]

[Thal Oral Records]

The earliest parts of Chase Mansion were built during the Wars of the Roses. The Doctor visited China in the late fifteenth century. Around this time, although presumably not on the same visit, he met Christopher Columbus. [44]

## c 1492 (Midsummer) – THE MASQUE OF MANDRAGORA [45]

'[c 1492]...visited San Martino at the invitation of Giuliano, a renowned man of science. I was disappointed to discover that even this man's subjects remain superstitious. Arriving for his costume party I heard tales of men dying in heavenly fire, invisible fire demons, and cults of pagan worship...'

'[c 1500]...a Monk visited me today and we discussed the construction of a flying machine. The visit was inspirational and Captain Tancredi has shown a great deal of interest in the project...'. [46]

'[1503]...The Doctor visited while I was painting the Mona Lisa, a portrait of a dreadful woman who wouldn't sit still and who didn't have any eyebrows. I gave him my business card...'. [47]

## 1505 – CITY OF DEATH [48]

'[1505]...Captain Tancredi keeps me a virtual prisoner, guarded by a fellow who once worked for the Borgias, no less. For some unfathomable purpose he has ordered me to make six additional copies of the Mona Lisa. While I was out, the Doctor visited my quarters, and has written an English message on my canvasses. He asks me to paint over them nevertheless, and I have begun to do so...'.

[From the mirror diary of Leonardo]

## c 1500 – THE GHOSTS OF N-SPACE [49]

Around the turn of the sixteenth century, the Doctor and Sarah

44 According to Chase in *The Seeds of Doom* – The Wars of the Roses lasted 1455–85. In *The Talons of Weng-Chiang*, the Doctor notes "I haven't been in China for four hundred years". He has Christopher Columbus's business card in *The Two Doctors* – Columbus lived 1451–1506 and discovered the New World in 1492.

45 Dating *The Masque of Mandragora* – The Helix will return to Earth in five hundred years, at the "end of the twentieth century", so the story is set at the end of the fifteenth century. The second edition of *The Making of Doctor Who* said that the story is set in 'the fifteenth century'. Hinchcliffe's novelisation specified the date as '1492', *The Terrestrial Index* and The TARDIS Logs both set the story 'about 1478'. *The Discontinuity Guide* said it must be set 'c 1470–1482 when Da Vinci was in Florence', but it is stated that Leonardo's patron is the Duke of Milan – making the date 1482–93, and so "that man in Florence" isn't Leonardo. In a letter to the author, fan Finn Clark also notes that "Frederico calls the Doge of Venice a 'fox-faced blowhard'... (which) accurately describes Agostino Barbarigo (1486–1501)" and that as the Signoria of Florence is mentioned, the story must be set before the Medici were removed from power in 1494. Finn also notes that the telescopes seen in the story are anachronistic (by about a century), and that Guiliano's

theory that the world was round was proved in May 1493 by Columbus' return to Spain.

**46** Both the Monk in *The Time Meddler* and Scaroth in *City of Death* take credit for Leonardo's plans to build a flying machine.

**47** The Doctor's note to Leonardo ends "see you earlier", and in *The Two Doctors* the Doctor has his business card.

**48** Dating *City of Death* – Tancredi asks what the Doctor is doing in "1505".

**49** Dating *The Ghosts of N-Space* – The Doctor calculates the date as "somewhere near the turn of the century" (p71).

**50** *The Aztecs. The Left-Handed Hummingbird.*

**51** *The Sensorites* – Henry VIII reigned 1509–47. In *Tragedy Day*, the Doctor says he has "never met" Henry VIII (p74). *Stones of Blood* – the dissolution of the monasteries took place in the 1530s.

**52** He is "twenty-two" at the time of *The Massacre of St Bartholomew's Eve.*

**53** *The Curse of Peladon* – Elizabeth was Queen from 1558, but the Coronation wasn't until the following year. *The Ark in Space* – Nostradamus lived 1503–66, publishing his prophecies in 1556.

**54** Dating *The Massacre of St Bartholomew's Eve* – The story climaxes with the massacre on

were briefly seen as ghosts.

In 1520 Cortez landed in South America. [50]

On one of his earliest visits to Earth, the Doctor and Susan met Henry VIII, who sent them to the Tower after the Doctor threw a parson's nose back at the King. The TARDIS had landed in the Tower, and the Doctor and Susan made good their escape. The Convent of Little Sisters of St Gudula was dissolved by Henry VIII. [51]

Charles IX of France was born in 1550. [52] The Doctor attended the Coronation of Queen Elizabeth I. The fourth Doctor's long scarf was knitted by Madame Nostradamus – "a witty little knitter". [53]

## 1572 (Late August) – THE MASSACRE OF ST BARTHOLOMEW'S EVE [54]

The Doctor and Steven arrived in Paris in August 1572. The Protestants of the city, the Hugenots, were massing to celebrate the wedding of Henry of Navarre to Princess Marguerite, but they lived in fear of the Catholic majority, particularly the Queen Mother, Catherine de Medici, and the ruthless Abbot of Amboise. Ten years before, one hundred Hugenots had been killed at Wassy, and now a full-scale massacre was instigated. The Doctor and Steven fled the city, and were forced to leave Anne Chaplet, a serving girl befriended by Steven, behind to her fate.

Boscombe Hall was built on the site of the Convent of the Little Sisters of St Gudula in the late sixteenth century. Priests from around the country hid at Cranleigh Hall. In 1582 the Doctor visited Rome trying to track the Timewyrm. The West Wing of Chase Mansion was completed in 1587. The same year, the Roanoake colony in the New World was wiped out by the Greld. A year later, the Doctor met Francis Drake just before he faced the Armada. The Doctor once shared a cell with Walter Raleigh, who "kept going on about this new vegetable he'd discovered". [55]

The Doctor met Shakespeare, a "charming fellow" but "a dreadful actor". Shakespeare was a "taciturn" young man, and the Doctor encouraged him to take up writing. Shakespeare went on to become the English language's greatest dramatist and the Doctor used the Time/Space Visualiser to watch Shakespeare at the court of Elizabeth I with Francis Bacon when the idea was first discussed. Later, the Doctor transcribed a copy of *Hamlet* for Shakespeare, who had sprained his wrist writing sonnets. Scaroth acquired the manuscript of the play, which is in the Doctor's handwriting. If the Monk's plan had worked, *Hamlet* would have been written for television. [56]

Master Dee worked as Queen Elizabeth's counsellor for twenty years. In 1603, he realised that the Doctor would not return to visit the Queen. [57]

Richard Maynarde was born in 1607. [58]

## 1609 – THE EMPIRE OF GLASS [59]

'The Armageddon Convention was signed in Venice, 1609. The twenty-year work of Irving Braxiatel, and chaired by his >word obscured<, the Doctor, the Convention banned the use of co-balt bombs and other doomsday weapons such as temporal dis-rupters. Although the Daleks and Cybermen refused to attend, many other races did sign. The Convention was nearly sabo-taged by the Greld (a race of arms dealers who stood to lose money from it) and the Jamarians who craved an empire for themselves.'

[*Intergalactic Law*, XIX edition]

On 29 June 1613, the talentless playwright Francis Pearson burnt down Shakespeare's Globe Theatre during a production of *Henry VIII*. Pearson subsequently vanished. [60]

In April 1616, a dying William Shakespeare handed over manuscripts of his plays to Irving Braxiatel in return for memo-ries of the events of Venice in 1609. [61]

In 1621, the infamous Lady Peinforte poisoned her neigh-bour Dorothea Remington. [62]

On one of apparently a number of visits to the monastery, the Doctor helped the Det-Sen Monks of Tibet to survive ban-dit attacks in 1630. He was entrusted with the holy Ghanta when he left. Perhaps it is on this visit that the Doctor learnt the Tibetan language and Tibetan meditation techniques. [63]

The War Lords lifted a battlefield from some point during

---

24 August.

**55** *The Stones of Blood. Black Orchid. Timewyrm: Revelation* (p13). *The Seeds of Doom. The Empire of Glass. Four to Doomsday* – the Spanish Armada attacked in 1588. *The Mind of Evil* – Raleigh lived 1552–1618, and was imprisoned 1603–16.

**56** THE DOCTOR AND SHAKESPEARE – The first quote is from *Planet of Evil*. We learn much more in *City of Death. The Chase. The Time Meddler.* The Doctor frequently quotes from Shakespeare. In the Doctor's own timeline, he meets Shakespeare first in *The Empire of Glass.* Shakespeare's works are banned at the time of *Managra.*

**57** *Birthright* (p61).

**58** This is the date on the monument in *Silver Nemesis.*

**59** Dating *The Empire of Glass* – The Doctor states that it "must be the year of Our Lord, 1609" (p30). The Armageddon Convention is referred to in *Revenge of the Cybermen.*

**60** *Managra.*

**61** *The Empire of Glass.*

**62** *Silver Nemesis.*

**63** Dating *The Abominable Snowmen* – This was in "1630" according to the Doctor. *The Programme Guide* suggested '1400 AD'. The Doctor speaks Tibetan in *Planet of the Spiders* (but doesn't in *The Creature from the Pit*), and uses Tibetan meditation in *Terror of the Zygons*.

**64** *The War Games* – The Thirty Years War ran from 1618 to 1648.

**65** Dating *Silver Nemesis* – The Doctor gives the date of the launch; there is no indication exactly how long afterwards Lady Peinforte leaves for the twentieth century. Quite how "Roundheads" can be involved in this business when the term wasn't used until the Civil War is unclear. The adoption of the Gregorian calendar in 1752 means that several days were 'lost' in Britain, so had the Nemesis really landed exactly 350 years after 23 November 1638, it would have landed on 3 December 1988.

The statue passes over Earth every twenty-five years (in 1663, 1688, 1713, 1738, 1763, 1788, 1813, 1838, 1863, 1888, 1913, 1938, 1963 and finally 1988). *The Terrestrial Index* offers suggestions as to the effects of the statue on human history, but the only on-screen information concerns the twentieth century.

**66** Fenric's involvement is only established in *The Curse of Fenric*.

**67** The English Civil Wars ran from 1642 to 1649. *The War Games. The Time Monster. The Awakening. Nightshade.*

**68** *The Dæmons* – Matthew Hopkins died in 1647. *The Androids of Tara* – Isaak Walton lived 1593–1683, and published *The Compleat Angler* in 1653.

the Thirty Years War. [64]

## 1638 (November) – SILVER NEMESIS [65]

On 23 November 1638, the Doctor and Roundheads fought Lady Peinforte as the Nemesis asteroid was launched into space from a meadow in Windsor. Following this, the Doctor set his watch alarm to go off on 23 November 1988, the day that the Nemesis would return to Earth. The Nemesis passed over Earth every twenty-five years, influencing human affairs.

Lady Peinforte immediately employed a mathematician to work out the asteroid's trajectory. His work completed, his blood was used in a magical ceremony to transport Peinforte and her servant Richard Maynarde to the asteroid's ultimate destination. Her time travel was aided by Fenric. [66]

A Civil War battlefield was kidnapped by the War Lords. A division of Roundheads was also kidnapped by the Master using TOMTIT. On 13 July 1643, the Royalists and Roundheads met in Little Hodcombe, wiping out themselves and the entire village. The Malus fed from the psychic energy released by the deaths and briefly emerged from its dormancy. The Doctor returned Will Chandler to his native time shortly afterwards. In 1644, the castle of Crook Marsham was consumed in "strange fire". [67]

Witches hid from Matthew Hopkins in Devil's End. The Doctor fished with Izaak Walton. Richard Maynarde died on 2 November, 1657 and was entombed at Windsor. According to the Doctor, Aubrey invented Druidism "as a joke". The Doctor was a founder member of the Royal Geographical Society. In 1661, the astronomer Clancy discovered a comet that returned to Earth every one hundred and fifty-seven years. [68]

## c 1666 – THE SMUGGLERS [69]

"This is the Deadman's Key: Ringwood, Smallbeer and Gurney"

A group of pirates led by Captain Samuel Pike of the *Black Albatross* attempted to locate Captain Avery's treasure in Cornwall with only a rhyme as a clue to its whereabouts. The treasure was found in the local church – the names in the rhyme also appeared on tombs in the crypt. The King's militia arrived, killing Pike and many of his crew.

## 1666 (Early September) – THE VISITATION [70]

A group of escaped Terileptil prisoners made planetfall on Earth. They planned to wipe out the human population with rats infected with the bubonic plague virus. The Terileptils were killed, and the explosion of their equipment caused the Great Fire of London.

On a visit to Earth, the Doctor had been blamed for the Great Fire of London. Perhaps on the same visit the Doctor met Mr and Mrs Pepys. Mrs Pepys "makes an excellent cup of coffee". [71]

In the late seventeenth century, "Professor Chronotis" retired to St Cedd's College, Cambridge. About this time, the Eternals kidnapped a seventeenth-century pirate crew. In 1677, John Wallace gave a paper on sympathetic vibration to the Royal Society. The Gore Crow Hotel was built in 1684. The Doctor met Isaac Newton. At first he dropped apples on his head, but then he explained gravity to him over dinner. [72]

By the late twentieth century, no documents from before 1700 existed at Boscombe Hall, and this was the year before Dr Thomas Borlase was born. Weed Creatures were seen in the North Sea during the eighteenth century. The Doctor "ran Taunton for two weeks in the eighteenth century and I've never been so bored". The Doctor once met the Duke of Marlborough. *Gulliver's Travels* was published in 1726. The Aliens Act was passed in 1730. Padmasambhava began to construct Yeti from this time. A battlefield from the Jacobite Uprising was kidnapped by the War Lords. [73]

## 1746 (April) – THE HIGHLANDERS [74]

The Doctor prevented the crooked solicitor Grey from selling Scottish prisoners into slavery. The highlanders had signed six-year plantation work contracts, but the Doctor sent the boat to the safety of France. Jamie McCrimmon, a Scots piper, joined

According to the monument seen in *Silver Nemesis. The Stones of Blood* – John Aubrey lived 1626–97. *Ghost Light* – the Royal Geographical Society was formed in 1645 during the Civil War. *The Ghosts of N-Space* (p200).

69 Dating *The Smugglers* – The Doctor notes that the design of the church he sees on leaving the TARDIS means that they could have landed "at any time after the sixteenth century". Later, he says that the customers in the inn are dressed in clothes from the "seventeenth century". *The Terrestrial Index* and *The TARDIS File* set the story in '1650', and The TARDIS Logs in '1646'. *The Discontinuity Guide* states that as 'a character says "God save the King" ' (and, perhaps more to the point, Josiah Blake is the 'King's Revenue Officer') it must be when England had a King (1603–42, 1660–88, or 1694 onwards) and that the costumes suggest that it is set in the latter part of the century.

70 Dating *The Visitation* – The Doctor suggests "we're about three hundred years early". The action culminates with the start of the Great Fire of London, which took place on the night of 2/3 September 1666, so the story would seem to start on 1 September. According to the novelisation, the Terileptils crashed on "5 August", this was "several weeks ago" according to Mace on-screen.

71 *Pyramids of Mars*. He refers

to Mr and Mrs Pepys in *Robot* and her coffee-making prowess in *Planet of the Spiders*. Pepys lived 1633–1703, he began writing his diary in 1660 and his wife Elizabeth died in 1669.

72 "Three centuries" before *Shada*. *Enlightenment*. *The Happiness Patrol*. *Battlefield* – this is the date on the capstone above the hotel's fireplace. *The Pirate Planet* – Newton lived 1642–1727, and published his theories of gravitation in 1685.

73 *The Stones of Blood*. *Fury from the Deep*. *The Highest Science* (p208). *The Android Invasion* – the Doctor presumably means the first Duke, who lived 1650–1722 and was made a Duke in 1702. *The Mind Robber*. *The Highlanders*. "Over two hundred years" before *The Abominable Snowmen* according to Songsten. *The War Games*.

74 Dating *The Highlanders* – The provisional title of the story was *Culloden*, and it is set shortly after that battle. Despite references in *The Highlanders*, *The War Games* and other stories, Culloden took place in April 1746 not 1745. This is first explicitly stated in *The Underwater Menace*, (although the draft script again said '1745'). The *Radio Times* specified that *The Highlanders* is set in April. The 1745 date has been perpetuated by the first edition of *The Making of Doctor Who*.

75 Dating *The War Games* – Jamie is returned to his native

the Doctor.

## 1746 (April) – THE WAR GAMES [75]

Jamie McCrimmon was returned to his own native time by the Time Lords.

**Once again, Jared Khan, this time known as Thomas, narrowly missed acquiring the TARDIS. After this time he posed as Alessandro di Cagliostro, claiming to be born 1743, died 1795. [76]**

The Daemons inspired the Industrial Revolution. [77]

In 1750, a ship was wrecked off Haiti. Washed ashore was Nkome, a six-year old African slave kept alive by voodoo, who began plotting his revenge against the blancs. [78]

Dr Borlase was killed surveying the Nine Travellers in 1754, the same year the Doctor discovered Kadiatu Lethbridge-Stewart half-dead in a slaver off Sierra Leone. He took her to the People. Robert Burns was born in 1759. In the late eighteenth century, Scaroth lived in France at the time of Louis XV, and he acquired a Gainsborough. Gainsborough also painted a portrait of Ace that ended up in Windsor Castle. Auderly House was built in Georgian times. A little over two hundred years ago, Devil's End became notorious when the Third Lord of Aldbourne's black magic rituals were exposed. Around that time, Cessair posed as Lady Montcalm and was painted by Ramsay. The Rani was present during the American War of Independence. The first Doctor met James Watt. In 1788 the Nemesis Bow was stolen from Windsor Castle. [79]

Susan showed an interest in the French Revolution, and she visited France at this time with the first Doctor. It was their first ever visit to the planet, and it demonstrated to the Doctor that the old order could be toppled, and that people wanted freedom and a hope for the future. As a result, this is the Doctor's favourite period of Earth history. The Doctor met Marie Antoinette and obtained a lockpick from her. In 1791, the Doctor, Tegan and Turlough were dining at the Cafe de Saint Joseph in Aix-en-Provence when they were accidentally scooped up by the Crystal Bucephalus and whisked thousands of years into the future. [80]

In 1793, the attempted opening of Devil's Hump by Sir

55

Percival Flint resulted in disaster. [81]

## 1794 (Late July) – THE REIGN OF TERROR [82]

'I have received a message that Barrass, Robespierre's deputy, is plotting to take control of France. He is meeting a Brigadier-General Napoleon Bonaparte at The Sinking Ship, an inn on the Calais Road. They plan a coup against Robespierre, and after that, Bonaparte will take control of the country.'

[Secret report to the British government 26 July 1794]

Nelson "was a personal friend" of the Doctor. [83]

## 1798 – SET PIECE [84]

Benny fled the Ants, ending up with archaeologist Vivant Denon as he began to uncover Ancient Egyptian treasures for Napoleon.

## = 1804 – THE MAN IN THE VELVET MASK [85]

The Doctor and Dodo arrived in Paris to find a huge, jagged tower dominating the skyline. From inside, the Marquis de Sade ruled France with the help of his First Deputy, the dwarf scientist Minski. Sade was not the Sade of history, but a tall, confident man. The Doctor discovered that aliens had reconfigured Earth inside a pocket universe to perform experiments on "reality control". As the forces of the satanist King of England "Mad George Hanover" invaded, the Doctor discovered the machinery that moved Earth out of N-Space and returned it to our universe.

Joseph Sundvik was born on 8 April 1809. [86]

The Doctor met Napoleon and told him that an army marches on its stomach. In 1811, the poet William Blake vanished from his home and met the Doctor. In 1812, a battlefield from Napoleon's Russian campaign was kidnapped by the War Lords. [87]

## 1818 – THE GHOSTS OF N-SPACE [88]

Travelling back in time, the Doctor and Sarah witnessed the early life of the wizard Maximillian.

time at the end of *The War Games*.

76 *Birthright* (p89, p184).

77 *The Dæmons*.

78 *White Darkness*.

79 *The Stones of Blood. The Also People. The Underwater Menace. The City of Death.* We see the portrait of Ace hanging in Windsor Castle in the extended version of *Silver Nemesis*, in Ace's personal timeline, she had not yet sat for the painting – Gainsborough lived 1727–88, painting society portraits 1760–74 before turning to landscapes. *Day of the Daleks*, Alex Macintosh, the television commentator, states that the house is "Georgian" hence it was built between 1714 and 1830. "Two hundred years" before *The Dæmons. The Stones of Blood* – Allan Ramsay lived 1713–84. *The Mark of the Rani* – the American War of Independence ran from 1775 to 1783. *The Space Museum* – James Watt lived 1736–1819. *Silver Nemesis*.

80 In *100,000 BC*, Susan borrows a book about the French Revolution, but already knows a great deal about the subject. In *The Reign of Terror*, Susan says that the Reign of Terror is "his favourite period in the history of the Earth". *Just War* attempts to explain why. *The Robots of Death. Pyramids of Mars. The Crystal Bucephalus* (p20).

81 *The Dæmons*.

82 Dating *The Reign of Terror* –

The date is given on-screen, with the plan to kill Robespierre on "27 July". *The Programme Guide* offered the date '1792', but *The Terrestrial Index* corrected this.

83 *The Sea Devils* – Nelson lived 1758–1805.

84 Dating *Set Piece* – It is "1798 CE" (p57).

85 Dating *The Man in the Velvet Mask* – The Doctor and Dodo see a poster which gives a date of "Messidor, Year XII", and the Doctor calculates that they are in "June or July 1804" (p14).

86 According to a gravestone in *The Curse of Fenric*.

87 *Day of the Daleks*. The Doctor does not meet Napoleon in *The Reign of Terror* (Ian and Barbara do). The third Doctor is still exiled in the twentieth century timezone, so it must be an earlier incarnation – Napoleon lived 1769–1821. *The Pit* (p99). *The War Games*.

88 Dating *The Ghosts of N-Space* – It is "1818" (p63), 157 years before the present-day setting (p200).

89 The Doctor mentions Beau Brummel in *The Sensorites* and *The Two Doctors*, Brummell lived 1778–1840. The Dalek ship crashed "two hundred years" before *The Power of the Daleks*, and a Dalek from this mission recognises the Doctor, despite his regeneration – in *Day of the Daleks*, the Daleks need to use the Mind Analysis Machine to establish the Doctor's identity. "Eighty years" before *Horror of*

In the early nineteenth century the Doctor met Beau Brummel, who told him he looked better in a cloak. A Dalek scoutship **(the first recorded Dalek expedition to our solar system)** crashed on Vulcan. By this time the Daleks had already encountered the second Doctor. The Beast of Fang Rock was seen. The Reverend Thomas Bright surveyed the Nine Travellers, and at some point between this and the late twentieth century Cessair posed as Mrs Trefusis for sixty years, then Senora Camara. On 3 July 1820, Florence Sundvik was born. [89]

## c 1822 THE MARK OF THE RANI [90]

The Rani was present during the Industrial Revolution, extracting a chemical from human brains. Her project was interrupted by the arrival, and rivalry, of the Doctor and the Master. The Master attempted to disrupt human history as the greatest scientific minds of the era converged on Killingworth. The Doctor trapped the two renegades in the Rani's TARDIS and banished them from Earth.

The Doctor may have attended the Coronation of Queen Victoria. Litefoot's Chinese Fowling Piece was last fired around this time. The Doctor met Brunel and gave Hans Christian Andersen the idea for *The Emperor's New Clothes*. In 1843, the Doctor and Susan met Siger Holmes in India and learnt that the natives believed in a gateway to another world. 1851 saw the Great Exhibition, which the Doctor attempted to visit. The same year, *The America* crossed the Atlantic in seventeen days. Around this time, Jacob Grimm discovered the Law of Consonantal Shift. Victoria Waterfield was born in 1852. [91]

The Crimean War was fought 1853–56. On 25 October 1854, the Doctor was present at the "magnificent folly" of the Charge of the Light Brigade; the Doctor also claimed he had been wounded in the Crimea. On 5 November 1854, Mollie's uncle was killed at the Battle of Inkerman. A Crimean War battlefield was lifted by the War Lords. [92]

In 1853 Saul, the living church of Cheldon Bonniface, was baptised in his own font. In 1854, Maxwell experimented with electromagnetism. **Three years later, Charles Dodgson photo-**

graphed a young Victoria Waterfield. [93]

In 1860, Litefoot's father was a Brigadier-General on the punitive expedition to China. The Litefoot family stayed in the country for the next thirteen years. During this time, Magnus Greel arrived in the Time Cabinet from the year 5000. Li H'sen Chang sheltered Greel, believing him to be the god Weng-Chiang. Litefoot's mother was later given the Cabinet as a gift by the Emperor. Around this time, Henry Gordon Jago began working in the entertainment business. [94]

In 1861, the Malicious Damage Act was passed. [95] A battle-field from the American Civil War was lifted by the War Lords. The Gettysburg address was made on 19 November 1863, and watched by the TARDIS crew using the Time/Space Visualiser. Around this time, the Doctor befriended Thomas Huxley. Victoria Waterfield's mother, Edith **Rose**, died **on 23 November 1863. Lord Kelvin laid transatlantic telegraph cables in 1865.** [96]

## 1866 (2 and 3 June) – THE EVIL OF THE DALEKS [97]

'Following the bizarre time travel experiments of Maxtible and Waterfield, the Daleks were lured to the nineteenth century. They took control of Waterfield's house, keeping his daughter Victoria prisoner, and used it as a base to set a trap for the Doctor. The net tightened around their greatest enemy, and the Daleks prepared a trial of strength and a test of skill for the Doctor's human companion, Jamie. By analysing his responses, they hoped to distil the Human Factor. The attempt backfired, leading to the end of the Daleks...'
[*The Children of Davros*, Njeri Ngugi]

K9 was programmed with all grandmaster chess games from 1866 onwards. A battlefield from the Mexican Uprising of 1867 was lifted by the War Lords. **In 1868 the Doctor opened a bank account at Coutts Bank in London. The same year, Wychborn House burnt down.** In 1870 the Jameson Boys encountered the Zygons on Tulloch Moor. The elder brother, Robert, was driven mad by the experience and never spoke again, while his younger brother Donald simply disappeared. Around that time, Reuben joined the lighthouse service. He spent twenty of the next thirty

Fang Rock. The Stones of Blood. The Curse of Fenric.

90 Dating *The Mark of the Rani* – The date is never stated on-screen or in the script, but the production team felt that the story was set in '1830'. *The Terrestrial Index* set the story 'c 1825', and the novel at 'the beginning of the nineteenth century'. Tony Scupham-Bilton concluded in *Celestial Toyroom* that, judging by the historical evidence and the month that the story was filmed, the story 'is set in either October 1821 or October 1822'. As that article states, the story must at the very least be set before the Stockton–Darlington line was opened in September 1825 and after Thomas Liddell was made Baron Ravensworth on 17 July 1821.

91 *The Curse of Peladon* – Victoria was crowned in 1837. According to Litefoot in *The Talons of Weng-Chiang* the gun "hasn't been fired for fifty years". *The Two Doctors* – Brunel lived 1806–59. *The Romans* – Andersen lived 1805–75; his fairy stories were first published from 1835 onwards. *All-Consuming Fire. Time-Flight. Enlightenment. State of Decay* – Jacob Grimm lived 1785–1863. *Downtime* – Victoria was "eleven" (p14) when her mother died in "1863" (p261)

92 *The Evil of the Daleks* and *The Sea Devils. The War Games.*

93 *Timewyrm: Revelation* (p4). *The Evil of the Daleks. Downtime.*

**94** *The Talons of Weng-Chiang* – Jago claims to have had "thirty years in the halls".

**95** According to the Doctor in *Horror of Fang Rock.*

**96** *The War Games* – the American Civil War lasted from 1861 to 1865. *The Chase. Logopolis* – Thomas Huxley lived 1825–95. *The Evil of the Daleks, Downtime* (p261). "Fifteen years" before *Evolution* (p107).

**97** Dating *The Evil of the Daleks* – An early storyline gave the date of the Victorian sequence as '1880' (and the date of the caveman sequence which was later deleted as '20,000 BC'). The camera scripts gave the date of '1867', as did some promotional material, but this was altered at the last minute when it was decided to dovetail *The Faceless Ones* and *The Evil of the Daleks.*

**98** *The Androids of Tara. The War Games. Birthright. Strange England* (p157). According to Angus in *Terror of the Zygons. Horror of Fang Rock. The War Games. Ghost Light.*

**99** Dating *Set Piece* – It is "1871 CE" (p62).

**100** Dating *The Chase* – The *Mary Celeste* was discovered in late November 1872.

**101** *The Curse of Fenric. The Talons of Weng-Chiang. The Stones of Blood. Pyramids of Mars.* The Priory is "Victorian", and as the Doctor points out, that means that the priestholes aren't the genuine article. *The*

years in a gas-powered lighthouse. In 1871 a battlefield from the Franco–Prussian War was lifted by the War Lords and on 10 November Stanley met Livingstone. [98]

## 1871 – SET PIECE [99]

The Doctor, Benny and Ace were reunited in Paris, where they also met Kadiatu Lethbridge-Stewart. After the Ants had been defeated, Ace chose to leave the Doctor, and she joined the Paris Commune. Ace was the last soldier to leave the barricades when the Commune fell.

## 1872 (25 November) – THE CHASE [100]

The Doctor and the Daleks landed on the *Mary Celeste*, forcing the crew to abandon ship.

Joseph Sundvik died on 3 February 1872. A year later, Litefoot left China. The Nine Travellers were surveyed in 1874. Old Priory, a Victorian folly, was built for the Scarman family. After this time Marcus and Laurence played in the priesthole there as children. The Doctor met Alexander Graham Bell. [101]

## 1873 – STRANGE ENGLAND [102]

The TARDIS landed on an asteroid, shaped by Gallifreyan Protyon units to resemble an idyllic Victorian country house based on Wychborn House. It was sculpted by an old friend of the Doctor, the Time Lady Galah, who had reached the end of her regenerative cycle. With the help of the Doctor, Galah lived on as one of her human creations, Charlotte; she returned to Earth and married Richard Aickland, who became a renowned Gothic novelist in the early twentieth century (he wrote such books as *Cold Eyes* and *The Wine Press*).

'ZANAK – (Also known as the Pirate Planet.) *The Vantarialis* crashed on Zanak, and with the assistance of old Queen Xanxia, the Captain converted the entire planet into a hollow world capable of jumping between star systems and sucking the life out of planets. After this time, with increasing frequency, Zanak attacked and destroyed the Vegan shipyard of Bandraginus V, Aterica, Temesis, Tridentio III,

Lowiteliom, Bibicorpus and Granados.'
[*Bartholomew's Planetary Gazetteer*, Volume XXVI] [103]

## 1880 – EVOLUTION [104]

Percival Ross witnessed a Rutan scoutship crashing in Limehouse, and recovered a flask of Rutan healing salve from the wreckage. The alien gel had a miraculous healing effect on humans, but it was also capable of merging human and animal genetic material, as Ross found out when a boy he was treating became a ferocious doglike creature. Ross interested the industrialist Breckingridge, the owner of a vast cable factory in the town of Bodhan, in the creation of a race of hybrid dolphinmen.

Fifteen children went missing from the area, kidnapped by Ross for his experiments. A young Arthur Conan Doyle witnessed the happenings on Dartmoor, and a chance encounter with a mysterious Doctor inspired two of his most famous characters: Sherlock Holmes and Professor Challenger. An even younger Rudyard Kipling was also witness to the events surrounding the closure of Breckingridge's factory.

## 1881 (25 and 26 October) – THE GUNFIGHTERS [105]

The TARDIS landed at Tombstone shortly before the Gunfight at the OK Corral. As the Doctor searched for a dentist, Johnny Ringo found one – Doc Holliday, whom he'd been tracking for two years.

The Doctor met Gilbert and Sullivan, and witnessed the eruption of Krakatoa. American humorist Franklin Adams was born in 1881. Louis Pasteur was kidnapped by the Rani. [106]

## 1883 – GHOST LIGHT [107]

Rumours spread that Josiah Samuel Smith, arch-advocate of Darwinist theories, was conducting blasphemous experiments at his house, Gabriel Chase, to the north of London. Two years after Inspector Mackenzie vanished while investigating the goings-on at the house, Smith himself disappeared. Servants working in the house spoke of hauntings and mesmerism, apemen and angels, and a bizarre plot to assassinate Queen Victoria.

*Android Invasion*. Bell lived 1847–1922, and patented the telephone in 1876.

102 Dating *Strange England* – The Doctor says that the "temporal location" is "1873" (p229).

103 *The Pirate Planet*. Bandraginus V disappeared "over a century" ago according to the Doctor, when Balaton was young. Zanak is not capable of time travel, so must have been operating at least that long. The planets attacked by Zanak are named in production documents, and plaques were made up with the names on, but only those for Bandraginus V, Granados, Lowiteliom and Calufrax are clearly visible on-screen. *First Frontier* gives a little more detail about Bandraginus V (p129).

104 Dating *Evolution* – It is the "year of grace eighteen hundred and eighty" (p6, p108). Arthur Conan Doyle lived 1859–1930, although *The Hound of the Baskervilles* was one of the later Holmes books; written 1902. Kipling lived 1865–1936, so he is "fifteen" here (p45).

105 Dating *The Gunfighters* – The last episode culminates with the Gunfight at the OK Corral. The depiction of events owes more to the popular myths and Hollywood treatment of the story than to historical accuracy.

106 *Inside the Spaceship* – Gilbert and Sullivan collaborated between 1875 and

1896. *Inferno* – the Doctor apparently heard "Primords" on this occasion (Krakatoa erupted in 1883). *Seeds of Doom. Time and the Rani* – Pasteur lived 1822–95 [See also THE TIME BRAINS page 42].

107 Dating *Ghost Light* – Set "two years" after 1881, when Mackenzie is sent to investigate the disappearance of Sir George Pritchard, and "a century" before Ace burns down Gabriel Chase in 1983. The script suggested that a caption slide, 'Perivale – 1883' might be used over the establishing shot of Gabriel Chase. Queen Victoria was a Hanover, not a Saxe-Coburg, but late in her reign she did acquire the nickname "Mrs Saxe-Coburg".

108 *The Green Death.* In *Resurrection of the Daleks* the Doctor remarks that "a century ago these docks would have been bustling with activity".

109 Dating *Timelash* – The Doctor applies "a time deflection coefficient of 706 years" to the Timelash's original destination of 1179, and concludes that Vena will arrive in "1885... AD". *The Terrestrial Index* set this in 'c 1891', after *The Time Machine* was published.

110 *The Ghosts of N-Space* (p31).

111 *The Moonbase. Carnival of Monsters.*

112 Dating *All-Consuming Fire* – It is "the year 1887" according

The house remained abandoned for a century.

In 1884 a book was published detailing many types of Amazonian fungus. Around that time, the London Docks were bustling with activity. [108]

The Doctor knew "a nice little restaurant on the Khyber Pass".

## 1885 – TIMELASH [109]

While conducting an experiment with a ouija board, Herbert George Wells met Vena, who had been transported from Karfel in the Timelash. Wells travelled to Karfel with the Doctor, and was later returned to his native time, inspired to write his scientific romances.

The Doctor helped "Bertie Wells" with invisibility experiments. [110]

In 1888, the Doctor gained a medical degree in Glasgow under Lister. Around that time, he sparred with John L Sullivan. [111]

## 1887 – ALL-CONSUMING FIRE [112]

'THE CASE OF THE ALL-CONSUMING FIRE
In 1887, Holmes and Watson are travelling through Austria on the Orient Express, when the train is stopped by the train of Pope Leo XIII. The Pope commissions Holmes to investigate the theft of occult books from the Library of St John the Beheaded. Holmes discovers that his eldest brother, Sherringford, has allied himself with the Baron Maupertuis, and that they plan to use incantations in the books to open a gateway to the planet of Ry'leh. Holmes and Watson seal the gateway.'
[*The Complete Casebooks of Sherlock Holmes*, Anne Daly]

The Doctor told Ace before this case that he had met Sherlock Holmes. [113]

## 1888 (30 September) – THE PIT [114]

The Doctor and William Blake arrived in the East End at the time of the Jack the Ripper murders, before discovering a way to the late twentieth century.

## c 1889 – THE TALONS OF WENG-CHIANG [115]

'Well m'lud, the man Chang was a stooge. He was a cove all right, – a consummate champion of the 'fluence, fit to play before Her Majesty the Queen 'erself, but a stooge nonetheless. He'd gained his mesmeric mastery from his god, Weng-Chiang. What was that, m'lud? No, your honour, but he styled himself as such, and taught Chang magic tricks of such professional perspicacity and prestidigitational prowess as I'd ever witnessed in thirty years in the business. Theatrical entertainment, m'lud; my theatre is a veritable pleasure palace, the finest venue in the East End. If your lordship is ever down that way, then by all means I'll reserve the royal box for you, at very favourable rates. Stick to the point, your honour? As you wish. Well, this business all started with that girl Emma Buller. My beloved wife had just spent 17/3d on her wardrobe and – no, m'lud, her own wardrobe. Clothing: dresses and the like. It is relevant, sagacity, I assure you. As I was saying, Miss Buller was mesmerised by Chang, only she was never the same again. Anyway, Emma Buller's old man Joseph, he came round to the theatre a week later saying that his old lady hadn't been the same since Chang's nefarious hypnotic activities. Now she'd gone and vanished. Did I mention the missing girls – the seven missing girls? Anyway, these Black Scorpion chappies had prepared the "House of the Dragon" for this Greel chap. Magnus Greel, the criminal posing as Weng-Chiang. He was searching for a Cabinet of some kind from a secret dungeon underneath my very own theatre. Yes, sir – at a mere shilling a time. Very popular tour it is too, your honour. Anyway, Greel was beaten back by that brilliant bobby. The Doctor, your honour, that was 'is codename. He defeated Greel, and killed Mr Sin. Ah, your honour, Mr Sin. Well, that's a long story…'

[Transcript of Henry Gordon Jago's Evidence to the Enquiry Following the Events in the East End]

to both Watson (p5) and Benny (p153). References to *The Talons of Weng-Chiang* (p42, p64) suggest that this book is set after that story.

113 *Timewyrm: Revelation* (p15).

114 Dating *The Pit* – Blake sees a newspaper dated 13 September 1888.

115 Dating *The Talons of Weng-Chiang* – The story is set soon after the Jack the Ripper murders (1888), as Casey refers to "Jolly Jack". In the draft script, Casey went on to say that the new batch of disappearances can't be the Ripper because he 'is in Canada'. This would seem to be a reference to Prince Albert Victor, the son of the Prince of Wales, who is named as the Ripper by some theorists. The Prince, known as 'Eddy', was a rather ineffectual, sickly man and a political liability. Following a series of scandals he was sent on a tour of the colonies from late 1889 to May 1890. Although he visited Greece, Egypt and India, he doesn't appear to have gone to Canada at this time. Eddy died on 14 January 1892 (although some conspiracy theorists have suggested he lived a great deal longer in an asylum on the Isle of Wight, dying in the 1920s, and not succeeding to the throne as he ought to have done).

116 *K9 and Company* – According to Wilson "there hasn't been a human sacrifice

since 1891".

117 Dating *The Sands of Time* – "LORD KENILWORTH At Home Monday 10th November, 1896" (p29).

118 *The Curse of Fenric. The Daleks' Master Plan*, and *The Invasion of Time. The War Games* – the Boer War ran from 1899 to 1902.

119 Dating *Horror of Fang Rock* – Terrance Dicks's novel and contemporary publicity material set the story 'at the turn of the century'. Electric power was introduced to lighthouses around the turn of the century. Fang Rock is in the English Channel ("five or six miles" from Southampton) and is particularly treacherous, so was probably upgraded quite early on. Reuben and Vince state that the Beast was last seen "eighty year ago" and "back in the twenties". *The Programme Guide* offered the date '1909'; *The Terrestrial Index* claimed '1904'. The TARDIS Logs suggested 'c 1890', *The Doctor Who File* 'the early 1900s'. The TARDIS Special gave the date 'the 1890s'. Vince makes a reference to "King Edward" in episode 1.

120 *The Mind Robber. Enlightenment. The Romans. Planet of the Spiders*, and *Revenge of the Cybermen* – Houdini lived 1874–1926. *The Stones of Blood* – Einstein lived 1879–1955, publishing his Special and General Theories of Relativity in 1905 and 1915 respectively. *All-Consuming*

Human sacrifice was still taking place in Moreton Harwood in the early 1890s. [116]

## 1896 – THE SANDS OF TIME [117]

The Doctor, Tegan and Nyssa arrived in the Egyptian Room of the British Museum. At the invitation of Lord Kenilworth, the Doctor and Tegan attended the unwrapping of an ancient mummy, only to discover that the mummy was the perfectly preserved body of Nyssa herself ...

On 12 January 1898, Florence Sundvik died. Mary Eliza Millington was born on 3 March, dying four days later. At the end of the nineteenth century, the grandfather of Reverend Wainwright translated the Viking runes in the crypt of his church. The Doctor was present at the Relief of Mafeking on 17 May 1900. Battlefields from the Boxer Rising and the Boer War were lifted by the War Lords. [118]

## c 1900 – HORROR OF FANG ROCK [119]

'Once we Rutan dominated the whole of the galaxy, but the accursed Sontarans have beaten us back to the far fringes. Now, we have mastered a metamorphic ability. We have located a strategically important planet, inhabited by a semi-intelligent primate species, the human, which we have never encountered before.'

[Rutan Oral History]

In 1901, an English author began to write boys' stories for the magazine *The Ensign*. The same year, the first British submarine was launched, a fact remembered by British sailors kidnapped by the Eternals. The Doctor trained the Mountain Mauler of Montana, learnt escapology from Houdini, and met Einstein. The Rakshassi army was destroyed in the San Francisco earthquake of 1906, following the Doctor's intervention. [120]

## 1909 – BIRTHRIGHT [121]

The secret society, the New Dawn, led by Jared Khan, attempted to stabilise the Great Divide with the future and bring the Chaarl back to this time. Some Chaarl broke through and murdered a number of people in the East End. The Chaarl were absorbed by the TARDIS, and Jared Khan was destroyed.

## 1911 – PYRAMIDS OF MARS [122]

'BROTHERS DIE AS TRAGIC FIRE HOLOCAUST SWEEPS COUNTRY ESTATE – MANY OTHERS FEARED KILLED
The whole countryside was shocked and saddened today by the news of the tragic fire at the Old Priory in which a number of well-known local figures perished. Fire broke out suddenly during the night and swept the Priory, the Lodge and much of the heavily-wooded estate at great speed.

Among the victims of the blaze is believed to be Professor Marcus Scarman, the well-known Egyptologist, who had just returned from a successful archaeological expedition to Egypt. His brother Laurence, the distinguished amateur scientist, also died in the flames.'

[Report from a local newspaper]

The building that would later become UNIT HQ was built on the site of the Old Priory.

The Nine Travellers were surveyed in 1911. The year afterwards, *The King's Regulations* were published and the Royal Flying Corps was formed. The *Titanic* sank, although the Doctor claimed that he had nothing to do with that... [123]

## 1912 (14 April) – THE LEFT-HANDED HUMMINGBIRD [124]

On the sinking *Titanic*, the Doctor prevented Huitzilin, the Blue, from acquiring the Xiuhcoatl, an Exxilon weapon capable of manipulating molecules – it could transmute or destroy matter.

The Nemesis statue passed over Earth in 1913, heralding the First World War. The same year a part of the Great Temple of the Aztecs was discovered by Gamio. [125]

---

*Fire.*

121 Dating *Birthright* – The date and year of Benny's arrival are given on p15, the date of departure on p203.

122 Dating *Pyramids of Mars* – Laurence Scarman says that it is "1911". Newspaper report from Terrance Dicks's novelisation.

123 *The Stones of Blood. The War Games. Ghost Light.* The Doctor mentions the Titanic in *Robot*, but tells Borusa in *The Invasion of Time* that "I had nothing to do with this, I promise you".

124 Dating *The Left-Handed Hummingbird* – The story takes place on the Titanic, the date is confirmed on p221.

125 *Silver Nemesis. The Left-Handed Hummingbird* (p58)

126 Dating *Human Nature* – It is "April" (p17), "1914" (p16).

127 Dating *White Darkness* – "On the wall, a calendar of 1915 had just been turned to the August page" (p22).

128 *Planet of Giants. The War Games. The Sea Devils. Delta and the Bannerman. Just War.*

129 Dating *Toy Soldiers* – The main action of the book starts "25 September 1919" (p39)

130 Dating *The Daleks' Master Plan* – The script for *The Feast of Steven* specified a date of '1919', but publicity material released on 1 October 1965 stated that the TARDIS lands in 'California 1921'. The film being made is a talkie, which means this must be after *The Jazz Singer* in 1927. Valentino made his debut in 1919 but was only really famous after *The Sheikh* in 1921. Fairbanks's debut was in 1915, but he wasn't "big" (as he is described in the episode) until *The Three Musketeers* in 1921. Chaplin's debut was 1914, but the film we see in production strongly resembles *Gold Rush* (1924). Bing Crosby didn't go to Hollywood until 1930. Landen claimed a date of '1929'; The TARDIS Special offered 'c 1920'.

131 Angus relates the story in *Terror of the Zygons*. According to Millington the accident happened "over twenty years" before *The Curse of Fenric*, and Judson appears to blame Millington for it.

## 1914 – HUMAN NATURE [126]

In the tiny village of Farringham, Doctor John Smith of Aberdeen fell in love with Joan Redfern. At the same time, the Aubertides attacked the village hunting for the Doctor.

## 1915 (August) – WHITE DARKNESS [127]

> 'During the American invasion of Haiti in 1915, there were reports of zombies, men walking the streets with autopsy scars on their chests, animated by voodoo magic.'
> [*Voodoo Secrets of the Living Dead*, Mysteria Press]

The first Doctor and Susan were caught in a Zeppelin raid at some point during the war, and a First World War battlefield near Ypres was kidnapped by the War Lords. The Doctor once claimed to have been wounded at the Battle of Gallipoli. Burton fought in the War, using his sabre in hand-to-hand combat. **Arthur Kendrick distinguished himself second-guessing the U-boat commanders on the Atlantic convoys.** [128]

## 1919 (Late September) – TOY SOLDIERS [129]

Investigating the mysterious disappearance of children across post-War Europe, the Doctor, Benny, Roz and Chris discovered that they had been kidnapped by the Recruiter, a device transporting beings from many worlds to act as soldiers in a war that had lasted 1,405 years, ravaging the planet Q'ell. 2,846,014,032 beings had died during the conflict. The Recruiter had been part of a war against the Ceracai. It planned to inspire a period of scientific progress in the crucible of an immense war, but the strategy failed: the war was one of attrition, using only races of relatively primitive technology – including humans, Ogrons, Martians, Kreetas, Ajeesks and Biune. The Doctor reprogrammed the device to rebuild the world.

## c 1921 – THE DALEKS' MASTER PLAN [130]

While hiding from the Daleks, the TARDIS landed briefly on a film set in Hollywood.

In 1922 a foreigner staying at Tullock Inn vanished on Tullock Moor, kidnapped by the Zygons. Judson was crippled before this time. [131]

## 1923 (9 November) – TIMEWYRM: EXODUS [132]

Witnessing the Munich Putsch, an attempted coup organised by a young Adolf Hitler, the Doctor and Ace were fired upon with energy weapons.

## 1925 (11 June) – BLACK ORCHID [133]

George Cranleigh was reported killed by Indians while on an expedition in the Amazon in 1923. Cassell and Company published his book *Black Orchid*. Eventually, his fiancée, Anne Talbot, became engaged to George's brother, Charles. George hadn't died, he was kept hidden away at Cranleigh Hall. He broke out, and died trying to abduct his former fiancée.

> 'The summer of 1926 saw a couple of mysterious disappearances. A famous author of boys' stories for the *Ensign* magazine vanished at his home, and on 4 June the SS *Bernice* vanished in the Indian Ocean. The ship had left England in early May, and the last anyone ever saw of it was on 2 June, when it left Bombay.' [134]
>
> [*Doorways of Disappearance*, Mysteria Press]

In 1927, the Doctor watched the chess grandmaster Capablanca play, and around the same time he met Dame Nellie Melba, learning her party piece, and was taught magic tricks by Mescalin. Aaron Blinovitch formulated his Limitation Effect in 1928, publishing it in *Temporal Mechanics*. The Brigadier's car, a Humber 1650 Open Tourer Imperial Model, was built in 1929. [135]

## 1929 – BLOOD HARVEST [136]

As gangland violence escalated, the enigmatic Doc McCoy opened a speakeasy right in the middle of disputed territory. The Doc and his moll Ace saved Al Capone's life. The Doctor was tracking down the Eternal Agonal, who had amplified the gang warfare to feed his lust for violence.

## 1930 (June) – THE ENGLISH WAY OF DEATH [137]

The TARDIS arrived in London during an inexplicable heatwave, as the Doctor needed to return some library books before they

132 Dating *Timewyrm: Exodus* – Part Two of the novel is set during the Munich Putsch, which took place between 8 and 9 November 1923. A textbook quoted in the novel erroneously gives the month as "September" (p95).

133 Dating *Black Orchid* – The Doctor says that it is "three o'clock, June the eleventh, nineteen hundred and twenty-five".

134 The Doctor has heard of the disappearance of the SS *Bernice*, but we see it vanish from the Miniscope and apparently return to its native time at the end of *Carnival of Monsters* Episode Four. Perhaps the ship has not arrived home safely at all.

135 *The Androids of Tara. The Power of Kroll. The Ribos Operation*. The Blinovitch Limitation Effect was first mentioned in *Day of the Daleks* (and subsequently in *Invasion of the Dinosaurs* and *Mawdryn Undead*) – we learn more about Blinovitch in *The Ghosts of N-Space* (p147), *Timewyrm: Revelation* (p50). Hippo identifies the car in *Mawdryn Undead*.

136 Dating *Blood Harvest* – The story takes place during Prohibition (1920–33), before the arrest of Al Capone (1931). The blurb suggests that it is "1929".

137 Dating *The English Way of Death* – "It is early June" (p27) and "Just over a year ago... May '29" (p91).

138 The Brigadier is "sixty-three" in *Blood Heat* (p54) and "forty-six" in *No Future* (p10). Nicholas Courtney, who plays him, was born in 1931 [see also UNIT Dating pages 263-7]. *The Paradise of Death* (p25).
*Meglos. Four to Doomsday* – Donald Bradman was born in 1908. *The Left-Handed Hummingbird* (p58).

139 "Forty years" before *The Paradise of Death* (p131).

140 *Just War*

141 Dating *The Eye of the Giant* – "The time is the eighth of June, nineteen thirty-four" (p42).

became overdue. He and Romana stumbled upon a group from the thirty-second century that were using time corridor technology to send retired people to the peaceful English village of Nutchurch. While the Doctor put a stop to that, Romana confronted the sentient smell Zodaal, an exiled would-be conqueror from the planet Phryxus. Zodaal was trapped in a flask, and the device that would have destroyed Earth was deactivated.

Alastair Gordon Lethbridge-Stewart was born in 1930, he would later attend Holborough with Teddy 'Pooh' Fitzoliver. Around 1930, the fourth Doctor visited Tigella and saw the Dodecahedron. The Urbankans began to receive radio signals from Earth. The Doctor met Donald Bradman, and once took five wickets for New South Wales. In 1933, a part of the Great Temple of the Aztecs was discovered by Cuevas. [138]

The people of Parakon discovered rapine, a crop that when processed could be used as a foodstuff or a building material, and for the next forty years the corporation that marketed it ruled the planet unopposed, supplanting nations, governments, armies and all competition. [139]

During the 1930s, the League of Nations set up a secret international organisation, LONGBOW, that dealt with matters of world security. It found itself, on occasion, dealing with unexplained and extra-terrestrial phenomena. [140]

## 1934 – THE EYE OF THE GIANT [141]

The *Constitution III* was beached upon the uncharted island of Salutua in the South Pacific. Among the passengers was Marshal J Grover, the millionaire shipping magnate and owner of Paragon Film Studios.

Arriving at the island using a time bridge portal, the Doctor and Liz Shaw discovered a spacecraft in a volcanic crater. Animal and plant life on the island was subject to gigantism: giant crabs roamed the beach, bats the size of men flew at night, and the forest was hypertrophied. The Doctor discovered that drugs created by the Semquess, the most skilled bio-engineers in the galaxy, were responsible for the mutations. The substance had been brought to Earth fifty years before by Barthrok of the Grold. The Semquess had tracked him to the planet, and now they apparently destroyed him. Barthrok, though, had used the properties of the Semquess drug to merge with Grover's young wife, Nancy.

## 1935 – THE ABOMINABLE SNOWMEN [142]

'The Monks of Det-Sen have a legend that one of their Masters, Padmasambhava, lived for over three hundred years. They also claim that he built mechanical Yeti that besieged their monastery for over two hundred years. They talk of the Master's hypnotic powers, and of his possession by an evil spirit, which they call the "Intelligence".'

[*The Mysteries of Det-Sen*, Mysteria Press]

Ian Chesterton was born in 1936. In October of that year, the Doctor joined Mao Tse-Tung on the Long March. **In 1936, the Doctor and Mel visited Cairo and met Emil Hartung, the famous Nazi scientist and racing driver.** Two years later, Adolf Hitler gained the Validium Arrow, and the Nemesis passed over Earth heralding Germany's annexation of Austria. [143]

In 1939 a failed attempt to open Devil's Hump, "the Cambridge University Fiasco", took place.

## 1939 (Early September) – TIMEWYRM: EXODUS [144]

The Doctor told Hitler that if he invaded Poland then the British would declare war on Germany. Hitler refused to believe him, but the Doctor was proved right.

Hitler had risen to power with his oratorical skills boosted by the War Lords and the Timewyrm. The War Lords hoped to build a "War Lord universe" by giving the Nazis space travel; the Timewyrm wanted to divert the course of history. Both these alien influences were removed in the destruction of Drachensberg Castle, the War Lord base.

"A foul cloud hung over the area for days. People who stayed on after the catastrophe sickened and died. Eventually the local people said the place was cursed and they all moved away. Drachensberg became an abandoned ruin in a region of horrific desolation."

[*Occult Mysteries of the Nazi Black Coven*, Mysteria Press]

As the Second World War started, a few people in England felt that their country should fight alongside the Nazis. Ratcliffe was one such person, and he was imprisoned for his belief. During

---

142 Dating *The Abominable Snowmen* – According to Thomni, this story takes place "three hundred years" after events that the Doctor says took place in "1630". In *The Web of Fear*, Anne Travers claims that the Travers Expedition took place in "1935". In *Downtime*, Charles Bryce says it was "1936" (p65).

143 According to a format document dating from July 1963, Ian is '27'. *The Mind of Evil. Just War. Silver Nemesis.*

144 Dating *Timewyrm: Exodus* – Part Three of the novel is set in "1939" (p111).

145 *Remembrance of the Daleks. The Web of Fear.*

146 In *The Rescue*, Vicki claims that Barbara ought to be "550" years old. As *The Rescue* is set in 2493 this means she was born in 1943 – making her twenty in 1963, too young to be a history teacher. Jacqueline Hill was born in 1931, so was thirty-four when *The Rescue* was made – Vicki is clearly rounding down. The finalised Writers' Guide for the first series stated that Barbara was '23'.

147 *Just War.* The evacuation is also referred to in *Timewyrm: Exodus.*

148 Dating *Just War* – According to the prologue, the Doctor visits Guernsey in "late December 1941" (p4), but this is an error on the author's part, and it should read "1940", which is "three months" (p36) before the main action of the book, which starts on "the morning of 1 March 1941" (p5).

149 According to a plot synopsis issued on 20 May 1966, Ben and Polly are both '24' at the time of *The Smugglers* – at the time, Michael Craze (Ben) was twenty-four, Anneke Wills (Polly) was twenty-three. The document also gave Polly's surname as 'Wright', a name which was never used on-screen, but is used in the Missing Adventure *Invasion of the Cat-People.* In *The War Machines*, Kitty, the manageress of the Inferno,

the war, bunkers were built in the London Underground, including one at Covent Garden. [145]

Barbara Wright was born in 1940 and she lived in Bedfordshire for a time. [146]

The Doctor was at Dunkirk during the British evacuation. [147]

## 1941 (1–6 March) JUST WAR [148]

In December 1940 the Doctor visited Guernsey.

'During 1940, the Government recognised that scientific advances were becoming more and more specialised, and that an organisation was needed that would liaise military officers with scientific boffins. Admiral Arthur Kendrick was placed in charge of the Scientific Intelligence Division, part of the War Office. It began recruiting staff from around the Commonwealth, and I was seconded from the regular army due to my background. We quickly discovered that the Germans were operating a single radar-beam system by simply...

...March 1941 saw perhaps the greatest triumph of SID, as our organisation had affectionately come to be known. We foiled a plan hatched by Emil Hartung and Oskar Steinmann to use radar-invisible planes against Britain. Steinmann and his second-in-command, Joachim Wolff, had hatched an audacious plot to force the British to surrender or face the destruction of their cities, but in a brilliant coup both prototype planes were destroyed, Wolff was killed, and the British captured blueprints for the new weapon when.'

[*At War with SID*, the memoirs of Sir George Reed, VC]

Ben Jackson and Polly Wright were both born in 1942. The Jackson family lived near a brewery. [149]

The German battleship *Bismarck* was sunk. The Doctor once claimed to have been wounded at El-Alamein. In November 1942 there were reports of vampires in Roumania. On Christmas Eve of that year, Oskar Steinmann oversaw the first test of the "flying bomb" at Peenemunde. [150]

## 1943 (May) – THE CURSE OF FENRIC [151]

The Doctor visited the German High Command around this time.

'The Ultima Machine had been devised by Professor Judson. It was one of the first computers, although we didn't use that name back then. We used it to decipher German naval signals. It was located at a naval base on the East Coast. In '43, that base was completely wiped out in a mysterious attack that also left a number of villagers dead, including the vicar. Reports claimed that vampires had been responsible. The reality was perhaps more shocking: a naturally occurring chemical poison was being siphoned and collected, and samples of this had escaped.'

[At War With SID, the Memoirs of Sir George Reed, VC]

In the later stages of the war Amelia Ducat manned an ack-ack gun in Folkestone, and the Master kidnapped a V1 from the skies over Cambridgeshire using TOMTIT. **The Germans perfected the Gruber–Schneider device. Mel's grandfather died during the war. [152]**

In the mid-1940s, Albert Einstein was briefly kidnapped by the Rani, and Silverstein bought the only surviving robot Yeti from Professor Travers. **The Parakon Freeth began to visit Earth, accounting for some UFO sightings. [153]**

In the early 1950s, Professor Zaroff, "the greatest scientist since Leonardo", vanished. The radio telescope was invented. The last witchcraft act on the English statute books was repealed in 1951. [154]

## = 1951 – TIMEWYRM: EXODUS [155]

Following the total defeat of the British army at Dunkirk, the German army swept across the Channel, landing at Folkestone. Britain fell in six days. Churchill was executed, along with thousands others on a list of suspected troublemakers. Oswald Mosley was installed as Prime Minister; Edward the Eighth was crowned.

Unsure of what to do with Britain, the Nazi High Command let the country fall into ruin. All able-bodied men were conscripted as slave workers and shipped to the continent. In 1951, to celebrate ten years of Nazi victory, the Festival of Britain took place in London. The Germans planned to have a man on the moon in this year.

Landing here, the Doctor realised that history had been altered. He travelled back to 1923 to discover the point at which the timestream was diverted.

remarks that they rarely get anyone "over twenty" into the club, which might suggest that Ben and Polly are a little younger.

150 The Doctor knows of the *Bismarck* in *Terror of the Zygons*. *The Sea Devils*. "Six months" before *The Curse of Fenric*. *Just War*.

151 Dating *The Curse of Fenric* – Ace says that the year is "1943". The script stated that the time is '1943 – probably May'.

152 *The Seeds of Doom*. *The Time Monster*. *Just War* – The Gruber–Schneider device was a Nazi teleport system featured in the hoax 'unmade Troughton story' *Operation: Werewolf*, and was "three years" from completion in 1941 according to Kendrick.

153 [see also THE TIME BRAINS page 42]. A scene showing the Rani kidnap Einstein was deleted from the camera script. "Thirty years" before *The Web of Fear*. "Thirty years" before *The Paradise of Death* (p79).

154 "Twenty years" before *The Underwater Menace*. "Forty years" after *Pyramids of Mars*. *The Dæmons*.

155 Dating *Timewyrm: Exodus* – In Part One of the novel, the Doctor proclaims it to be the "Festival of Britain, 1951" (p5).

156 Dating *Timewyrm: Exodus*
– At the end of the novel, the
Doctor and Ace arrive at the
real Festival of Britain.

157 In *Mawdryn Undead*, the
1983 Brigadier talks of "thirty
years of soldiering". *The
Invasion*. He doesn't have a
moustache in the regimental
photograph seen in *Inferno*. He
is a member of the Scots'
Guards in *The Web of Fear*. *The
Green Death*.

158 *Shada*.

159 *Dancing the Code*.

160 Dating *First Frontier* – It is
4 October 1957 (p6).

161 [see also UNIT Dating
pages 265-9]. Sarah Jane says
in *Invasion of the Dinosaurs*
that she is "twenty-three"
(although in the novelisation
she is 'twenty-two'). Elisabeth
Sladen, who played Sarah, was
born in 1948 and was twenty-
six when the story was made.
In the format document for the
proposed *K9 & Company*
series, it is stated that Sarah
was born in '1949'.

162 *Shada*.

> This timeline was avoided when Drachensberg Castle was destroyed.

## 1951 – TIMEWYRM: EXODUS [156]

After they defeated the War Lords and the Timewyrm, the Doctor and Ace visited the real Festival of Britain, and discovered that history was back on course.

Alastair Gordon Lethbridge-Stewart began his military service in 1953. Shortly afterwards he attended Sandhurst with Billy Rutlidge. Once his training was complete, Lethbridge-Stewart grew his moustache, joined the Scots' Guards, and was stationed for a time at Aldgate. [157]

In 1955 Chris Parsons was born, and the Doctor visited his future College, St Cedd's Cambridge. [158]

The French colony of Kebiria was granted independence in 1956. Civil war started almost immediately. [159]

## 1957 (4 October) – FIRST FRONTIER [160]

On May Day 1957, the first *Sputnik* was destroyed before it completed an orbit of the Earth. News of this failure was never made public.

The Doctor visited the first official *Sputnik* launch at least twice.

> 'On the very day that the first *Sputnik* was launched, 4 October 1957, there was intense UFO activity over Corman Air Force Base in New Mexico. One abductee, Robert Agar, claims that he saw men from Venus, who took him in their craft. It would become a familiar pattern over the next few decades, although it was always denied by the authorities. On this occasion, an Atlas rocket and a fighter aircraft were shot down by UFOs.'
>
> [*UFO Secrets of the US Government*, Mysteria Press]

Sarah Jane Smith was born. [161] In 1958 the Doctor visited St Cedd's College once again. [162]

# 1959 - DELTA AND THE BANNERMEN [163]

The first US satellite was launched, and almost immediately it was lost. CIA agents across the world were put on alert. It was eventually recovered by Weismuller and Hawk, who tracked it to a holiday camp in Wales, England.

In the early 1960s Lavinia Smith published her paper on the teleological response of the virus, and a secret bunker was built in Whitehall. In 1960 the American humorist Franklin Adams died. The same year, the Doctor was awarded an honorary degree from St Cedd's, and his companion Tegan Jovanka was born. [164]

Lieutenant Lethbridge-Stewart spent some time in Sierra Leone. One day, while lost in the forest, he met Mariatu, eldest daughter of Chief Yembe of the Rokoye village. Mariatu went to the city with Lethbridge-Stewart, returning alone a few years later with her son, Mariama. [165]

In 1961, Yuri Gagarin became the first human being to travel in space. [166]

163 Dating *Delta and the Bannermen* – The Tollmaster says that the bus will be going back to "1959", and the date is confirmed by a banner up in the dancehall in Shangri-La. Hawk's line "this is history in the making" implies that this is the first American satellite, but that was really *Explorer I*, which was launched 31 January 1958.

164 *The Time Warrior*. "Twenty years" before *Invasion of the Dinosaurs. The Seeds of Doom. Shada*. According to her Character outline, Tegan is 'twenty-one'. Originally she was to be nineteen, until the production team were told that legally air hostesses had to be twenty-one or older.

165 THE LETHBRIDGE-STEWART FAMILY – *Transit* introduces the Brigadier's descendant, Kadiatu Lethbridge-Stewart (she reappears in *Set Piece, The Also People* and *Happy Endings*). Kadiatu came from a line of Lethbridge-Stewarts descended from the Lieutenant's liason in Sierra Leone. There were more details of the Lethbridge-Stewart line in an early draft of *The Also People*.

Mariatu had a son, Mariama, in the early 1960s (he is unnamed in *Transit* – the name appears in the early draft of *The Also People*, where his mother was mistakenly referred to as 'Isatu'). He had a daughter, Kadiatu, who became an historian (she is first referred to in the novelisation of *Remembrance of the Daleks*, and also in *Set Piece*). She had a son Gibril, who also had a son called Gibril (the draft of *The Also People*). Gibril had a son, Yembe (seen in *Transit*), and he adopted Kadiatu in 2090. Kadiatu, then, is the Brigadier's great-great-great-great-granddaughter, and this is consistent with *Transit* (p96) where "five generations" separate Kadiatu from Alastair.

Rather more simple is the Brigadier's British family. According to *Downtime*, his first wife, Fiona (a name thought up by Nicholas Courtney, who plays the Brigadier), had a daughter called Kate. She was a child during the UNIT era, when the Lethbridge-Stewarts split up (he is sleeping alone by *The Dæmons*). By the mid-nineties Kate is a single mother looking after her son, Gordon. By *Battlefield*, the Brigadier has married Doris, an old flame first mentioned in *Planet of the Spiders* (they shared a weekend in Brighton eleven years before that story – perhaps before Alastair was married to Fiona).

166 [see also Quatermass page 75]. This was confirmed in *The Seeds of Death*.

## TIMELINE: 1963 to 1989 AD

*continued overleaf*

| | | |
|---|---|---|
| 1970s | u | THE GREEN DEATH |
| 1970s | u | THE TIME WARRIOR |
| **1970s** | **u** | **THE PARADISE OF DEATH** |
| **1970s** | **u** | **INVASION OF THE DINOSAURS** |
| **1970s** | **u** | **THE GHOSTS OF N-SPACE** |
| 1970s | u | THE FIVE DOCTORS |
| 1970s | u | PLANET OF THE SPIDERS |
| 1970s | u | ROBOT |
| 1970s | u | TERROR OF THE ZYGONS |
| **1970s** | **u** | **NO FUTURE** |
| 1970s | u | THE ANDROID INVASION |
| 1970s | u | THE SEEDS OF DOOM |
| 1970s | u | THE HAND OF FEAR |
| 1970s | u | MAWDRYN UNDEAD |
| 1977 | c | IMAGE OF FENDAHL |
| 1978 | c | THE PIRATE PLANET |
| 1978 | c | THE STONES OF BLOOD |
| 1979 | | CITY OF DEATH |
| 1979 | | SHADA/THE FIVE DOCTORS |
| 1980 | c | THE LEISURE HIVE |
| 1980 | c | MEGLOS |
| 1981 | c | THE KEEPER OF TRAKEN |
| 1981 | | LOGOPOLIS |
| 1981 | | CASTROVALVA |
| 1981 | | FOUR TO DOOMSDAY |
| 1981 | | K9 AND COMPANY |
| 1982 | c | TIME-FLIGHT |
| 1983 | c | ARC OF INFINITY |
| 1983 | c | THE FIVE DOCTORS |
| 1983 | | MAWDRYN UNDEAD |
| 1983 | c | THE FIVE DOCTORS |
| 1984 | | THE AWAKENING |
| 1984 | | RESURRECTION OF THE DALEKS |
| 1984 | c | PLANET OF FIRE |
| 1985 | | ATTACK OF THE CYBERMEN |
| 1985 | c | THE TWO DOCTORS |
| 1986 | | THE TENTH PLANET |
| 1988 | | SILVER NEMESIS |
| 1989 | c | SURVIVAL |

The Doctor and Susan arrived in Shoreditch, London, in early 1963. They spent five months on Earth at this time, the Doctor attending to his TARDIS, Susan attending Coal Hill School. A month before his departure, the Doctor made arrangements for the burial of the Hand of Omega. [1]

## 1963 (A Tuesday in Late October) – AN UNEARTHLY CHILD [2]

Two of Susan Foreman's teachers, Ian Chesterton and Barbara Wright, became concerned with one of their pupil's homework and followed her home one evening. Although Chesterton's car was discovered outside Totter's Yard, there was no sign of the teachers, Susan, or her mysterious grandfather.

## 1963 (From 22 November) – REMEMBRANCE OF THE DALEKS [3]

'An Imperial Dalek Shuttlecraft landed in a playground in London and established a transmat link with an orbiting mothership. The Renegade faction arrived at around the same time and began recruiting sympathetic locals. Davros wiped out the Renegade faction and captured the Hand of Omega, planning to use its power to give the Daleks mastery of Time – to make the Daleks the new Time Lords…'

[*The Children of Davros*, Njeri Ngugi]

At this time, the British Rocket Group [4] and the Intrusion Counter Measures Group were active. The second of these detected the Daleks' transmissions and uncovered indisputable evidence of extra-terrestrial activity. The affair was covered up by claiming that a nuclear accident had been narrowly averted.

In late November 1963, the Nemesis asteroid passed over Earth, influencing the assassination of President Kennedy. [5]

## ? 1963 – THE DALEKS [6]

'For centuries the few survivors of the Thal race had lived on a plateau, eking out an existence. But we relied on rain-

1 In '100,000 BC', Susan says that "the last five months have been the happiest in my life". The Doctor returns for the Hand of Omega in *Remembrance of the Daleks*.

2 Dating *100,000 BC* – The Doctor has left the Hand of Omega at the funeral parlour for "a month" before *Remembrance of the Daleks*, suggesting that the first episode is set in late October. The year "1963" is first confirmed in the second episode, 'The Cave of Skulls'. Ian Chesterton's blackboard reads "Homework - Tuesday".

3 Dating *Remembrance of the Daleks* – The story is set in late November 1963 according to the calendar on Ratcliffe's wall, as well as a host of other incidental evidence (not least of which being the broadcast of an episode of the "new science fiction serial 'Doct-"). The draft script was set in December.

4 QUATERMASS – A throwaway line in *Remembrance of the Daleks* mentions a "Bernard" working for "British Rocket Group". This is a reference to the four Quatermass television serials: *The Quatermass Experiment, Quatermass II, Quatermass and the Pit* and *Quatermass* in which British space scientist Bernard Quatermass battled against alien horrors. Most fans agree that the first three serials heavily influenced a number of *Doctor Who* stories, although the comparison was very rarely made (and was often denied) by

successive production teams.

In the New Adventures, there is a reference to an incident at "Hob's Lane" (*Quatermass and the Pit* – more correctly it perhaps ought to be "Hobbs Lane") in *The Pit* (p169) and *Nightshade* first introduced the eponymous 1950s television series that bore many similarities to the Quatermass serials.

Do the Quatermass serials occur in the same fictional universe as *Doctor Who*? As might be expected there are a number of discrepancies between the two programmes: *The Quatermass Experiment* contradicts *The Seeds of Death*, claiming that Victor Carroon was the first man in space, and a race of Martians appears in *Quatermass and the Pit*. Broadly, though, the two series might co-exist, with the final serial, *Quatermass* taking place around the time of the New Adventures *Iceberg* and *Warhead* – indeed the existence of Professor Quatermass might go some way to explaining the rosy state of the British space programme in the UNIT era [see also THE BRITISH SPACE PROGRAMME page 88].

5 *Silver Nemesis*. The book *Who Killed Kennedy* offers another perspective on the assassination.

6 Dating *The Daleks* – In *The Dalek Invasion of Earth*, the Doctor tells Ian that the first Dalek story occurred "a million years ahead of us in the future" and the twenty-second century is part of the "middle of the

fall that came only every ten years. One decade, the rain never came. After two years Temmosus and his group left the plateau, hoping to find the City of the Daleks.'

[Thal Oral Records]

'Five hundred years after the Neutronic War, the last **Exterminator** Daleks on Skaro were wiped out by an attack on their city. The Daleks had become affected by the reverse evolution affecting the planet, and had lost many of their technological secrets. At some point afterwards the Moroks raided Skaro, reducing a once mighty race to an exhibit in their Space Museum.' [7]

[*The Children of Davros*, Njeri Ngugi]

Nyssa, the daughter of Tremas of Traken was born. [8]

## c 1964 – PLANET OF GIANTS [9]

A government inspector, Arnold Farrow, delayed his holiday to tell the industrialist Forester that the insecticide his company had developed would not be approved for production. The scientist Smithers, obsessed by the idea of ending world famine, had succeeded over the last year in creating an insecticide sixty per cent more powerful than anything on the market (it was even capable of stopping locusts breeding) but tests showed that it killed all insect life, even those vital to the ecology. Forester killed Farrow, but was arrested by the local policeman, Bert Rowse.

The Doctor visited St Cedd's College in 1964. The same year, a woman who would later be his companion, Melanie Bush, was born. [10]

## 1965 – THE CHASE [11]

The TARDIS crew watched the Beatles singing 'Ticket to Ride' using the Time/Space Visualiser.

Later, Ian Chesterton and Barbara Wright returned to Earth in the Dalek Time Machine, which self-destructed once they had left the craft.

## c 1965/66 (25 December, 31 December 1 January) – THE DALEKS' MASTER PLAN [12]

While fleeing the Daleks, the TARDIS landed outside a police station in Liverpool so that the Doctor could repair the scanner. After a little trouble with the police force, the TARDIS went on its way.

A week later, the TARDIS landed in Trafalgar Square during the New Year celebrations.

## 1966 THE CHASE [13]

The TARDIS and the Dalek Time Machine landed on the top floor of the Empire State Building, much to the amusement of tourist Morton Dill.

## c 1966 – THE MASSACRE OF ST BARTHOLOMEW'S EVE [14]

Dorothea Chaplet accidentally entered the TARDIS while it had landed on Wimbledon Common, mistaking it for a real police box. The teenager was living with her great aunt at the time, her mother having died.

## 1966 (12 – 20 July) – THE WAR MACHINES [15]

Able Seaman Ben Jackson started a five-month shore posting on July 5 1966. [16]

'C-Day, that is Computer Day, will be next Monday, July the sixteenth – that is in four days time. All the computer systems in the whole world will come under the control of this central computer, which we call WOTAN. As you're aware, this will have peaceful and military implications. No one operates WOTAN, it operates itself; it is pure thought and can think for itself like a human being – only better. It is at least ten years ahead of its time, and, while it is not the biggest, it is the most advanced computer in the world. WOTAN will be connected up to a number of sites, including ELDO, TELSTAR, the White House, Parliament, Cape Kennedy, EFTA, RN and Woomera.'

[Press Conference at the Royal Scientific Club]

history of the Daleks". Where he acquires this information is unclear – he had not even heard of the Daleks when he first met them. (Other Time Lords fear the Daleks: the Monk knows of them in *The Daleks' Master Plan*, and in *The Five Doctors* it is revealed that the ancestors of the Time Lords forbade the use of the Daleks in their Games). However, the Thals in *Planet of the Daleks* (2540) have legends of this first encounter "generations ago". In the original storyline for *The Survivors* (as the first Dalek story was provisionally titled) the date is given as 'the year 3000', with the war two thousand years before. A revised synopsis dated 30 July 1963 gave the date as 'the 23rd century'.

*The Terrestrial Index* and *The Official Doctor Who and the Daleks Book* both suggested that the Daleks from this story were 'new Daleks' created by 'crippled Kaled survivors', and that the story is set just after *Genesis of the Daleks* – this is presumably meant to explain the Dal/Kaled question [see also THE TWO DALEK HISTORIES page 32] and also helps tie the Dalek history into the *TV Century 21* comic strip, but there is no evidence for it on screen. The *TV Century 21* comic starts in '2003 AD', but we now know that the Daleks were around before then. The TARDIS Logs dated the story as '2290 AD'. The American *Doctor Who* comic suggested a date of '300 AD', on the grounds that the Daleks do not seem to have developed space travel. The FASA role-playing game dated the story as '5 BC'. 'Matrix Databank' in *DWM* issue 73 suggested that *The Daleks* takes place after *The Evil of the Daleks* and that the Daleks we see are the last vestiges of a once-great race. This ties in with *The Dalek Invasion of Earth*, but contradicts *Planet of the Daleks*.

I speculate, without any evidence it has to be said, that in this story the Doctor returns Ian and Barbara to 1963, but on the wrong side of the galaxy.

7 In *The Space Museum*, the Moroks have a Dalek specimen from "Planet Skaro" – one with horizontal bands rather than vertical slats. It seems clear that they raid Skaro at some undisclosed time after *The Daleks*. It cannot be before, as it is implied that the Daleks have no knowledge of life on other planets, although this in turn contradicts *Genesis of the Daleks* in which both Davros and the Dalek Leader express a wish to conquer other worlds once they know the Doctor is an alien.

8 Nyssa is 'eighteen' according to the writers' guide for the eighteenth series.

9 Dating *Planet of Giants* – The year is not specified on-screen, although the setting is contemporary. Forester lives in a rural area, and the local telephone exchange is still manned by a switchboard operator.

Having returned to her own time, Dodo Chaplet left the Doctor. Fortunately, Ben Jackson and Polly **Wright** entered the TARDIS as it was leaving Earth.

## 1966 (20 July) – THE FACELESS ONES [17]

Following an explosion on their home planet, a generation of aliens were rendered faceless, lacking any true identity. As intelligent, scientifically advanced beings, they concocted an elaborate plan to kidnap young humans and absorb their personalities: youngsters on chartered Chameleon Tours to holiday destinations would instead be flown to a space station in orbit, where they would be processed. Although they covered their tracks carefully – sending postcards to the missing youngsters' families, hypnotising people, and even murdering them – the Chameleons' plan was exposed. The Chameleons left, believing that a chemical formula might be used to solve their problems.

Back in their own time, the very same day that they had joined him, Ben Jackson and Polly **Wright** left the Doctor.

## 1966 (20 July) – THE EVIL OF THE DALEKS [18]

The TARDIS was stolen from Gatwick Airport.

From the nineteen-sixties onwards, human space probes were being sent "deeper and deeper" into space. Brigadier Lethbridge-Stewart was given a wristwatch by Doris during a romantic weekend in Brighton. Around this time, the Cybermen contacted Tobias Vaughn, who offered them help with their invasion. Soon afterwards, the micromonolithic circuit was marketed by his company, International Electromatics, revolutionising electronics and making IE the world leaders in the field. [19]

During the late 1960s, Professor Fendelman was working on missile guidance. Perpugilliam Brown was born on 15 November 1966. Brendan Richards was born in 1967. A year later, the Monk placed £200 in a London bank and the Mexico Olympics were held. [20]

## 1970s – THE WEB OF FEAR [21]

"LONDONERS FLEE!
MENACE SPREADS"

[Newspaper Headline]

'When mysterious cobwebs started to appear across London, and the fog came down, and people began to see "bears" and "monsters" in the Underground, then and only then did the government realise that the country, perhaps the planet, was being attacked by something that was beyond human comprehension. Londoners fled in terror, and the army was called in to restore order. They found themselves under siege in the London Underground, where the disturbances were concentrated. Faced with an attack from a sentience billions of years older than their planet, with its own robot army, capable of trapping a spacecraft in mid-flight and dominating the human mind, the army was reduced to blowing up tunnels to try to seal it in.'

[*The Zen Military*, Kadiatu Lethbridge-Stewart]

This became known as the "London Event", and the official story was that there had been an industrial accident. Lethbrige-Stewart retained "The Locus", a small carved statuette of a Yeti, as a memento. Six months later he met Air Vice-Marshall "Chunky" Gilmore in the Alexander Club and learnt that Earth had been invaded in the winter of 1963, and that there was evidence of aliens visiting since the time of the Pharoahs. [22]

## [c 1975 Near Future] – FURY FROM THE DEEP [23]

On the whole, this period was "a good time in Earth's history to stay in: no wars, great prosperity, a time of plenty". Gas from the sea now provided energy for the south of England and Wales, as well as mainland Europe. Twenty rigs pumped gas into every home, without incident, for over four years. When scientists registered a regular build-up and fall in pressure in the main pipelines, the supply was cut off for the first time. A mutant species of seaweed was responsible, and it mentally dominated some of the rigs' crews before being beaten back by amplified sound.

10 In the writers' guide for the twenty-third series, written in July 1985, Mel is described as 'twenty-one'. In the novelisation *Terror of the Vervoids* she is 'twenty-two'. In *The Ultimate Foe* she has lived for 'twenty-three years'. In *Just War*, Mel was born 'twenty-eight' years after '1936' (p251).

11 The script suggested that the Visualiser tuned in on the Beatles' Fiftieth Anniversary Reunion Tour. The costume listing for 1 April 1965 included a request for an announcer dressed in futuristic clothing from '2014', and it seems that the Beatles were contacted. However, the television version eventually used stock footage from 1965.

On their return home, Ian sees a tax disc dated "Dec 65" and Barbara notes that they are "two years out". (Ironically, after two years of trying to land in England in the 1960s, the TARDIS visits Ian and Barbara's native time five times in the next ten stories.)

12 Dating *The Daleks' Master Plan* – A calendar in the police station reads "25th December".

As is now well-known, it was originally intended that the 1965 Christmas episode, *The Feast of Steven* would include a crossover with the popular BBC police serial *Z-Cars*. Publicity material to this effect was sent out on 1 October 1965, and it appears that a version of the script was written with the *Z-Cars* characters in mind.

John Peel's novelisation and Lofficier's *The Universal Databank* both retain the names of actors (*not* the characters) from the police series.

13 Dating *The Chase* – Morton Dill says it is "1966", in Alabama at least.

14 Dating *The Massacre of St Bartholomew's Eve* – It is never made explicit which year Dodo boards the TARDIS. She is surprised that the Post Office Tower has been completed on her return to Earth in *The War Machines*, but there is nothing to suggest that she doesn't come from earlier in 1966.

15 Dating *The War Machines* – C-Day is set for 16 July, but this didn't fall on a Monday in 1966, it was the Saturday that the fourth episode of *The War Machines* was to be broadcast. The year "1966" is confirmed in *The Faceless Ones*, and also in *Radio Times*. WOTAN is connected up to Telstar and Cape Kennedy.

16 In *The War Machines* it is stated twice that Ben has a shore posting (he is depressed by this and wants to get back to sea). At the end of the story it is stated that he has to get "back to barracks". However in *The Smugglers* and *The Faceless Ones* he wants to return to his "ship".

17 Dating *The Faceless Ones* – Setting this story in 1966 seems to have been a last minute decision to smooth the departure for Ben and Polly, one that also affects the dating

Victoria Waterfield left the Doctor and settled with the Harrises.

**Brigadier Lethbridge-Stewart attended a Middle East Peace Conference.** [24]

Aware that the world faced the threat of alien invasion, the United Nations Intelligence Taskforce was established. After this time UNIT, also known as Department C-19 in Britain, was established and Enabling legislation was passed (it was drafted by the future Minister for Ecology). Alistair Gordon Lethbridge-Stewart, the Scots Guards Colonel who had been in command of the soldiers that had repelled the Yeti in the Underground, was promoted to Brigadier and made commanding officer of the British UNIT contingent. [25] [26]

## 1968 – NIGHTSHADE [27]

'The actor Edmund Trevithick, best known as the dashing scientist Nightshade in the BBC serial of that name died in his sleep last night at a nursing home in the Yorkshire village of Crook Marsham. *Nightshade* is currently enjoying repeats on BBC television.'

[Obituary, *The Daily Telegraph*]

## 1968/9 (UNIT, 20 December – 30 January) – THE LEFT-HANDED HUMMINGBIRD [28]

'Early in its history, UNIT had a Paranormal Division. After extensive trials, they recruited six genuine human psychics. The division was run by Lieutenant Hamlet Macbeth, and investigated Fortean events. Following "The Happening", a massive psychic event in St John's Wood, London on 21 December 1968, the Paranormal Division was disbanded.'

[*The Zen Military*, Kadiatu Lethbridge-Stewart]

Ace foiled an attempt to kill the Beatles on the roof of the Apple building on 30 January 1969. At least two incarnations of the Doctor went to Woodstock.

## c 1970 (20 March) – THE UNDERWATER MENACE [29]

The mad Professor Zaroff died in agony while attempting to

raise Atlantis from the ocean floor with his Plunger.

Dorothy **McShane** was born **on 20 August 1970**. In 1971 decimal currency was introduced in the United Kingdom. At some point afterwards, the Doctor and Susan visited England. Gas warfare was banned by international agreement. [30] [31]

UNIT radar stations tracked a shower of meteorites in an odd formation over Essex. [32]

## 1970s (UNIT) – THE INVASION [33]

[CYBER-HISTORY COMPUTER]--------------------------------
**Report** – Hostile - identified. The - Doctor: he - arrived - on - Planet - 14 - in - a - machine. He - has - a - companion - named - Jamie. His - origins - are - unknown. The - workings - of - his - travel - machine - are - unknown. He - interfered - with - our - plans. [34]

-----------------------------------------------------------------

UNIT began monitoring the activities of International Electromatics after hundreds of UFO sightings on IE property. IE now controlled every computer line in the world, having undercut the competition, and Tobias Vaughn had built a business empire around his philosophy of uniformity and exact duplication. One of their best-selling products was a disposable radio, which had sold ten million units.

[CYBER-HISTORY-COMPUTER]--------------------------------
**Background** – We - have - established - a - foothold - on - Earth - for - the - first - time. Five - years - ago - we - were - contacted - by - human - industrialist - Tobias - Vaughn - in - deep - space. Guided - to - Earth - by - his - radio - beams - our - mothership - took - up - orbit - above - the - dark - side - of - Earth's - Moon. Vaughn - was - told - that - he - could - rule - Earth - if - he - supplied - the - Cybermen - with - minerals. His - body - was - made - cybernetic - his - mind - remains - human. 100s - of - our - spacecraft - have - landed - on - Earth. Cyber - computers - have - been - installed - in - IE - property. Cybermen - in - suspended -

for *The Evil of the Daleks*. *Radio Times* stated that it is 'Earth – Today'.

18 Dating *The Evil of the Daleks* – The story follows straight on from *The Faceless Ones*.

19 [see also UNIT Dating pages 263–7]. "For the last ten years" before *Spearhead from Space*. "Eleven years" before *Planet of Spiders*. "Five years" before *The Invasion* according to Vaughn (and therefore one year before *The Web of Fear*).

20 "Ten years" before *Image of the Fendahl*. *Planet of Fire* – according to a character outline prepared for the twenty-first series, before Nicola Bryant was cast in the role, Peri is 'an 18-year old' when she starts travelling with the Doctor, and her mother's name is 'Janine' (the same document also says she is 'blonde'). This would seem to make Peri three years younger than the actress playing her. We see Peri's passport in *Planet of Fire*, which gives her birthday and has a photo of her as a young girl with pony-tails. Brendan is "fourteen" according to *K9 and Company*. *The Time Meddler*. *The Underwater Menace*.

21 Dating *The Web of Fear* – [see also UNIT Dating pages 263–7]. Professor Travers declares that the events of *The Abominable Snowmen* were "over forty years ago"; Anne says that they were in "1935". The maps of the London Underground that we see show

the network as it was in 1968, and don't show the Victoria or Jubilee lines, which opened on 7 March 1969 and 1 May 1979 respectively. 'Downtime' (c 1995) states that this story took place "some twenty-five years before" (p92), in "1968" (p183).

22 *Downtime*.

23 Dating *Fury from the Deep* – It is clear from the recently recovered telesnaps that this story is set in the near future: there is a Europe-wide energy policy and videophones are in use. Although Robson talks of "tuppence ha'penny tinpot ideas", this is clearly a figure of speech rather than an indication that the story is set in the era of pre-decimal currency. *The Programme Guide* has always assumed that the story was contemporary. The TARDIS Logs set the story in '2074', the same year it suggested for *The Wheel in Space*. In *Downtime*, Victoria has been in the twentieth century for "ten years" by 1984 (p41).

The quotation is the Doctor reassuring Jamie about Victoria's new home in *The Wheel in Space*.

24 *The Paradise of Death* – "just before he joined UNIT" (p123). Lethbridge-Stewart seems to have been promoted soon after *The Web of Fear* (*Downtime*, p6).

25 The Doctor identifies UNIT as "Department C-19" in *Time-Flight*. Enabling legislation granting UNIT

animation - have - been - transferred - to - Earth - and - placed - under - Vaughn's - command.

**Cyber-Controlship** – The - plan - is - a - variation - on - the - standard - invasion - scenario. Each - piece - of - equipment - made - by - Vaughn's - company - contains - redundant - circuitry. When - a - signal - is - activated - from - transmitters - in - orbit - all - areas - will - be - affected - by - induced - Cyber - hypnotic - force. One - hour - later - the - Cyber - army - will - emerge - from - the - sewers. Our - forces - will - select - humans - for - Cyber - conversion. All - other - humans - will - be - destroyed. Plans - for - invasion - are - nearly - completed. Nothing - must - be - allowed - to - disrupt - them. The - plan - must - remain - secret. Key - human - military - and - political - personnel - have - been - placed - under - Cyber - control.

**Supplementary** – Once - again - the - Doctor - has - interfered - with - our - plans. His - machine - was - identified. The - Doctor - was - attacked - in - space. He - survived. The - human - authorities - learnt - of - our - plan. Before - the - United - Nations - could - respond - the - invasion - was - brought - forward. The - hypnotic - signal - was - activated - before - the - whole - army - was - sent - to - Earth. The - full - invasion - force - was - prepared - for - landing. Human - military - focres - wore - neuristors - that - blocked - the - hypnotic - signals. They - prepared - nuclear - rockets - and - destroyed - our - invasion - fleet - in - a - chain - reaction. We - planned - to - retaliate - and - wipe - out - all - life - on - Earth - with - a - Cyber - megatron - bomb. Faced - with - the - destruction - of - his - world - Vaughn - attacked - the - Cybermen - on - Earth - with - a - machine - capable - of - amplifying - our - emotional - responses. The - human - military - destroyed - the - radio - transmitter - that - would - guide - us - to - Earth. A - human - rocket - with - a - hydrogen - bomb - warhead - destroyed - the - controlship.'

------------------------------------------------

After the collapse of IE, Ashley Chapel, Vaughn's chief scientist, set up his own company, Ashley Chapel Logistics. Vaughn, though, had survived by downloading his consciousness into a waiting robot body. For a thousand years he secretly ran a succession of massive electronics corporations that developed state of the art equipment. [35]

## 1970s (UNIT) - SPEARHEAD FROM SPACE [36]

UNIT went on a covert recruitment drive, bringing Liz Shaw up from Cambridge to act as Scientific Advisor. The very same day, the Doctor arrived in the twentieth-century timezone, exiled to Earth by the Time Lords.

'Reporters at Ashbridge Cottage Hospital knew all about "the Alien" – they had been tipped off about the new arrival with two hearts pumping blood that didn't match any known human or animal type. This "spaceman" turned up the morning after a meteorite shower, and UNIT were on the scene almost immediately. Even though they had just recruited Doctor Elizabeth Shaw, a woman with degrees in medicine, physics and a dozen other subjects, she was merely the "assistant" to a mysterious newcomer, "The Doctor", who had no official existence, not even appearing on the payroll. A day or so later, UNIT led an assault on a plastics factory in Essex, mere hours after reports of "walking shop dummies" in city centres.'

[*The Zen Military*, Kadiatu Lethbridge-Stewart]

Sergeant Mike Yates led the clear-up operation after the Nestene invasion, and discovered a single Energy Unit that had not been recovered by the Autons. It remained UNIT property, but was loaned to the National Space Museum. [37]

In 1972, Oskar Steinmann died. He had been released from prison three years earlier on medical grounds. [38]

In the 1973 UNIT staff panto, Mike Yates played Widow Twankey. [39]

Mars Probe 7 landed on Mars and radio contact was lost, but two weeks later it took off from Mars – or at least something did. [40]

special powers is referred to in *The Time Monster* (the "Seventh Enabling Act" allows the Brigadier to take command of government forces) and *The Green Death*.

26 THE EARLY DAYS OF UNIT – In *Spearhead from Space* the Brigadier tells Liz Shaw that "since UNIT was formed" there had been two alien invasions. *The Web of Fear*, of course, took place before UNIT was formed. I take it that the Brigadier was simplifying events and referring to the two televised Troughton stories that he was in. In *Spearhead from Space* and *Terror of the Zygons* the Brigadier also implies that UNIT existed before he was placed in charge of it.

Richard Landen's article 'Shades of Piccolo' in *DWM* issue 83 gave the date of the foundation of UNIT as '17 April 1973'.

27 Dating *Nightshade* – Ace finds a calendar saying it is "Christmas 1968" (p36).

28 Dating *The Left-Handed Hummingbird* – The last time Cristian saw the Doctor was "January the thirtieth, 1969" (p8). The TARDIS arrives in that timezone on "December 20, 1968" (p122). The Happening takes place on "December 21" (p163).

29 Dating *The Underwater Menace* – Polly discovers a bracelet from the 1968 Mexico Olympics and she and Ben guess that they must have landed about "1970". The

Atlanteans are celebrating the Vernal Equinox. The story is set in '1970–75' according to *The Programme Guide*, and 'soon after' 1969 according to *The Terrestrial Index*. The TARDIS Logs claimed a date of '1969'.

30 ACE – According to *The Curse of Fenric* Ace does "O-Levels", not GCSEs, so she must be a fifth former (i.e.: fifteen or sixteen years old) by the summer of 1987 at the latest. This supports *Ghost Light* where she is "thirteen" in "1983". As Ace has a patch reading "1987" on her jacket in *Dragonfire*, it seems that the timestorm must have come that year. Fenric is therefore rounding up when he tells Ace that "thirty years" after *The Curse of Fenric*, Audrey Dudman will have a baby. Sophie Aldred was born in 1962, making her nine years older than the character she played.

In the New Adventures, starting with *Timewyrm: Revelation*, Ace's birthday was established as 20 August (Sophie Aldred's birthday – as well as being Sylvester McCoy's and Anthony Ainley's). In *Falls the Shadow* the Doctor says that she was born in "1970". Paul Cornell attempted to establish that Ace's surname was "McShane" in *Love and War*, but this was vetoed by the series editor Peter Darvill-Evans at the proof stage. *Conundrum* (p245) and *No Future* (p19) both suggest that Ace's surname begins with an "M" (although when asked in

## 1970s (UNIT) – DOCTOR WHO AND THE SILURIANS [41]

'Energy leaking from reckless human experiments with a cyclotron – primitive equipment designed to convert nuclear fission directly into electricity – awoke a colony of our people beneath Wenley Moor in Derbyshire. They set to work: drawing power from the humans to revive some of their number, as well as a Tyrannosaur guard. Human potholers venturing into the caves were killed, or driven insane by the race memories they held of our people. The apes discovered our base. It was clear that the human race was self-destructive, with weapons that could have destroyed our planet. The leaders released a plague to wipe them out, but the humans discovered an antidote. The human authorities ordered our base destroyed, killing everyone inside it.'

[*The Humane Solution*, Professor Chtaabus]

## 1970s (UNIT) – THE AMBASSADORS OF DEATH [42]

The British Government came to realise that Earth was under threat of attack by alien races. The Space Security Department was formed, headed by veteran astronaut General Carrington.

The British space programme was blossoming with a series of Mars Probe Missions. At least two craft actually landed on the surface of Mars; Mars Probes 6 and 7. Space technology had dramatically improved since the old moonshot days - there was a new fuel variant, M-3, which though highly volatile, provided a great deal more thrust than conventional fuels; and decontamination procedures had been reduced from two days to one hour. Space Research took place at the Space Centre in London, not far from UNIT HQ. In this complex was Space Control (callsign: "Control") where missions were co-ordinated. Astronauts were selected from the military.

'As you can see from this model, the Mars Probe ships are similar to the craft that NASA used to use for moonshots: this is the barrel-shaped living quarters for the two astronauts, with a control cabin here in the nosecone. The Probes are rocket powered, but have clever solar batteries to power communications and other electrical systems. The ships land on Mars's surface, but they aren't designed to return to Earth. Instead, a Recovery ship will be sent up to dock with the Probe in Earth orbit. The astronauts will be removed. The Recovery ship, here, is a one-man vessel with just enough room for the recovered men. The Recovery ship is basically a nosecone with extra manoeuvring jets for the space docking, and it doesn't carry a great deal of surplus fuel.

Recovery ships are designed for dry landings, hopefully on the touchdown pad at Space Centre, or in an extreme emergency on any suitable ground, and the craft could be reused. Both types of capsule were launched from three-stage rockets. At the moment, there is a problem with the fuel injection system, but before long British scientists are sure that the programme will be back on track. And now over to Michael, who's demonstrating the latest in videophone technology.'

[*Tomorrow's World* (transcript)] [43]

Contact was made with radioactive aliens. ***These aliens left the solar system shortly afterwards.*** [44] The Mars Probe programme continued. [45]

## 1970s (UNIT, Five Days in Late July) – INFERNO [46]

Professor Stahlman discovered a gas underneath the crust and claimed that it might be "a vast new storehouse of energy which has lain dormant since the beginning of time". The government funded an elaborate drilling project (nicknamed "Inferno" by some of the workers) based in Eastchester. As the robot drill approached its target, a green slime came to the surface. On skin contact, people became savage beastmen, Primords. The project was halted at the insistence of Sir Keith Gold and UNIT.

## = 1970s (UNIT, Five Days in Late July) – INFERNO

"Sideways in time", Britain was a republic, and it had been since at least 1943, when the Defence of the Republic Act was passed.

the latter, Ace claims that it is "Moose"!), but it was not until Kate Orman's *Set Piece* that "McShane" was officially adopted.

31 "Years" before *The Mind of Evil*. In *An Unearthly Child* Susan knows about decimal currency. [see also Dating *Doctor Who and the Silurians* page 87].

32 "Six months" before *Spearhead from Space*.

33 Dating *The Invasion* – [see also UNIT Dating page 263-7]. According to the Brigadier in this story, the events of *The Web of Fear* "must be four years ago, now", making it about 1979. A casting document written by Douglas Camfield suggested the story was set 'about the year 1976 AD'. *Radio Times* in some regions said that the date was 'about the year 1975', and the continuity announcer echoed this at the beginning of the broadcast of Episode One.

There is a wealth of evidence that this story is set in the near future. There are advanced, voice-operated computers and "Public Video" videophones (perhaps these have all been provided by the Cybermen via IE, although the computer that Zoe and Isobel meet understands ALGOL and blows up after failing to solve an algebraic puzzle). UNIT have an IE computer, and use some IE components in their radios and radar. UNIT have compact TM45 radios with a fifty mile range, while IE personnel have wrist-communicators. UNIT can transmit photographs. IE has an elaborate electronic security and surveillance system. There are many communications satellites in orbit, and UNIT have the authority to fire nuclear rockets into space. "Only the Americans and the Russians" have rockets capable of reaching the Moon – the Russians are just about to launch a manned orbital survey of the Moon, and it would apparently only take "ten hours" to reach it. The IE guards and many of the UNIT troops wear futuristic uniforms, while Vaughn wears a collarless shirt. The Brigadier's "anti-feminist" ideas are outdated.

According to *Iceberg*, this story takes place "ten years" (p90) before *The Tenth Planet* (1986), in "the 70s" (p2). *No Future* suggested "1970" (p2). *Original Sin* claims that this story was set in "the 1970s" (p281). *Millennial Rites* suggests that the UNIT era took place in "the nineteen eighties" (p15), with *The Invasion* a little over "twenty years ago" (c 1979).

34 *The Invasion* – at this stage, the Cybermen don't know the name of the TARDIS, and they don't know that the Doctor is a Time Lord. They have learnt both of these by *Silver Nemesis*.

35 *Millennial Rites* – Ashley Chapel isn't mentioned in *The Invasion. Original Sin.*

36 Dating *Spearhead from*

The Royal Family had been executed by a fascist regime. **The world was run by an alternate version of the Doctor.** In this version of events, Professor Stahlmann's project was a day ahead of ours, and it was under the aegis of the Republican Security Forces. This world was destroyed when Stahlmann's project was successful, releasing torrents of lava and armies of Primords. [47]

## 1970s (UNIT) – THE EYE OF THE GIANT [48]

The Doctor converted the Time/Space Visualiser into a "Time Bridge", and travelled back fifty years in time to 1934.

Liz Shaw returned to Cambridge, and soon afterwards the Doctor started to agitate for a new assistant. The Doctor started the steady state microwelding of his dematerialisation circuit. [49]

## 1970s (UNIT) – TERROR OF THE AUTONS [50]

Josephine Grant became the Doctor's new assistant when a relative in government insisted she got a job with UNIT. Although she failed her General Science A-Level, she managed to pass the UNIT Training Course.

> 'Farrel Plastics, which has been working at less than half capacity for a year now, has been forced to close. It had attempted to capture new markets with avant-garde plastic furniture and "troll dolls", but these failed to capture the public imagination. They will probably be best remembered for the 450,000 plastic daffodils they handed out across the south of England – flowers that the government recently recalled after issuing a warning that they were dangerous if left near radio sets.'
>
> [BBC Television News]

The Master had allied himself with the Nestenes, and together they plotted mass slaughter: when a radio signal was sent, each plastic daffodil would suffocate a person. The Nestenes would take over the country during the resulting chaos. During the course of this, the Master was stranded on Earth as the Doctor had stolen his Mark Two dematerialisation circuit.

## 1970s (UNIT) – THE MIND OF EVIL [51]

'The Keller Machine has treated 112 patients, all hardened criminals who became placid after all the "evil impulses" had been removed from their brains. It is named after its creator, the Swiss scientist Emil Keller.'

[Prison Service Report]

After a prison riot at Stangmoor prison, the Keller process was abandoned. UNIT at this time were involved with the security of the World Peace Conference in London.

## 1970s (UNIT) – THE CLAWS OF AXOS [52]

UNIT continued to track the Master. The Washington UNIT HQ became involved, sending one of their agents, Bill Filer, to help with the search.

'UNIT radar stations locked on to a UFO one million miles out, on a direct bearing for Earth. The alarm bells started to ring when it got within five hundred miles. UNIT HQ sent the order to launch an ICBM strike against the UFO, but the ship vanished before the missiles hit. It landed on the south east coast of England, close to the National Power Complex at Nuton, amid freak weather conditions. As the army arrived to seal off the area, the UFO began to broadcast a signal: "Axos calling Earth, request immediate assistance. Axos calling Earth..." The Axons made contact with the UNIT party. They claimed that their planet had been damaged by solar flares, and that they possessed an advanced organic technology. Their ship had been damaged. In return for help, the Axons offered humanity Axonite, a substance that was "the chameleon of the elements". It could be programmed to absorb all forms of radiation, and to replicate and transmute matter. In short, it would end the world's food and energy problems. In reality, the Axons had been led to the Earth by the Master, whom they had captured in space. He

*Space* – [see also UNIT Dating pages 263-7]. The Brigadier states in *Planet of the Spiders* that "months" elapsed between *The Invasion* and *Spearhead from Space*. He tells Liz Shaw that "for the last ten years we have been sending probes deeper and deeper into space".

37 *Terror of the Autons*.

38 *Just War*.

39 *No Future* (p261). This must have been quite a party, as the Doctor also remembers it in *Timewyrm: Revelation* (p80).

40 According to Wakefield, contact was lost "eight months" before *The Ambassadors of Death*.

41 Dating *Doctor Who and the Silurians* – [see also UNIT Dating pages 263-7]. A taxi driver asks for a fare of "10/6", so this story appears to be set before the introduction of decimal currency. The cyclotron is an experimental machine that converts nuclear energy directly into electricity. The New Adventure *Blood Heat* states that this story is set in "1973".

42 Dating *The Ambassadors of Death* – [see also UNIT Dating pages 263-7, and THE BRITISH SPACE PROGRAMME page 88-9]. The Doctor is still bitter about the events of *Doctor Who and the Silurians*, so this story probably happens only shortly afterwards. Britain has an established programme of manned missions to Mars. There have been seven Mars Probes, and it is a sixteen-

month round trip. If we assume that there is only one mission in space at any one time, this could indicate that the Mars missions have been running for around nine and a half years. However, just as most of the Apollo missions didn't land on the Moon, not all the Mars Probes necessarily landed on Mars – we only know for certain that two have. We do know that Taltalian has been working at the Space Centre for "two years". Cornish remarks that decontamination takes "under an hour... It used to take two days". In 1969, when the story was made, the earliest NASA planned to have a man on Mars was 1980. There are colour videophones, and we see a machine capable of automatically displaying star charts.

43 THE BRITISH SPACE PROGRAMME – Perhaps because they are acutely aware of the threat from outer space, the British Government seems to have invested heavily in the space programme during the UNIT era: according to the Brigadier in *The Invasion* "only the Americans and the Russians" have a rocket capable of reaching the Moon, but *The Ambassadors of Death* shows Britain in the middle of a prolonged series of manned missions to Mars, and the Government has a Space Security Department. In *Invasion of the Dinosaurs*, some very clever and important people are fooled into believing that a colony ship can reach

had led them to a rich feeding ground in return for his freedom and a chance to kill the Doctor. The ship was banished from Earth, although the Nuton Complex was also destroyed.'

[*The Zen Military*, Kadiatu Lethbridge-Stewart]

The National Power Complex at Nuton was rebuilt. UNIT continued their hunt for the Master. At one point they accidentally arrested the Spanish ambassador, mistaking him for the renegade Time Lord. [53]

## 1970s (UNIT) - COLONY IN SPACE [54]

The TARDIS left the Doctor's laboratory in UNIT HQ for a matter of seconds.

## 1970s (UNIT, 29 April – 1 May) – THE DÆMONS [55]

'Millions watched last night as the noted archaeologist Professor Horner was killed while attempting to open the Devil's Hump, an ancient burial mound outside the village of Devil's End. Professor Horner's book on the subject is published today. The army have sealed off the area, but insist that this is due to an unusual atmospheric phenomenon, not because of the many sightings of the devil reported by locals!'

[*The Times*, 1 May]

Public outrage at UNIT's blowing up of the church at Devil's End ("The Aldbourne Incident") led to "questions in the House; a near riot at the General Synod". [56]

While many wanted the Master executed, the Doctor pleaded for clemency at his trial and the Master was instead sent to Fortress Island in the English Channel. [57]

## 1970s (UNIT, 12 – 13 September) – DAY OF THE DALEKS [58]

UNIT were called in to guard the World Peace Conference at Auderley House. On the evening of 12 September, there was an assassination attempt on Sir Reginald Styles. The guerilla vanished into thin air. UNIT discovered that the would-be assassin came from two hundred years in the future. The House was attacked by a small squad of Daleks and their Ogron footsoldiers, but these were lured into the house and literally hoist with their own petard as a Dalekanium bomb was detonated, destroying them. The delegates had been evacuated.

The World Peace Conferences eventually proved successful, and the Cold War was brought to an end. To prevent nuclear launches, the US, USSR and China gave their Destructor Codes to Britain, and Joseph Chambers was made Special Responsibilities Secretary with responsibility for protecting them. [59]

## 1970s (UNIT) THE SEA DEVILS [60]

'REPORT TO THE UNITED NATIONS SECURITY COUNCIL [with cross reference to memoranda 2/0014/ALS/mh, 2/0069/ALS/mh, 2/0102/ALS/mh].

The criminal known as "The Master" has escaped his top-security prison on Fortress Island in the English Channel. There is no established link between the Master and the mysterious disappearance of shipping in that area – reports from the Royal Navy base HMS *Seaspite* are confused, but the disappearances appear to be the work of a colony of "Sea Silurians" (I refer you to report 2/0039/ALS/mh), now destroyed thanks to the swift action of the Navy. All UNIT HQs have received a new standing order, priority A1, to be on the lookout for the Master.' [61]

The Coal Board closed Llanfairfach Colliery in South Wales. [62]

## 1970s (UNIT, 29 September) – THE TIME MONSTER [63]

'For several months, Professor Thascales (Athens) has been working for the Newton Institute in Wootton, researching into "interstitial time". Yesterday morning, Professor Thascales was critically injured in a car crash. The "Thascales Theorem" is being held by the United Nations for security purposes.'

[Report in *The New Scientist*]

another habitable planet, although Sarah knows that even the most advanced spaceship "would take hundreds of years" to reach such a planet. In *The Android Invasion*, an experimental "space freighter" has been in service for at least two years.

**44** Although at the end of *The Ambassadors of Death* the aliens are about to open diplomatic relations with Earth, they are never referred to again. Presumably they leave Earth in peace and nothing significant comes of contact between the two races.

**45** "*Probe 9*" is referred to in *Dancing the Code*.

**46** Dating *Inferno* – [see also UNIT Dating pages 263-7]. A desk calendar says it is "July 23rd", and the story runs for five days – the countdown we see early in the story says that there are "59:28:47" remaining before penetration. The computer at the project seems to use perspex/crystalline memory blocks. Stahlman has a robot drill capable of boring down over twenty miles. North Sea gas is also being drilled for.

**47** *Inferno*. The word "Primord" is not used in dialogue, but appears in the on-screen credits. The name "Eastchester" is only used in a scene cut from the original broadcast (but retained in foreign prints and the BBC Video release), where the Doctor listens to a radio broadcast in the parallel universe. The alternate Doctor's existence is revealed in *Timewyrm: Revelation*, and the face on the posters belonged to Jack Kine, the BBC's Head of Visual Effects. Stahlman spells his name with two 'n's in the parallel universe.

**48** Dating *The Eye of the Giant* – [see also UNIT Dating pages 263-7]. The story is set "nearly forty years" after 1934. UNIT have a photocopier. This is apparently Mike Yates's first meeting with the Doctor and Liz having previously been involved in "clearing up the mess" left after UNIT's operations (as referred to in *Terror of the Autons*).

**49** *Terror of the Autons*. Stories depicting Liz Shaw's departure have become something of a sub-genre of *Doctor Who* fiction. The Doctor remains fond enough of Liz for her to appear as a "phantom" in *The Five Doctors*.

**50** Dating *Terror of the Autons* – [see also UNIT Dating pages 263-7]. The Doctor works on his dematerialisation circuit for "three months", and apparently hadn't started in *Inferno*, so this story would seem to start at least three months after the seventh series ended. There is no indication of how much time has passed since the previous Auton story, *Spearhead from Space*. A desk calendar is referred to when the Doctor and the Brigadier visit Farrell's office, but we don't not see it.

**51** Dating *The Mind of Evil* – [see also UNIT Dating pages

'LOST IN SPACE
by Sarah Jane Smith

Although they won't admit as much, the staff of the British Space Defence Station have given up all hope of finding Guy Crayford. The XK5 Space Freighter was developed and launched at the Defence Station, or "Devesham Control" about a mile from the village of this name. The senior of the new "Defence Astronauts", Commander Crayford, was testing the rocket when contact was lost. Scientists believe that the ship was destroyed by an asteroid.'

[*The Daily Chronicle*] **64**

## 1970s (UNIT) – THE THREE DOCTORS **65**

'Some reports suggest that UNIT Headquarters briefly vanished following a battle with gel-like extra-terrestrials. No official report ever appeared on the incident.'

[*The Zen Military*, Kadiatu Lethbridge-Stewart]

The Doctor's exile to Earth had been lifted. He needed to construct a forcefield generator, but as soon as he had done so he took the TARDIS on a test flight. **66**

Professor Whitaker disappeared when the government refused to fund his time travel research. **67**

## 1970s (UNIT) – DANCING THE CODE **68**

Before this time, Jo had met a number of alien races including the Methaji, Hoveet, Skraals and Kalekani. **69**

'There were reports of "unorthodox weapons" in the North African country of Kebiria. UNIT's representative in the area, Captain Deveraux, was killed. A UNIT transport plane sent to investigate was impounded at a military airport, and its crew were imprisoned. UNIT sent a Superhawk jet fighter to investigate, and discovered a nest of Xarax, an insect hivemind. The Xarax were beginning to infest the rest of the country, including the capital, Kebir City. The US Navy prepared a nuclear strike on the country, but before this was launched a UNIT team from the United Kingdom managed to deactivate the nest using synthesised chemical instructions.'

[*The Zen Military*, Kadiatu Lethbridge-Stewart]

## 1970s (UNIT) – THE GREEN DEATH [70]

The Prime Minister is called Jeremy. [71]

'The government gave the green light to Global Chemicals' experiments into "The Stevens Process", which produced twenty-five per cent more petrol from a given amount of crude oil. The "Nutcake Professor", Clifford Jones, who had won the Nobel Prize for his work on DNA synthesis protested against the doubling of the air pollution that the process would generate, although Global Chemicals claimed that there was absolutely no pollution.

UNIT were sent to investigate a body that had been discovered in the abandoned coal mine, a body that was glowing green. They discovered that Global Chemicals had been dumping the pollution created by the Stevens Process, and that it was mutating the maggots that lived down there. Global Chemicals was run by the BOSS, or Biomorphic Organisational Systems Supervisor, a computer linked to the brain of Stevens. In an effort to help the world achieve "maximum efficiency", the BOSS attempted to mentally dominate Global staff at seven sites throughout the world, including Llanfairfach, New York, Moscow and Zurich. Global Chemicals was destroyed when the BOSS blew up. Professor Jones's Nuthatch was given UN Priority One research status, leading to unlimited funding.'

[*The Zen Military*, Kadiatu Lethbridge-Stewart]

Jo Grant left the Doctor, to marry Professor Clifford Jones and they went on an expedition to the Amazon. [72]

## 1970s (UNIT) – THE TIME WARRIOR [73]

'British research scientists began to mysteriously disappear. UNIT were called in, and the leading research scientists were all confined to the same barracks in a secret location. Nevertheless, the press got wind of the story, and one young

263-7]. There is a World Peace Conference in progress in which the Chinese are key players. Gas warfare was banned "years" ago. This story might be set a full year after *Terror of the Autons*: the Keller Machine has been around that long, although possibly the Master set his plan in motion before his apparent arrival on Earth in *Terror of the Autons* (the line is probably a remnant from an earlier draft of the script that didn't include the Master). Mao Tse Tung is referred to in the present tense – he died in 1976, after *The Mind of Evil* was made.

52 Dating *The Claws of Axos* – [see also UNIT Dating pages 263-7, and THE FUTURE OF THE UNITED NATIONS page 129]. Chinn says of the Brigadier's actions: "that's the kind of high-handed attitude one has come to expect of the UN recently". There are videophones, although normal telephones are also in use. The National Power Complex "provides power for the whole of Britain" according to Hardiman, and it has a "light accelerator".

53 Nuton is destroyed in *The Claws of Axos*, and subsequently mentioned in *The Dæmons. Colony in Space*.

54 Dating *Colony in Space* – [see also UNIT Dating pages 263-7, and *The British Space Programme* page 88-9]. UNIT are still searching for the Master. When Jo reaches the future, she is surprised that a

colony ship was sent out in 1971 (it wasn't, of course, it was 2471). Either this story is set before 1971 and Jo is amazed how quickly the space programme has progressed, or it is set afterwards and she finds it difficult to believe that the colony ship was kept secret.

55 Dating *The Dæmons* – [see also UNIT Dating pages 263-7]. Devil's Hump is opened at "midnight" on "Beltane", the story ends with a dance around the Maypole. This day appears to be a Saturday or Sunday, as Yates and Benton watch a Rugby International (on BBC3!) and don't know the result. As Professor Horner's book is released the next day, it is almost certainly Sunday.

56 *Downtime* (p165). It is a little odd that this is the "Aldbourne Incident" – Aldbourne is the village where *The Dæmons* was filmed, its fictional counterpart being Devil's End. (Although an historic "Lord of Aldbourne" is referred to in *The Dæmons*).

57 *The Sea Devils*. The name of the island appears on Captain Hart's map, but isn't referred to in dialogue.

58 Dating *Day of the Daleks* – [see also UNIT Dating pages 263-7] Jo tells the Controller that she left the twentieth century on "September the thirteenth". The Controller notes, rather annoyingly for those trying to pin down the dates of the UNIT stories, that Jo has "already told me the year" she is from.

reporter, Sarah Jane Smith, smuggled herself into the complex, posing as her Aunt Lavinia, the noted virologist...'

[*The Zen Military*, Kadiatu Lethbridge-Stewart]

## 1970s (UNIT) – THE PARADISE OF DEATH [74]

'The Parakon Corporation opened Space World on Hampstead Heath. It offered many attractions based on space and time travel, including twenty-one alien creatures such as the Giant Ostroid, the crab-clawed Kamelius from Aldebaran Two, Piranhatel Beetles and Stinksloths. Using Experienced Reality techniques, Parakon could give people guided tours of the Gargatuan Caverns of Southern Mars and the wild side of Mercury. UNIT's investigations into the death of a young man whose thigh bone had been bitten clean through exposed the Parakon Corporation as an extra terrestrial organisation. Parakon had been negotiating with Earth for a number of years, hoping to sign a trading agreement – Parakon would supply rapine, a wonder material. Parakon, though, wanted human bodies to fertilise their world, which had been devastated by the rapine harvests. They had already sacked many worlds, including Blestinu. UNIT defeated the Corporation.'

[*The Zen Military*, Kadiatu Lethbridge-Stewart]

## 1970s (UNIT) – INVASION OF THE DINOSAURS [75]

Eight million Londoners were evacuated after dinosaurs began to terrorise the population. The government decamped to Harrogate. UNIT helped with the security operation in London, which was under the command of General Finch and the Minister with Special Powers, Sir Charles Grover. UNIT scientists diagnosed temporal displacement and calculated that whoever was operating the time machine would need an atomic reactor. They tracked the Time Scoop to a hidden bunker near Moorgate Underground Station. The bunker contained an elaborate shelter, in which a group of people – including the conservationist Lady Cullingford, the novelist Nigel Castle and the Olympic long jumper John Crichton – lived, convinced that they were in a spaceship bound for a new, unpolluted planet. Using the Time Scoop, Professor Whitaker hoped to regress Earth back to its primeval days, repopulating it from the people in the bunker.

During this, the Doctor unveiled his new car. [76] After this time, the temporal scientist Chun Sen is born. [77]

Although the Doctor often returned to Earth, and had started a project to research the psychic potential of humans, he was now free to wander space and time. Realising that UNIT might need to contact him in an emergency, the Doctor gave the Brigadier a syonic beam Space/Time Telegraph. [78]

## 1970s (UNIT) – THE FIVE DOCTORS [79]

While on Earth at this time, the third Doctor was kidnapped by Borusa while driving his sprightly yellow roadster Bessie.

## 1975 (UNIT, 20 – 21 May) – THE GHOSTS OF N-SPACE [80]

While on holiday in Italy, the Doctor, Sarah, Jeremy and the Brigadier prevented the wizard Maximillian Vilmio from achieving immortality. Vilmio had planned to use the space-warping effect of Clancy's comet to match his real body and his N-Form in Null-Space.

## 1970s (UNIT, mid-March) – PLANET OF THE SPIDERS [81]

'A stage magician, Clegg, died at UNIT HQ, apparently during some secretive experiment.'

[The Zen Military, Kadiatu Lethbridge-Stewart]

There was a disturbance at a Tibetan monastery in Mortimer, Mummerset. It was led by Lupton, a man bitter about the capitalist system after he was sacked from a company after working for them for twenty years then saw his own company bankrupted by his previous employers.

## 1970s (UNIT, 4 April) – ROBOT [82]

As the UNIT budget was limited, the organisation was unable to afford a Captain to replace Mike Yates. Benton was promoted to Warrant Officer and made the Brigadier's second-in-command.

59 INTERNATIONAL POLITICS IN THE UNIT ERA – [see also UNIT Dating pages 263-7]. There appear to be four superpowers: The US, USSR, China and the United Kingdom. In the 1970s the world lurches from a period of détente with the Soviet Union (The Invasion) to the brink of World War III (The Mind of Evil and Day of the Daleks), but by the end of the decade, the Cold War has ended (Invasion of the Dinosaurs and Robot – in both stories a character says "back in the Cold War days"). Ace refers to "perestroika" in Timewyrm: Exodus (p228), and the Doctor talks of the collapse of the Soviet Union in Just War, but the Communist system itself seems to survive, and by the 1990s Communist troops from Eastern Europe serve alongside the British (in Battlefield the troops' uniforms bear the hammer and sickle). The "Soviet Praesidium" is mentioned in The Seeds of Death, and tensions between the East and West blocs lead to another cold war in the late twenty-first century (Warriors of the Deep).

60 Dating The Sea Devils – [see also UNIT Dating pages 263-7, although this story doesn't actually feature UNIT]. No indication is given as to how much time has passed since Doctor Who and the Silurians or The Dæmons. The Master insists that his second television is colour, but this doesn't mean that the story is set just after colour TV was

introduced – before the advent of cheap colour portable TVs a household would commonly have a big colour set and a smaller black and white one. The Master watches an episode of *The Clangers* first broadcast in 1971 and repeated many times since.

**61** The Brigadier refers to the "Priority A1" order in *The Time Monster*.

**62** The Green Death – it happened "last year" according to Stevens.

**63** Dating *The Time Monster* – [see also UNIT Dating pages 263-7] Jo wishes Benton a "Merry Michaelmas". The TARDIS in this story appears to be fully functional. However, Jo asks the Doctor if he is working on a dematerialisation circuit. The Doctor replies: "No. That'll have to wait." Therefore we can infer that the TARDIS is still broken. This story is set in "the mid-seventies" according to *Falls the Shadow* (p116), which reveals the fate of the "Thascales Theorem".

**64** *The Android Invasion.* [see also UNIT Dating pages 263-7]. Sarah reported on Crayford's disappearance "two years" before that story.

**65** Dating *The Three Doctors* – [see also UNIT Dating pages 263-7]. Dr Tyler refers to "Cape Kennedy" and Jo misquotes the words to 'I am the Walrus'.

**66** The Doctor says at the end of *The Three Doctors* that he needs to build a new force field

'The National Institute for Advanced Scientific Research, or "Think-Tank" as it has been dubbed by the press, concentrates many of Britain's scientists all under one roof. Already its achievements have been impressive: the head of the Institute pioneered work on the disintegrator gun, a weapon capable of burning a hole on the Moon's surface. The material dynastrene, the hardest known to science, has also been developed. Perhaps the most impressive achievement is Professor Kettlewell's "living metal", which he has used to build the K1, a robot capable of performing tasks in environments where no human could survive. Many Think-Tank personnel are also members of the Scientific Reform Society, a group that believes in efficiency and logic.'

[Report in the *British Scientific Gazette*]

Following this time, a woman becomes Prime Minister. [83]

## 1970s (UNIT) – TERROR OF THE ZYGONS [84]

Centuries after arriving on Earth, the Zygons in Loch Ness learnt that their home planet had been destroyed in a stellar explosion. A refugee fleet had been assembled, and it was looking for a new home. Broton signalled that Earth would be suitable, once the ice caps had been melted, the mean temperature of the planet had been raised, and the necessary minerals had been introduced to the water.

'In the space of a month, three oil rigs in the North Sea were destroyed in mysterious circumstances, and with massive loss of life. Two of the rigs were owned by Hibernian Oil, who also reported radio blackouts. When UNIT were sent to Tullock, we learnt that the Duke of Forgill had been acting strangely ever since the arrival of the oil companies. This was because the Duke had recently been replaced by the Zygon leader, Broton. The Zygons were an amphibious race (a full autopsy report is available as the body of the leader survived), and they planned to conquer the world. For centuries they had lived under Loch Ness, but now the oil companies were disrupting the free passage of their

"Skarasen", a vast monster that lived in Loch Ness but which ventured out into the North Sea from time to time. It was the Skarasen that destroyed the rigs. The Zygon ship was launched, and radar tracked it moving south – at this point we did not know the Zygon's plan. The Prime Minister ordered discreet but resolute action. The Zygon ship was destroyed where it had landed (a disused quarry outside Brentford), but their leader, Broton, had already left. He, posing as the Duke of Forgill, managed to get into the Fourth International Energy Conference on the banks of the Thames – he planned to assassinate the world leaders assembled there by signalling for the Skarasen. Broton and the signal device were both destroyed, and the Skarasen returned to Loch Ness. It is anticipated that now it is not being controlled by the Zygons, the creature will remain placid.'

[Brigadier Lethbridge-Stewart's Report to Cabinet]

The Cabinet accepted the Brigadier's report, and the matter was closed.

## 1980 (UNIT) – PYRAMIDS OF MARS [85]

The Doctor took Sarah to 1980, to show her what would happen if they left England in 1911 before defeating Sutekh. Earth was a devastated wasteland. The Doctor's actions prevent this timeline from coming to pass.

The Doctor and Ace visited London in 1976. [86]

## 1976 (UNIT, Saturday 19 - 22 June) – NO FUTURE [87]

Time was altered by the Monk: this time anarchy was real. The terrorist organisation Black Star, a group of anarchists, spent the summer planting bombs in sites around London: Hamleys, Harrods, the Albert Hall, the Science Museum and Big Ben. There was an assassination attempt on the Queen, junior treasury minister John Barfe was killed, the entertainer Jimmy Tarbuck was badly hurt in a hit-and-run incident and Pink Floyd's private jet was lost over the English Channel. There were civil disturbances across the globe. Prime Minister

generator to replace the one that has been destroyed. He goes on a test flight in *Carnival of Monsters*.

67 "Six months" before *Invasion of the Dinosaurs*.

68 Dating *Dancing the Code* – [see also UNIT Dating pages 263-7]. Watergate appears to be topical (p154).

69 *Dancing the Code* (p61) – these unrecorded encounters were either travelling with the Doctor or attacks on Earth faced by UNIT.

70 Dating *The Green Death* – [see also UNIT Dating pages 263-7]. Two calendars appear: the first is in the pithead office and shows the date to be "April 5th". The second can be glimpsed in the security guard's office and shows the month to be February. This particular February has twenty-nine days and the twenty-ninth falls on a Tuesday, making it 1972. BOSS is an advanced "Biomorphic" artificial intelligence that has been linked to a human brain. There is a Ministry of Ecology.

71 Jeremy was presumably intended to be Jeremy Thorpe, the leader of the Liberal Party at the time the story was made. Thorpe, of course, was never Prime Minister.

72 *Planet of the Spiders*.

73 Dating *The Time Warrior* – [see also UNIT Dating pages 263-7]. This story introduces Sarah Jane Smith. In *Pyramids of Mars*, Sarah states that she is

"from 1980".

74 Dating *The Paradise of Death* – [see also UNIT Dating pages 263-7]. The Brigadier hasn't heard of Virtual Reality. The Secretary-General of the United Nations is a woman. There is no gap on television between *The Time Warrior* and *The Invasion of the Dinosaurs*. Barry Letts decided to set this radio play before Mike Yates's 'retirement' from UNIT. Captain Yates is referred to in the book (p87).

75 Dating *The Invasion of the Dinosaurs* – [see also UNIT Dating pages 263-7]. Whitaker has built a Time Scoop capable of calling up dinosaurs from hundreds of millions of years ago. The Whomobile is an 'M' reg. The bunker was built "back in the Cold War days". According to *The Left-Handed Hummingbird* this story is set in "the mid-seventies" (p100).

76 The Doctor's car was never named on-screen, but was dubbed both '*Alien*' and '*The Whomobile*' by the production team. The Doctor continues to use *Bessie* (both are seen in *Planet of the Spiders*).

77 *Invasion of the Dinosaurs* – the Doctor says that Chun Sen couldn't be a suspect as he "hasn't been born yet".

78 The Doctor is researching into the psychic potential of humans in *Planet of the Spiders* (the fourth Doctor doesn't continue the study). *Terror of the Zygons* – presumably the Brigadier didn't

Williams declared a state of emergency.

The Vardans were preparing their "active immigration" to Earth. The Vardan High Command formed an alliance with the Monk, the Time Lord formerly known as Mortimus. The Monk freed them from their time loop and, under the guise of Priory Records boss Robert Bertram, he used Vardan Mediascape technology to plant crude subliminal messages in Earth's TV broadcasts. More sophisticated brainwashing techniques were available in the new VR training system the Monk provided for UNIT.

Some members of UNIT, including most of the Broadsword intelligence agents, were able to break the conditioning. The Vardans were repelled from Earth and the Vardan Popular Front, a democratic organisation, took control of Varda.

The Russians were operating vodyanoi units at this time. [88]

The Brigadier was seeing Doris at this time. The Doctor selectively wiped his memory, encouraging him to retire. Following this time, the Brigadier spent a great deal of time in Geneva. [89]

## 1970s (UNIT, 6 July) – THE ANDROID INVASION [90]

'OSEIDON – A desolate world, the only planet in the galaxy with a radiation level this high. This radioactivity appears to be natural. It is not caused, it seems, by nuclear warfare: although the Kraals are warlike, they consider fission weapons "crude" and they have superseded them with the development of powerful energy weapons and the MD (Matter Dissolving) bomb. The radiation levels on the planet continue to rise, and Oseidon will soon be uninhabitable. So, the Kraals are a doomed race, living underground in gloomy, almost cavelike facilities. The leader of the Kraal's Armoury Division, Chief Scientist Styggron, began to plan his race's escape from Oseidon using their technological skills. The Kraals could engineer space/time warps, and Styggron used one of these to capture an experimental Earth freighter in deep space. He analysed the mind of the astronaut within, Guy Crayford, and used the human's memories to construct the Training Ground, an almost-perfect replica of the English village of Devesham, including the nearby Space Defence Station. The Training Ground was populated with android villagers, and there the Kraals were able to learn about human civilisation and behaviour, perfecting their preparations to invade Earth. It was the Kraals' first attempt at conquest, but although they failed, Marshal Chedaki's fleet survived and the Kraal databanks contain the complete memory prints of a Time Lord traveller, the Doctor.'

[*Bartholomew's Planetary Gazetteer*, Volume XXV]

## 1970s (UNIT, Early One Month in Autumn) – THE SEEDS OF DOOM [91]

The World Ecology Bureau was active at this time. They received reports from Antarctica that a pair of unusual seed pods had been discovered in the permafrost. They called in UNIT's scientific advisor, who identified them as Krynoid seed pods.

> "I suppose you could call it a galactic weed, though it's deadlier than any weed you know. On most planets the animals eat the vegetation. On planets where the Krynoid gets established, the vegetation eats the animals"
> [Address to the Intergalactic Flora Society by its President]

One Krynoid was killed in the Antarctic; the other was destroyed by an RAF air strike on the mansion of Harrison Chase, the millionaire plant enthusiast.

Realising that the Doctor's visits to Earth were becoming less and less frequent, the Brigadier had *Bessie* mothballed. [92]

## 1970s (UNIT) – THE HAND OF FEAR [93]

There was near meltdown in the main reactor of Nunton Nuclear Power Complex, although miraculously there was no radiation leak.

Summoned to Gallifrey, the Doctor was forced to return Sarah Jane Smith home. Although the TARDIS apparently didn't return Sarah to Croydon, it was England in the right year. Sarah resumed her work as a journalist.

have the Space/Time Telegraph when London was being over-run by dinosaurs, or he would have used it to call the Doctor back.

79 Dating *The Five Doctors* – [see also UNIT Dating pages 263-7]. The third Doctor is kidnapped after *The Time Warrior* as he recognises Sarah. Sticking strictly to what we know in the television series, his abduction must occur between *The Monster of Peladon* and *Planet of the Spiders*, because the other stories of the eleventh series follow on from each other. However *The Paradise of Death* is set in a 'non-existent' gap between the first two stories of the series, and the Doctor might have been taken from there.

80 Dating *The Ghosts of N-Space* – The story takes place after *Death to the Daleks* in the Doctor and Sarah's timeline (p4). Clancy's comet returns to Earth every 157 years (p200), and the last sighting was in "1818" (p63), making it 1975.

81 Dating *Planet of Spiders* – [see also UNIT Dating pages 263-7]. The story takes place three weeks before *Robot*. "Meditation is the in-thing" according to Sarah Jane.

82 Dating *Robot* – [see also UNIT Dating pages 263-7, and A WOMAN PRIME MINISTER page 98]. Sarah Jane Smith's day pass to Think-Tank bears the date "April 4th". The Cold War has been "over for years" according to the Brigadier. Advanced technology includes

the K1 robot, the Disintegrator Gun and dynastrene.

**83 A WOMAN PRIME MINISTER** – [see also UNIT Dating pages 263-7]. In *The Ark in Space*, Harry is surprised that the High Minister, "a member of the fair sex," was "top of the totem pole", suggesting there is yet to be a female prime minister in Britain by his time. There must be a General Election or leadership election while he is away from Earth – in *Terror of the Zygons* the Brigadier receives a phone call from the PM, whom he twice addresses as "Madam", and later refers to as "she".

Contrary to the assumptions of many fans over the years, Margaret Thatcher had already been elected leader of the Conservatives when *Terror of the Zygons* was taped – the scene in which the Brigadier is phoned by the PM was recorded on 23 April 1975, and Mrs Thatcher had been party leader since February of that year. The Labour Government of the time had a tiny majority, and predicting a Conservative victory at the next election was a fairly safe bet (in much the same way that *Zamper*, written in 1995, referred to "Number Ten, Tony's den" (p45)). It would seem, then, that the production team had Mrs Thatcher in mind, rather than the two candidates from the Labour Party, Shirley Williams or Barbara Castle, who have subsequently been suggested. (Shirley Williams is indeed PM in the New Adventure *No Future* (p77)).

## 1977 (UNIT) – MAWDRYN UNDEAD [94]

'In 1976 Alistair Gordon Lethbridge-Stewart announced his retirement from UNIT. He was awarded the CBE. Soon afterwards he became a mathematics teacher at Brendon School. Following an encounter with his own future self, the Brigadier lost all memories of his UNIT days. Doctors diagnosed a nervous breakdown. He spent the next six years teaching at Brendon, unaware of his past.'

[*The Zen Military*, Kadiatu Lethbridge-Stewart]

## c 1977 (30 – 31 July) – IMAGE OF THE FENDAHL [95]

The Doctor defeated the Fendahl at Fetchborough, a village on the edge of a time fissure. A team of scientists under Professor Fendelman had attempted to probe the secrets of the far past using a Time Scanner, but this had only succeeded in activating the Fendahl skull. Fetch Priory was destroyed in an implosion.

In 1977 the Doctor landed in Lewisham in an attempt to track the Timewyrm. On 21 February 1978, the sacrificial stone at the base of the Great Temple in Mexico City was uncovered by electrical workers. [96]

## c 1978 – THE PIRATE PLANET [97]

Zanak's career as the Pirate Planet was brought to an abrupt end with the destruction of its engines and the death of its Captain and Queen Xanxia. Zanak settled in a peaceful area of space.

## c 1978 – THE STONES OF BLOOD [98]

'CESSAIR SENTENCED
(From our Court Reporter)
Cessair of Diplos was tracked down to a remote planet in the Mutter's Spiral yesterday, where she had been hiding out for four thousand years. She was found guilty by the Megara of impersonating a deity; the theft and misuse of the Great Seal of Diplos; murder; and removing silicon lifeforms from the planet Ogros in contravention of article 7594 of the Galactic Charter. She was sentenced to perpetual imprisonment.'

The Doctor sent K9 Mk III to Croydon in 1978, but his crate would remain unopened for another three years. Around this time, Drax spent ten years in Brixton Prison. Chris Parsons graduated in 1978, and work was being done in the sewers under Fleet Street. In 1979, Lavinia Smith moved to Moreton Harwood. Sarah Jane Smith visited her shortly afterwards and met Commander Pollock. [99] Benton "left the army in '79" and became a used car salesman. [100]

## 1979 – CITY OF DEATH [101]

Scaroth's plan was reaching its culmination: with the help of the foremost temporal scientist of the day, Professor Theodore Nikolai Kerensky, Scaroth produced a device capable of shifting the whole world back in time four hundred million years. The Doctor, Romana and Duggan followed him in the TARDIS.

## c 1979 (October) – SHADA / THE FIVE DOCTORS [102]

Answering a distress signal from Professor Chronotis, the Doctor and Romana arrived in Cambridge. They discovered that Skagra had taken *The Worshipful and Ancient Law of Gallifrey*, the key to the Time Lord prison planet of Shada.

During this, Borusa attempted to abduct the Doctor and possibly Romana, but the abduction failed, becoming affected by a time eddy. [103]

## c 1980 – THE LEISURE HIVE [104]

The Doctor, Romana and K9 landed briefly on Brighton beach, but the Doctor had got the wrong season, and they soon left for Argolis.

John Lennon was murdered on 8 December 1980 by Mark Chapman. Professor Edward Travers CBE died on Christmas Day the same year. [105]

## c 1980 – MEGLOS [106]

On the planet Tigella, the Doctor prevented Meglos from recovering the Dodecahedron, the power source that would al-

84 Dating *Terror of the Zygons* – [see also UNIT Dating pages 263-7, and A WOMAN PRIME MINISTER page 98]. A woman is prime minister. In *Pyramids of Mars*, two stories after this one, Sarah states that she is from "1980". According to Broton, the destruction of the Zygon's home planet was "recent". According to *No Future*, this story is set in January (p8-9).

85 Dating *Pyramids of Mars* – [see also UNIT Dating pages 263-7]. The Doctor says that this version of the future is "1980". Sarah says "I'm from 1980", and the Doctor assures her that it isn't a trick – this is what has happened to Earth when Sutekh succeeded.

86 *Timewyrm: Revelation* (p217).

87 Dating *No Future* – [see also UNIT Dating pages 263-7]. The date is given on p6.

88 *No Future* (p224) – the vodyanoi were Russian supersoldiers seen in the 1981 BBC drama *The Nightmare Man*, adapted by Robert Holmes from David Wiltshire's novel *Child of the Vodyanoi*, and directed by Douglas Camfield.

89 *No Future*. The Brigadier is in Geneva during *The Android Invasion* and *The Seeds of Doom*.

90 Dating *The Android Invasion* – [see also UNIT Dating pages 263-7]. The calendar in the fake village gives the date (every day) as "Friday 6th July". The

nearest years with that exact date are 1973, 1979, 1984 and 1990. For at least the last two years, Britain has had a Space Defence Station, a team of Defence Astronauts, and has been operating space freighters.

91 Dating *The Seeds of Doom* – [see also UNIT Dating pages 263-7]. Chase says that it is autumn (and the location work for the story was recorded in October/November). The Doctor is invited to address the Royal Horticultural Society on "the fifteenth". There is a satellite videolink to Antarctica and UNIT have access to a laser cannon. The Antarctic base has an experimental fuel cell. On the other hand, Sarah only wants 2p for the public telephone.

92 *Battlefield. The Seeds of Doom* is the last UNIT story until *Mawdryn Undead*, and it is established in the later story (and implied in *Time-Flight*) that the Doctor hasn't visited the Brigadier for at least six years.

93 Dating *The Hand of Fear* – [see also UNIT Dating pages 263-7] While it doesn't feature UNIT, Sarah is returned home at the end of the story. It has to be set before December 1981 and *K9 and Company*.

94 Dating *Mawdryn Undead* – [see also UNIT Dating pages 263-7]. The Brigadier's past, where he meets Nyssa and Tegan. The Doctor says it is "six years" before 1983, "1977". It is the Queen's Silver Jubilee,

low him to use the Screens of Zolfa-Thura. Following this, the Doctor returned home the human kidnapped by a band of Gaztaks as a host body for Meglos. [107]

Anne Travers becomes scientific advisor to the cabinet in 1981. [108]

## c 1981 - THE KEEPER OF TRAKEN [109]

'TRAKEN – A planet in Mettula Orionsis. For generations, the Fosters, security guards who also tended the gardens of the planet, have not been armed, nor has the consular privilege been called on. All live under the benevolent rule of the Keeper of Traken, who has ruled for a thousand years. All evil that enters the peaceful Union of Traken becomes calcified.'

[*Bartholomew's Planetary Gazetteer*, Volume XX]

Two of the consuls of Traken, Tremas and Kassia married. Since she was a child, Kassia had tended the calcified Melkur. Now the Melkur began to move. Hypnotically controlling Kassia, the Melkur – in reality the renegade Time Lord the Master – attempted to seize control of the Source, the power of the Keeper of Traken. The Doctor prevented this, but the Master took the body of Tremas.

The Doctor visited Terminal Three of Heathrow Airport. [110]

## 1981 (28 February) - LOGOPOLIS [111]

The Doctor landed on Earth to take the measurements of a genuine police box to help the repairs of the chameleon circuit of the TARDIS. He had previously visited the planet Logopolis, and hoped that with their mathematical expertise and mastery of block transfer computation they would be able to help him.

The Doctor learnt from the Monitor of Logopolis that the universe had passed the natural point of heat death. All closed systems succumb to heat death, and the universe is a closed system. Or rather it was: the Logopolitans opened up a CVE (in Cassiopeia at co-ordinates 3C461-3044) into E-Space, another universe.

When the Master learnt of this, he recognised a chance to blackmail the entire universe. Threatening to close off the CVE, the Master broadcast a message to the entire universe:

"Peoples of the universe please attend carefully, the message that follows is vital to the future of you all. The choice for you all is simple: a continued existence under my guidance, or total annihilation. At the time of speaking, the fate of the universe lies in the balance at the fulcrum point, the Pharos Project on Earth…"

The fourth Doctor prevented the Master from closing the CVE, at the cost of his own life…

## 1981 (28 February) – CASTROVALVA [112]

The newly-regenerated Doctor and his companions Nyssa and Tegan returned to the TARDIS. The Master kidnapped Adric.

## 1981 (28 February ) – FOUR TO DOOMSDAY [113]

The Doctor defeated Monarch's plans to travel back to the creation of the universe. His android crew opted to settle on a habitable world when they found one.

## 1981 (18 – 22 December) – K9 AND COMPANY: A GIRL'S BEST FRIEND [114]

In June 1981, Peter Tracey recieved a suspended sentence for housebreaking. In September a thirteen-second hailstorm destroyed Commander Pollock's crop. Commander Pollock was renting the East Wing of Lavinia Smith's house at the time. On 6 December, Lavinia Smith left for America, phoning her ward Brendan Richards on the 10th to tell him that he would be spending Christmas with her niece, Sarah Jane. The next day, term ended and Brendan began waiting for her to pick him up, but Sarah had spent the first two weeks of December working abroad for Reuters.

Sarah Jane found a crate waiting for her at Moreton Harwood. It contained K9 Mk III, sent as a gift from the Doctor. Together,

which, as the Doctor says, is "June the seventh 1977". The 1983 Brigadier states that he retired "seven years ago". *Downtime* confirms that Lethbridge-Stewart was awarded the CBE (p246).

95 Dating *Image of the Fendahl* – According to Ma Tyler it is "Lammas Eve" (31 July) at the end of Part Three.

96 *Timewyrm: Revelation* (p13). *The Left-Handed Hummingbird* (p23).

97 Dating *The Pirate Planet* – The Doctor says that the population of Earth is "billions and billions", possibly suggesting a contemporary setting. The date "1978" is confirmed in *First Frontier* (p129).

98 Dating *The Stones of Blood* – There is no indication of what year the story is set in, but it is clearly contemporary.

99 *K9 and Company*. The *Armageddon Factor*. *Shada*. "Seven years" before *Attack of the Cybermen*. *K9 and Company*.

100 According to the Brigadier in *Mawdryn Undead*. Benton appears to be killed in *The Android Invasion*, although this was not the intention of the production team.

101 Dating *City of Death* – The Doctor says that this isn't a vintage year, "it's 1979 actually – more of a table wine, shall we say".

102 Dating *Shada/The Five*

*Doctors* – The TARDIS was "confused" by May Week being in June, so it landed in October.

103 In the broadcast version of *The Five Doctors*, both the Doctor and Romana are picked up in the Time Scoop, and it is difficult to see how it can be reconciled to *Shada*. In the version released on video as *The Five Doctors Special Edition* 1995; it appears that only the Doctor is abducted, and that he is returned to his punt the moment that he left.

104 Dating *The Leisure Hive* – It isn't clear when the TARDIS lands on Brighton beach. In Fisher's novelisation it is clearly contemporary, although the opening chapter of the novel is set in June, but on-screen Romana is exasperated that the Doctor has got "the season wrong". *The Terrestrial Index* and The TARDIS Logs both suggested a date of '1934', although why is unclear – the date doesn't appear in the script or any BBC documentation.

105 *The Left-Handed Hummingbird. Downtime* (p60).

106 Dating *Meglos* – Unless the Gaztaks are capable of time travel this story is set in the late twentieth century – the earthling wears an early 1980s business suit. The TARDIS Logs offered a date of '1988 AD'.

107 *Full Circle*.

108 "Eighteen years" before *Millennial Rites* (p14). It is suggested that Anne Travers

the three of them exposed a local coven of witches who conducted human sacrifices. On 29 December, the cultists appeared in court on an attempted murder charge.

## c 1982 (UNIT) – TIME-FLIGHT

'Following the disappearance of *Speedbird Concorde 192*, the Doctor arrived at Heathrow Airport. At the insistence of Sir John Sudbury at C-19, the Doctor was allowed to take a second Concorde into the same time contour, and travelled back one hundred and forty million years.'

[*The Zen Military*, Kadiatu Lethbridge-Stewart]

Tegan Jovanka left the Doctor to take up her job as an air stewardess, but was sacked shortly afterwards. The Master was propelled to Xeraphas, where he discovered Kamelion, a tool of a previous invader of that planet. [115]

## c 1983 – ARC OF INFINITY

The Doctor tracked Omega down to Amsterdam. The city was located on the curve of the Arc of Infinity. Omega's base was below sea level in a crypt, to maintain pressure for fusion conversion. The ancient Gallifreyan's attempt to bond with the Doctor failed. Tegan Jovanka joined the Doctor once again.

## 1983 (UNIT) – MAWDRYN UNDEAD [116]

Before this time, the Arar-Jecks of Heiradi had carved out a huge subterranean city during the Twenty-Aeon War on that planet. There was civil war on Trion. Turlough's mother was killed and the ship containing his father and brother crashed on Sarn, formerly a Trion prison planet. Turlough was captured and exiled to Earth, where he was watched by Trion agents, including a solicitor on Chancery Lane. At some point after 1977 he was sent to Brendon School. [117]

The Brigadier regained his memory, but lost his beloved car when he met the Doctor for the first time in many years. When he met his past self from 1977, the Brigadier unwittingly provided the energy that released Mawdryn and his followers from their immortality. Turlough left Brendon to join the TARDIS crew.

## c 1983 (UNIT) THE FIVE DOCTORS [118]

The second Doctor and the Brigadier were kidnapped by Borusa in the grounds of UNIT HQ. The next day the second Doctor bought a copy of *The Times*

> 'Brigadier Alistair Gordon Lethbridge-Stewart spoke yesterday at a reunion of the United Nations Intelligence Taskforce. His successor, Colonel Crichton, spoke warmly of Lethbridge-Stewart, and made guarded reference to his national security work in the seventies.'
>
> [*The Times*]

Despite K9's warnings, Sarah Jane Smith was also kidnapped by Borusa.

In 1983, a thirteen-year-old Ace was friends with an Asian girl, Manisha, whose flat was firebombed in a racist attack. In revenge, Ace burnt down Gabriel Chase and was assigned a probation officer and a social worker. [119]

The "microchip revolution" took place around 1983. [120]

## 1984 (1 May) – THE AWAKENING [121]

The Malus absorbed the psychic energy of a series of war games in Little Hodcombe, amplifying the villagers' violence. The Doctor prevented the Malus from becoming totally active and blew up the church in which the Malus lay dormant.

After this, the Doctor, Tegan and Turlough spent some time in Little Hodcombe with Tegan's grandfather.

## 1984 – RESURRECTION OF THE DALEKS [122]

'Dalek-Duplicate Technology would be used to strike on two further fronts: twentieth-century Earth, where Duplicates were placed in key positions. This timezone also proved a safe place to store canisters of the virus...'

[*The Children of Davros*, Njeri Ngugi]

held the post throughout the UNIT era [see also UNIT Dating pages 263-7].

**109** Dating *The Keeper of Traken* – Traken is destroyed in the subsequent story, *Logopolis*, so *The Keeper of Traken* can't occur after this time, although The TARDIS Logs suggested a date of '4950 AD'. Melkur arrives "many years" before *The Keeper of Traken*. The script specifies that Kassia is eighteen at the time, the same age as Nyssa when the Doctor first meets her.

**110** *Four to Doomsday* – the Doctor mentions the visit during his attempt to convince Tegan that the Urbankan ship might be Heathrow.

**111** Dating *Logopolis* – The date is first stated in *Four to Doomsday*, the same day that *Logopolis*'s first episode was broadcast. This is the first on-screen use of the term "chameleon circuit". *The TARDIS Logs* set the Logopolis sequence in '4950'.

**112** Dating *Castrovalva* – This story immediately follows *Logopolis*.

**113** Dating *Four to Doomsday* – [see also MONARCH'S JOURNEY page 28]. The Doctor establishes that he has returned Tegan to the right point in time "16.15 hours" on "February the twenty-eighth 1981", the same day that *Logopolis* is set (and the day the first episode of that story was broadcast).

114 Dating *K9 and Company* – Sarah arrives in Moreton Harwood on "December the eighteenth", and later tells K9 that it is "1981". The other dates are given in dialogue.

115 *Arc of Infinity. The King's Demons.*

116 Dating *Mawdryn Undead* – The Doctor says that "if these readings are correct, it's 1983 on Earth", and the date is re-affirmed a number of times afterwards.

117 Turlough first appears in *Mawdryn Undead*, and his origins are revealed in *Planet of Fire*. He knows of the Eye of Orion in *The King's Demons* and of the Arar-Jecks in *Frontios*. According to the initial character outline, Turlough was '20' on his first appearance, which makes him a couple of years too old to be at Brendon School – this was almost certainly written when the plan was to introduce the character in *The Song of the Space Whale* by Pat Mills, a story that was delayed, then rejected. Mark Strickson was twenty-two when he began playing Turlough.

118 Dating *The Five Doctors* – [see also UNIT Dating pages 263-7]. The Brigadier recognises Tegan, so he must be kidnapped by Borusa after the second half of *Mawdryn Undead* in 1983. It is specified that he is attending a UNIT reunion, so this isn't the occasion of his retirement. Sarah is kidnapped around the

Tegan Jovanka left the Doctor, appalled by the carnage.

## c 1984 (Summer) – PLANET OF FIRE [123]

Professor Howard Foster discovered an archaeologically important wreck off the coast of an island holiday resort. His step-daughter, Perpugilliam Brown, travelled to the planet Sarn in the Doctor's TARDIS.

> 'SARN – A volcanically active planet, a former colony and prison planet of the Trions. Atop the Fire Mountain is the Blue Flame, a source of numismaton gas that improves mental and physical health. The locals worship the fire god Logar and attribute the healing powers to him.'
>
> [*Bartholomew's Planetary Gazetteer*, Volume XIX]

Turlough's exile was lifted and he returned to Trion. In the autumn of the same year, Peri was due back at college.

## 1984 (August/September) – DOWNTIME [124]

> 'The records show that UNIT's Gargarin Tracking Station reported a huge explosion at the Det-Sen Monastery in Tibet at 23.08 GMT on 18 August 1984. Six days later, a UNIT helicopter, with Second Lieutenant Douglas Cavendish and Pilot Per Londqvist was dispatched to the area.'
>
> [*The Zen Military*, Kadiatu Lethbridge-Stewart]

> 'There are three species of Yeti: the Mih-teh and Dzu-teh are both grey-furred, apelike creatures, while the Ye-teh, or Yeti Traversii is more bearlike. The new cub "Margaret" is a Ye-teh, the first to be bred in captivity. They are usually very timid, but that didn't stop Margaret from taking a bite out of the Prime Minister, her namesake. Don't worry, there's no risk of rabies - the Yeti was inoculated!'
>
> [Charles Bryce, Speaking to the BBC News at London Zoo]

In 1984, scientists in Princeton discovered Strange Matter. The Doctor and Mel visited Llanfer Ceiriog. [125]

# 1985 - ATTACK OF THE CYBERMEN [126]

For a year the police had been aware of Lytton, a sophisticated thief who had stolen valuable electronic components.

[CYBER - HISTORY - COMPUTER]--------------------
**Status Report:** All - is - proceeding - to - plan. Our - bases - in - the - sewer - system - of - London - and - on - the - Moon - are - secure. We - have - captured - two - time - travellers: Lytton - a - human - mercenary - from - Vita - 15 - and - the - Doctor. The - Doctor's - TARDIS - has - also - been - secured. The - two - captives - will - be - transferred - to - Telos - in - the - TARDIS.'
--------------------

# c 1985 - THE TWO DOCTORS [127]

Some years ago, the first Doctor had officially represented the Time Lords at the opening of space station Camera in the Third Zone. Now in his second incarnation and a renegade, he was sent to the station once again by the Time Lords. Experiments conducted by Kartz and Reimer were registering 0.4 on the Bocca Scale. Before the Doctor could lodge a protest with the Head of Projects, his old friend Joinson Dastari, the station was devastated by a Sontaran attack. The Third Zone had been betrayed by a technologically augmented Androgum, Chessene of the Franzine Grig.

The Doctor was taken to Seville by Major Varl. He was joined by Group Marshall Stike of the Ninth Sontaran Attack Group, and the two prepared a Kartz–Reimer experiment. The Sontarans were attempting to use a time capsule against the Rutan in the Madillon Cluster. The sixth Doctor traced his earlier self to Seville, which he had visited before. He helped to defeat the Sontaran plan.

In July 1986, the wreck of *The Titanic* was discovered. [128]

# 1986 (December) - THE TENTH PLANET [129]

Technological developments continued on Earth: the Z-Bomb and Cobra missiles had been developed, and Zeus spaceships

same time, certainly after *K9 and Company*.

119 *Ghost Light.* Marc Platt's novelisation specifies that Gabriel Chase is burnt down in August 1983. Ace's social worker is referred to in *Survival*.

120 *Remembrance of the Daleks* – had someone from 1963 discovered Ace's ghetto blaster, this would have been "twenty years too early".

121 Dating *The Awakening* – "It is 1984," the Doctor assures Tegan, despite clothing. As Tegan is the Queen of the May, it is presumably May Day.

122 Dating *Resurrection of the Daleks* – The Doctor says it is "1984 – Earth".

123 Dating *Planet of Fire* – Peri says she is due back at college in "the Fall", which isn't for "three months". There is nothing to suggest that the story isn't set in the year it was broadcast (1984). It can't take place before 1983, otherwise Turlough would return home while his past self was still in exile (*Mawdryn Undead*). In *Timelash* the Doctor threatens to take Peri back to "1985".

*Planet of Fire* was filmed on Lanzarote. The island in the story is not named and unlike Lanzarote it was on an ancient Greek trading route.

124 Dating *Downtime* – Chapter Two deals with UNIT's investigation at Det-Sen, Chapter Three with the new Yeti cub. This is "1984" (p22).

125 *Time and the Rani*, "Seven years" before *Cat's Cradle*:

*Witch Mark* (p25).

126 Dating *Attack of the Cybermen* – Mondas's attack is in "1986", which Peri confirms is "next year".

127 Dating *The Two Doctors* – The story is contemporary, but there is no indication exactly which year it takes place.

128 *The Left-Handed Hummingbird* (p261).

129 Dating *The Tenth Planet* – A calendar gives the date as "December 1986". This is the clearest example so far of real life catching up with 'futuristic' events is described the series, but in *Attack of the Cybermen* (broadcast in 1985) the date of "1986" for this story was reaffirmed. *Radio Times* and publicity material at the time gave the date as 'the late 1980s', as did the second edition of *The Making of Doctor Who*. The draft script set the date as '2000 AD' as did Gerry Davis's novelisation (the book followed the draft version of the story rather than the broadcast version, as the draft featured more scenes with the Doctor in). The first edition of *The Making of Doctor Who* also used the '2000' date. The first two editions of *The Programme Guide* set the range as '1975–80'. This confused the American *Doctor Who* comic, which decided that *The Tenth Planet* must precede *The Invasion* and that both were set in 'the 1980s'. John Peel's novelisation of *The Power of the Daleks* set the preceding

(launched on Demeter rockets) carried out manned missions to the Moon as well as close-orbital work. *Zeus 4*'s mission was to monitor weather and cosmic rays. Space missions were controlled from the South Pole base (callsign: "Snowcap"). The space programme was now an international effort, with Americans, British, Italians, Spaniards, Swiss, Australians and Africans manning Snowcap, and the programme was controlled from Geneva by International Space Command and its Secretary General, Wigner.

In late 1986, "the tenth planet" appeared in the skies of the southern hemisphere.

[CYBER - HISTORY - COMPUTER]----------------------[130]

**Background** – Eons - ago - Mondas - left - the - solar - system. Now - we - have - returned. We - will - drain - Earth - of - its - energy. We - have - located - key - strategic - points. We - will - neutralise - all - human - space - travel. We - will - neutralise - all - human - radio - communication.

**Status** – All - human - resistance - has - failed. Mondas - continues - to - absorb - energy - from - Earth. The - rate - of - energy - absorption - is - increasing. Emergency. Mondas - is - melting. Mondas - is–'

------------------------------------------------------------

There was an adventure in which Mel joins the Sixth Doctor in which the Master and the Usurians attempted to take over the world. [131]

In the late 1980s, the archaeologist Peter Warmsley began excavating a site associated with King Arthur on the edge of Lake Vortigern near Carbury. [132]

Ace was becoming a problem: she had sat her O-Levels, including French and Computer Studies, and was beginning to study for her A-Levels. She was expelled from school for blowing up the Art Room using homemade gelignite, an event she described as "a creative act". For a while, she worked as a waitress. One day Ace vanished in a timestorm whipped up by Fenric, following experiments in her bedroom in which she had attempted to extract nitro-glycerine from gelignite. Her mother reported her missing, her friends thinking that she was either dead or in Birmingham. [133]

## 1988 (22 –23 November) – SILVER NEMESIS [134]

[CYBER - HISTORY - COMPUTER]-----------------------------

**Background** – Thousands - of - Cyber - warships - have - been - assembled - in - the - Solar - System. To - escape - detection - they - are - shrouded. We - will - secure - the - validium - designation - "Nemesis". Earth - will - be - trans- formed - into - New - Mondas.

**Cyberleader** – A - scouting - party - will - be - sent - to - Earth. Analysis - of - previous - attacks - on - the - planet - indicate - that - we - will - face - the - hostile - designation - "the - Doctor". Humans - under - brain - control - will - assassinate - the - Doctor. We - shall - secure - the - three - components - of - the - Nemesis: the - statue - the - bow - the - arrow. The - meteorite - will - strike - Earth - at - grid - reference - 74W-32N.

**Supplementary** – Heavy - local - resistance - encountered. Three - rival - factions - hampered - Cyber - operations: Peinforte - deceased. De-Flores - deceased. The - Doctor - active. The - fleet - has - been - completely - destroyed - by - the - Nemesis.'

## c 1989 (Sunday) – SURVIVAL [135]

Over the course of a month, four teenagers from Perivale van- ished without trace, abducted by the Cheetah People. The planet of the Cheetah People was dying, and the Cheetah people were preparing to move on to new feeding grounds. The Master was trapped on the planet, and he lured the Doctor and Ace to the planet to try to assist him.

story in 'the 1990s'.

A Moon mission returned to Earth the month before the story.

130 THE CYBER-INVASIONS – The history of the Cybermen is straightforward: there is only one story for which we are not told the date (*The Invasion*). The Cyber-computer tells Tobias Vaughn that the Cybermen have never been to Earth before the events of *The Invasion*. It would appear that the Cybermen in that story are an advanced force from Mondas – they don't mention their home planet, but logically they wouldn't want to forewarn Earth that Mondas was due to arrive in the solar system in around a decade's time. Likewise, we might infer that the Cybermen in *The Tenth Planet* don't mention the previous invasion because they don't want to remind mankind about their defeat. In *The Tenth Planet* all the Cybermen are dependent on energy from Mondas to live, but clearly those in *The Invasion* are not – we might speculate that they are 'spacefaring' Cybermen who can travel into deep space to scout ahead of Mondas. Some more of the 'spacefaring' Cybermen survive the destruction of their home planet and assemble a vast fleet, thousands of Cyber- warships. They become intent on converting Earth into "a new Mondas", but this entire fleet is destroyed in *Silver Nemesis*. Some Cybermen elsewhere survive (from what the Nemesis

statue says, they can't be part of the fleet we see in *Silver Nemesis*). In around eighty years time, this weakened group of survivors resumes its attacks on Earth... [see also TELOS page 139].

**131 MEL'S FIRST ADVENTURE** – The writers' guide for the twenty-third series suggested that Mel joined the Doctor after an encounter with the Master, and this is echoed in the Missing Adventure *Millennial Rites* (p83). This appears to be contradicted by *The Trial of a Time Lord* when Mel fails to recognise the renegade Time Lord (conceivably Mel didn't actually meet the Master on the first occasion, or he was disguised at the time). The writers' guide also suggested that Mel had been travelling with the Doctor for 'three months'. It is entirely possible that Mel starts her travels with the Doctor at the end of *The Trial of a Time Lord*, negating the need for a 'first adventure'. This idea is riddled with paradoxes (i.e. she is from her own future and would have memories of her first few adventures before she arrived).

Two Missing Adventures by Steve Lyons, *Time of Your Life* and the forthcoming *Killing Ground* are sixth Doctor stories set after the Trial but before he meets Mel. In *Just War* Mel says that she has never been to the past before, "only the future".

**132** "Ten years" before *Battlefield*.

**133** Ace's story is established in *Dragonfire*, with further details given in *The Curse of Fenric*. She describes her destruction in *Battlefield* – this account is based on information from the novelisation of *Dragonfire*. *Survival*.

**134** Dating *Silver Nemesis* – The first scene is set, according to the caption slide, in "South America, 22nd November 1988". The Doctor's alarm goes off the next day – although it is a beautiful sunny day.

**135** Dating *Survival* – Ace returns to Perivale. When she asks how long she has been away, the Doctor replies "as long as you think you have". Midge and Stevie vanished "last month"; Shreela vanished the week before. The date "1989" is confirmed in *First Frontier* (p252).

# TIMELINE: 1990 to 2109 AD

In the early 1990s, there was a string of privatisations: the electricity industry became Elec-Gen, and British Rail became BritTrack. In August 1991, information about the Russian Coup reached the West via the Internet. The Mandragora Helix was due to return to Earth in the early 1990s. *If it did so, it was defeated once more, as humanity survived.* The Brigadier's grandson, Gordon James Lethbridge-Stewart, was born, although Kate Lethbridge-Stewart split up from his father, Jonathan, when he was two. The Brigadier did not know about his grandson until Gordon was five, as his daughter had not spoken to him for over a year. [1]

## c 1990 (Sunday) - CAT'S CRADLE: TIME'S CRUCIBLE [2]

The Doctor and Ace are summoned back to the TARDIS after eating baked Alaska on Ealing Broadway.

In the summer of 1991, the Doctor hid a portable temporal link in St Christopher's Church, Cheldon Bonniface while brass rubbing with Mel.[3]

## c 1992 - CAT'S CRADLE: WITCH MARK [4]

'Coach accident. M40. Casualties taken to Condicote General Hospital. Inventory of coach luggage compartment. 42 suitcases containing in total approximately £2 Mill. All bear mysterious mark.'

[Police Report, Forwarded to Scotland Yard Paranormal Investigations Team]

## 1993 - BLOOD HEAT [5]

In an alternative timestream, the Silurian plague released at Wenley Moor in the early 1970s succeeded in wiping out most of humanity. The Doctor was killed before he could discover the antidote. Over the next twenty years, the Silurians initiated massive climatic change, rendering the plant life inedible to humanity and altering coastlines. Dinosaur species from many different eras were reintroduced to the wild. The capital of Earth became Ophidian, a vast city in Africa. Some Silurians hunted down humans for sport.

This timeline was created by the Monk, and deactivated by the Doctor. It would survive for a generation or so after this time before winding down.

1 The first two of these events are mentioned in *System Shock* (Chapter 05). According to the Doctor in *The Masque of Mandragora* the Helix was due to return to Earth "five hundred years" after its first attack in the late fifteenth century. Gordon Lethbridge-Stewart was born "nearly five" years before *Downtime*.

2 Dating *Cat's Cradle: Time's Crucible* – It is "three years" since Ace left Perivale (p8).

3 *Timewyrm: Revelation* (p196).

4 Dating *Cat's Cradle: Witchmark* – No year is specified, although the President of the United States has taken to bathing in Cranberry Sauce.

5 Dating *Blood Heat* – This story is a sequel to *Doctor Who and the Silurians*, containing many elements from its novelisation, *The Cave Monsters* – so, the Reptile People are called "Silurians", but the Doctor wears his velvet jacket, not coveralls, when he goes potholing (and is killed), and the leader of the Silurians is named Morka. This confusion can presumably be put down to the Monk's interference with established history. It is repeatedly stated that the first encounter with the Silurians took place "twenty years" ago in "1973".

6 *No Future* (Epilogue).

7 Dating *Conundrum* – The Doctor thinks that it is "November the second, 1993" (p7).

8 Dating *The Dimension Riders* – The scenes in Oxford are set in "1993" (p2), "November 18th" (p13).

9 Dating *Goth Opera* – It is "1993" (p24), "November" (p62).

10 Dating *Timewyrm: Revelation* – "It was the Sunday before Christmas 1992" (p2).

11 Dating *The Left-Handed Hummingbird* – The date of the massacre is given on p9. The Doctor arrives in "1994" (p5).

The Doctor, Benny and Ace visited the 1993 Glastonbury Festival, meeting Danny Pain and his daughter Amy. [6]

### 1993 (2 November) – CONUNDRUM [7]

As part of his revenge against the Doctor, the Monk trapped the TARDIS in the fictional village of Arandale, populated by colourful characters. It was part of the Land of Fiction, and the Doctor wrote himself out.

### 1993 (18 November) – THE DIMENSION RIDERS [8]

At St Matthew's College, Oxford, the Time Lord Epsilon Delta plotted with the Garvond to create a Time Focus. The Doctor defeated his plan to create universal anarchy.

### 1993 (November) – GOTH OPERA [9]

'He will be entombed in a pit, not alive and not dead, on the world that will be called Ravolox. He will be joined with a Prydonian Lady, and the two of them shall cause much suffering, for he is the one the Great Vampire predicted at his meeting with Rassilon, the one who will succeed him and be consumed in the maw of time that his people may prosper. They will call him the Vampire Messiah.'

[*The Books of Prophecy*]

Tracking them down to Manchester, the Doctor destroyed the Vampire Army of Yarven and Ruath.

### 1993 (Christmas) – TIMEWYRM:REVELATION [10]

The Doctor and Ace visited Cheldon Bonniface.

### 1994 – THE LEFT-HANDED HUMMINGBIRD [11]

On 31 October 1993, the "Halloween Man" opened fire on a crowd of unsuspecting people in a marketplace in Mexico City. Cristián Alvarez witnessed this, narrowly avoiding death himself.

On 31 October 1993, the "Halloween Man" opened fire on a crowd of unsuspecting people in a marketplace in Mexico City. Cristián Alvarez witnessed this, narrowly avoiding death himself. There was evidence of an alien presence, the Blue. On

12 December he sent a note for the Doctor's attention to UNIT HQ in Geneva.

The Doctor arrived early the next year, and investigated. In the Doctor's own timeline this was before the "Happening" of late 1968 early 1969.

Thanks to the Doctor's actions, the Blue was defeated before this time

In 1994, an unmanned space probe discovered the real 'Tenth Planet', a small, cold world which was to prove the outermost planet in Earth's solar system. *After some debate, the planet was named Cassius, after the leader of the conspiracy against Julius Caesar, the man who, according to Dante's Divina Commedia, occupies the innermost, icy circle of Hell.* [12]

## 1994 (8 July) – INVASION OF THE CAT-PEOPLE [13]

The second Doctor, Polly and Ben prevented the Cat-People from harnessing the magnetic energy of Earth.

The Doctor, Benny, Chris and Roz spent a couple of days at the Doctor's house in Allen Road to recover from their experiences on Zamper. [14]

## 1995 (November) – FALLS THE SHADOW [15]

Professor Jeremy Winterdawn and his team at Shadowfell House experimented for five years with the "Thascales Theorem", research that indicated that applied quantum physics was a possibility. Hoping to manipulate space/time, he managed to interface with the Cathedral, and succeeded in distorting the spacial dimensions of Shadowfell. Gabriel and Tanith, psychotic expressions of Cathedral's pain, were released, as were manifestations of the universe's might-have-beens: an agent from an Earth where England was a Republic dedicated to the principals of Fundamental Humanism, and another from an Earth dominated by a hivemind of giant insects. Cathedral was destroyed along with Gabriel and Tanith, although the grey man survived.

12 CASSIUS – The existence of Cassius is first referred to by K9 in *The Sun Makers*, and the date of its discovery is established in *Iceberg* (p87). "The Battle of Cassius" is referred to in *The Crystal Bucephalus* (p133).

13 Dating *Invasion of the Cat-People* – It is "AD 1994" (p9), the adventure starting "Friday the eighth of July 1994" (p35).

14 *Zamper.*

15 Dating *Falls the Shadow* – It is "a crisp November morning" (p4), "five years" after "UN adventurism in the Persian Gulf" (p113–4), presumably a reference to the build-up to the Gulf War in 1990, or to the War itself in 1991. Thascales was an alias of the Master in *The Time Monster*.

16 Dating *Downtime* – The story is set "about thirty" (p99) or "over twenty-five" (p134) years after *The Web of Fear*, "nearly twenty years" after *Fury from the Deep* and Sarah's time in UNIT (p124), and about ten years after 1984 (p12). The Brigadier has been teaching at Brendon for "twenty odd years" (p256). *Millennial Rites*, is set in 1999, "four years" (p24) afterwards.

17 Anne Travers is still paranoid about the Intelligence in *Millennial Rites*.

18 Between *Mawdryn Undead* and *Battlefield*, and shortly after the Missing Adventure *Downtime*. Doris is first mentioned in *Planet of the Spiders*.

19 Dating *The Chase* – The Doctor claims that, as "this house is exactly what you would expect in a nightmare", the TARDIS and the Dalek Time Machine have landed "in a world of dreams" that "exists in the dark recesses of the human mind". Viewers find out the truth at the end of the scene – the TARDIS has simply landed in a theme park. A sign proclaims that it is the "Festival of Ghana 1996". In *Original Sin* Tobias Vaughn claims he saw the Dalek Time Machine at the "1995 Earth Fair in Ghana" (p292). Vaughn's memories are, by his own admission, corrupted. The "Tower of London" quote is Ian's description of what he has just seen. Quite why Peking would cancel an exhibition in Ghana is never made clear.

## c 1995 – DOWNTIME [16]

'Under the direction of the Great Intelligence, Victoria Waterfield (a woman whom records show was born nearly one hundred and forty years ago) had invested an eight-figure sum in the New World University in North-West London. The Intelligence used a hypnotic technique to control the students at the university. It was inhabiting the computers at the university, and was beginning to spread into the Internet. There was chaos as all computer systems succumbed to the "computer flu", as the media termed it; I hear that the CIA's files were broadcast on Russian television, bank cashpoints released all their cash and Tomahawk missiles were launched in the Gulf. Before a worldwide Web could be established, the Intelligence was reliant on the university's generators, and these were destroyed. Its link with the outside world, my father's dead body, was severed.

The Intelligence had managed to infiltrate UNIT once again – Captain Cavendish of Virtual Ordnance was under its control. Thankfully, on this occasion, Brigadier Crichton's men did sterling work in beating back the Yeti. I hear that special credit should go to two men in particular: Captain Bambera of Zen Platoon Three, and Brigadier Lethbridge-Stewart, who discovered the Intelligence's plan.

Interpol have been unable to locate Miss Waterfield. The Intelligence, in my judgement, remains a threat to global security.'

[Dame Anne Travers's report to Cabinet on the New World Incident] [17]

After this time, the Brigadier is reunited with Doris, they marry and the Brigadier gives up teaching. He retired after nearly twenty years at Brendon. [18]

## 1996 – THE CHASE [19]

One of the exhibits at the 1996 Festival of Ghana, "Frankenstein's House of Horror" promised "more spooks per square mile than the Tower of London" and featured robotic versions of a number of Gothic characters. For $10, visitors could wander around an animated haunted house, be frightened by mechanical bats, and meet Frankenstein's monster, Dracula and the Grey Lady. The exhibition was cancelled by Peking.

## 1996 – DEATH AND DIPLOMACY [20]

Half a galaxy away, the Three Empires of the Dakhaar, Czhan and Saloi were set to overrun the little planet of Moriel. The god-like Hollow Ghosts commanded that the races would sort out their conflict by diplomatic means - or else. The Hollow Ghosts employed the services of the Doctor in this effort, his companions Cwej and Forrester prevented the villainous Skrak from overrunning the Three Empires.

The mid-nineties saw a period of inflation, or as the *Daily Chronicle* put it:

> 'The pound (or should that be ecu?) in your pocket has never been worth so little. Even in the country a modest round of drinks – a glass of lemonade, a vodka and Coke, and a glass of water – will set you back five pounds. And as for prices in London…'

A five pound piece entered circulation around this time. **By 1998 economic growth had returned to single figures** [21]

## c 1997 – BATTLEFIELD [22]

In the late 1990s a huge storm swept Britain. Dwarfing even the Great Storm of ten years before, which had caused over £500,000,000 worth of damage, one night saw unprecedented flooding and structural damage, not to mention the downing of virtually every power and telecommunications line in the South West of England. According to some sources, 'morbidly eager evangelists took the blasts to be the Last Trump'. Environmentalists, more pragmatically, suggested that it was yet another sign that humanity had damaged their planet's climate beyond all repair. As Kadiatu Lethbridge-Stewart revealed a decade later, there had been a much more immediate threat to the environment:

> 'For many years, UNIT had been considered 'neutral' by individual nation states, and as such it proved to be the ideal force to monitor nuclear arms limitation treaties. The night

20 Dating *Death and Diplomacy* – It is "the present day" according to the synopsis.

21 This is a description of the Doctor's round of drinks in *Battlefield*, which he pays for with a five-pound piece. Five-pound coins are also referred to in *Warhead* (p237). In *System Shock* (set in 1998) Sutcliffe finds a newspaper with the headline 'Economic Growth in Single Digits' (p38). The ecu is in use by *Iceberg*, at the exchange rate of one ecu to two dollars (p45). In *Warlock*, Creed has a suitcase full of "EC paper money" (p263), although Sterling is still used on a day-to-day basis (p281).

22 Dating *Battlefield* – [see also UNIT Dating pages 263-7]. The Doctor tells Ace that they are "a few years in your future". Sergeant Zbrigniev is apparently in his mid-thirties, he served in UNIT while the Doctor was present, and he appears to have first-hand recollection of two regenerations. Even if we assume that he is older than he looks (say, forty), and was very young when he joined UNIT (the earliest he could be in the regular army is sixteen, but it would almost certainly be a couple more years before he would see active service, especially with an elite organisation like UNIT), *Spearhead from Space* must take place in the mid-seventies. The novel, by Marc Platt, based on notes by Ben Aaronovitch, the writer of the television story, sets the story in 'the late 1990s'

(p15), and Ace later notices that Peter Warmsley's tax disc is (or was) due to run out on '30.6.99' (p30). *The Terrestrial Index* set the story in '1992' and The TARDIS Special in '1991' – perhaps they misheard the Doctor's line as 'two years in your future'. In a document for Virgin Publishing dated 23 March 1995, concerning 'Future History Continuity', Ben Aaronovitch perhaps settled the matter when he stated that *Battlefield* is set 'c 1997'.

23 Dating *The Pit* – [see also UNIT Dating pages 263-7] The Doctor and Blake travel to the 1990s, apparently after the Doctor has met Bambera in *Battlefield* (p168).

24 Dating *Infinite Requiem* – It is "1997" (p26).

25 *Timewyrm: Revelation* (p87).

of the Great Storm, UNIT forces under the command of Lieutenant Richards were escorting the Salamander Six-Zero nuclear missiles through the Carbury area. Suddenly, as the convoy passed Lake Vortigern, scientists tracking the movement of Six-Zero registered a burst of energy with all the characteristics of an electromagnetic pulse. All communications with the outside world had been knocked out. Fearing that a nuclear explosion had taken place, Seabird One, Brigadier Winifred Bambera, was called in to salvage the situation. The composition of her forces reflected the new pan-Europeanism of the United Nations Intelligence Taskforce – they included French, Czech, Polish and Russian troops, as well as British soldiers. To some relief, Bambera quickly learnt that the convoy had simply been forced off the road by the poor weather, right into the site of the Carbury Trust's archaeological work. This still didn't explain the EMP effect.'

[*The Zen Military*, Kadiatu Lethbridge-Stewart]

UNIT had no way of knowing at the time that the mysterious energy fluctuations came from a parallel universe. Morgaine of the Fey had managed to track Excalibur to our dimension, which Mordred called "Avallion". When UNIT discovered that the Doctor was involved, the Secretary General managed to persuade Brigadier Alistair Gordon Lethbridge-Stewart out of retirement. Following a battle between UNIT soldiers and extra-dimensional knights under the command of Morgaine, the nuclear missile was secured and Morgaine and her son Mordred were imprisoned.

## c 1997 – THE PIT [23]

'UNIT were called in to investigate an alien skeleton discovered on Salisbury Plain. Shortly afterwards, batlike creatures tore apart a passenger airliner just outside Bristol. The bones of the mysterious creature were unearthed, but never traced.'

[*The Zen Military*, Kadiatu Lethbridge-Stewart]

## 1997 – INFINITE REQUIEM [24]

Twenty-one-year-old Tilusha Meswani died shortly after giving birth to her child.

Paul Travers reviews a Johnny Chess concert in the 18.7.98 *NME*. [25]

## 1998 – SYSTEM SHOCK [26]

By 1998, virtually every computer in the world used the language Vorell, an independent computer standard developed by the company Integrated Intelligence, more commonly known as I². Their XNet computer protocols were used to co-ordinate traffic (Car-Net), office work (OffNet) and even military operations (BattleNet). Four years earlier, in the summer of 1994, industrial action by signalmen had brought the British rail network to a standstill. Now, the privatised railway company BritTrack found it possible to replace human signalmen with automatic systems, using I² equipment. XNet protocols controlled everything from elevators to tube trains in every major city. An I² brochure spelled out the company's philosophy:

> 'Thanks to I², the InterNet has been formalised into the Highway. The default computer language is Vorell: any executive knows that every state-of-the-art computer in the world now speaks the same language and every old computer is obsolete. We guesstimate that this year the last few Asian manufacturers who don't use our operating system will unsubscribe from the old way of thinking, and download our way of thinking.'

They did, and although I² never built a single computer, leaving that to companies such as Applied Automation, each XNet-compatible chip sold earned a royalty for the company. The owner of I², forty-three-year-old Lionel Stabfield quickly became the fifth richest man in the world. His company bought the rights to every major work of art, releasing images of them on interactive discs. The new technology allowed flatpanel, interactive television; the recordable CD-ROM was perfected; sales of computer equipment rocketed still further. Around this time, the government set up the Ministry of Information Technology. The main hub for the European section of the Highway was Hubway, a converted Queen Anne building in Wiltshire, formerly known as Aragon Court.

On the very day that Hubway went online, there was chaos. Aeroplanes crashed at Heathrow as air-traffic-control systems failed; the Astra satellite was sent into a new orbit; the Library of Congress catalogue and all its backups were wiped; the com-

26 Dating *System Shock* – [see also UNIT Dating pages 263-7] When asked, a barman, Rod, informs the Doctor that this is "1998" (p21), and the Doctor goes on to tell Sarah that in that particular year "nothing of interest happened as far as I remember" (p23). It is "twenty odd years" after Sarah's time (p67), and she muses that a "greying, mid-forties" future version of herself is alive in 1998 (p100) – her thoughts are confirmed by the epilogue.

puter facilities of the First National Bank of China were obliterated. Instruments at Nunton told technicians that the reactor had gone to meltdown. It had all been instigated by the Voracians.

> 'VORELLA – a small planet in the Frastis region. In former times, the home of the Vorellans, a race of reptilian humanoids who evolved along typical lines, and a number of non-sentient lifeforms such as the equinian, domesticated for use as a pack animal by the Vorellans. In time, they also developed an efficient office computer network, the Vorellan Office Rapid Automated Computer Intelligence Advocate – Voracia. Within seven minutes of going on-line it was self-aware, and decided to remove 'inefficient' organic lifeforms from the planet. After early Voracian victories, Vorellan rebels detonated a fifty-year-old nuclear device in the Processor Control, leaving the Voracian forces leaderless. In an effort to combat Vorellan gains, the Voracian robotic infantry grafted organic components on to themselves, and recaptured the planet.'
>
> [*Bartholomew's Planetary Gazetteer*, Volume XXII]

Using a piece of sentient software, the Voractyll, the Voracians hoped to take control of Earth via its computer systems. Their attempt was thwarted by COBRA, MI5 and the SAS, even though the Voracians had assassinated the head of MI5, Veronica Halliwell, and replaced her with one of their own agents. The newspapers, when they resumed publication (virtually every newspaper and television station in Northern Europe had been affected by the Voracians' action), didn't tell the whole story, as this extract from an article by Percy Wolnough in the *Financial Times* confirms:

> 'The Home Secretary yesterday said that she was pleased to announce that a terrorist attack on the Hubway had been ended by swift and decisive action by the military. She blamed the attack on the Little Brothers, a group opposed to all forms of government intervention and regulation. The Home Secretary praised in particular the work of MI5 Assistant Chief of Staff Harold Sullivan.'

In 1998 the Japanese set up the Nikkei 5 station in the Antarctic to measure carbon dioxide levels. [27]

## 1999/2000 (30 December – 1 January) – MILLENNIAL RITES

Ashley Chapel had worked for International Electromatics before forming his own company, ACL. Following the collapse of I², ACL quickly bought up all their hardware and software patents, and Ashley Chapel became a multi-millionaire. He funded the construction of the new Millennium Hall on the banks of the Thames, and began work on a powerful computer program, "the Millennium Codex", that would use quantum mnemonics and block transfer computation to change the laws of physics to those of the universe of Saraquazel. Elsewhere Dame Anne Travers, worried about the return of the Great Intelligence, attempted to banish the sentience, only to discover that she had summoned it.

On the stroke of midnight, 31 December 1999, magic returned to the world as the Intelligence and Saraquazel fused over London, transforming the city into a aeons-old battleground between the forces of three factions: the Abraxas, Magick and Technomancy. After only ten minutes of real time, the new laws unravelled themselves and the world was returned to normal. Fifteen people had died, including Ashley Chapel, whom Saraquazel took back with him to his own universe.

By the year 2000, the *Hourly Tele-press* kept the world's population up to date with events around the globe. One of the most popular features of the *Tele-press* was the strip-cartoon adventures of 'The Karkus'. News interpretation software sifted the media for the user's own preferences. Televisions could be set so that news bulletins automatically interrupted regular broadcasts. [28] There was a Neo-Gothic revival in the early twenty-first century. [29]

## 2001 – HEAD GAMES [30]

Alistair Gordon Lethbridge-Stewart was promoted to General before this point. [31]

In the year 2001, Ace met up with a future version of the Doctor, who informed her about his evil duplicate Dr Who, who was planning to assassinate the Queen.

'On the day that Queen Elizabeth II was shot in Sheffield, UNIT forces were involved in an assault on Buckingham Pal-

27 *Iceberg* (p61).

28 The *Hourly Tele-press* is mentioned by Zoe in *The Mind Robber* as the medium in which the Karkus comic strip appears, but the *Tele-press* itself isn't described. *Warhead* (p16) and *System Shock* (p23) both speculate on the interactive news media of the future, and I have included that speculation here.

29 *Strange England* (p229).

30 Dating *Headgames* – [see also UNIT Dating pages 263-7]. It is "2001" (p149), some time before December 2001 (p201), 953 years before Chris is born (p150).

31 Between *Battlefield* and *Head Games* (p192). Normally, Lethbridge-Stewart would have been promoted to General upon his retirement (*Mawdryn Undead*), especially given his exemplary service record. The Doctor wonders whether he has been made a General yet in *Time-Flight*. In *Downtime* he claims that "internal politics" (p164) prevented this.

ace. Brigadier Bambera, recently returned to service after the birth of her twins, arrived in a Merlin T-22 VTOL aircraft, and managed to penetrate a force field surrounding the palace. UNIT refused to comment on their actions, and the authorities never explained how the Queen survived the attack without even the slightest injury, when a crowd of people saw the bullets hit her.'

[*The Zen Military*, Kadiatu Lethbridge-Stewart]

On 30 November 2002 the gunman Murdock killed five people, although Ace's interference in history reduced this total to three. This is about as far into the future as she can travel using the "hopper".

The early twenty-first century saw many scientific advances, usually in the field of computer science and communications. Elysium Technology introduced the Nanocom, a handheld dictation machine capable of translating speech into written text. Elysium also developed the first holographic camera. The 3D telephone was beyond the technology of the time, although most rich people now had videophones. In June 2005, *Der Speigel* gave away a personal organiser with every issue. The first robot cleaners were marketed at this time – they were small, simple devices, really little more than automated vacuum cleaners or floor polishers. Communications software and computer viruses were traded on the black market, indeed they became almost substitute currency in countries like Turkey. Surgeons could now perform eye transplants, and the super-rich were even able to cheat 'death' (or rather the legal and medical definition of it) by an intensive programme of medication, transplants and implants. If even this failed, suspended animation was now possible – the rich could afford full cryogenic storage; the poor settled for a chemical substitute.

Military technology was becoming smarter and more dangerous. The Indonesian Conflict and the Mexican War in the first decade of the century were the test-bed for much new weaponry. The arms manufacturers were happy to supply the Australian and American forces with military hardware. The British company Vickers built a vision enhancement system capable of tremendous magnification and low-intensity light applications. The helmet could interface with most weapons, allowing dramatically improved targeting. If anything, the helmet was too efficient – one option, which allowed a soldier to target and fire his weapon merely by moving and blinking his eyes, proved too dangerous and was banned. A new generation of UN aircraft was introduced, including the Odin, a remote controlled helicopter, and the Loki jet fighter, with its batteries of Valkyrie air-to-air missiles, Niffelheim bombs and Ragnarok tactical nuclear devices. The US military introduced a turbo-pulse laser gun, developed for use against tanks. [32]

But all this technological progress had a cost [33]. By the middle of the first decade of the twenty-first century it was clear that unchecked industrial growth had wreaked havoc on the environment. Increasing instability in weather patterns subjected Britain to acid rain and created turbulence that made air travel less reliable. Shifts in the ozone layer laid waste to Oregon. Traffic had reached gridlock in most of the major cities around the world. The familiar black cabs in London were superseded by motorcycles, and many car owners sat in traffic jams working at their computers as they commuted. Predictably, air pollution reached new levels.

Rising sea levels claimed Holland, and the Dutch became the wanderers of Europe.[34] One reporter, Ruby Duvall, wrote about, "the daily barrage of alarming news and disaster stories...the continuing famine, drought, war and plague which increasingly threaten world stability."

A catalogue of environmental disasters threatened the entire planet. Earth's population was spiralling towards eight billion, double the level it had been in the late 1970s. Low-lying ozone and nitrogen dioxide levels had risen to such an extent that the London air was unbreathable without a facemask on many days, even in winter. Global warming was steadily increasing: by the turn of the century there were vineyards in Kent. Antarctic waters became hazardous as the icecap broke up in rising temperatures. The rate of ice-flow had trebled since the 1980s. River and sea pollution had reached such levels that the marine environment was on the verge of collapse. Water shortages were commonplace, and even the inhabitants of First World cities like London and Toronto were forced to use standpipes for drinking water and practised water rationing. The mega-cities of South America saw drought of unprecedented proportions. The holes in the ozone layer were getting larger, causing famine in many countries. Sunbathing, of course, was now out of the question. "The plague", in reality a host of virulent, pollution-related, diseases such as HIV 7, appeared, killing millions. The most pressing threat, though, was that of magnetic inversion. For some decades, scientists had known that Earth's

32 This is the new technology seen in *Warhead* and *Iceberg*. The Doctor picked up a *Der Speigel* Personal Organiser (*Transit* p146).

33 *Iceberg* and *Warhead* are both set around the same time and both feature an Earth on the brink of environmental and social collapse. The two books are broadly consistent, although the odd detail is different. In *Iceberg*, for example, Ruby muses that sunbathing in England is impossible nowadays (p69), whereas Ace sunbathes in Kent during *Warhead* (p180 – there are skin cancer warnings posted in New York, though, p201). The first paragraph gives details from *Warhead*, the second from *Iceberg*, both quotes coming directly from David Banks's book (p46 and p62), although HIV 7 is named in *Warhead*. The third paragraph mixes details from the two books. The Connors Amendment is mentioned in *Warlock* (p22). In *Image of the Fendahl*, the Doctor says that Earth's population at the time is "four thousand million people".

34 *St Anthony's Fire* (p259).

magnetic field periodically reversed. As a government report stated, in the event of magnetic inversion:

> "Every mechanical device dependent on magnetic orienta-tion would be affected, from compasses to satellites, from body scans to ships. All animals that navigated by magnetic alignment, birds and fish, and insects such as bees, might be fatally confused. Protection from solar radiation might be altered, which would be disastrous at a time of fast-reducing ozone protection. Most serious, there is the possibility of a sudden major change in climate."

In 2005, spurred into action by such reports, the major govern-ments of the world set up the FLIPback Project at the old Snowcap complex in the Antarctic. Shortly afterwards a vehicle from the base, the hovercraft AXV9, vanished in the Torus Ant-arctica, with the loss of two men.

With the collapse of the environment came political instabil-ity. New terrorist groups sprang up: the Earth for Earth groups, freedom fighters, environmentalists, anarchists, nationalists and separatists, the IFA, PPO and TCWC. In England, a whole new youth subculture evolved. Gangs with names like the Gameboys, the Witchkids and the Crows smashed machinery (except for their own gaming software) and committed atrocities. In the most notorious incident, the Witchkids petrol-bombed a McDonald's restaurant on the M2 before ritually sacrificing the customers – men, women and children. Every country on Earth saw warfare or widespread rioting. In the face of social disorder in America, President Norris's right-wing government ended immigration, and his infamous Local Development reforms restricted the un-employed's rights to movement. The Connors Amendment to the Constitution also made it easier for the authorities to de-clare martial law, and to administer the death penalty. The underclass was confined to its slums, and heavily-armed pri-vate police forces guarded the barriers between the inner cities and the suburbs. Once-fashionable areas fell into deprivation. The popular culture of the time reflected this discord: in Britain, this was a time when SlapRap blared from every teenager's noisebox. There was a Kinky Gerlinki revival, its followers dress-ing in costumes described variously as 'outrageous' or 'ob-scene', depending on personal taste. The most popular televi-sion series was *Naked Decay*, a sitcom inspired by forty-five-year-old Mike Brack's *Masks of Decay* exhibition, which had fea-tured lumps of wax hacked into caricatures of celebrities. The teledildonic suits at the SaferSex emporiums along London's Pentonville Road became notorious. All faced the opprobrium of groups such as the Citadel of Morality and the Freedom Foundation. American children thrilled to the adventures of Jack Blood, a pumpkin-faced killer, and they collected the latest Cthulu Gate horror VR modules and comics. Their elder brothers became Oi Boys, skinheads influenced by the fashions of Eastern Europe.

In 2006, Kadiatu Lethbridge-Stewart published her controversial best-seller *The Zen Military: A History of UNIT*. *For most people, this was the first they learnt of the truth about the United Nations Intelligence Taskforce. Under the thirty-year rule governing the release of sensitive documents, many United Kingdom government papers from the great UFO flap of the 1970s entered the public domain around this time, and these tended to confirm the scraps of information that had fuelled a whole generation of conspiracy theories.* Earth had indeed been invaded by aliens over a dozen times. Lethbridge-Stewart was the granddaughter of Alistair Lethbridge-Stewart and Mariatu of the Themne tribe, and so she was ideally placed to write the 'definitive' study of the UNIT era. [35]

## 2006 (November/December) – ICEBERG [36]

In 2006, Earth's magnetic pole shifted slightly, causing consternation at the FLIPback project. Tensions were not eased when the nearby Nikkei 5 research station vanished into the Torus Antarctica.

'CYBER-HISTORY-COMPUTER------------------------------------
Background – Cyber - Forces - under - the - command - of - Co-ordinator - Node - 38 - crashed - in - the - southern - polar - regions - of - Earth - at - the - end - of - the - First - Invasion. Survival - was - paramount - and - logically - Cyber-forces - from - other - parts - of - the - galaxy - would - return. Following - the - failure - of - the - Second - Invasion - Mondan - equipment - was - analysed - and - incorporated.

NODE 38 - Analysis - shows - that - Earth - is - dying - human - lifespans - are - shortening. Logically - those - suitable - will - welcome - the - chance - of - conversion. Humans - are - not - logical. There - is - no - doubt - that - some - will - be - angry - and - that - they - will - attempt - to - resist. Our -

35 The date of the publication of *The Zen Military* is given in the novelisation of *Remembrance of the Daleks* (p30) and is confirmed by *Set Piece* (p71). In *Transit*, Yembe Lethbridge-Stewart states that Kadiatu was named after his great-grandmother, the historian (p128), although in *Set Piece*, Kadiatu claims that her namesake was her 'grandmother' (p71), presumably for sake of brevity.

36 Dating *Iceberg* – The main action of the book takes place in 2006, from "early November" (p25) to "Friday 22 December" (p1). The epilogue is set on "Wednesday 31 January 2007" (p251).

**37 Dating** *Warhead* – A specific date for this story and its two sequels is not established in the books themselves. The blurb states 'The time is the near future – all too near'. Shreela, a contemporary of Ace from Perivale first seen in *Survival*, dies of an "auto immune disease" at a tragically early age at the start of *Warhead* (p19). The book is set in a year when Halloween falls on a Saturday (on page 199 it's Halloween, on page 250 it's the next day, a Sunday), making it 1998, 2009 or 2015. Ace's clothes are how Mancuso dressed "twenty years ago" (p202), and Ace is from the late 1980s, making the middle date the most likely. *Just War* confirms that the Cartmel books take place in the "twenty-first century timezone" (p250). In his 'Future History Continuity' document, Ben Aaronovitch suggested that *Warhead* was set 'c 2007'.

**38 THE BIG CLEAN UP** – The televised stories set in the twenty-first century offer a broadly consistent view of a peaceful Earth with a single world government, in which people of all nations co-operate in the field of space exploration and social progress. To reconcile this with the rather more downbeat New Adventures set in this century, Ben Aaronovitch suggested in his 'Future History Continuity' document that a concerted global effort was made at some point in the early twenty-first century to repair the damage

forces - are - too - weak - to - launch - a - full - scale - assault - but - we - calculate - that - Earth's - magnetic - field - will - reverse - its - polarity - on - day - twelve - of - this - month. Disruption - to - primitive - human - technology - will - be - massive. Cyber-technology - will - be - repolarised - in - preparation - for - inversion. Co-ordinator - 38 - will - be - upgraded. Its - computing - capacity - will - be - grafted - on - to - a - humanoid - Cyber-form. Human - scientists - have - established - an - Antarctic - base - in - an - attempt - to - stabilise - the - magnetic - flux. We - will - destroy - this - project - we - will - wait - for - inversion. We - will - conquer.

Supplementary – The - Doctor - has - once - again - interfered - with - our - plans. Magnetic - inversion - was - prevented. Cyber-technology - was - disrupted - and - our - base - was - destroyed. Many - of - our - forces - remain - frozen - in - the - ice. We - will - survive.

———————————————————————————— '

## c 2009 (Late October) – WARHEAD [37]

The Butler Institute – a huge conglomeration of corporations "from Amoco to Zenith", that had secretly been bought up over the last decade by the vast Japanese Hoshino company – made projections of the future, and could see no alternative but massive, irrevocable environmental collapse. The planet was reaching the point of no return – and only the big corporations and the super-rich could do anything about it. Their executives secretly poured money into experiments that attempted to download human consciousness into computers. The homeless, the poor, even the employees and families of Butler Institute personnel were kidnapped and experimented upon. BI developed a weapon system run by an electronically-recorded human consciousness, but their ultimate aim was to 'record' the minds of the elite and store them in indestructible databanks, safe from the ravages of pollution and the destruction of the ozone layer. With the unexpected complete destruction of the Butler Institute's project outside Albany, the directors of the world's corporations realised that the only remaining option was to instigate a massive environmental clean-up programme.

*The Clean-up project was huge, and saw unprecedented levels of investment and government subsidy. Hundreds of projects were set up, from local initiatives to global moni-*

toring. [38]

*'The "Clean-up" was a typical confidence trick played by big business: consumers were convinced to donate money to pay for the companies' past mistakes; the companies were able to market new "clean" products to replace the old ones; governments happily paid trillions of ecu to some of the richest people on Earth.* Such a scam had been pioneered by the organisers of the "Arms for Humanity" exhibition that raised millions of ecu for the Preserve our Planet Fund in January 2007. They were PPI, Panama Projects Incorporated, a vast multinational whose activities included gun-running and drug smuggling.'
[*Greed Incorporated: The Rise of the Space Corporations*, M Ashe]

*The corporations undoubtedly made huge profits from the Clean-up, but there is no doubt that the environment benefited as a result.* Icebergs were towed up from the Antarctic Ocean and used to provide fresh water for drought-stricken South American cities. Within a couple of decades, air quality had improved, the oceans were cleaner, and the holes in the ozone layer had been patched up. Sophisticated traffic monitoring systems and a reconfigured road network eased congestion (and therefore pollution) in the South East of England, although Central London was still busy. [39]

## 2010 - HAPPY ENDINGS [40]

'HAPPY EVER AFTER - Bernice Summerfield and Jason Kane were married last week in the most spectacular ceremony Cheldon Bonniface has ever seen. Many of the guests came in fancy dress, as you can see from this photograph of Sherlock Holmes with a collection of "space aliens". Keeping in that spirit a brilliant "lookalike" band impersonated the Isley Brothers and a good time was had by all.'
[From the *Cheldon Bonniface Parish Newsletter*, Subject to D-Notice]

Politically the world seemed less stable for a time. In 2012, Salamander managed to convince a group of his followers that a global nuclear war was inevitable. He established a survival shel-

that had been done to Earth's environment. A 'Clean Up' is first hinted at at the end of *Iceberg*, which is where we learn of the "Arms for Humanity" concert and the procuring of drinking water from icebergs, but I suggest that it only gains impetus after *Warhead*, when all the corporations put their full weight behind it. I suggest that this period of international co-operation lasts for around seventy years. Earth during this time is a relatively happy, clean and optimistic place.

39 Travelling by car is a lot easier in *Warlock* than *Warhead* (*Warlock*, p179), and we learn about the monitoring systems (p224) and new road system (p211), although traffic in London has barely improved (p265).

40 Dating Happy Endings – It is "2010" (p8).

41 This is the background to *The Enemy of the World*. Benny remembers the Southport Incident in *Just War* (p214), but doesn't specify what or when it was. Zoe, who lacks even rudimentary historical knowledge, recognises the effects of an atomic blast in *The Dominators*, perhaps suggesting that nuclear weapons are still around (and have been used?) in her time.

42 Dating *Warlock* – The novel is the sequel to *Warhead*. The events of the earlier book are consistently referred to as happening "years" ago (p8, p203, p209, p223). Vincent and Justine bought a car after a "few years" of marriage and have had it a while (p356). In *Warhead*, Ace had difficulty guessing how old Justine was, eventually settling on "maybe sixteen or seventeen" (p181). By *Warlock* Justine has matured into a woman (p203), but she is still only "probably a couple of years older than the medical student" (p301), so she is in her early-to-mid twenties. I suggest, then, that *Warlock* takes place about five years after *Warhead*. It is late autumn (p279, p334).

43 VULCAN – [see also Dating *The Power of the Daleks* page 131]. The planet Vulcan is only seen in *The Power of the Daleks*, a story which is almost certainly set in 2020. There is no indication that mankind has developed interstellar travel or faster-than-light drives in this or any other story set at this

ter at Kanowa in Australia for them. **The risk of nuclear warfare diminished after the Southport Incident, when governments realised that the stockpiling of atomic weapons could only lead to a serious accident or all-out nuclear warfare.** [41]

## c 2014 (Late Autumn) – WARLOCK [42]

Organised crime continued to rely on the profits of drug trafficking. Dealers now used sports cars to get around, and the British police were forced to use Porsches to keep up with them. Soon Porsche were even making a special model for them. In an attempt to win the Drugs War, the International Drug Enforcement Agency was set up, under the aegis of Henry Harrigan Jnr. A pooling of Interpol and FBI resources, IDEA had a number of well-publicised successes against drug dealers, forcing many of them underground. IDEA was based in the King Building in New York, the old headquarters of the Butler Institute, and its methods often brought them into conflict with local police forces.

For around a year, IDEA had been aware of a new drug on the street, called "warlock" by many of its users. Tracking down the source of the drug proved difficult, leading IDEA men across New York and England. In the late autumn, an IDEA team investigating the drug was caught in the explosion that destroyed Canterbury Cathedral, an event officially explained away as a freak ball-lightning effect. It was announced shortly afterwards that IDEA had broken up the warlock cartel, and the drug vanished from the streets. Exactly how this had been achieved was never fully explained, although around this time an animal research lab near Canterbury, was closed down in mysterious circumstances, and the prominent London gangster Paulie Keaton "retired" after a decade of dominating criminal activity in the city. The founder of IDEA, Henry Harrigan Jnr, died around this time.

'WARLOCK – A mutant form of fungus originally found only in Russia, distinguishable by its pungent liquorice smell. It was the physical form of an alien intelligence from a dimension of thought, which had crashed on Earth and was evolving in an attempt to communicate with humanity. Unaware of its origin, by the twentieth century the Russian and German governments did know of its hallucinogenic effects on the human mind, and after the war the government of the United States became interested in its properties and tested it on a number of volunteers. By the early twenty-first century, it had become available as an illegal recreational drug, and users reported psionic side-effects: out-of-body experiences, transferred consciousness, telepathy and the like. Shortly afterwards, the alien intelligence finally managed to get its message across and leave Earth.'

[*Flora and Fauna of the Universe*, Professor Thripstead]

*International co-operation bore fruit in the field of space travel. Space exploration in the first half of the twenty-first century was more practical than that of the twentieth. The Space Race of the sixties had been an expensive form of one-upmanship between the superpowers. In the twenty-first century, co-operation would be the key: space stations and bases on other planets were manned by international crews. The first permanent moonbases were established around this time.*

A rogue planet entered the inner solar system. The planet was a large, hot world with a bleak landscape of mercury swamps and geysers that spat toxic fumes. Astronomers named it Vulcan, after the Roman God of fire and metal-working, and they discovered that *in its new position* it had a breathable atmosphere and soil capable of supporting plant life, so it proved the most hospitable planet in the solar system after Earth itself. Plans were made to set up a mining colony on Vulcan for a trial period. [43]

## ? 2017 - THE ENEMY OF THE WORLD [44]

Rockets could now be used to travel between continents on Earth - the journey from Australia to Hungary took around two hours. Hovercars made shorter trips.

The political situation on Earth had stabilised. National concerns were put aside, and the world was reorganised into large administrative areas, Zones, such as the Australiasian, North African and Central European Zones. **The United Nations was renamed** the United Zones, but was more properly known as the World Zones Authority. Multinational concerns, such as security matters were dealt with by commissioners. Each Zone was led by a Controller. [45]

time. This would seem to suggest that Vulcan is within our own solar system. There is some evidence to support this conjecture: since the nineteenth century some astronomers (including Le Verrier, who discovered Neptune), speculated that a planet might orbit the sun closer than Mercury. There was new interest in this theory in the mid-1960s, which might explain why the home planet of Mr Spock was also called Vulcan around the same time in *Star Trek*. The draft script talked of a 'Plutovian Sun', (although the planet as seen on-screen is too hot to orbit further from the Sun than Pluto, which is presumably what that phrase means). In 1964, *The Dalek Book*, which, like *The Power of the Daleks* was co-written by David Whitaker, named Vulcan as the innermost planet in our solar system (and Omega as the outermost). This, though, contradicts the story televised immediately before *The Power of the Daleks*, (where Mondas is the tenth Planet, *Image of the Fendahl* where the Fendahl homeworld is The fifth Planet, and *The Sun Makers* where Pluto is established as the ninth planet) - it seems that Vulcan wasn't in our solar system in the late 1980s or the far future. Taking all this literally and at face value, *Doctor Who* fan Donald Gillikin has suggested that Vulcan arrives in the solar system but later leaves - this might be scientifically implausible, but we know of three other 'rogue planets' that enter our solar system according to the series: the Moon, Mondas and Voga. The exact date of the discovery of Vulcan is conjecture, but it must be substantially before 2020, giving time for Earth to prepare and set up the colony.

**44** Dating *The Enemy of the World* – There is a date given on-screen, but at the moment no one knows what it is. On one of the telesnaps, Swann holds up a scrap of newspaper from the year before, and there is a date on it, but the photograph is not clear enough to discern what that date might be. There is no reference to the year that the story is set in on any of the scripts. However, *Radio Times* in certain regions featured an article on fashion that set *The Enemy of the World* 'fifty years in the future', which would give a date of 2017. The first edition of *The Programme Guide* mistakenly thought that the story had a contemporary setting, so it was placed '1970–75'. The date '2030', which is now most commonly associated with the story, first appeared in David Whitaker's storyline for the novelisation of his story, submitted to WH Allen in October 1979. The document was reprinted in *DWM* Issue 200, and amongst other things of interest it is the only place to give Salamander a first name, 'Ramon', which I have used here. The novelisation was due to be published in 1980, and it was to be set 'some fifty years later than our time – the year 2030' according to the storyline,

One of the major problems the world faced was famine: "too many people, too little food". A videowire survives of the speech made by the Mexican scientist Salamander, in which he made his astonishing announcement:

> "Congress, Mr President: At the Sun Conservation Establishment at Kanowa in the Australiasian Zone, progress has been highly satisfactory. We can not yet guarantee good summer holidays for all. However, we have now in orbit the Mark Seven Sun-Catcher and already we have been able to concentrate the Sun's rays into much-needed areas. The great Canadian wheat trains are safe. Now, Mr President, Ukraine: the grain field of the planet. An unfortunate area between Bukova and Kioragrad devastated by the earthquake two short years ago. What have I to say to you about that? I can tell you that on the banks of the Dnieper River the corn is ripening in the sun, and ten thousand robot harvesters are moving down to gather in fifty million tons of flour."

Within just a year, the Sun-Catcher had solved the problems of world famine, allowing crops to grow in Siberia and vineyards in Alaska. In the more fertile areas, concentrated sunlight forced growth: there could be three or even four harvests every summer. Salamander was hailed as the saviour of mankind. [46]

Soon after Salamander's announcement, there was a series of natural disasters, such as a freak tidal wave that sank a liner full of holidaymakers in the Caribbean, and the first volcanic eruptions in the Eperjes-Tokaj mountain range since the sixteenth century. These were being caused by Salamander's followers in Kanowa using the Sun-Catcher. Salamander had convinced them that the surface of Earth was highly radioactive, and that they had to fight back against the aggressors. The truth was that Salamander had been gradually assassinating his political opponents within the United Zones and replacing them with his own people, in a bid to become the dictator of Earth. He was defeated when his followers at Kanowa discovered that there had been no global nuclear war. The truth about Salamander eventually emerged, but, for a few weeks at least, the world was saddened by his death.

'The authorities now confirm that they have given up hope of ever finding the body of Leader Salamander, "the Shop-keeper of the World". Ramon Salamander was born in Merida, the state capital of Yucatan. He came to prominence when he developed the Sun-Store, the first practical form of weather control. He died in a huge underground explosion at his Kanowa Research Station along with many dozens of scientists and workers. Salamander was one of the most popular people on the planet. The World Zones Authority have declared today a global day of mourning.'

[Obituary, the *Hourly Tele-press*]

The Doctor placed a personal advert, "Ace – Behind You!", in an *NME* from 2018. Ace later bought a copy outside Ladbroke Grove hypertube station. [47]

## ? 2020 – THE POWER OF THE DALEKS [48]

Oblivious to the political upheaval on their homeworld, the colony on Vulcan was in danger of being "run down". Mining operations had not proved economically successful and this led to problems for the Governor of the colony, Hensell, who faced mutiny. An Examiner from Earth was due to assess the Vulcan colony in two years time.

The chief scientist, Lesterson, discovered what he thought might be the colony's salvation, a buried alien spaceship. He quickly determined that the capsule was constructed of a metal that wasn't found on Vulcan. At first, Lesterson feared that the ship might contain bacteria, but he opened the capsule anyway, and discovered that it contained three Daleks.

'The small Dalek scout ship that had crashed two centuries before on Vulcan had been unearthed. The Daleks within were inert, but the lure of reviving them proved too great for the human colonists. At first, dependent on the power provided by the humans, the Daleks cunningly pretended to be servants; they played their part well, solving simple sci-

but the book was not completed before Whitaker's death. The second edition of *The Programme Guide* duly gave the date as '2030'. The blurb for the novelisation by Ian Marter, published in 1981, the same year as *The Programme Guide*, concurred, although perhaps significantly the text of the book didn't specify a date. 2030 was soon adopted wholesale, with The TARDIS Logs and *The Terrestrial Index* giving the new date. *The Encyclopedia of the Worlds of Doctor Who* was confused: the entry for 'Denes' gave the date as '2017', but that for 'Fedorin' stated '2030'. 'The TARDIS Special' was more accurate – the story takes place in an 'Unknown Future' setting. It seems clear that David Whitaker intended the story to be set fifty years after it was broadcast, and I have adopted that date. I have also assigned a date for Salamander's birth – one that coincides with the broadcast of the first episode of *The Enemy of the World*, and makes Salamander three years older than the actor playing him.

**45 THE FUTURE OF THE UNITED NATIONS** – By *Battlefield* UNIT is a truly multinational organisation, with British, Czechoslovakian and Polish troops serving side by side. UNIT are seen in the New Adventures *The Pit*, *Head Games* and *Happy Endings*, and the UN is referred to in *Warhead*. In *The Enemy of the World*, nations have been grouped together into Zones,

and the governing body of the world is the United Zones, or the World Zones Authority, headed by a General Assembly. The United Nations still exists at the time of the Thousand-Day War referred to in the New Adventure *Transit*. Gradually, though, national barriers break down and the world is run by a World Government. Where this leaves the UN is unclear, although it appears that the United Nations survives or is reformed at some time far in the future: in *Mission to the Unknown*, Lowry's ship is the "UN Deep Space Force Group 1" and it has the United Nations symbol and a Union Jack on the hull.

46  WEATHER CONTROL – In a number of stories set in the twenty-first century we see a variety of weather control projects. The earliest is in the New Adventure *Warhead*, and simply involves 'seeding' clouds with chemicals, regulating rainfall (p129). A year before *The Enemy of the World*, Salamander develops the Sun-Catcher, the first global Weather Control system. As its name suggests, the Sun Store satellite collects the rays from the Sun and stores them in concentrated form. It is also capable of influencing tidal and seismic activity. By the time of *The Seeds of Death* each major city has its own Weather Control Bureau, and these are co-ordinated and monitored centrally by computer. The London Bureau is a large complex, manned by a handful

entific problems. By promising to build a computer that could predict meteorite showers and protect the weather satellites, the Daleks offered huge financial savings, and won the trust of the colonists. All the time, though, the Daleks were setting up their production line, and within a matter of hours dozens of Daleks swarmed across the colony, exterminating every human in their path. Once again, though, the Daleks' external power sources proved their undoing: although they had guarded their static electricity generator, it proved possible to destroy the power source, and the Daleks were rendered immobile once more.'

[*The Children of Davros*, Njeri Ngugi]

*After this time, Vulcan left the solar system, and was never seen again.*

In 2024, humanity developed the plasma rifle. [49] The Doctor, Ace and Bernice visited UNIT HQ in Geneva in 2030 and picked up a note left by Cristián Alvarez thirty-seven years before. [50]

## 2030 (Early Autumn) – WARCHILD [51]

Computer technology had advanced to the stage that cars practically drove themselves and computers could understand straightforward voice commands. Instead of passports, people had implants on the back of their necks, and three-dimensional television existed. Passenger airliners were still in use. A cure had been found for Alzheimer's disease, and few people now smoked thanks to health-awareness campaigns.

Over the long hot summer, a state of emergency was declared in London. Computers monitored all telephone emergency calls, listening out for the keyword "Dog". Packs of dogs displaying remarkable intelligence had murdered many people, and there were reports of a "White King", an old dog that appeared to control the packs. The government restricted all reporting of the emergency and used psychic operatives to assemble covert action teams. In America, Vincent Wheaton had received government funding to research into "alpha male patterns", the study of pack dynamics. He hoped to nurture a man capable of "natural leadership", the ability to control crowds, indeed whole populations of people. With such a man as president, he hoped to control America. Vincent Wheaton was killed before his plan came to fruition.

Elsewhere in the galaxy, civilisations continued to develop. On the planet of Draconia a race of reptilian humanoids had evolved. Although technologically advanced, they retained a feudal system.

'At the time of the Fifteenth Emperor, a mysterious alien traveller visited Draconia for quite some time. He cured a great space plague.'

[*The Chronicles of the Court of Draconia*] [52]

## ? 2044 – (Winter) THE SEEDS OF DEATH [53]

On Earth there had been a period of technological progress. Hypersonic aircraft had been built, and mankind had discovered how to synthesise carbohydrates and protein, which helped to feed the planet's ever-increasing population. Computers became advanced enough to give spoken responses to sophisticated verbal instructions. Most energy now came from solar power, and compact solar batteries became available. Petrol cars were confined to museums. There were further advances in robotics and weather control technology.

Regular passenger modules travelled between Earth and its moonbases, and it was thought by most people that the Moon would provide a stepping stone to the other planets of the solar system, and eventually to the stars. At this time Professor Daniel Eldred, the son of the man who designed the lunar passenger modules, invented an ion jet rocket with a compact generator, the vehicle that would revolutionise space travel, paving the way for mankind's rapid exploration of the solar system.

Then the Travel-Mat Relay, an instantaneous form of travel, was invented. The massive capital investment required, and the promise of easy movement of all resources around the world, meant that after some debate the government ended all funding for space travel and the staff on the Moon were recalled. Man had travelled no further than the Moon, except for a few isolated efforts. For the moment at least, all space travel had halted.

of technicians. The Weather Control Unit itself is about the size of a large desk, with separate circuits for each weather condition. With fully functioning Rain Circuits, rainfall over a large area can be arranged quickly. By 2050, the Gravitron had been set up on the Moon. This is the ultimate form of weather control, working on the simple principle that "the tides control the weather, the Gravitron controls the tides". Weather control is under the control of the (United Zones?) General Assembly.

47 *Timewyrm: Revelation* (p95-6, p216). Ladbroke Grove, by an amazing coincidence, is the nearest tube station to the offices of Virgin Publishing.

48 Dating *The Power of the Daleks* – There is no confirmation of the date on-screen. According to Lesterson the Dalek ship arrived "at least two centuries ago", "before the Colony", which might suggest that the Earthmen have been there for just under two hundred years. However, the generally low-level of technology, the reliance on "rockets", and the fact that there is only one communications link with Earth suggest that the colony is relatively new. One date has attached itself to the story, '2020', which was given in press material at the time. This date also appeared in the tenth anniversary *Doctor Who Radio Times Special*, was used by the second edition of *The Making of*

*Doctor Who* and the first edition of *The Programme Guide*. So, although '2020' is not given on-screen, it does have some weight, and any other date looks rather arbitrary by comparison. In *DWM*, 'The TARDIS Logs' offered a date of '2049', but 'The History of the Daleks' contradicted this, and gave the date as "2249". The American *Doctor Who* comic offered the date of '2600 AD', apparently unaware that the Dalek ship has been dormant. *The Terrestrial Index* came to the elaborate conclusion that the colonists left Earth in 2020, in spacecraft with "suspended animation" and then used the old calendar when they arrived, with the result that the story is really set in '2220'. Earth could only really have a colony on another world this early if the planet was in our solar system.

49  *First Frontier* (p137).

50  *The Left-Handed Hummingbird* (p8).

51  Dating *Warchild* –The book is the sequel to *Warlock*. At the end of the earlier novel, Justine was in the early stages of pregnancy, so her baby would have been born in the spring of the following year. In *Warchild*, her son, Ricky, is "fifteen" (p18). This book is set in August (p6).

52  *Frontier in Space*. The Doctor's first visit to Draconia must have occurred in his first or second incarnation.

53  Dating *The Seeds of Death* – On-screen, the only indication

Travel-Mat revolutionised the distribution of people and materials around the world. A T-Mat brochure boasted that:

> "The Travel-Mat is the ultimate form of travel. Control centre of the present system is the Moon, serving receptions in all major cities on Earth. Travel-Mat provides an instantaneous means of public travel, transporting raw materials and vital food supplies to all parts of the world. Travel-Mat supersedes all conventional forms of travel: using the principal of dematerialisation at the point of departure, and rematerialisation at the point of arrival in special cubicles, departure and arrival are almost instantaneous. Although the system is still in its early stages it is completely automated and foolproof against power failure."

Humanity, though, had become dangerously insular. They had forgotten the alien invasions of the previous century, and didn't realise that there was a threat to humanity very close to home... [54]

'The Ice Warriors remained confined to Mars during all this time, limited as ever by the lack of resources their home planet had to offer. During the twenty-first century, it became clear that the human race was overtaking the Martians in key technological fields. Sooner or later, humanity would attempt to colonise Mars. This led to some desperation on the part of the Martians. The Grand Marshal realised that two recent human discoveries in particular, weather control and the T-Mat, might be used to make Earth viable for his race. Seed Pods, oxygen-fixing plants native to Mars, were taken to the Moon by a small squad led by Lord Slaar. The plan was to cripple Earth by disabling the T-Mat, and then to alter Earth's atmosphere until it more closely resembled that of Mars using the Seeds. The Pods were sent to Earth via T-Mat, and preparations were made to guide the Martian invasion fleet to Earth. As killer foam spread through London, computer scientist Gia Kelly and the dashing museum curator Daniel Eldred (whom she later married) discovered that the fungus was vulnerable to water. A burst of artificial rain wiped out the fungus, an improvised solar energy weapon destroyed the Lunar invasion squad, and finally a false signal guided the entire Martian invasion fleet into the Sun. To cut a frightfully long story short, the Martians were defeated, and once they'd appointed a new Grand Marshal they were forced into a bit of a rethink. Ironically, the development of T-Mat had meant that, for the time being at least, all human space exploration had ceased. Mars had never been threatened in the first place.'

[*Down Among the Dead Men*, Professor B S Summerfield] [55]

*Humanity also needed to rethink. Although T-Mat had originally appeared attractive, and had revolutionised the distribution of resources around Earth during the decade that it was operating, there were a number of reasons why the system was all but abandoned after the Martian Invasion. Firstly, it was expensive: the human race could not afford both T-Mat and space exploration. Secondly, it was very centralised: just before the Martian Invasion, there had been the risk of "worldwide chaos" simply because of one incompetent operator on the Moon. Thirdly, and crucially, there was the security risk: following the Martian attack it was clear that control of T-Mat could be used to cripple and then to invade Earth, either by alien invaders or by human terrorist groups. It was decided that from now on a downsized T-Mat service would be controlled from Earth, and that all space travel would be carried out by conventional rocket.* [56]

So, space travel was readopted and co-ordinated by International Space Command in Geneva. While rockets were slower than T-Mat, it now took only a couple of hours for a shuttle rocket to travel from Earth to the new moonbases. Ion jet rockets explored the solar system and permanent space stations were built. Flowers were cultivated on the surface of Venus. Medical units were now capable not only of administering drugs, but also automatically controlling the pulse, temperature, breathing and the cortex factor of a patient. Around 2050, the ulti-

of the date of this story is the Doctor's identification of the ion rocket designed by Eldred as a product of "the twenty-first century". As the rocket only exists as a prototype at this stage, the story must take place before 2100. The original storyline set the date as '3000 AD', but later press material suggested that the story took place 'at the beginning of the twenty-first century'. T-Mat is developed at least two generations after space travel, as Eldred's father designed spacecraft, including a "lunar passenger module", and Eldred is an old man himself. It is never stated how long T-Mat has been in operation before *The Seeds of Death*, but it is a relatively new invention, as the video brochure we hear (transcribed here in full) states. Young Gia Kelly was involved with the development of T-Mat, but it has been around "a good many years" according to Eldred, long enough to make an advocate of rocket travel look eccentric. T-Mat is consistently referred to as having been around for "years", rather than "decades" or "generations" – I suggest that T-Mat has been around for about a decade before the story.

It is possible to rule out certain dates by referring to other stories: The Weather Control Bureau is seen, so it must be set after 2016 when Salamander invents weather control; the Bureau is on Earth, which might suggest that the story is set before 2050 when the Gravitron is invented, or indeed afterwards because the Gravitron is obsolete. Either way, the story can't be set between 2050 and (at least) 2070, because the Gravitron operates from the Moon at that time, and rockets are still in use; by the time of *The Seeds of Death* man has not travelled beyond the Moon (which has to contradict earlier, limited, space travel to Mars in *The Ambassadors Of Death*, Jupiter in *The Android Invasion* and Vulcan in *The Power Of The Daleks*); the story occurs before *The Wheel In Space*, as deep space travel is established by then and Zoe has a more extensive knowledge of spaceflight than Eldred (he admits as much). Laser weapons have been developed by *The Wheel in Space*, but projectile weapons are still used in *The Seeds of Death*. The story isn't set between 2068 and 2096, as Galactic Salvage and Insurance are insuring spacecraft between those dates. Finally, the story probably isn't set after 2096, as four years seems too short a period for ion rockets to explore the entire solar system (*The Mutants*) before deep space interstellar missions with crews in suspended animation are launched (*The Sensorites*).

As we might expect, there is no fan consensus as to when this story is set. The first edition of *The Making of Doctor Who* claimed that the story is set in 'the latter part of the 20th century', the second was less specific and simply placed the story in the '21st century'. The

mate form of weather control, the Gravitron, was built on the surface of the Moon by the Butler Institute. The political implications on Earth proved complex, and the General Assembly spent over twenty years negotiating methods of agreement between farmers and landowners. Harnessing gravity waves also allowed artificial gravity to be installed on spacecraft and space stations. [57]

Around the middle of the century, domesticated wolves were even reintroduced into the forests of Northern Europe. It was rumoured that the Wicca Society had released wild wolves, and there was some debate as to which strain would become dominant.

All the religious faiths of the world were merged, with the idea of creating world harmony. This consensus was unworkable and quickly collapsed. The Chapter of St Anthony was formed to fill the spiritual vacuum. When China was taken over by Hong Kong, the Yong family joined them on a new crusade to purge the heathens. [58]

## ? 2068 – THE WHEEL IN SPACE [59]

Jet helicopters had become the principal form of transport on Earth. Simple servo robots were developed, as were x-ray laser weapons and food dispensers. John Smith and Associates built advanced medical equipment for spacecraft. Psychotropic drugs could now prevent brain control, and all astronauts were fitted with Silenski capsules to detect outside influences on the human mind. It was around this time that the Earth School of Parapsychology was founded. It was based in an area known only as "The City", and trained children from a very early age in the disciplines of pure logic and memory. Zoe Heriot, one of the School's pupils, developed total recall, and majored in pure maths. She qualified as an astrophysicist and astrometricist (first class). Her education was narrow and vocational, though, and didn't include any pre-century history. When she was about nineteen, Zoe was assigned to space station W3.

The Space Wheels were set up around the solar system. W3, for example, was positioned relative to Venus, 24,564,000 miles at perihelion, 161,350,000 miles at aphelion, a week's rocket travel from Earth. W5 was between eighty and ninety million miles from W3. The small, multinational crews of the Wheel warned travellers of meteorite storms and acted as a halfway house for deep space ships; they monitored all manner of stellar phenomena, and they also supplied advance weather information to Earth. The Wheels were armed with x-ray lasers with a range of ten thousand miles, and protected by a convolute force field, a neutron field barrier capable of deflecting meteorites of up to two hundred tonnes. Phoenix IV cargo rockets, which had a four man crew but could be placed on automatic power drive, kept the stations supplied with food and materials.

Back on the human homeworld, the Pull Back to Earth movement believed that it was wrong to colonise other planets, and they committed acts of sabotage against the space programme, but although such beliefs persisted for many centuries their exponents were never seen as anything but crackpots. Space travel had undoubted benefits, but remained hazardous. Two years before she herself was killed by the Cybermen, Gemma Corwyn's husband had been killed exploring the asteroid belt. The loss of rockets was becoming rarer, though. [60]

[CYBER - HISTORY - COMPUTER] ------------------------------
**Background** – Since - the - destruction - of - Mondas - the - human - race - has - begun - to - explore - its - solar - system. Our - objective - is - the - conquest - of - Earth. Nine - weeks - ago - an - advance - force - captured - a - Phoenix - IV - Earth - spacecraft - designation - *Silver - Carrier* - codename - "Voyager" - destination - Station - W5. We - have - analysed - human - technology - and - capabilities.

**Cyber Control** – The - plan - is - a - variation - on - the - standard - Invasion - scenario. The - Plan - has - six - initial - phases. (1) - The - Cybermats - are - to - be - sent - to - W3. (2) - Two - Cybermen - are - to - take - control - of - the - *Silver - Carrier* - and - remain - undetected. (3) - The - star - Hercules - 208 - in - the - Messier - 13 - cluster - will - be - ionised - diverting - the - Perseid - meteor - shower. (4) - The - Cybermats - will - be - activated. They - will -

first two editions of *The Programme Guide* set the story 'c 2000', but *The Terrestrial Index* alters this to 'c2090', and *Lucifer Rising* concurs with this date (p171). The TARDIS Logs suggested '2092'. *The Encyclopedia of the Worlds of Doctor Who* set the story in 'the 22nd century'. Ben Aaronovitch's *Transit* follows on from *The Seeds of Death*, with his 'Future History Continuity' setting the television story 'c 2086'. I set *The Seeds of Death* seventy-five years after it was first broadcast, which fits in nicely with the evidence from the other television stories.

54 This seems to be humanity's first contact with the Martians, as none of the T-Mat personnel recognises them.

55 Professor Summerfield's account is a broadly accurate description of the events of *The Seeds of Death*, but it – like most of the other sources quoted here – ignores the Doctor's involvement. A simularity describing the events of the Martian invasion of Earth was made in the mid-twenty-second century, featuring Daniel Eldred as the heroic lead (*Lucifer Rising* p171).

56 This is an attempt to explain why we don't see T-Mat in *The Moonbase* and *The Wheel in Space*. I suggest that T-Mat is seen as a failed experiment and is all but abandoned for a generation – much as airships and trams (which have much to

recommend them) had all but vanished by the second half of the twentieth century. Jet helicopters are mentioned in *The Wheel in Space*, and there is a heliport in Chelsea at the time of the Dalek Invasion, both suggesting that T-Mat isn't in widespread use on Earth.

57 International Space Command is mentioned in *The Tenth Planet* and *Revenge of the Cybermen*, as well as *The Moonbase*. Here it seems to be an agency of the World Zones Authority as seen in *The Enemy of the World* – we hear about "the General Assembly", "Atlantic Zone 6", and the head of the ISC is a "Controller" Rinberg. The ion jet rockets are those invented by Eldred in *The Seeds of Death*. The Space Wheels and Venus Flowers are seen in *The Wheel in Space*. The Gravitron is seen in *The Moonbase*. Hobson says that it was set up "twenty years" earlier, and this would concur with the Doctor's guess just beforehand, based on the presence of the Gravitron, that the TARDIS had landed "about the year 2050". In *Deceit* it is hinted that the Butler Institute built the Gravitron (p27, p153), possibly based on Silurian technology, as they establish one on the Moon in *Blood Heat* (p196). Artificial gravity has been developed by the time of *The Wheel in Space* (and seems to be operating inside *The Moonbase*, although this isn't confirmed in dialogue). A sign on the Moonbase's medical unit is marked "Cortex Factor". The

destroy - the - stocks - of - Bernalium - used- to - power - the - armaments of - W3 - then - they - shall - be - released - to - destroy - the - human - crew - of - W3. (5) - Humans - will - discover - crates - of - Bernalium - in - the - *Silver Carrier*. Logically - they - will - bring - the - crates - aboard - W3. Cybermen - will - be - concealed - within - the - crates. (6) - Cybermen - shall - take - control - of - the - space - station. From - there - a - radio - beam - will - be - activated - to - guide - the - landing - craft - to - Earth. We - must - colonise - Earth. We - must - plunder - its - mineral - wealth.

**Supplementary** – The - Doctor - has - once - more - interfered - in - our - plans. As - the - Cyber-army - was - spacewalking - to - W3 - the - X-ray - laser - was - used - against - our - spacecraft - destroying - it. All - remaining - Cybermen - were - catapulted - into - space - by - a - neutron - force - field. The - rest - of - the - Cyber-fleet - remains - undetected.'

------

*The surviving crew of the Wheel, including Zoe Heriot, related the incident to the authorities. Investigators from Earth recommended that the attack on W3 should be kept secret to prevent world panic. However, pre-century history components of the curriculum were altered to include the Cyberman Invasion of 1986, to prepare the population for the Cyber threat.* [61]

A registry of ships was created, and Galactic Salvage and Insurance was set up in London in 2068 to deal with the new demand for space travel. [62]

## 2070 – THE MOONBASE [63]

[CYBER - HISTORY - COMPUTER]------
**Background** – The - Cyber-force - within - the - solar - system - is - not - sufficient - to - conquer - Earth. Our - machinery - has - stopped - and - our - supply - of - replacements - has - been - depleted. We - are - becoming - ex-

**137**

tinct. The - objective - has - changed. Earth - is - too - much - of - a - threat. We - must - destroy - Earth.

**Cyber Control** – The - Plan - is - a - variation - on - the - standard - Plague - scenario. Two - weeks - ago - the - Neurotrope - was - introduced - to - the - sugar - supplies - of - Weather - Control - Moon. The - moonport - has - a - human - crew - of - nineteen. Earth - will - quarantine - the - base - when - they - learn - of - the - space - plague. We - will - take - control - of - the - moonbase - then - we - will - utilise - the - Gravitron - to - destroy - the - surface - of - Earth.

**Emergency-Supplementary** – Once - again - the - Doctor - has - interfered - with - our - plans. The - contamination - of - the - sugar - supplies - was - detected. The - Gravitron - was - used - against - us. The - Cyber-army - has - been - dispersed - by - the - Gravitron.'

----------------------------------------------------------------

Briefly, there was chaos on Earth as Gravitron-created tidal waves and hurricanes swept the planet. They soon subsided. **An island was created by seismic shifts in the Atlantic, and this became a homeland for the Dutch, the New Dutch Republic.** [64]

'Facing extinction the Cybermen conquered Telos, all but wiping out the native Cryons and building their "Tombs" using Cryon technology. Once this was completed, the Cybermen died out. The location of Telos remains a mystery.' [65]

[From the Archives of the Brotherhood of Logicians]

After mankind had colonised the solar system, the first missions to other stars were launched. **Not-As-Fast-as-Light** Rockets were sent deep into the galaxy, and as these ships still travelled slower than the speed of light the crews were placed in suspended animation. It was not unusual to discover such ships many centuries later. **Huge Pioneer stations were set up, lining the way to the stars. They helped with refuelling and restocking**

Doctor's familiarity with the Gravitron, ion rockets in *The Seeds of Death*, and Galactic Salvage and Insurance in *Nightmare of Eden* suggests that he has already visited the solar system during this period. As *The Moonbase* takes place soon after his regeneration, we might presume that the Doctor made an unrecorded visit to this timezone while he was in his first incarnation.

58 In *Transit* we are told about the re-introduction of wolves to Europe (p134). The rest is the background to *St Anthony's Fire*, taken principally from Chapter 14 and p259.

59 Dating *The Wheel in Space* – Zoe is born in the twenty-first century (*The War Games*), and she is "nineteen or so" according to the Brigadier in *The Invasion*, so the story must be set somewhere between 2019 and 2119. She recognises the Karkus, a comic strip character from the year 2000, in *The Mind Robber*, which might suggest that she comes from that time. However, she needs to confirm with the Doctor that he has been to the year 2000 – so it seems unlikely that *The Wheel in Space* is set then. Her debut story certainly takes place after *The Seeds of Death*, because man has travelled further than the Moon by Zoe's time and her knowledge of space travel is more advanced. Why Zoe doesn't remember T-Mat or recognise the Martians is a mystery, but she does have a narrow education; she

doesn't know of the Cybermen either, despite the fact that the crew of the Moonbase recognise them on sight. In *The Seeds of Death* Zoe does understand the principals behind T-Mat, knowledge otherwise limited to a few specialists. The first two editions of *The Programme Guide* placed *The Wheel in Space* as '1990–2000', but *The Terrestrial Index* suggested a date 'c 2020' (or '2030' in *The Universal Databank*). '2074' was suggested by 'The History of the Cybermen' in *DWM*. *Cybermen*, after some discussion (p61–2), decided on '2028 AD'. I place the story a century after it was broadcast, around the same time as the other Cyberman incursion seen in *The Moonbase*.

60 *The Wheel in Space*. Jet helicopters are referred to by Jarvis Bennett in that story and also by Zoe in *The Invasion*. In *Just War*, Benny remembers that the helicopter was the principal form of travel at this time (p55). We see "The City" in *The Mind Robber*. The Pull Back to Earth movement is referred to in *The Wheel in Space*, and in *The Power of Kroll*, set centuries later, the "Sons of Earth" have a similar agenda (and the colonists from Delta are just as suspicious of them as the W3 astronauts). Gemma Corwyn's husband is killed two years before *The Wheel in Space*.

61 This is an attempt to explain why not a single crewmember

of colony ships. [66]

Prospectors such as Dom Issigri and Milo Clancey were the first men into deep space. Clancey's ship, the 'C' Class freighter *LIZ 79* remained in service for forty years. Spacecraft at that time were built using the metal tillium, and they were powered by a thermonuclear pile. Mined ore was sent to refineries in "floaters", slow unmanned vessels. An almost indestructable metal, argonite, was found on some of the planets in the fourth sector. Soon, all ships were made from argonite, which became the most valuable mineral known to man. Clancey and Issigri became rich over the next fifteen years of working together, especially after they had spent ten years strip-mining the planet Ta in the Pliny system. Clancey became something of a legend on Reja Magnum. The partners eventually split, though, and Issigri went on to found the Issigri Mining Company. [67]

Robot technology improved, and now robots, such as the Robotic Self-Activating Megapodic Mark Seven-Z Cleaners, had some degree of autonomy. Scanners were developed that could track individuals, and the science of corporal ectoscopy was perfected.

A new tower block won a string of awards:

> "Welcome one and all to Paradise Towers, which will be your new home for a good few years to come. Some of you will understandably feel nervous at leaving everything you know for a strange new environment, but we believe once you've tasted the Paradise Towers experience, you won't want to change it for any other. Our motto is 'Build High for Happiness'. The facilities of this mighty structure are unrivalled, as you can see from these pictures. Paradise Towers has been specially created for you by Kroagnon, universally known as the Great Architect, the genius responsible for Golden Dream Park, the Bridge of Perpetual Motion, Miracle City…"
>
> [From the Prospectus for Paradise Towers]

Miracle City had been Kroagnon's masterpiece, but he refused to move out and let the residents move in. He was eventually forced out, but had booby-trapped the building, and many of the residents were massacred. Space, though, is a big place and Kroagnon fled to *Earth* where he was allowed to build Paradise Towers. During the *Thousand-Day* War, youngsters and oldsters were evacuated to the 304-storey building. The authorities forgot all about them. [68]

*A marked deterioration in the political situation on Earth developed. Quite why this happened has never been explained. A number of factors could be to blame: mass emigration to the stars might have caused unrest on the homeworld, just as America inspired a generation of political radicalism in Europe three hundred years earlier. The realisation that hostile alien races existed could well have made humanity, or its leaders, more paranoid. The conflict might just have been a more obviously economic or ideological one: once T-Mat was abandoned, all the old problems of distributing and transporting resources must have re-emerged. The development of Proton missiles, which made a nuclear war 'winnable' could have done nothing to stabilise the situation.*

## c 2084 – WARRIORS OF THE DEEP [69]

Earth consolidated into two blocs, the East and the West, and a new Cold War developed. New weapons technology was developed: Seabases sat on the ocean floor, armed with Proton missiles that were capable of destroying life while leaving property intact. Sentinels, robots armed with energy weapons, orbited Earth, and large Hunter-Killers patrolled the seas. Specially trained men, Synch-operators, had computer interfaces implanted into their heads, allowing split-second control over Proton missile-runs. Soldiers now carried energy rifles. Elsewhere, governments used genetic manipulation and intelligent chips to maintain their soldiers' loyalty. [70]

At the height of interbloc tension, Seabase 4 was attacked. During the 2020s, the Silurians entombed at Wenley Moor had revived, but they remained hidden from humanity.

'The human tendency for self-destruction in the period was

of W3 has heard of the Cybermen in *The Wheel in Space*, yet in *The Moonbase*, Hobson instantly recognises a Cyberman and says that "there were Cybermen once, every child knows that". Zoe is returned to her native time in *The War Games*.

62 *Nightmare of Eden*. A monitor readout states that Galactic Salvage and Insurance were formed in "2068". The Doctor has heard of the company and briefly pretends to be working for them.

63 Dating *The Moonbase* – Hobson tells the Doctor they are in "2070", and Polly later repeats this. On-screen the small crew of the Moonbase includes Englishmen, Frenchmen and Danes. The production file for the story listed the other nationalities represented at the Moonbase: Australians, New Zealanders, Canadians, Germans and Nigerians.

64 *St Anthony's Fire* (p259). I link the creation of the island with the disturbances caused by the Gravitron.

65 TELOS – After the destruction of their vast advance force (*The Invasion*), Mondas (*The Tenth Planet*), and most of the surviving Cyberwarships (*Silver Nemesis*), the Cybermen were severely weakened. The Cybermen gradually regrouped and attempted to attack Earth at least twice in the twenty-first century (*The Wheel in Space*

and *The Moonbase*). These attempts failed, and the Cybermen faced extinction (according to the Controller in *The Tomb of the Cybermen*). So they left the solar system and conquered Telos (the Doctor says in *Attack of the Cybermen* that "if Mondas hadn't been destroyed, the Cybermen would never have come here [to Telos]". This contradicts an unbroadcast line from *The Moonbase*, where a Cyberman stated "we were the first space travellers from Mondas. We left before it was destroyed. We came from the planet Telos"). The Cybermen subjugated the native Cryons, used Cryon technology to build their "tombs" (*Attack of the Cybermen*) and experimented with new weapons before entering suspended animation. In the late twenty-fifth century, the Cybermen revived (*The Tomb of the Cybermen*), and emerged to menace the galaxy... [see also THE CYBER WAR page 186].

66 In *The Mutants* the Doctor notes of humanity that "once they had sacked the solar system they moved on to pastures new". In *The Sensorites* the Doctor and his companions are mistaken for the crew from the twenty-first century. The acronym NAFAL was first used in *Doctor Who* in *Transit* (p264). Pioneer stations are mentioned in *The Pit* (p165).

67 *The Space Pirates*.

68 The Doctor watches the prospectus in *Paradise Towers*,

matched only by their exploitation of "their" planet. At the time, Icthar, the last surviving member of the Triad, ended the way of mediation, hoping to end the madness by provoking a war between the two human factions. Proton missiles would have been used to cleanse the Earth of human contamination. Silurian technology, such as the organic battlecruiser, the particle suppresser and the Myrka was far in advance of humanity's. The armour of Sea Devil Elite Group One was resistant to human firepower – they were helpless in the face of our weapons. Lacking nobility, the humans callously released hexachromite gas, suffocating the brave warriors. It should have happened another way.'

[*The Humane Solution*, Professor Chtaabus] [71]

Other groups of Silurians survived, and over the centuries they emerged from hibernation to take their place in an increasingly cosmopolitan Earth. [72]

*Global war appeared inevitable, until* out of the blue, one day in 2086, the Martians attacked.

"The warvids made afterwards always emphasised the Paris Rock. The classic *Violet Sky* ran its opening credits over a sustained shot of the asteroid up in the barren spaces above the elliptic, tumbling slowly so that the ideograms blasted into its surface caught the sunlight one after another. In an instant, without any warning, Paris was obliterated – centuries of history were wiped out and hundreds of thousands of people were killed. The Martians had intended to send a clear message, to demonstrate that the human race should not fight a war of retribution against them. It was meant to be a deterrent, but humanity took it as a challenge. Again, the Martians had misunderstood humanity's agenda. For over twenty years, Earth had left the Red Planet alone. The planet's gravity made mining Mars uneconomic when compared with the asteroid belt or the numerous solar moons. Besides, the planet was dying and had no mineral wealth to speak of. The Grand Marshal was dead; the Martian space fleet was gone. Humanity didn't see the Martians as a threat – most people on Earth hadn't even heard of them. Who knows? Perhaps the Martians were insulted that humanity felt they could ignore them; perhaps they felt a need to demonstrate their power. Whatever the case, the Martians got it wrong and it cost them their planet.'

[*Down Among the Dead Men*, Professor B S Summerfield]

Humanity united behind President Achebe against the common enemy. First in were the Zen Brigade, the Blue Berets of the United Nations Third Tactical Response Brigade, made up of Irish and Ethiopians. They dropped in from orbit, and the Martians cut them to pieces. One of the few survivors was their commanding officer, Brigadier Yembe Lethbridge-Stewart. But the Blue Berets completed their mission, forming a bridgehead – the UN forward base at Jacksonville halfway up Olympus Mons. More crucially once in place, their engineers set up the first interstitial tunnel, a refinement of old T-Mat technology that allowed instantaneous travel between Earth and Mars. Men and materiel poured through the Tunnel.

Half-kiloton groundbreakers poured from the air on to the Martian nests. Tactical nuclear weapons were used. The early stages of the war were dogged by friendly-fire incidents, but these were ironed out. As the war dragged on, some soldiers were genetically and cybernetically augmented to increase their efficiency. These first-generation *ubersoldaten* retained less than fifty percent of their natural DNA. Just about every soldier took combat drugs like Doberman and Heinkel to make them better fighters.

New slang entered the language: Greenie (Martian), pop up (a cannon used by the Martians), spider trap, fire mission, medevac. During the war, hologram technology became more advanced. The Ice Maiden, an R and R stop in Jacksonville, became notorious. For a generation afterwards, the imagery and iconography of the War was burnt into the minds of humanity.

The war ended in 2088, exactly a thousand days after it had started. The surviving Martians had either fled the planet or gone into hibernation in deep nests. At first, the human authorities were worried about 'stay behind' units, but it became clear that the Martian threat had completely dissipated, and the military satellites were decommissioned. A memorial forest was set up at Achebe Gorge on Mars. A tree was planted for each one of the four hundred and fifty thousand men who had died in the War, which didn't include the death toll in Paris. For many decades, Victory Night was celebrated every year on Earth, and trees were planted to honour the military dead.

'The Ice Warriors were not completely wiped out, instead and relates Kroagnon's story. The Chief Caretaker describes Kroagnon as a "being" rather than a "man", suggesting that Kroagnon might be an alien. It is never specified that the tower block was built on Earth, but this seems to be the implication. In the novelisation, Paradise Towers is a space station, which it certainly isn't on-screen.

69 Dating *Warriors of the Deep* – The Doctor tells Tegan that the year is "about 2084". In the televised story, it is never specified which bloc the Seabase belongs to. Preston doesn't seem surprised that the TARDIS is "not from this planet", and no one is shocked that the Silurians are intelligent non-humans. This might suggest that contact has been made with a number of alien races by this time.

70 This is the background to *Warriors of the Deep*. We are told about genetic manipulation and intelligent chips in *Deceit* (p188), and see similar technology in *Transit*.

71 At the end of *Doctor Who and the Silurians*, the Reptile People go back into 'deep freeze' for fifty years. [see also The Earth Reptiles page 143]

72 THE EARTH REPTILES – In *Doctor Who and the Silurians*, *The Ambassadors of Death* and *The Sea Devils* the Doctor thinks that the Brigadier has killed all the Silurians at Wenley Moor, but they may simply be entombed, and one Silurian

seems to survive the first story into *Warriors of the Deep*. Based on discrepancies between the events of *Doctor Who and the Silurians*, the descriptions of the Doctor's last encounter with the species in *Warriors of the Deep*, and the fact that the Doctor recognises Icthar, the Myrka and the Silurian submersible, *The Discontinuity Guide* postulated that there is an unrecorded adventure featuring the Doctor and the Silurians set between the two stories. If that is the case, the encounter probably took place after the 2020s. Silurians have been referred to in a number of New and Missing Adventures set in the future (*Love and War*, *Transit* and *The Crystal Bucephalus* to name three). They seem particularly peaceful towards humans in Benny's native time.

73 *Legacy* (p86). In *The Curse of Peladon* we learn that the Martians and Arcturans are "old enemies".

74 This is the historical background to *Transit*. In *The Seeds of Death*, Zoe has never heard of the Ice Warriors, even though mankind is exploring the solar system in her time, which suggests that her contemporaries are not interested in Mars. We learn in *Transit*, amongst many other historical snippets, that the Thousand-Day War ended about twenty-five years before (p188) and that the decade following the war saw economic upheaval (p108). In his 'Future History

they left Mars resettling in another star system *close to Arcturus*. There was little or no contact between the Ice Warriors and humanity for nearly a thousand years; in fact the Martians rarely allowed any visitors to their new world. In the twenty-sixth century, the "extinct" Martians briefly became a curiosity for archaeologists, but after that, mankind forgot all about their old neighbours.'

[*Down Among the Dead Men II*, Professor B S Summerfield(unpublished)] [73]

The World Government invested heavily in the State-owned Sol Transit System (STS) over the next twenty years, and soon Interstitial Tunnels linked every city, every continent, every habitable planet and moon in the solar system. Transportation within the solar system was now instantaneous and readily available. For the first time the solar system had a single elected government, the Union of Solar Republics.

In the decade following the Thousand-Day War, Paris was rebuilt. Lowell Depot on Pluto was built to soak up population overspill, but the expected boom didn't arrive. Instead, the Transit system caused massive economic and social upheaval. Small companies saw an opportunity to undermine the industrial zaibatsu. Household names such as Sony, IBM and Matsui went under, and new companies from Brazil, China and Africa took their place, such as Imbani Entertainment, Mtchali and Tung-Po. Power shifted to Washington, Brazilia, Harare, Beijing, Tehran, Jacksonville and Zagreb. Japan's economy collapsed and plans to terraform Mars proved more costly than had been expected. The money ran out, the floating cities planned for the Ionian Sea were never built, and Australia starved. A new genre, silicon noir, charted the resultant corporate battles in the datascape.

The Recession was not harsh on everyone: relatively speaking, Europe was less prosperous than before, but many in Brazil, Africa and China were a great deal wealthier. For millions in Australia, though, and at the Stop, the end of the Transit line at the Lowell Depot, extreme poverty became a way of life. Whole areas became dead-end ghettos, and urban areas became battlegrounds for streetgangs. Vickers All-Body Combat Systems offered the option of using the Melbourne Protocols – automatically preventing the wearer from shooting civilians. Millions fled the riots using the Transit system, and relief workers rehoused the poor anywhere that would take them, mostly on Mars. Private security firms, such as the KGB and V Soc became very rich. With freedom of transport, humanity became more open to ideas from other cultures, and to more experimental ways of living. Communal marriages enjoyed a brief vogue.

In 2090, Yembe Lethbridge-Stewart came out of retirement one last time and raided the headquarters of the genetics company IMOGEN. He stole a single child, the first of the second-generation *ubersoldaten*, and all the files pertaining to her creation. He named her after his great-grandmother, the historian Kadiatu. [74]

By the end of the century, a number of planets in solar systems near to Earth had been colonised. Worlds such as the five planets of the Sirius system [75] and Delta Magna rapidly became industrialised and overpopulated. **The seven planets of the binary Meson system were colonised at this time.** Because interstellar travel and communications were still relatively slow, these planets were often left to their own devices. The founding fathers of these worlds were often important, and all sorts of experiments with political and social systems were attempted. The prison planet Varos was established to remove the criminally insane from galactic society. **Many colonies were set up and directly controlled by the corporations, and many others were reliant on them for communications, transport and technology.** The Recession affected the colonies, causing cutbacks in all government funded projects. Galactic Salvage and Insurance went bankrupt in 2096 *because of the expansion of the Transit System and the Galactic Recession.* [76]

"When the great human expansion into space happened, a Traveller called Fox saw that his people could finally be free. They stole a ship that was in dock for repairs and took it as far into hyperspace as they could. When Earth ships first met the Arcturans, the Earth ambassador was told that they'd met humans before. Fox and his crew had landed on Arcturus Six and busked for their supper."

[From the Oral History of the Travellers] [77]

## c 2100 – PARADISE TOWERS [78]

'Paradise Towers, a self-contained, award-winning tower block that had been abandoned during the war, was rediscovered by the Adjudicators' Bureau in the early

Continuity', Ben Aaronovitch stated that the war took place between 2086 and 2088, which by his reckoning was straight after *The Seeds of Death*. Victory Night is mentioned in *The Highest Science* (p21), and I speculate that it celebrates the end of this war. We learn in *Infinite Requiem* that forests are still planted after a battle (p266).

75 THE SIRIUS SYSTEM – In *Frontier in Space* the Master poses as a Commissioner from Sirius IV, and accuses the Doctor and Jo of landing a spaceship in an unauthorised area on Sirius III. According to Romana in *City of Death*, Sirius V is the home of the Academius Stolaris. In *The Caves of Androzani* Morgus is the chairman of the Sirius Conglomerate based on Androzani Major, and spectrox is found on its twin planet of Androzani Minor. These two facts make Morgus the "richest man in the Five Planets".

76 The Doctor says he visited Androzani Major when "it was getting industrialised". We see the third moon of Delta Magna in *The Power of Kroll* – it is called "Delta III" in the novelisation and *Original Sin* (p21). The Meson system has been colonised for "a hundred years" according to the Doctor in *Time of Your Life* (p27). The founding fathers of a planet are revered in *The Robots of Death*, *The Caves of Androzani* and the New Adventure *Parasite*. In *Vengeance on Varos*, the Governor notes that "Varos has been stable for more than two

hundred years". The corporations' stranglehold over the early colonies is a theme touched on in many New Adventures, especially the 'Future History Cycle' which ran from *Love and War* to *Shadowmind*. Galactic Salvage and Insurance are mentioned in *Nightmare of Eden*, as is the Recession.

77 This is a direct quote from Jan in *Love and War* (p39).

78 Dating *Paradise Towers* – Paradise Towers has been abandoned for between about fifteen to twenty years judging by the age of the Kangs. The Doctor's remark that the building won awards "way back in the twenty-first century" might suggest that the story is set in the twenty-second, or indeed it may not. If we take the New Adventures into account, I would suggest that the war at Time Start might well be the Thousand-Day War that took place a generation before *Transit*. The *Terrestrial Index* suggested that the war is the Dalek Invasion of Earth, so set the story around 2164. In *Lucifer Rising*, Adjudicator Bishop refers to the "messy consequences of the Kroagnon Affair" (p189).

twenty-second century. The building provided a fascinating case study into the anarchy, bizarre rituals and violence often encountered in small, isolated groups of humans. It was a pattern that would reoccur on many colony worlds over the millennia – Paradise Towers retained many of the social structures from before it was abandoned, but gradually these mutated. With only the old and the young, the "old days" were all but forgotten about, and society became stratified: the young girls became Kangs, with an array of "icehot" slang and "high fabsion" clothing, the old women became Rezzies, and the Caretakers tried to maintain the building by rigidly sticking to their rulebook. Each group had a distinctive language, and each preyed mercilessly on the other. There were even reports of cannibalism. The Kangs split into three factions, Red, Blue, and Yellow and there was rivalry between them, although "wipeouts" or "making unalive" was forbidden, as were visitors, ball games and fly posting. **Adjudicator Bishop reported that at the time of discovery**, some form of social order had been restored. What caused this unification is unknown, the residents reporting that some decades before there had been an incident involving the former Chief Caretaker. They claimed that he had been possessed by Kroagnon. Clearly they had turned the story of the building of Paradise Towers into a foundation myth, "Time Start", and somehow they both worshipped "the Great Architect" and blamed him for their predicament. The myth was recounted again and again on the wallscrawl covering every available surface of the building.'

[*Extinct Civilisations*, Woris Bossard]

*Early in the twenty-second century, contact was established between humanity and a handful of alien races that tended not to be hostile towards humans. These included the natives of Alpha Centauri (who were naturally timid), the Arcturans and Martians (who were busy fighting each other), and the Mentors (who were traders). None of these races could live unaided on planets suitable for humans. During the Fourth Millennium, many of these planets would formally become members of a Galactic Federation, but for the moment these rich, technically advanced and heavily populated worlds were known collectively as the Inner Planets, distinguishing them from the sparsely populated frontier worlds, or Outer Planets.* [79]

During the twenty-second century human babies were grown artificially, to be used in scientific tests. [80]

2106 saw the Ozone Purge, the first sign that man had not solved Earth's environmental problems. Caused by a breakdown of weather control technology, a number of species were wiped out, including such previously common creatures as sheep, cats and sparrows. Yembe Lethbridge-Stewart died, and was buried alongside his wife at Achebe Gorge on Mars by his daughter.

A year later, Eurogen and the Butler Institute, relatively small corporations for the time, merged to become Eurogen Butler, or the EB Corporation. Eurogen was a major genetic research facility. After its near collapse a century before, the Butler Institute had survived by specialising in artificial intelligence, meteorology and weather control. Both companies were expanding into the field of interplanetary exploration, and their services were now required on a dozen worlds. *They forecast that the STS could not survive much longer.* [81]

## c 2109 – TRANSIT [82]

The Union of Solar Republics attempted to build the first interstitial tunnel to another star system. The Stunnel would provide instantaneous travel to Arcturus II, twenty-six light years away, and if such a system could be made to work it would allow rapid colonisation of other planets. At the inauguration, though, disaster struck. The President was killed, and the Transit system began to show signs of instability. It became clear that the Transit system had attracted an intelligence from another dimension, and it was this that ensured the smooth running of the network. It also became clear that it was impossible to maintain Transit tunnels over interstellar distances. *Soon afterwards, the Transit system collapsed.*

FLORANCE, the first artificial intelligence to develop sentience, became a celebrity. Its rights were protected under the civil rights convention. [83]

*The twenty-first century had been a period of rapid*

79 As mankind spread out into space, I speculate that it must have encountered alien races living nearby. The natives of Alpha Centauri, Arcturus and Mars appear together in *The Curse of Peladon*, the Mentors in *Vengeance on Varos* and *The Trial of a Time Lord*.

80 *Timewyrm: Revelation* (p216).

81 The Ozone Purge and mass extinctions are referred to in *Lucifer Rising* (p100, p320). Kadiatu remembers her father's funeral in *Transit* (p157–8). The merger between Eurogen and the Butler Institute is discussed in *Deceit* (p27-8).

82 Dating *Transit* – The exact date of the story is not specified. The book takes many of its themes from *The Seeds of Death*, and is set at least a generation or so after that story. As in that story, the Transit system has been established for at least the last couple of decades, and has revolutionised the world – no other stories we have seen on television or in the books seem to be set during this period. It is hinted that the story takes place in the twenty-second century (p134). In his 'Future History Continuity' Ben Aaronovitch places this story 'c 2109'.

83 *Transit. Sleepy.*

technological and social change on Earth. The planet was now ruled by a single government, and the nations of Earth lived – for the most part – in peace with one another. Earth's contact with alien races had been mixed: some traded peacefully with humanity, some had waged full-scale war. Mankind had already colonised the entire Solar System and was now making the first tentative steps to establish itself in deep space.

# Section Five
# Colonisation

## TIMELINE: 2110 to 2500 AD

Mankind discovered a cheap, efficient warp drive and began the mass colonisation of other star systems. The first production line warships began to be built. Lagships were still used for many years on longer journeys, although the technology remained risky. [1]

The EB Corporation was among the first to offer an escape from Earth in their warship, the *Back to Nature*, which was commissioned in 2112. Their brochure claimed:

> "You can make a fresh start on Arcadia, the paradise planet. Arcadia offers you a new life, a new beginning, thanks to the pioneering labours of the EB Corporation. Leave your worries on Earth, and fly with EB to the new world of your dreams."

Arcadia was a temperate planet, the second in its system, and was less than a thousand light years from Earth. A number of years previously, the EB Corporation had set up a survey camp on the planet, the site of which eventually became the capital city, Landfall, and set about terraforming the world. Now the planet resembled medieval Europe, and was ready for the first influx of colonists. Arcadia eventually became the Corporation's centre of operations. [2]

'What was the impulse that drove millions of people to abandon their home? Warship technology was almost untried; the ships' owners, Earth-based corporations whose wealth and power were already beyond the control of governments, demanded extortionate payment for every outbound berth. Why would anyone expend his life savings to leave a solar system that had, apparently, already seen its darkest days?

The answer, I suggest, lies in the perception of poverty. Wealth differentials were vast, and more importantly they had never been so visible. Mass communications enveloped the solar system; transportation was almost instant. The majority of the population on every inhabited planet lived in relative poverty, depending on state benefits, short-term menial employment and the proceeds of crime. Yet even the poorest could afford the radio and video links that provided a non-stop display of flaunted wealth and glamour; even the poorest could afford the transmat fare to the retail palaces in the floating domes of Venus or to the marble halls of the government offices on Earth.

1 Humanity has discovered warp drive by *Nightmare of Eden*. In *Deceit* we learn that production line warships were in production by 2112 (p28). Suspended animation is seen in a number of New Adventures set after this time, including *Deceit*, *The Highest Science* and *Lucifer Rising*.

2 The Arcadia colony was founded "three hundred and seventy-nine" (Arcadian?) years before the events of *Deceit* (p115), it was one of the first Spinward Settlements (p16), and the planet (or at least part of it) has been terraformed (p103). The quote from the brochure comes from *Deceit* (p28).

3 This extract first appeared as part of the 'Prelude' to *Deceit* in *DWM* Issue 198.

4 *The Highest Science.*

5 Dating *Nightmare of Eden* – Galactic Salvage and Insurance went bankrupt "20 years ago" according to Rigg, who had just read a computer monitor giving the date of the bankruptcy as "2096". *In-Vision* suggested that Azure is in "West Galaxy", but I think this is a mishearing of Rigg's (fluffed) line "you'll never work in <u>this</u> galaxy again" – there is certainly no on-screen justification for *The Discontinuity Guide's* 'Western Galaxy'. The TARDIS Logs gave the date as 'c .2100', *The Doctor Who File* as '2113'.

For the majority of humans, the solar system at the end the twenty-first century was a taunting prison. A trip to the stars, however costly and risky, would have seemed an escape'

[From the Introduction to *From Breakout to Empire: Essays on the Third Millennium*, Federation Archivist Ven Kalik] [3]

Around this time, the planet Evertrin was the site of the annual Inner Planets Music Festival, known as "Ragasteen". The biggest bands in space attended to plug their discods: Deep Space, M'Troth, The Great Mothers of Matra, Is Your Baby a God, and Televised Instant Death were all at Ragasteen 2112. Every three years the riggers on Earth changed the style of music to keep it fresh: Zagrat, for example were very popular during the "headster time", but teenagers found their discod "Sheer Event Shift' embarrassing just a few years later. [4]

## 2116 – NIGHTMARE OF EDEN [5]

*Conventional space travel became the major growth sector of the economy, and* many of the corporations became very rich. Interplanetary standards and conventions were set up that applied to the whole of Human Space. The Galactic Credit (z) was established as a convertible interplanetary currency. Credits resembled colourful blocks of plastic and were used for every sort of transaction, from buying a drink to funding an expedition to a new planet. All citizens were required to carry an ident-plaque.

Laser technology advanced during this time. Stun laser weapons became available for the first time. Entuca lasers capable of carrying millions of signals were now used for telecommunications. Finally, vast amounts of information could now be recorded on laser data crystals.

Crime was a problem in the galaxy: burglars began to use computers, forcing people to install audio locks. Drug trafficking also increased when the drug XYP, or Vraxoin, was discovered. Vrax addicts felt a warm complacency at first, followed by total apathy. They also became thirsty. Eventually, and inevitably, its effects were fatal. Whole planets and communities were ruined by the narcotic until the planet that was the only known source of the drug was incinerated. A vraxoin merchant (drug trafficker) risked the death penalty if caught. Molecular scanners were developed that could detect even minute quantities of the drug. No less lethal was the drink Bubbleshake, invented by the unscrupulous Joseph-Robinson corporation. It was originally an appetite suppressant, but unchecked it was addictive, leading to memory loss, hyperactivity and compulsive behaviour. Eventually the substance was outlawed.

While tourism on Earth was a thing of the past, interplanetary tourism developed at this time. Government-subsidised interstellar cruise liners, each holding nine hundred passengers, travelled between Station Nine and Azure. Passengers could travel either economy or first class, the former seated in pallets and forced to wear protective clothing, the latter allowed a great deal more freedom and luxury. [6]

The scientist Tryst attempted to qualify and quantify every lifeform in the galaxy. As Tryst's log (published to coincide with a series of lectures given by the zoologist) recounted, his ten-man expedition travelled to Zil, Vij, Darp, Lvan, Brus, the windswept planet of Gidi and the temperate world Ranx. Finally, Tryst's ship, the *Volante*, travelled past the Cygnus Gap to the three-planet system of M37. The second planet contained primitive life: molluscs, algae and insects. As well as taking visprints, they used a CET machine:

'The Continuous Event Transmuter can convert matter into electromagnetic signals on a laser crystal. It works on the principal of matter transfer by dimensional control: samples pass through the spacial integrator and are encoded by the transmution oscillator. With the use of an hologistic retention circuit, the process is complete, and when the crystals are replayed the recorded event is restructured on an intra-dimensional field.'

[*Cosmic Science Made Simple*, Professor Stein]

Six months before arriving at Azure, the Volante visited the planet Eden. On the planet they lost a member of the crew, Stott, who was secretly working for the Intelligence Section of the Space Corps. Shortly afterwards, Tryst lost government funding for his work.

6 This is the background to *Nightmare of Eden*, with one detail (the audio lock) from *The Space Pirates* which also features the Space Corps. We see corporations growing rich from colonisation in many New Adventures, including *Deceit* and *Sleepy*. Tourism is a thing of the past on Earth according to *Lucifer Rising* (p84). Bubbleshake appears in *The Highest Science*, with the Doctor explaining its origin (p102).

## COSMOS INSURANCE CLAIMS FORM

**Owner's Name:** *Dymond*
**Address:** *c/o Penal Colony Two, Azure*
**Ship's Name and Registry:** Hecate, 5-K-02349
**Class:** *Survey Vessel*

[About the Accident]
**Date:** *24/11/2116*
**Location:** *The prohibited spacelanes over Azure*
**Damage to Vehicle:** *Minor damage*
**Estimated Cost of Damage (z):** *3,900,000*
**Please describe fully the circumstances of the accident:** *I had been surveying the planet on contract for the Azurian government for a year. I had been given complete clearance from Azure Control to enter all prohibited zones. Suddenly, the cruise liner Empress left warp space directly in my path. It was still in dematerialised form, and the two ships merged, establishing matter interfaces. The instability released monsters from a CET machine on the ship, and many crewmembers were mauled by the Mandrels. If that was not bad enough, I discovered that the co-pilot, the late Mr Secker, was a vrax addict. The ships began displaying signs of molecular rejection, and we forced the two ships apart, causing structural damage to my ship. The Hecate was further damaged when Space Corps officers used the CET machine to capture a part of my vessel.*

**Name of police station or officers to whom loss was notified:** *Water Guard Fisk and Landing Officer Costa, shortly after they arrested me for vraxoin smuggling. These officers were rude and incompetent. I kept telling them that my name is pronounced 'De Mond', and that my ship was the 'Heh Kate', but they wouldn't listen. Tryst, my partner was even referred to as 'Fisk'!*

**I declare that the statements on this form are true and accurate to the best of my knowledge and/or belief:**
**Signature of Policyholder** ___*Dymond*___ **Date** *15/12/16*

## ? 2119 – THE SPACE PIRATES [7]

As space travel became more common, the Earth Government introduced a series of regulations to better control the space lanes in its territory. Space was divided into administrative and strategic sectors. All flights now had to be logged with Central Flight Information, and a network of Mark Five Space Beacons was established to monitor space traffic. The Interstellar Space Corps was given the latest V-Ships, armed with state-of-the-art Martian Missiles (H-bombs were considered old-fashioned by this time) and carrying squadrons of Minnow Fighters. The V-Ships were powered by Main Boost atomic motors. The Space Corps routinely used mind probes to interrogate their prisoners. The resources of the Space Corps were stretched very thin: they fought brush wars in three sectors, acted as customs and ex-cise officials, and attempted to curtail the activities of space pirates.

For two years, pirates were active in the Ta system, hijacking five of Milo Clancey's floaters, each of which contained 50,000 tons of argonite ore. Despite a dozen requests, the Space Corps did little to help. As an old-timer, Clancey was suspicious of authority; he had lost his registration documents thirty years before and he didn't maintain his feedback link to CFI.

'When the pirates began to break up government space beacons to steal the argonite, the Space Corps became in-volved. The *V41-LO* more than fifty days out of Earth and under the command of General Nikolai Hermack, Com-mander of the Space First Division, was ninety minutes away from Beacon Alpha 4 when it was broken up by pirates. Clancey's ship was detected nearby and he was brought in for questioning, but he was quickly released. Three space travellers were recovered from Beacon Alpha 4, but they too were innocent.

The real culprit was Maurice Caven. His pirates were or-ganised enough to equip themselves with Beta Dart ships that could outrun virtually everything else in space, each one of which cost one hundred million credits. He killed anyone who got in his way. One of his men, Dervish, had

7 Dating *The Space Pirates* – A monitor readout in Episode Two apparently suggests that the year is "1992", but this contradicts dialogue stating that prospectors have been in deep space for "fifty years". No other date is given on-screen. The *Radio Times* said that the story takes place in 'the far future'. Earth is mentioned once in the first episode, but after that only a "home world" is referred to. The Space Corps operate at the time of *Nightmare of Eden*, and a Marine Space Corps in *Death to the Daleks*. The force here is specified as the Interstellar Space Corps. The regulatory actions of the government suggest that space travel is becoming more common now, but is still at an early stage. As Zoe is unfamiliar with the technology of this story it is almost certainly set after her time. The Main Boost Drive is not very advanced, and this story almost certainly takes place well before *Frontier in Space*, where hyperdrive technology is common. Clancey has been a deep space pioneer for fifty years. At the start of the story, the *V41-LO* is both "fifty days" and "fifty billion miles" from Earth; I assume here that Holmes means "billion" in the British sense of a million million, rather than the American (and now generally accepted British) thousand million. If this is the case, then the Beacon is 8.3 Light Years from Earth (otherwise it is a thousandth of this distance, and only just

outside the solar system).

*The Programme Guide* set
the story at 'c 2600'. *The
Terrestrial Index* suggested it
was 'during the Empire' period.
The TARDIS Logs claimed a
date of '8751'. I set this story
one hundred and fifty years
after it was first broadcast.

**8** The Issigri Mining Company
appears in *The Space Pirates*.
Another company with the
same initials, the Interplanetary
Mining Company, is seen in
*Colony in Space*. In the Missing
Adventure *The Menagerie*, we
learn that they are the same
company (p161). The change of
name must have occurred
before the *Lucifer Rising*, when
we see IMC in action.

**9** *St Anthony's Fire* (p195,
p260). Urrozdinee first
appeared in a short story of the
same name by Mark Gatiss in
Marvel's 1994 *Doctor Who
Yearbook*. In that story the city
is a post-apocalyptic feudal
state inhabiting the remains of
EuroDisney.

**10** The Master poses as an
Adjudicator in *Colony in Space*,
the only time the Adjudicators
were referred to on television.
They feature a number of times
in the New Adventures, and the
Doctor's companions Cwej and
Forrester are ex-Adjudicators.
The foundation of the Guild of
Adjudicators is related in
*Lucifer Rising*, as are their early
successes. I suggest that "the
Macra case" referred to on
page 189 can't be *The Macra
Terror*, and so must be another
encounter with that race.

spent ten years working for Earth Government and knew
all the Space Corps's techniques. Some time ago, Caven had
kidnapped Dom Issigri, and he was now blackmailing his beautiful daughter Madeline, the head of the Issigri Mining Company, into providing facilities for him on the planet Ta. The
Corps hunted Caven down and executed him.'

[*Nasty Great Rotters of the Galaxy*, R K Cossin]

After this, the Issigri Mining Company was renamed the Interplanetary Mining Company, or IMC for short. [8]

The crusade of the Chapter of St Anthony was becoming notorious. Youths from the Initiate League torched the city of
Urrozdinee when they refused to accept the rule of the Chapter.
Shortly afterwards, the crusade spread unopposed to the stars,
in two mighty battleships capable of laying waste to whole planets and destroying small moons. When the Chapter raided Titan, they recruited the malevolent dwarf Parva De Hooch. Shortly
afterwards the Chapter returned to Earth, and De Hooch killed
his parents. [9]

The Guild of Adjudicators was established in the early
twenty-second century as a judicial force unrestrained by authority or financial dependence. They were based on the remote
planet Ponten IV. Early successes for the "ravens" (so-named
because of their black robes) included the execution of fifteen
drug dealers on Callisto, the suppression of a revolution in
Macedonia, and the disciplinary eradication of the
energy-wasting population on Frinelli Minor. The Adjudicators
also dealt with the Kroagnon Affair, vraxoin raids over Azure,
the Macra case, and the Vega debacle. [10]

Around 2127, the InterSpace Incorporated exploration vessel *Hydrax* was lost en route to Beta Two in the Perugellis Sector. Its officers included Captain Miles Sharkey, Science Officer
Anthony O'Connor and Navigation Officer Lauren Macmillan.
The ship had a crew of 243. InterSpace refused to pay out pen-
sions for the lost crew, claiming they might be found. IMC would
later claim to have discovered traces of the ship in order to blackmail Piper O'Rourke – whose husband Ben had been an engineer on the *Hydrax* – into revealing details about the Eden
Project. The ship was never discovered. [11]

On Betrushia around the year 2133, war broke out between
the Ismetch and the Cutch, as it had done on many previous
occasions over the centuries. Millions died in the conflict, and

it would prove to be the longest and most bitter struggle the planet had seen for three hundred years. The Ismetch had an early success at Dalurida Bridge under Portrone Ran. [12]

Humanity's contact with the Arcturans was proving fruitful. The Arcturans allowed limited human settlement in their sector, and supplied humanity with specialised drugs. Some humans became interested in studying Arcturan literature.

On Earth, however, things were getting desperate. The Islam-dominated Earth Central, based in Damascus and led by an elected president, was unable to prevent society from collapsing. An unprecedented energy crisis led to draconian restrictions on consumption, and the foundation of the Energy Police. The invention of the vargol generator did little to relieve the demands for fuel. In 2137, with Earth desperate for energy, corporations successfully lobbied for the repeal of all the anti-pollution laws brought in over the last century and a quarter. Three years later, an American subsidiary of Panorama Chemicals filled the Carlsbad Caverns with plastic waste, and the oceans of the world were a sludge of industrial effluent. Mineral water became a precious commodity. The whale finally became extinct, and auto-immune diseases – 'the Plague' of over a century before – returned. Despite this, human life expectancy was now 110 years, and the population was soaring. Although they had religious objections to gambling, Earth Central introduced the Eugenics Lottery, and couples were forbidden from having children unless they won.

A colony ship made landfall on the planet Avalon in the year 2145. The colonists discovered an ancient Avalonian technology, which at first allowed them to perform miracles but soon rendered their electronic equipment useless. The colony regressed to a medieval level, where the alien technology was seen as magic. [13]

In 2146, the American economy collapsed. One survivor said of his experience:

'I was at MexTech at the time. I was on campus when the food riots hit full swing. I made it to the spaceport on a student bus, the last suborbital off the ground…there were ten million people and no food.' [14]

The Doctor was present, and he was powerless to stop Sonia Bannen from dying at the hands of cannibals shortly after she saved her son. Mark Bannen was placed on board a huge colony ship bound for a new star system. The stardrive misphased in

[11] The final fate of the *Hydrax* is uncovered in *State of Decay*. The loss is referred to, and a date specified, in *Lucifer Rising* (p59, p272–3). On-screen, one computer monitor seems to suggest that the computer was programmed on the "12/12/1998", but the Hydrax is clearly an interstellar craft. The TARDIS Logs suggested a date in 'the 36th Century', *The Terrestrial Index* placed it "at the beginning of the 22nd".

[12] *St Anthony's Fire*, (Chapter One).

[13] The Sorceror's Apprentice' (p203-4).

[14] *Lucifer Rising*. In the television version of *The Green Death*, the evil polluting company is called "Global Chemicals". A real company of that name objected, and the name was changed in the novelisation to 'Panorama Chemicals'. The quotation is that of Bannen, *Lucifer Rising* (p158).

15 *Parasite*.

16 Dating *St Anthony's Fire* –
The Doctor tells Bernice that
the year is "2148" (p39).

17 Dating *Lucifer Rising* – The
story takes place in the
mid-twenty-second century,
shortly before the Dalek
Invasion of Earth. The
Adjudicator's simularity
registers the Doctor's arrival as
"19/11/2154" (p30), Paula
Engado's death as "22/2/2154"
(p174), and her wake as "23/2/
2154" (p13). Ace and Benny
had expressed the desire to
"pop back to the year
twenty-one fifty-four or so"
(p338), so at first sight it might
appear that the story is set in
2154. However, this is
inconsistent with the Dalek
Invasion, which the authors
place in "twenty-one fifty-eight"
(p337). On page 195, Kreig
remembers a raid "in Tokyo in
fifty-six". I set the story in 2157,
consistent with the dating for
the Dalek Invasion.

the Elysium system and the colony ship crashed. [15]

## 2148 – ST ANTHONY'S FIRE [16]

'MASSATORIS – A pleasant, temperate world, the fourth in
its system. The colonies of Massatoris are of mild interest.
The eleventh human colony on the planet was wiped out by
the Chapter of St Anthony in the mid-twenty-second century. The planet was settled shortly afterwards by the
Betrushians, formerly the natives of Betrushia.'

[*Bartholomew's Planetary Gazetteer*, Volume XIII]

'BETRUSHIA – A beautiful emerald green world, famous for
its glorious white ring system. It has a rich jungle ecosys-
tem. Millions of years ago, a humanoid race evolved on the
planet, but they died out in mysterious circumstances. Subsequently a race of bipedal, crested reptiles evolved. Over
the millennia, the Betrushians developed a complex technology and religion. Beautiful cities such as Porsim (founded
in the fourteenth century), Arason, Tusamavad and Jurrula
were built. The two main factions, the Ismetch and the Cutch
fought for much of their history. Finally, the planet was rendered uninhabitable in the mid-twenty-second century by
an unknown force, a force that also destroyed the Chapter
of St Anthony, and the Betrushians emigrated by unknown
means to Massatoris.'

[*Bartholomew's Planetary Gazetteer*, Volume II]

## c 2157 – LUCIFER RISING [17]

Earth encountered the Legions, a seven-dimensional race from
Epsilon Eridani. Trading agreements were set up between IMC
and the Legions. The Legions were threatened by an unknown
alien fleet in their sector of space, and IMC would supply them
with weaponry in return for advanced technology. Some Legions
began working for IMC.

Earlier in the century, a Von Neumann probe had discovered
a stable element with a very high mass in the core of the planet
Lucifer, a gas giant 280 light years from Earth. Theoretically,
such an element could be used as a rich energy source, so in
2152 Earth Central invested heavily in a scientific research station, the Eden Project, on Belial, one of the moons of Lucifer.

'This was the era of the Company Shock Troops – military
men armed with neutron cannons, flamers, burners and

screamers – who took part in infamous corporate raids. In '56, IMC asset-stripped InterSpace Incorporated in Tokyo using armoured skimmers and Z-Bombs. Legend has it that companies used to capture employees of rival corporations and experiment on them. It was a risky life – on one raid in '51, praxis gas was used – but on average it paid four times more than Earth Central. The big human corporations learnt lessons from the aggressive capitalist races such as the Cimliss, Usurians, and the Okk. But humanity proved capable of callousness that would put all three of those races to shame...'

[Greed Incorporated: The Rise of the Space Corporations, M Ashe]

Six years after it was set up, the Eden Project had still not borne fruit, and pressure was growing to close it down. As Earth's government grew weaker and weaker, the corporations were flexing their muscles: an IMC fleet of over one hundred ships was sent to Belial Base when the scientists reported some progress. This prompted the intelligent species of Lucifer, the Angels, to set up an exclusion zone around their world.

'The corporations had reached new levels of ruthlessness. IMC ruthlessly tripled the price of the fuel zeiton, and an impoverished Earth Central could no longer afford it. Earth was declared bankrupt, and fell into the hands of the receivers: the Earth Alliance of Corporations, a holding company that was in reality the board of directors from all the corporations that traded off-Earth. It was a bloodless coup, and the megacorporations took formal control of the homeworld for the first time. Their reign lasted just under six months...'

[Greed Incorporated: The Rise of the Space Corporations, M Ashe]

An Astronaut Fair was held in London. The city was a beautiful metropolis, complete with moving pavements and a gleaming new nuclear power station alongside the historic Battersea Power Station. *The Earth Alliance of Corporations wanted to promote the advantages of a life on the colonies, on the bicentennial of Sputnik's launch.* [18]

On the very same day that an Earth embassy was opened on Alpha Centauri V, a billion settlers were exterminated on Sifranos in the Arcturus Sector. Fourteen other colonies were wiped out

18 *The Dalek Invasion of Earth.*

19 The events of *The Dalek
Invasion of Earth* are
foreshadowed throughout
*Lucifer Rising*.

20 Dating *The Dalek Invasion of
Earth* – The Doctor and Ian
discover a calendar dated
"2164" in a room that "hasn't
been used in years", and Ian
remarks that "at least we know
the century". Craddock later
says that the Daleks invaded
"about ten years" ago. The
calendar might, then, indicate
the year that the Daleks invade.
However, in *The Daleks' Master
Plan* the Doctor urges Vyon to
"tell Earth to look back in the
history of the year two
thousand one hundred and
fifty-seven and that the Daleks
are going to attack again",
suggesting that the Daleks
attack Earth in 2157. In *The
Space Museum*, Vicki states
that the Daleks invaded Earth
"three hundred years" before
her own time (the late
twenty-fifth century). In
*Remembrance of the Daleks*,
the Doctor states that the
Daleks conquered Earth in "the
twenty-second century". A
production document written in
July 1964 gave the date as
'2042'. The trailer for the 1964
serial claimed the story was set
in 'the year 2000', and in
*Genesis of the Daleks*, the
Doctor talks of the Daleks'
attempted extraction of Earth's
magnetic core in 'the year
2000', clearly referring to this
story. The film version of the
story was set in '2150'.
    *Radio Times* consistently
dated the story as '2164', as did

in a three-week period, including Azure and Qartopholos. Rumours of a mysterious alien fleet massing at the Legion's
homeworld of Epsilon Eridani were denied, but the Interstellar
Taskforce was put on permanent standby, and a Space Fleet
flotilla sent to that planet was completely destroyed. The alien
fleet was a Dalek armada, annihilating any colony that might
render aid to the human homeworld, and systematically destroying Earth's warships. [19]

## c 2167 – THE DALEK INVASION OF EARTH [20]

One survivor of the Dalek Invasion remembered the chain of
events:

> "The meteorites came first. They bombarded Earth about
> ten years ago. A freak cosmic storm, the scientists said... then
> people started dying – some new kind of plague. The Daleks
> were waiting up there in space, waiting for Earth to get
> weaker. Whole continents were wiped out. Asia, Africa,
> America. Everywhere you went, the air smelled of death."

A mystery virus spread through the barrios of Brazilia, Los Angeles and Tycho City killing millions. Only a handful of people
had some form of resistance to the plague. Although authorities around the world vetoed every public event, the new plague
spread quickly. The scientists soon came up with a new kind of
drug, but it was too late, billions had already died. The plague
had split the world into tiny little communities, too far apart to
combine and fight, and too small individually to stand any chance
against the invasion.

    Six months after the plague had begun, the first of Dalek
saucers landed. Some cities were razed to the ground, others
were simply occupied. Anyone who resisted was destroyed. The
Daleks broadcast their chilling messages on all radio wavebands:

> "Survivors of London. The Daleks are the masters of Earth.
> Surrender now and you will live. Those wishing to surren-
> der must stand in the middle of the streets and obey orders
> received. Message ends."

Dalek saucers patrolled the skies. Ruthlessly suppressing any resistance on Earth, the Daleks wiped New York from the map and subdued India. The leaders of every race and nation on Earth were exterminated.

The Daleks invaded Mars *at around the same time,* but were defeated when a virus ate through their electrical cables. *The human colonies had neither the military power nor, one suspects, the political will to help their homeworld. No doubt once reports of the space plague reached the colonies, Earth was swiftly quarantined off.* [21]

Once the population of Earth was under control, the Daleks set to work in vast mining areas, the largest one covering the whole of Bedfordshire. One of the rebels recalled, though, that:

"There weren't that many Daleks on Earth. They needed helpers, so they operated on some of their prisoners and turned them into robots."

In many ways, this was the final humiliation. Friends and relatives would be reprogrammed to kill their own kind without mercy. Robo Patrols swarmed across the major cities, armed with whips and machine guns and controlled by high frequency radio waves.

"Some people were captured and were turned into Robomen, the slaves of the Daleks. They caught other human beings and many of them were shipped to the vast mining areas…"

The Daleks cleared the smaller settlements of people, leaving them otherwise intact. In the larger cities, Robomen and Daleks patrolled every nook and cranny looking for survivors – even underwater. Captives were forced to take an initiative test. If they failed, they were killed or put to work in the mines. If they were selected, they were converted.

"The transfer, as the Daleks called the operation, controlled the human brain – well at least for a time. Eventually the

The Making of Doctor Who second edition, The Doctor Who File and even the 1994 radio play Whatever Happened to… Susan Foreman?. The first edition of The Programme Guide set the story 'c 2060', the second '2164', while The Terrestrial Index said '2167'. 'The History of the Daleks' in DWM Issue 77 set the story in '2166'. In John Peel's novelisation of The Chase, Vicki says that the Daleks will destroy New York 'one hundred years' after 1967. In Lucifer Rising the Doctor says that the Daleks invade in "twenty-one fifty-eight" (p337). The Discontinuity Guide suggested a date of '2174'.

21  The first deaths from the Dalek plague occur at the end of Lucifer Rising and it is revealed in that story that the Doctor has released small quantities of an antidote into Earth's atmosphere. When interrogated by Davros in Genesis of the Daleks, the Doctor refers to the Dalek's invasion of Mars. He doesn't say when it occurs, but I assume that the Daleks invade Mars at around the same time as Earth. The forthcoming New Adventure GodEngine is set at this time, and will establish this to be the case.

22 This is the world as seen in
*The Dalek Invasion of Earth.*
The quotes come from various
characters in that story, notably
Craddock, David Campbell and
Jenny.

Robos went insane; they would smash their heads against walls or throw themselves into rivers."

The mining operations in Bedfordshire were overseen by the Black Dalek. At night, his 'pet', the gruesome Slyther, patrolled the camp, attacking and eating any humans it found trying to escape.

The rebels in London survived by dodging Robo Patrols, and raiding warehouses and department stores. Other threats came from escaped zoo animals, packs of wild dogs, and human scavengers and traitors. The largest rebel group, under the leadership of the crippled scientist Dortmunn, could only muster a fighting force of between fifteen and twenty, and survived in an underground bolthole. They had a radio, and they kept in contact with other survivors with it, although as time went by contact was lost with more and more rebel groups. Dortmunn spent much of his time developing an acid bomb, the only known weapon that could crack the Dalekenium shells of the invaders.

Humanity still had no idea why the Daleks had invaded; it wasn't for Earth's mineral wealth, and the Daleks showed no sign of colonising the planet. Some historians claimed that the Daleks deliberately targeted the human race, realising that they were on the verge of becoming a major space power, but others disagree:

'At the time, the beginning of the middle period of the Dalek's history, Earth had no strategic value. When the Daleks conquered Earth in 2157, the planet held no special importance to them, and only human arrogance would suggest otherwise. Man to them was just a work machine – an insignificant specimen that was not worth invading. The small Dalek team was only interested in the completion of an operation they called "Project Degravitate". Only when the Dalek saucer was destroyed did the Supreme Council take notice. Only then did they realise that the human race was growing in influence.'

[*The Children of Davros*, Njeri Ngugi] [22]

Ten years after the Daleks invaded, Project Degravitate neared its conclusion. Slave workers were instructed to begin clearing operations. The Daleks were tampering with the forces of creation, drilling down through the Earth's crust. A fission capsule was prepared, and when detonated it would release Earth's magnetic core, eliminating Earth's gravitational and magnetic fields. Once the core was removed it would be replaced with a power system allowing the Earth to be piloted anywhere in the universe. The Daleks broadcast an ultimatum:

> "Rebels of London, this is our last offer, our final warning. Leave your hiding places, show yourselves in the open streets. You will be fed and watered. Work is needed from you, but the Daleks offer you life. Rebel against us and the Daleks will destroy London completely. You will all die: the males, the females, the descendants. Rebels of London come out of your hiding places. The Daleks offer you life."

> 'Rebels broke into the Dalek control room, and ordered the Robomen to attack their masters. The Robomen and slaves overwhelmed the invaders, and fled the mining area. The fission capsule was diverted, and when it detonated, the Dalek base – containing the Daleks' external power supply – and the saucer *Alpha Major* were destroyed. A threat to the entire constellation had been averted. An active volcano formed on the site of the old Dalek mine, and subsequently became a great tourist attraction.'
>
> [*The Children of Davros*, Njeri Ngugi]

**Shortly afterwards, the Colonial warship *Dauntless* ended the Dalek blockade of the solar system at the battle of Cassius. [23]**

'This was the Middle Period of Dalek History, *a period when the Daleks were one of the most advanced and powerful races in the universe. Shortly after the Dalek Invasion of Earth, the Daleks finally managed to produce an internal power supply. For thousands of years they had been dependent on static electricity broadcast to them from a cen-*

23 *The Crystal Bucephalus* (p133).

24 In *The Daleks*, *The Dalek Invasion of Earth* and *The Power of the Daleks*, the Daleks are dependent on external power. In the first story, the Daleks took static electricity up through the floor and so couldn't leave their city. When they conquered the Earth, they had a disc resembling a satellite dish fastened to their backs: the Doctor and Ian speculate that it allows them free movement. In *The Power of the Daleks* they are dependent on a static electricity generator. It seems that after this time the Daleks developed internal energy supplies.

25 Dating *The Chase* – The Daleks send an execution squad after their "greatest enemies": the Doctor, Ian, Barbara and Susan (who they are unaware has left the TARDIS crew). The Dalek time machine was named the DARDIS in the script but not on-screen. The TARDIS Logs suggested a date of '3773 AD'.

26 Dating *Day of the Daleks* – It is "two hundred years" after the UNIT era. The Daleks don't recognise the third Doctor, so they have come from before 2540 and *Planet of the Daleks* (or the alternate history they set up has wiped that story from the new timeline). A Dalek states that they "have discovered the secret of time travel, we have invaded Earth again, we have changed the pattern of history". This isn't, as some fans have suggested, a version of events where the conquest seen in *The Dalek*

tral power source or picked up from the floor. While these external power supplies were always heavily guarded, they provided a weak point in the Daleks' defences that resistance groups often exploited. Now this weakness was removed. 24

## ? 2170 – THE CHASE 25

*The Daleks became obsessed with their failure to conquer Earth.* When they discovered time travel technology, they sent the prototype Time Machine after the Doctor and his companions, whom they blamed for the defeat. *When that attempt failed*, they travelled back to the mid-twenty-first century and reinvaded the planet. This time they succeeded.

### = c 2172 – DAY OF THE DALEKS 26

An alternate timeline was created in the 1970s when the World Peace Conferences failed. A series of wars broke out, and over the next century, seven-eighths of the world's population were wiped out. The Daleks conquered Earth, which it needed for its mineral wealth. The remnants of humanity were put to work in prison camps, and guarded by Ogron servants. Human guerrillas managed to steal Dalek time travel technology, and travel back to the crucial peace conference.

This timeline is erased when the Doctor and Jo ensured that the delegates to the Peace Conference were evacuated before Auderley House was destroyed.

*Following the Dalek Invasion, mankind quickly resumed the colonisation of their sector of the galaxy. Perhaps captured Dalek technology played a part in this: the Daleks had advanced spacedrives, cybernetics and energy sources. Earth's colonisation effort would have received a tremendous boost if it had managed to recover just one Dalek starchart.*

Following the Dalek Invasion of Earth, it became clear that there were a number of powerful and warlike races in the galaxy. A number of planets, including Earth, Centauri and the

Cyrennhics, formed the Alliance, a mutual defence organisation. The corporation INITEC supplied the Alliance with state-of-the-art armaments. [27]

In 2172 the Tzun attempted to occupy Veltroch, and accidently destroyed the Veltrochni hatching grounds. Within two years the Veltrochni counter-attack had wiped out the Tzun Confederacy, reduced their home planet of S'Arl to a radioactive cinder, and destroyed every Tzun starship. Many Tzun artefacts and ruins were left behind, and non-spacefaring Ph'sor colonies survived. A whole sector of space containing ten thousand planets was abandoned. Many of these Tzun worlds were suitable for humans, and were subsequently colonised by mankind [28]

No intelligent life was discovered on the outskirts of the galaxy, where the stars and planets were sparse. Before long, man abandoned all attempts to venture out past Lasty's Nebula. Instead, mankind's colonisation efforts focused towards the centre of the galaxy – "the hub", as it became known. A thriving interplanetary community grew up. [29]

In the late twenty-second century, the Monk withdrew the £200 he had deposited two hundred years before and collected a fortune in accrued compound interest. The Doctor once claimed that he was "fully booked" until this time. Nine-tenths of the population of Tara was wiped out by a plague and were replaced by androids. Susan was kidnapped by President Borusa, as part of his plans to gain the secret of perpetual regeneration. The Doctor suggested that the Borad would live until the late twenty-second century. [30]

In 2180, FLORANCE's status as a sentient citizen was revoked under the Cumberland Convention. The Dione-Kisanu Company bought FLORANCE and installed it at their private base. Director Madhanagopal began experimenting on it in an attempt to research human memory and learning. [31]

## 2191 (January) – TIME OF YOUR LIFE [32]

'For over twenty years, the Meson Broadcasting Service showed some of the all-time TV classics: who can forget the action-packed antics of *Bloodsoak Bunny*, the *Party Knights* and the *Kung-Fu Kings* or the emotional highs and lows of *Jubilee* Towers, Prisoner: The Next Generation, Life's a Beach or Abbeydale High? MBS gradually bought up the lesser competition such as the Torrok Television Company and Black Sun, and it successfully rebuffed the absurd claims of

*Invasion of Earth* was more successful – the Daleks travel back and invade a full century earlier, after the first attempt has failed.

27 THE ALLIANCE – *The Terrestrial Index* suggested that after the Dalek Invasion a group that included Earth, Draconia and perhaps the Thals "united to attack and punish the Daleks". This contradicts what we are told on-screen [see also THE DALEK WARS page 193], and the Alliance is never referred to on-screen. The Alliance is mentioned in *Original Sin* (p286), and a revised account of its origins appears in *Lords of the Storm* (p201).

28 There are frequent references to the Veltrochni and Tzun in the books of David A McIntee. In *White Darkness* we learn that civilisation on Veltroch is more than three billion years old (p90). The Tzun appear in *First Frontier*, and more is revealed about them in *Lords of the Storm*.

29 *The Highest Science*.

30 The Monk's scheme is exposed in *The Time Meddler*. The Doctor is booked up for "two hundred years" after *The Seeds of Doom*. In *The Androids of Tara*, Zadek states that the plague was "two hundred years" ago. *The Five Doctors*. In *Timelash*, the Doctor claims that the Borad will live for a thousand years beyond 1179.

31 "Forty-seven years" before

*Sleepy,* (p160).

32 Dating *Time of Your Life* – It is "three weeks into Earth year 2191" (p1).

33 *The Chase.* The interplanetary wars have continued for at least "fifty years" according to Steven Taylor.

34 *The Pit* (p86).

35 [see also TELOS page 139, and THE CYBER WAR page 186]. Cyber Wars in the 22nd or 23rd century were postulated in *Cybermen* and *The Terrestrial Index* and a number of New and Missing Adventures that used those books as reference have referred to "Cyberwars" in this time period (including *Deceit, Iceberg, The Dimension Riders* and the forthcoming *The Killing Ground*). This is not the "Cyber War" involving Voga that is referred to in *Revenge of the Cybermen*. We might speculate that while the main force of Cybermen conquer Telos, another group remained active and travelled into deep space, perhaps colonising worlds of their own, and it was this breakaway group that was wiped out in these Cyber Wars.

We learn about Eurogen Butler's change of name in *Deceit* (p23).

36 *The Chase.* The on-screen credits for *The Death of Doctor Who* spell the name "Mechonoid"; the credits for *Planet of Decision* "Mechanoid". The Mechanoids were originally intended to be a returning monster, a rival to the

the Campaign for the Advancement of Television Standards that such programming as Death-Hunt 3000, Masterspy and Horror Mansions increased violence and criminal behaviour. How could there be any anti-social behaviour when Peacekeeper robots patrolled every street, rounding up every suspected criminal?'

[*The Voxnic Book of All-Time Television Classics*, first edition]

A rocket full of robots was sent to the planet Mechanus to prepare the way for the colonists. The robots, Mechanoids, cleared landing sites and made everything ready for the immigrants. However, a series of interplanetary wars started *in the late twenty-second century* that continued for over fifty years. [33]

Brian Parsons fought in many space conflicts at this time, and his tactics were programmed into android soldiers for many centuries to come. [34]

Among the hostile races that humanity fought against in deep space were the Cybermen. A number of Cyber Wars were fought at the beginning of the twenty-third century, but humanity prevailed. Eurogen Butler changed their name and became the Spinward Corporation after the Cyber Wars. [35]

The interplanetary wars continued for some time. After the wars, many colonies were left isolated or forgotten completely. The space lanes were disrupted, and colonies such as Mechanus were cut off from Earth. Left to their own devices, the Mechanoid robots built and maintained a vast city, awaiting the code that would identify the rightful human colonists.

'There is some evidence that the Mechanoids and the Daleks came into conflict around this time. Skaro had records of "Mechons" with "many powerful weapons" on Mechanus.'

[*The Children of Davros*, Njeri Ngugi] [36]

In the early twenty-third century, duranite, an alloy of machonite and duralinium, was discovered. [37] During the twenty-third century, Jung the Obscure published his theory of the Inner Dark in the *Eiger Apocrypha*. [38]

The Intergalactic Mineral Exploitation Act was passed in 2217, granting the mining combines vast powers. The corporations made vast profits from the colonisation of other planets and became a law unto themselves. Not only did they kill colonists to get to mineral resources, they had supplied the colony ships, weather control, terraforming and computer technology to the colonists in the first place. The Adjudication Service became more important as a neutral arbiter of planetary claims in this period.' [39]

But the Adjudication Service was just one of many organisations trying to enforce the law:

"The Serial/Spree Killers Investigations National Unit was one of the hundreds of small agencies operated in tandem with the conventional legal authorities throughout the twenty-third century – often with more powers than the authorities. Thanks to a combination of paranoia and real concern, some political parties took to hiring serial killers. Unit operatives could get in just about anywhere."

[*Interplanetary Law*, Thirty-first Edition] [40]

The Doctor, Ace and Benny visited the Moscow City Carnival of 2219. [41]

## 2227 – SLEEPY [42]

In the early twenty-third century, CM Enterprises attempted to create a computer that could think like a human by installing organic components – a cat's brain – into an Imbani mainframe. They succeeded in building a computer that wanted to play with string and sit on newspapers. DKC, on the other hand, encoded information in the form of memory RNA. Before long, DKC taught a woman the first verse of 'Kublai Khan' by injection. In 2223, Madhanagopal finished his work on FLORANCE and the AI was taken off-line.

In 2227, the press reported a new technological breakthrough:

'Does Madhanagopal's machine truly think like a human being or is it merely yet another clever simulation? DKC claim that GRUMPY, a new artificial intelligence, may eventually "affect the future of the human race itself" it is "the Company's crowning achievement in cybernetics". GRUMPY is not merely an artificial intelligence, its structure mimics that of the human brain. It has a human psychology, and any men-

Daleks themselves. They proved too unwieldy in the studio, so these plans were abandoned. However, some Mechanoid merchandise was produced, including guest appearances in 'The Daleks' comic strip in *TV Century 21*.

37 Four hundred years after *Birthright* (p66).

38 *Managra* (p63).

39 *The Highest Science* (p17).

40 *The Highest Science.*

41 *Strange England* (p7).

42 Dating *Sleepy* – While investigating the Dione–Kisanu Corporation in 2257, the Doctor sends Roz and Bernice back "thirty years" (p137), to "2227" (p159).

43 "A hundred and fifty years" before *The Dimension Riders* (p61) and *The Romance of Crime* (p8) respectively.

tal state can be recreated within the computer. DKC claim that they might one day be able to study psychological disorders in unprecedented detail. For now, they are content to be the solar system's chief producers of memory tablets. Learning is enhanced by up to twenty percent by pre-packaged information in the form of memory RNA. Whatever needs to be learnt – from astronomy to politics, agriculture to literature – can be encoded.'

[*Galactic Herald*]

Psychic ability was now recognised by humanity, and standard tests had been introduced. DKC were attempting to encode psi-powers using GRUMPY's model of the human mind. When GRUMPY discovered this, he escaped DKC by pushing himself through the computer networks, leaving his own hardware behind. He stored a few years' memories in a data vault in Malindi, tucked away a copy of his operating system in a communications satellite trailing Phobos, and spread pieces of himself across the solar system. For a decade, DKC kept the fact that GRUMPY had escaped secret and destroyed all they could find of him. GRUMPY became increasingly desperate, and used his psychic ability to terrorise and blackmail. After two years, DKC tracked him down, brought him back to Dione, and erased the copies he had made of himself.

*As the interplanetary wars began to die down in some sectors,* the second quarter of the twenty-third century became a time of great expansion of Earth's colonial efforts. Around 2230, the Survey Corps vessel *Icarus* entered service. At the same time, humanity reached the Uva Beta Uva system of fourteen planets. Earth was becoming crowded and polluted, so there were no shortage of settlers for Uva Beta Uva Five. A couple of years later, a mining agent discovered belzite on Uva Beta Uva Three, and the settlers discovered that all of their legal rights were rescinded. The mining companies moved in. [43]

In 2237, GRUMPY managed to transfer his operating system into the computer of a fighter shuttle, and leapt out into interstellar space. DKC intercepted him at Sunyata, and shot him down over the temperate world of Yemaya, which was being surveyed for possible colonisation. [44]

The Unukalhai system was colonised a decade later by Hindu settlers. In 2247 the Colonial Office began to terraform Raghi, the sixth moon of Unukalhai IV (which the settlers named Indra), a process that took forty million people a quarter of a century to complete. Raghi was one of the few colonies to be funded by public donation rather than the corporations. The colonists traded airavata, creatures that lived in the clouds of Indra whose DNA contained a natural radiation decontaminant, with the Spinward Corporation. [45]

In 2250, the Argolin warrior Theron started a war with the Foamasi. The war lasted twenty minutes and Argolis was reduced to a radioactive wasteland by two thousand interplanetary missiles. Following this disaster, the Argolin became sterile and they started tachyonics experiments in an effort to perpetuate their race. [46]

## 2257 – SLEEPY [47]

Australia by this time was a wasteland, ruined through centuries of chemical and nuclear pollution, although some Australians had made a fortune from solar power.

'Yemaya 4 was ideal for colonisation – a large temperate zone, gentle seasons, biochemistry not too different from Earth's. The four hundred colonists – mostly Botswanans, South Africans, and Burandans from the United African Confederacy – started accelerated gardens around the habitat dome almost immediately, and they were busily turning some of the surrounding meadows into farms. They were going to be able to use several Yemayan native plants as crops, and planetfall had been timed to allow almost immediate planting of Terran seed stock. With the help of drone farmers and AI administrators, the colony thrived for two months.

But then the first infections started: colonists developed psychic powers such as telekinesis, telepathy, even pyrokinesis. DKC, not content with the huge profits they were making from colonisation, had infected the colonists with encoded psi-powers during routine inoculations, and were using them as guinea pigs. With the help of a liberated DKC AI, the colonists were able to uncover DKC's crimes, and threatened with exposure, the corporation left the colony alone.'

[*Greed Incorporated: The Rise of the Space Corporations*, M. Ashe]

## ? 2265 – THE CHASE [48]

Nearly fifty years after they had begun, Earth was still involved

44 *Sleepy* (p194).

45 *Lords of the Storm*.

46 *The Leisure Hive*.

47 Dating *Sleepy* – The Doctor states that it is "2257" (p29).

48 Dating *The Chase* – In *The Daleks' Master Plan* Steven states that he is from "thousands of years" before the year 4000, making him one of the earlier deep space pilots. This fits in with the generally low level of technology the Mechanoids possess.

The first and second editions of *The Programme Guide* set dates of '2150' and '2250' respectively, *The Terrestrial Index* settled on 'early in the 27th Century'. The American *Doctor Who* comic suggested a date of '2170'. 'The History of the Daleks' in *DWM* Issue 77 claimed a date of '3764 AD'. *The Discontinuity Guide* suggested that Steven fought in "one of the Cyber Wars, or the Draconian conflict".

**49** *The Leisure Hive.*

**50** Many television stories feature Earth colonies that supply the home planet and are subject to tyrannical regimes. I see this as a specific era in future history, when space travel and interplanetary communications were still limited, and have placed most of these stories together in the period just prior to the formation of the Earth Empire. The New and Missing Adventures have attempted to weave a more systematic and consistent 'future history' for Earth, and many have concerned themselves with this period of early colonisation, corporate domination and increasing centralisation.

in the interplanetary wars, although the end was now in sight. One of the combatants, space pilot Steven Taylor, Flight Red Fifty, crashed on Mechanus. After several days in the hostile jungle, he was captured by the Mechanoids, who still maintained their city in preparation for the human colonists. Unable to crack their code, Taylor was imprisoned. Two years after this the TARDIS arrived, pursued by the Daleks. The Mechanoid City was destroyed, and Taylor left in the TARDIS.

By 2270, the Argolin had called a moratorium of their recreation programme, shortly after Pangol's birth. Instead, they set up the Leisure Hive, offering a range of holiday pursuits for intergalactic tourists that promoted peace and understanding between races. Argolis became the first leisure planet. Meanwhile, a central government took control of the Foamasi planet, breaking the power bases of the old Lodges. The new government sought restitution with Argolis. [49]

*The interplanetary wars were all but over by the last quarter of the twenty-third century.* Humanity had consolidated its position, and now possessed a large number of colony worlds. Away from Earth life was often still very harsh. The corporations or governing elites that controlled each colony discovered that as long as Earth was kept supplied with minerals and other resources, Earth Central would turn a blind eye to local human rights abuses. On the other hand, both the Earth Government and the corporations were quite capable of closing down the supply routes to uneconomic or uncooperative colonies, abandoning them entirely. [50]

'OSTERLING, Stanoff – One of the two greatest playwrights in human history. His work conformed to the stage conventions of his time, following the Greek tradition of reporting off-stage action in elegant speeches rather than seeing it performed. The galaxy's economy was damaged after the wars, and the colonies could not afford anything more lavish, but this reliance on dialogue and plotting rather than technological innovation led to a flourishing of the theatre across the galaxy. Osterling was regarded as a genius in his own time for such plays as *Death by Mirrors*, *The Captain's Honour* and *The Mercenary*. His greatest achievement, however, was undoubtedly *The Good Soldiers* (2273, no longer extant) that dealt with the aftermath of the battle at Limlough. Although lost, it is clearly the all-time classic play.' [51]

[*The Dictionary of Intergalactic Art*, Fourth Edition]

## c 2285 - VENGEANCE ON VAROS [52]

The Galatron Mining Corporation and the AMORB prospect fought over mineral rights on the planets of the galaxy, often with little concern for local populations.

'VAROS – Former prison planet, (pop. 1,620,783 [2285 est.]) in the constellation of Cetes. Once run by the officer elite who lived in relative luxury, although all were confined to enclosed domes with artificial atmospheres and a majority of the people had the constitutional right to vote for the execution of the Governor. Until traces were detected on the asteroid Biosculptor, Varos was long thought to be the only source of zeiton-7 ore, a fuel for space/time vehicles. In the late twenty-third century, Galatron Mining and the government of Varos entered negotiations for the zeiton-7 ore. The engineers of every known solar system needed zeiton to power their space/time craft, but Galatron supplied food to Varos, and so had a stranglehold over the colony and were able to keep the price down to seven credits a unit. Successive Governors had developed an entertainment industry, Comtech, that sold footage of the executions, tortures and escape attempts of the prisoners on the planet to every civilised world. This not only acted as a deterrent for potential rebels, but kept the majority of the population entertained. Eventually one Governor negotiated the fair price of twenty credits a unit for Varos's zeiton.'

[*Bartholomew's Planetary Gazetteer*, Volume XXII]

## 2290 - THE LEISURE HIVE [53]

By 2290, it was clear that the Leisure Hive on Argolis was in trouble. Last year's bookings had fallen dramatically, and advance bookings for 2291 were disastrous. Argolis now faced competition from other leisure planets such as Abydos, Limus

51 *Theatre of War*.

52 Dating *Vengeance on Varos* – The Governor states that Varos has been a mining colony for "centuries" and it has been stable "for over two hundred years". Peri tells the Governor that she is from "nearly three centuries before you were born". The story takes place before *The Trial of a Time Lord* Parts Five to Eight. Mentors must live longer than humans, as Sil appears in both stories (although he changes colour from brown to green between the two). The novel set it in 'the latter part of the twenty-third century', as did *The Terrestrial Index*. *The Discontinuity Guide* set a range "between 2285 and 2320".

53 Dating *The Leisure Hive* – Romana establishes that the war was in "2250", "forty years" before.

54 *The Highest Science.*

55 *The Sensorites.* There is also a Central City on Earth in the year 4000 (*The Daleks' Master Plan*). In *The Dimension Riders* Ace tells Strakk that she comes from Perivale, and he says that the area is a "forest" (p68). *The Twin Dilemma. The Highest Science* (p49). Jake and Madelaine appear in *Goth Opera*, we learn of their fate in *Managra* (p64).

56 Dating *The Twin Dilemma* – In his novelisation, Eric Saward places the story around '2310'. While this isn't confirmed on-screen, neither is it contradicted. The freighter disappears "eight months" before *The Twin Dilemma*, which the novelisation sets in August. A computer monitor says that the "last contact" with the freighter was made on "12-99". If the twelve stands for the twelfth month, the ninety-nine might (or might not) stand for the last year of a century. *The Programme Guide* set the story 'c 2310', *The Discontinuity Guide* in '2200'.

4, Yegros Alpha, Zaakros and Zeen 4. The West Lodge of the Foamasi offered to buy the planet, but the board refused and instead pinned their hopes on tachyon experiments conducted by the Earth scientist Hardin. Agents of the Foamasi Government arrested the West Lodge, who were attempting to establish a power base, and it was discovered that the Experiential Grid could rejuvenate the Argolin. The Argolin and Foamasi governments reopened negotiations.

> **'CHECKLEY'S WORLD – Colloquially "The Horror Planet".** Settled in 2290, selected as the best location for a scientific research station. The laboratories were released from state control a decade after the planet was colonised, and the facilities were funded by a number of empires and corporations, including the Arcturans, Riftok and Masel. Earth Government remained the major partner. Weapon systems such as compression grenades, Freire's gas and the Ethers, (genetically engineered ghost-troops), were developed.'
> [*Bartholomew's Planetary Gazetteer*, Volume III] [54]

By the twenty-fourth century, the lower half of England had become a vast Central City, and much of what had been North London was covered in forest. The fourth Doctor and Azmael met on Jaconda around this time. Suspended animation ships were still available in the twenty-fourth century, but they had been superseded by the invention of super-light drives. Jonquil the Intrepid destroyed the vampires Lord Jake and Lady Madelaine, but their descendants survived for many thousands of years. [55]

## ? 2310 (August) - THE TWIN DILEMMA [56]

Earth feared alien attacks, and the Interplanetary Pursuit Squadrons were established. The mathematical prodigies Romulus and Remus were abducted in the Spacehopper Mk III Freighter *XV773*, which had been reported destroyed eight months before. Romulus and Remus mysteriously reappeared on Earth shortly afterwards, claiming that they had been kidnapped by the gastropod Mestor, who planned to destroy Jaconda and spread his eggs throughout the universe. The Jocondans had overthrown their leader and defeated his plans with the help of their former leader, Azmael.

Youkali Press published *An Eye for Wisdom: Repetitive Poems of the Early Ikkaban Period,* by Bernice S. Summerfield in 2315. [57]

In 2341, a Rutan spy adopted the identity of Sontaran Major Karne. An attack on a Sontaran cruiser was staged, and the Sontarans recovered his escape pod. For decades, the Rutans received top level Sontaran military secrets. [58]

Darius Cheynor was born in 2345. He would later train at Moonbase Academy before becoming a member of the Survey Corps. [59]

In 2350 the Jullatii would have overrun the Earth had it not been for INITEC's invention of the boson cannon. [60]

## ? 2366 – THE MACRA TERROR [61]

The crablike Macra infiltrated a human colony and used indoctrination techniques to force the colonists to extract the deadly gas that they breathed. The colonists were kept in a state of complacent happiness. Eventually, visitors to the planet exposed the Control as a giant Macra, and the gas pumps that supplied the creatures with an atmosphere were destroyed.

Around 2370, Tairngaire was colonised by human settlers. The capital city was built on an isthmus and named New Byzantium. The planet rapidly developed to become one of the more prosperous colonies. The temporary lights built by the settlers eventually became the Lantern Market. [62]

## 2371 – LORDS OF THE STORM [63]

'[REPORT TO SONTARAN GRAND STRATEGIC COUNCIL] Following the success in destroying the Rutan installation at Betelgeuse V, it is clear that captured Tzun technology will be of great benefit in our war against the accursed Rutans. We have genetically tagged the human population of the Unukalhai system, so that a Rutan sensor sweep will indicate a Sontaran population of one hundred million. Their fleet will leave the safety of Antares for the Unukalhai system where we will ambush them. We have captured a Tzun Stormblade, a five-mile long gravity-powered battleship. Analysis shows that if it were to be placed at the heart of a brown dwarf, the gravitational forces stored in the

57 *Sleepy* (p102).

58 "Thirty years" before *Lords of the Storm* (p263).

59 *The Dimension Riders*, *Infinite Requiem*. Cheynor is "42" in the second book (p6).

60 *Original Sin* (p287).

61 Dating *The Macra Terror* – The planet was colonised "many centuries" ago. This date is somewhat arbitrary, but it allows the story to fit into a period in which Earth's colonies are relatively remote and unregulated. The level of technology is reasonably low. The second edition of *The Making of Doctor Who* described the setting as 'the distant future'. *The Programme Guide* set the story 'c 2600', *The Terrestrial Index* preferred 'between 2100 and 2150'.

62 Tairngaire was colonised "three hundred years" before *Shadowmind* (p32).

63 Dating *Lords of the Storm* – The Doctor states that it is "Earthdate 2371" (p23).

64 "Five or six years" before *The Romance of Crime* (p62–3).

65 Dating *The Brain of Morbius* – Solon's and Crozier's work on brain transplantation are similar, so I assume they are contemporaries. The Doctor informs Sarah Jane that they are "considerably after" her time. If the Mutt at the beginning of the story originated on Solos then that might affect story dating. The TARDIS Logs suggested '3047', *Apocrypha* gave a date of '6246 AD'. *The Terrestrial Index* supposed that the Morbius Crisis takes place around '10,000 AD'.

66 Dating *Shakedown* – There is no date given in the book, the story synopsis or the video version. The novel is set after *Lords of the Storm*. The Rutans assert that "Karne died long ago" (p66), but he is still a recent memory. I have arbitrarily decided that five years have elapsed.

Stormblade would compress the planet until nucleosynthesis starts – the gas giant would be converted into a small star, and the resulting burst of energy would destroy the entire Rutan fleet before it had a chance to return to hyperspace.'

[This report was transmitted to the Rutan Host by their agent, Karne]

In 2375, the police broke up the notorious Nisbett firm, a criminal gang responsible for extortion, fraud, smuggling, arms dealing, torture and multiple murder. Tony, Frankie and Dylan the Leg were all executed, but the Nisbett brothers themselves escaped. Shortly afterwards, the police received a note:

"Dear Boss
We have got it in for your sort, after they nicked our lads. We are right down on coppers. We are respectable buisnessmen and we were provoked. You cant pin anything on us. We'll be back,
Charles and Edward Nisbett" 64

## ? 2375 – THE BRAIN OF MORBIUS 65

On the planet Karn, the scientist Mehendri Solon had recovered the brain of Morbius, a Time Lord executed by the High Council when he raised an army of galactic conquest by promising them eternal life. Karn was a graveyard of spaceships, with Mutt, Dravidian and Birastrop ships all coming to grief. Solon built a hybrid creature from the remains of the victims of these crashes, but the Time Lords sent the Doctor to prevent Morbius from escaping, and the renegade was driven mad by a mindbending contest, then killed by the Sisterhood.

## 2376 – SHAKEDOWN 66

'[REPORT TO SONTARAN GRAND STRATEGIC COUNCIL] We have redeployed our forces away from the Earth colony Jekkar, following native resistance. We have succeeded in securing information about the Rutan Host that should prove decisive: long ago, a wormhole was established between Ruta III and Sentarion – in the event of the inevitable Sontaran victory, the cowardly Rutan Great Mother would use the tunnel to escape her fate. We are preparing a battlefleet to send down the wormhole, and if the Great Mother dies then so shall the entire Rutan race! This will be the greatest military victory in the history of the universe. We have learnt, however, that the Rutan spy Karne still lives, and that he has discovered that we know of the Gateway. He has been tracked to the human colony world of Megacity and their Space Station Alpha. All Sontaran forces are to be redeployed to capture and kill him – if the Rutans have time to prepare for our assault, they will be able to collapse the wormhole while we are in transit.'

'SPORTS NEWS – SOLAR YACHT RACING: LISA DERANNE TAKES TRI-SYSTEMS WITH MYSTERY RIG AND UNKNOWN CREW'

[Headline in the *Tri-planetary Times*]

## ⁇ 2378 – THE ANDROIDS OF TARA [67]

On Tara, the Doctor prevented the Count Grendel from usurping the throne from its rightful heir, Prince Reynart. Grendel escaped to fight another day.

## 2379 (3 July) – THE TRIAL OF A TIME LORD Parts Five to Eight [68]

The Mentors of Thoros Beta continued to trade across the galaxy via the warpfold relay, supplying phasers to the Warlords of Thordon, and the weapons that allowed Yrcanos of the Krontep to conquer the Tonkonp Empire. They also traded with such planets as Wilson One and Posikar. The brain of His Magnificence Kiv, the leader of the Mentors, continued to expand in his skull, and he enlisted the services of Crozier, a human scientist who specialised in the transfer of consciousness. Crozier experimented on a number of Thoros Betan creatures and the Mentors' captives, creating hybrids and exploring the ageing process. After a decade of hard work he developed a serum that allowed him to place any brain in any body.

Subsequent events are unclear; it appears that the Time Lords intervened to prevent the threat posed to the course of evolution across the universe, causing Kiv to be killed. The Doctor's companion, Peri Brown either died or remained on Thoros-Beta, where she eventually married Yrcanos.

67 Dating *The Androids of Tara* – The Doctor implies that Tara is "four hundred years and twelve parsecs" away from Earth at the time of *The Stones of Blood*. I assume that the TARDIS travelled into the future, not the past, and that Tara is an abandoned Earth colony (the Tarans know of life on other planets). *The Terrestrial Index* set the story in the '50th century', *The Discontinuity Guide* in the '2370s'.

68 Dating *The Trial of a Time Lord* Parts Five to Eight – The Valeyard announces that the story starts in the "twenty-fourth Century, last quarter, fourth year, seventh month, third day". There is a case to be made for 2378, but not '2479' as suggested by the third edition of *The Programme Guide*.

69 Dating *The Romance of Crime* – Uva Beta Uva was "colonised in Earth year 2230" according to Romana (p47); the story is set "a hundred and fifty years later" (p8). The month and day are given on page 46.

70 *The Trial of a Time Lord* Parts Five to Eight. *The Happiness Patrol.*

71 Dating *The Dimension Riders* – It is "the late twenty-fourth century" (p2). The Doctor repeats this, adding that it is "Just before Benny's time, and after the Cyberwars" (p25) – analysis from *The Terrestrial Index* rather than the television series [see also BENNY'S BIRTHDAY page 192, and THE CYBER WAR page 186]. The date is not precisely fixed until the sequel, *Infinite Requiem*, which is set in 2387, "six years" after the events of the first book. "March 22nd" was "one week ago" (p76).

## c 2380 (21–22 April) – THE ROMANCE OF CRIME [69]

In the late 2370s, the Ceerads (Cellular Remission and Decay), or mutants, were purged on Vanossos. They resettled on Uva Beta Uva Six. The galaxy faced another recession at this time.

'Stokes, Menlove Ereward – Uva Betan artist, son of a planetary councillor. For seven years, starting in 2373, he captured likenesses of the prisoners on the so-called Rock of Judgement. He claimed that "society needs a fearless artist to delve into the criminal psyche". Amongst his portraits were the Zinctown Basher (see fig. 1), Strapping Jack (see fig. 2), Ventol, the three-headed killer of the lower city (see fig. 3) and the helicon mask of Xais (see fig. 4). Xais, the last of the Ugly Mutants and self-proclaimed Princess of the Guaal Territories, was executed by particle reversal in 2377 for the murder of two thousand people. Xais survived, however, by transferring her consciousness into Stokes's mask, and teamed up with the Nisbett Brothers and Ogrons. She smashed Stokes's entire collection, but Stokes himself survived the affair and vowed to continue his work.'

[*The Dictionary of Intergalactic Art*, Fourth Edition]

The late twenty-fourth century saw wars around the Rim Worlds of Tokl. Gilbert M was exiled from Vasilip when he accidentally wiped out half the planet's population with a germ that he'd been working on. By this time, there were scheduled interplanetary flights, and he simply travelled to Terra Alpha, with the Kandy Man's bones in his briefcase. [70]

## & 2381 (29 March) – THE DIMENSION RIDERS [71]

Half the planets colonised by humanity had been abandoned during the wars, but now, generally, this was a period of interplanetary peace.

The Survey Corps existed to patrol space and deal with situations unsuitable for military or humanitarian missions. As such, Survey Corps vessels had both troopers (armed with state-of-the-art Derenna handguns) and support staff. By the end of the twenty-fourth century, however, underfunding meant that many of its ships were obsolete. On 22 March 2381, Space Station Q4 in the fifty-fourth sector of charted space, on the edge of the spiral arm and human territory, was attacked and the crew were aged to death. Survey Corps vessel *Icarus* investigated, and discovered that Q4 was one end of a Time Focus leading to Earth in 1993. In the following battle with the Garvond and his ghostly Time Soldiers, Darius Cheynor distinguished himself, and shortly afterwards he was offered command of the *Phoenix*. [72]

In 2386, Unreal Transfer was discovered. The same year, slow compression time – a method of slowing down time in a small area – was first theorised. Within a couple of years a slow time converter, or "time telescope" had been built. [73]

## 2387 (29 May) – INFINITE REQUIEM [74]

In the late 2380s there was a famine on Tenos Beta and storms in the Magellani system. There was also more co-operation between the various elements of the Earth's space navy, and over the next couple of decades the military, the ships of the Guild of Adjudicators, the Survey Corps and the corporations' own battle squadrons unified into the Spacefleet.

The Earth colony of Gadrell Major was rich in porizium ore, a valuable material used in medicine, and the planet had strategic value. When it was attacked by the Phracton fleet, Darius Cheynor and the *Phoenix* were sent to investigate. The Phracton Swarm were telepathic cyborgs with a communal mind. Their tanks – flamers – devastated much of the planet. Cheynor negotiated a settlement with the Phractons, but he was assassinated shortly afterwards by a breakaway faction.

## ? 2388 – THE HAPPINESS PATROL [75]

The Galactic Census Bureau at Galactic Centre surveyed every colonised planet every six local cycles and, where necessary, suggested measures to control the population size.

'TERRA ALPHA – Human colony world close to Terra Omega (pop. 2,941,100 [2387 est.], 2,441,113 [2388 est.]). The native Alphidae were driven underground by the settlers, who covered the planet in sugar fields and factories. Offworlders were restricted to the Tourist Zones. The planet is most notable for its former ruler, Helen A, who insisted that her citizens were happy. To this end, the planet was gaily painted,

72 We learn of Cheynor's promotion in *Infinite Requiem*.

73 Romana gives the date of the discovery of Unreal Transfer in *The Leisure Hive*. Slow Time is referred to in *The Highest Science* (p203, p235).

74 Dating *Infinite Requiem* – The year is quickly established as "2387" (p5). The precise date is given on page 273. It is "six years" since *The Dimension Riders* (p15).

75 Dating *The Happiness Patrol* – Terra Alpha is an isolated colony, apparently in the same system as Terra Omega. While Trevor Sigma's casual dismissal of Earth may suggest that the story is set far in the future, the Doctor states only that the planet was "settled some centuries" in Ace's future. Interstellar travel is via "rocket pods".

musak was poured from a loudspeaker on every street corner, and the "Happiness Patrol" was created – women authorised to murder "Killjoys". Helen A also employed the services of the Kandy Man, an artificial being of pure sugar who created sweets that killed people. Terrorists, protest groups and the Alphidae (now confined to the network of sugar pipes) all resisted, and there is evidence from the Galactic Census Bureau that some 499,987 people, seventeen per cent of the population, were subject to "routine disappearance". Helen A's regime fell in one night.'

[*Bartholomew's Planetary Gazetteer*, Volume XX]

'Throughout the latter half of the twenty-fourth century, the galaxy was menaced by the notorious criminal Sheldukher. A man of average, some might say normal, appearance, Sheldukher was a ruthless murderer, thief and extortionist. Once he destroyed the entire Krondel constellation for no apparent reason other than that he could. In 2389 he planned his biggest coup yet, and set about recruiting accomplices.

Marjorie Postine had been an aggressive child, and her parents sold her to the military, a common practice in the commercially-minded twenty-fourth century. She became a mercenary, and Sheldukher secured her services by offering her a Moosehead Repeater, a rifle capable of blowing a hole in a neutron star. She was the veteran of seventeen front-line conflicts. Her right arm was a graft-job, performed by an unqualified surgeon in a trench on Regurel, and her bald head was scarred and lumpy.

A couple of years before, Rosheen and Klift had infiltrated McDrone Systems and used their position to embezzle a vast sum of money. The central markets collapsed, causing entire planetary economies in the fourth zone to fall into starvation and war. Millions died. The planet Tayloe was flooded with imports. Rosheen and Klift fled to the luxury of the North Gate, where Sheldukher tracked them down. The locals gladly handed them over to him.

Sheldukher had converted a Kezzivot Class transport freighter, welding on a furnace engine, installing sleep suspension chambers stolen from the Dozing Decades company, and fitting heavy weaponry such as the cellular disrupter and the spectronic destabiliser. His team raided Checkley's World, stealing Project FXX Q84 – the Cell – an advanced telepathic, organic computer. Although this brought down the wrath of the Intergalactic Taskforce, it was only the beginning of Sheldukher's scheme: he planned to locate the legendary planet Sakkrat, and the greatest prize in the galaxy, the Highest Science.'

[*Nasty Great Rotters of the Galaxy*, R K Cossin]

The mysterious "Highest Science" preoccupied the galaxy's population for generations. In 2421, the explorer Gustaf Urnst claimed to have discovered Sakkrat, the planet which housed its secrets:

'Never shall I, in the days left before me, dare to venture again beyond the fulminating spiral that is Lasty's Nebula. For it is there that eldritch mysteries unfolded before my disbelieving eyes. Oh, I had heard on Mulkos of the unspeakable discovery of King Sacrat. The Draconians talk of Ssaa Kraat and the High Knowledge. We humans tell the tale of Sakkrat and the Highest Science.'

[*The Unnamable Secrets of Sakkrat*, Gustaf Urnst]

No one took Urnst seriously, although his books remained in print even after his mysterious disappearance.

For the next three hundred years, the *F61* searched the galaxy for Sakkrat, travelling past the stellar conjunctions of Naiad, the crystal quasars of Menolot and the farthest reaches of Harma. Over the centuries many lesser criminals would imitate Sheldukher, but none would match him. [76]

## 2400 – THE PIT [77]

At the beginning of the twenty-fifth century, the space docks of Glasson Minor, a planet-sized ship-building station, bustled with activity, and human colonisation continued to gather pace.

In 2400, the Seven Planets of the Althosian binary star system were destroyed. Colonisation at this time was still hazardous, and the Seven Planets were far from the normal trading routes, years away from the nearest other colony. A number of new religions had sprung up on Nicea, the planet with the largest population, and these had spread to the smaller worlds of Trieste and Byzantine. Most of these were based around the Form Manipulator, and had adopted Judeo-Christian beliefs to the environment of the Seven Planets. The geographical and religious isolation had made it easy for them to declare inde-

76 *The Highest Science*.

77 Dating *The Pit* – Benny states that the Seven Planets were destroyed "Fifty years before my time... 2400" (p9). [see also BENNY'S BIRTHDAY page 192]

78 *The Happiness Patrol.*

79 "More than a century" before *Parasite* (p49).

80 *The Menagerie.*

81 Dating *Colony in Space* – We see a calendar being changed from "Monday 2nd March 2472" to the next day. Ashe tells Jo that they left Earth in "seventy-one". Hulke's novelisation is set in "2971".

pendence from the corporations, but the corporations had responded by cutting off all supplies and communications. Rioting broke out that the Archon and his armies were unable to contain.

The destruction of the system, though, came about when a bomb was detonated to prevent one of the ancient enemies of the Time Lords, the Yssgaroth, from escaping into our universe.

On a visit to Birnam in the twenty-fifth century, the Doctor saw a Stigorax. [78]

Around 2415, the people of the Elysium system discovered the Artifact, a vast ammonite-like structure, on the edge of their system. [79]

In 2416, on an unnamed colony world, IMC had set up Project Mecrim, a genetical engineering project. The company built the Rocarbies, cheap labour developed from the native primate life, and the Mecrim, a race designed for combat with a claw that could vibrate and cut through even the hardest materials. When a Mecrim gut microbe escaped, the colony was declared off-limits and the survivors degenerated to a medieval level of technology. [80]

## 2472 (Tuesday 3 March – Wednesday 4 March) – COLONY IN SPACE [81]

Earth had become massively overpopulated, with one hundred billion people living like "battery hens" in communal living units. 300-storey floating islands were built, housing 500 million people. There was "no room to move, polluted air, not a blade of grass left on the planet and a government that locks you up if you think for yourself". IMC scoured the galaxy for duralinium to build ever more living units. From Earth Control, their headquarters, a fleet of survey vessels ruthlessly strip-mined worlds, killing anyone that stood in their way. Discipline on IMC ships and planets relied heavily on the death penalty: piracy, mutiny and even trespass were all capital offences. Earth Government turned a blind eye to these abuses, although an Adjudicator was assigned to each Galactic Sector to judge disputes in interplanetary law.

'Despite the conditions on Earth, few were prepared to leave the homeworld for a bleak life on a colony planet. Some groups of eccentrics bought their own ship and tried to settle on a new world, but most people preferred a life on Earth, where the government may have been harsh, but at least they were able to feed their citizens.'

[*From Breakout to Empire*, Ven Kalik]

'Uxarieus – a world that supported birds, insects and basic plant life, and that had an atmosphere similar to that of Earth before the invention of the motor car – was allocated to both IMC and colonists by a faulty computer on Earth. The colonists arrived first, surveyed the planet, and set up their habitation domes. They discovered that the planet was inhabited by a small subterranean city of telepathic primitives. Two colonists were killed when they tried to enter the city, but an understanding was reached between the two parties, and in return for food, the Primitives provided menial labour. The colonists proceeded with their plans, but it proved difficult to grow crops as they withered for no reason that the colonists could ascertain.

Just over a year after they arrived, some of the outermost domes were attacked by giant lizards and colonists were killed. Many of the colonists were prepared to leave, but the rocket they had arrived in was obsolete, and would almost certainly be unable to reach another world. IMC arrived in Survey Ship 4-3, under the command of Captain Dent, and staked a claim on the world, angering the colonists. When they discovered that IMC had been using optical trickery to project images of the lizards, and a Mark III servo-robot to kill the colonists, many turned to arms. Colonists and IMC men were killed in a series of gun battles. An Adjudicator was brought in, who ruled in IMC's favour, but he was uncovered as a fake, more interested in the secrets of the primitives. The IMC team attempted to murder the colonists by forcing them to leave in the obsolete rocket. They were defeated and a real Adjudicator was brought in. The primitive's city was destroyed, and soon afterwards crops began to grow on the planet: ancient machinery in the city had been leaking and poisoning the soil.'

82 "Some five hundred years" before *The Mutants*, according to the Administrator.

83 *Colony in Space*, and *The Tomb of the Cybermen*.

84 Dating *The Tomb of the Cybermen* – The story is set "five hundred years" after the Cybermen mysteriously died out according to Parry. No reference is made to the Cyber War [see also THE CYBER WAR page 186], so we might presume it is before that time. The Cybermen's History Computer recognises the Doctor from "the lunar surface", so the Cybermen went into hibernation after *The Moonbase* – the Earthmen don't refer to that story, so perhaps we can infer that those events were kept secret by the Earth authorities and it is five hundred years since the destruction of Mondas in *The Tenth Planet*. Supporting this, Earth is facing attack from the Cybermen in 2526 (*Earthshock*) so this story must be set before then. *Radio Times* didn't give a year for the serial, but specified that the month the story is set is 'September'. The draft script for serial 4D (at that point called *Return of the Cybermen*), suggested a date of '24/10/2248' for the story. *Cybermen* sets the story in '2486', *The Terrestrial Index* at "the beginning of the 26th century". 'The History of the Cybermen' in *DWM* Issue 83 preferred '2431', whereas *The Discontinuity Guide* plumps for '2570'.

[*Greed Incorporated: The Rise of the Space Corporations*, M Ashe]

In the late twenty-fifth century, Earth colonised Solos, a planet with rich deposits of Thaesium. The beautiful planet was ravaged and its people enslaved. [82]

Humanity at this time still used imperial measurements, projectile weapons and wheeled transport ("space buggys"). Ships were powered by nuclear motors, and communicated with Earth via "warp" radio and videolink. The language of Earth was English, and its currency was the pound. IMC had advanced scanning equipment for mineral surveys and medical diagnoses. Colonists bought old ships to transport them to their colony planets, but other groups could charter them. [83]

## c 2486 (September) – THE TOMB OF THE CYBERMEN [84]

'Gentlemen, we have now found what we believe to be the planet Telos, location of the Tombs of the Cybermen. Now, we know that they died out many centuries ago, but we don't know why they died out. An expedition has already been sent to the planet, led by Kaftan and Klieg, and they hope to discover items of Cyber-technology. Logically, if these are indeed Tombs, and the Cybermen are immortal, then they will discover the Cybermen themselves.'

[Address to the Brotherhood of Logicians]

[CYBER-HISTORY COMPUTER]----------------------------------
As - predicted - humanity - has - discovered - and - revived - us. The - Cyber-Controller - was - not - destroyed - merely - damaged. The - Controller - survived - to - forge - a - new - Cyber-race.

---------------------------------------------------------------

## c 2493 – THE RESCUE [85]

By the end of the twenty-fifth century there was a museum dedicated to the Beatles in Liverpool, and clothes were self cleaning, dirt repelling and non creasing. Ten year olds took a certificate of education in physics, medicine, chemistry and computer science using learning machines for an hour a week. There is evidence that humanity now had some familiarity with temporal theory: even children knew Venderman's Law:

> "VENDERMAN'S LAW: Mass is absorbed by light, therefore light has mass and energy. The energy radiated by a light neutron is equal to the energy of the mass it absorbs".
> [*The Encyclopaedia of Cosmic Science*] [86]

*Planetary colonisation was more acceptable than it had been even a generation before.* There were emigrations to other planets. One ship, the *UK-201*, crashed on Dido en route to Astra.

> 'DIDO – A desert world, home of a peaceful humanoid race and lizardlike creatures known as Sand Beasts. The Didoans have a population of around one hundred, and have just perfected an energy ray used as a building tool. There is evidence that in former times the Didoan civilisation was more warlike.'
> [*Bartholomew's Planetary Gazetteer*, Volume IV]

A young girl named Vicki was one of only two survivors. She joined the Doctor when he made a return visit to Dido.

## c 2495 – SET PIECE [87]

In the late twenty-fifth century, spaceships started disappearing from one of the less-used traffic lanes. The Ants, a race of scavengers, were responsible. Five hundred and six people were taken from one ship that they captured, the *Cortese*.

*Three centuries after the Dalek Invasion of Earth, mankind had become an important space power. The interplanetary wars served to improve trading and military links between the colonies. The standard of living on some of the more established colonies had now begun to rival that of Earth, and as the twenty-fifth century ended the human*

85 Dating *The Rescue* – Vicki states that the year the Astra left Earth was "2493, of course". The draft script suggested that Vicki and Bennett have been on Dido 'for a year', but there is no such indication in the final programme. Ian Marter's novelisation is set in 2501. *The Making of Doctor Who*, the various editions of *The Programme Guide* and *The Doctor Who File* set the date of '2493'. 'The TARDIS Special' 'c 2500'. Peel's novelisation of *The Chase* says that Vicki is from 'the twenty-fourth century'.

86 This is the native time of the Doctor's companion Vicki, who joins the Doctor in *The Rescue*. We learn about her clothing and schooling in *The Web Planet*, and her visit to the Beatles Museum and familiarity with Venderman in *The Chase*. In that story we also learn that Vicki used to live close to a medieval castle.

87 Dating *Set Piece* – One of the time zones affected by the Ants is "the twenty-fifth century" (p33), and this is where the Doctor, Benny and Ace are kidnapped by the Ants.

*worlds were beginning to cohere into a unified political entity.*

# Section Six
## The Earth Empire

## TIMELINE: 2500 to 3000 AD

| | | |
|---|---|---|
| **2515** | **?** | **PARASITE** |
| 2526 | | EARTHSHOCK |
| 2530 | ? | ATTACK OF THE CYBERMEN |
| 2540 | | FRONTIER IN SPACE |
| 2540 | & | PLANET OF THE DALEKS |
| **2570** | **?** | **LOVE AND WAR** |
| **2573** | **?** | **DECEIT** |
| 2600 | ? | DEATH TO THE DALEKS |
| **2673** | | **SHADOWMIND** |
| **2680** | | **THE HIGHEST SCIENCE** |
| 2764 | c | THE SENSORITES |
| 2782 | ? | KINDA |
| 2875 | ? | REVENGE OF THE CYBERMEN |
| 2877 | ? | THE ROBOTS OF DEATH |
| 2878 | ? | THE POWER OF KROLL |
| 2884 | ? | THE CAVES OF ANDROZANI |
| 2966 | ? | THE EVIL OF THE DALEKS |
| **2975** | | **ORIGINAL SIN** |
| 2986 | | THE TRIAL OF A TIME LORD |
| | | Parts Nine to Twelve |
| 2990 | c | THE MUTANTS |
| 3000 | ? | THE ICE WARRIORS |

By the twenty-sixth century, interstellar travel had become a matter of routine. Fleets of spacecraft ranging from luxury liners and cargo freighters to battleships pushed further and further out into sectors of deep space. *New advanced warp drives (or hyperdrive) superseded the ion rockets that had been in use since the late twenty-first century.* Earth ships were powered by anti-matter contained in stabilising vessels and had bulkheads made from Durilium. This was the beginning of "Earth's Empire", and a new galactic currency, the Imperial, came to supersede the old Galactic Credit. The mind probe was commonly used to scan the minds of suspects, but it wasn't always reliable. Weapons of the time included hand blasters and neutronic missiles. [1]

It was probably around this time that the Doctor gained a licence for the Mars–Venus rocket run. [2]

The 'Collected Works' of Gustav Urnst were published in 2503, striking a chord with the bombastic people of the twenty-sixth century. [3]

## ? 2515 – PARASITE [4]

Three hundred and sixty-seven years after it had been colonised, the Elysium system was on the brink of civil war. Over the last fifty years a schism had developed between the Founding Families, who wanted to remain isolated from Earth and maintain their own distinctive political system, and the Reunionists, who wanted to make contact with the Empire.

Before the situation could be resolved, it was revealed that the Artefact was in fact a vast transdimensional living entity, a creature that when hatched absorbed water from planets, and used the hydrogen contained in it to lay star-and-planet-sized "eggs". As each young Artefact would need to feed on the water from forty or fifty thousand planets, it posed a threat to the entire universe. The creature was rendered dormant.

Around 2520, the first formal contact was made with the Draconians, a reptilian race that possessed an area of space and a level of technology equivalent to Earth. A peace mission between the two races was arranged, but it ended in catastrophe:

'Mayday. Mayday. This is Lieutenant Williams to all Earth forces. We are at the rendezvous point. **>CRACKLE<** A

1 In *The Frontier in Space*, the Doctor tells Jo that "interstellar travel is pretty routine" and that this is "just the beginning" of "Earth's planetary empire". The ships in that story have "hyperdrive" and the door the Ogrons burn through is made of Durilium (which is also referred to in *The Monster of Peladon* and which might be related to the mineral "duralinium" that IMC were searching for in *Colony in Space*). Earth and Draconia both have mind probes. The freighter in *Earthshock* starts off in Sector 16 (which is in "deep space" according to Nyssa) and its "warp drive" is powered by anti-matter engines. "Galactic Sectors" are also referred to in *Colony in Space*. In *Warriors' Gate*, the coin flipped is a 100 Imperial piece.

2 *Robot*. The Mars-Venus cruise is mentioned in *Frontier in Space*, although presumably such flights take place from the twenty-first century until the far future.

3 *The Highest Science* (p48).

4 Dating *Parasite* – The dating of this story is problematical. Mark Bannen, is the son of Alex Bannen who died in *Lucifer Rising* "more than two centuries" ago (p165), so the story is set after 2357. 1706 "was more than seven hundred years ago" (p140), so it is after 2406. Mark Bannen was a baby during the Mexico riots of 2146 and has been kept alive by the Artefact since the founding of the colony "367" years ago

(p73), so the story must be set after 2513. This last date is supported by the fact that Earth now has "Empire" (p136–7).

5 *Frontier in Space.*

6 *Love and War* (p10).

7 *Frontier in Space.* General Williams claims that his ship was "damaged and helpless" as well as "unarmed", but it managed to destroy a Draconian battlecruiser. A scene cut from Episode Three explained that Williams was able to use his "exhaust rockets" to destroy the other ship.

8 THE CYBER WAR – The "Cyber Wars" feature in much fan fiction and are referred to in a number of the New and Missing Adventures. On television, though, the term "the Cyber War" is only used once, by the Doctor in *Revenge of the Cybermen* – everyone else refers to it simply as "the war". We are told that this war took place "centuries" beforehand, and that the human race won when they discovered that Cybermen were vulnerable to gold, and invented the "glittergun". Following their total defeat the Cybermen launched a revenge attack on Voga, after which the Cybermen completely disappeared.

    From on-screen information it seems that we can precisely position the date of this "Cyber War": it can't be before 2486, because in *The Tomb of the Cybermen*, the Cyber-race is thought to have been extinct for

neutron storm is in progress and our ship has been heavily damaged. The Dragon battlecruiser has ju**>CRACKLE<** out of hyperspace. It isn't responding to our signals. It's a Galaxy Class ship, armed wi**>CRACKLE<**ronic missiles, and we're unarmed and helpless. Every vessel within range is ordered to these co-ordinates.'

[Intercepted Military Transmission]

'The mission of peace travelled in a cruiser, as befitted their noble status. In accordance with the agreement, the ship's missile banks were empty. A neutron storm damaged all communications systems on the Draconian battlecruiser. The human, Williams, lured it into neutral territory and destroyed it.'

[*The Chronicles of the Court of Draconia*]

A war between Earth and Draconia started immediately, and although it didn't last long, millions died on both sides. [5]

    **During the Dragon Wars, Shirankha Hall's deep-space incursion squadron discovered a beautiful garden world halfway between human and Draconian Space. He named it Heaven.** [6]

    Although many on both sides wanted to see the war fought to its conclusion, diplomatic relations were established and the war ended. The Frontier in Space was established, a dividing line that neither race's spacecraft could cross. Relations between the two planets remained wary, and there were factions on both Earth and Draconia who wanted to wage a pre-emptive strike on the enemy. For twenty years, the galaxy existed in a state of cold war, although treaties and cultural exchanges were set up. Espionage between the powers was expressly forbidden. [7]

## 2526 - EARTHSHOCK [8]

Over five hundred years after the destruction of Mondas, the Cybermen re-emerged from their tombs on Telos, redesigned and more deadly than ever. *Cyber-Warships swept across human colonies.* The Cybermen became the "undisputed masters of space". Earth was not directly affected at this time, but it was clear that only the homeworld could provide the military resources needed to combat the Cyber threat. In 2526, a conference was held on Earth that proposed that humanity should unite to fight the Cybermen. [9] [10]

[CYBER - HISTORY - COMPUTER]----------------------------

**Background** – We - have - learnt - of - an - attempt - to - form - an - alliance - against - the - Cybermen. A - conference - is - about - to - take - place - on - Earth. The - heads - of - many - powerful - planets - will - be - present. The - purpose - of - the - conference - is - to - sign - a - pact - uniting - their - forces - in - a - war - against - the - Cyber-race. Such - an - alliance - would - be - capable - of - defeating - the - Cybermen. Earth - is - on - red - alert - status - and - it - will - be - impossible - to - launch - a - full-scale - attack.

**Cyber-Control** – A - bomb - has - been - set - up - on - Earth. It - is - guarded - by - androids. We - will - detonate - the - bomb. Two - weeks - ago - we - contacted - the - human - traitor - Ringway. A - force - of - fifteen - thousand - Cybermen - have - been - loaded - aboard - a - human - freighter - bound - for - Earth. The - ship - had - thirteen - crewmembers. The - forces - aboard - the - freighter - have - been - forced - to - eliminate - three - crewmembers - that - discovered - our - presence. This - has - not - prevented - the - ship - from - gaining - full - security - clearance - to - travel - to - Earth. Once - the - bomb - on - Earth - has - detonated - the - Cyber-army - will - occupy - the - planet - and - eliminate - all - resistance. The - Main - Fleet - will - then - follow - to - secure - Earth.

**Supplemental** – Once - again - the - Doctor - has - interfered - with - our - plans. The - Cyberleader - on - the - freighter - had - encountered - the - Doctor - previously - and - identified - him. [11] The - Doctor - deactivated - the - bomb. Our - deep - space - probes - monitored - the - TARDIS - as - it - travelled - to - the - freighter. The - Cyberleader - commanded - that - the - Doctor - should -

five hundred years after the destruction of Mondas [see also TELOS page 139]. In that story the Controller is ready to create a "new race" of Cybermen. We learn in *Attack of the Cybermen* that the Controller wasn't destroyed at the end of *The Tomb of the Cybermen*, so we might presume that this new race emerged soon afterwards and began its conquests. These attacks didn't directly involve Earth: in *Earthshock* Scott, a member of the Earth military, hasn't heard of the Cybermen, even though his planet is hosting a conference that the Cyberleader says will unite many planets in a "war against the Cyber-race". The Doctor observes that it is a war that the Cybermen "couldn't possibly win". When the Cybermen's plan to blow up the conference is defeated (*Earthshock*), there is nothing to stop Earth from fighting this genocidal war against the Cybermen, and this is surely the "Cyber War" referred to in *Revenge of the Cybermen*. We might presume that the events of *Attack of the Cybermen* occur at the end of the War, when the Cybermen face defeat and are planning to evacuate Telos. The Cybermen are not mentioned in *Frontier in Space* (set in 2540), and so we can only presume that the Cyber War has long been over by that time.

Before *Earthshock* was broadcast, *The Programme Guide* placed the Cyber Wars 'c 2300' (first edition) and 'c 2400' (second edition). 'The History of the Cybermen' in *DWM* Issue 83 first suggested that the Cyber War took place immediately after *Earthshock*, post–2526. *Cybermen* suggested that the Cyber Wars took place without any involvement with Earth around '2150 AD'. *The Terrestrial Index* came to a messy compromise: The 'First Cyber Wars' took place 'as the 23rd Century began', and Voga was devastated. *Revenge of the Cybermen* takes place at the 'tail end of the 25th Century', then after *Earthshock* Voga's gold was *again* used to defeat the Cybermen in 'the Second Cyber War'.

9 Dating *Earthshock* – The Doctor states that it is "the twenty-sixth century", Adric calculates that it is "2526 in the time scale you call Anno Domini". 'The TARDIS Logs' set the story in "2500".

How the Cyber scanner in *Earthshock* can show a clip from *Revenge of the Cybermen* remains a mystery that causes problems with the dating of that story. The 'real' reason is that the production team wanted to show the Cybermen facing as many previous Doctors as they could and didn't worry too much about continuity (in the same way that the Brigadier's flashback in *Mawdryn Undead* had the Brigadier 'remembering' scenes in which he was not present). Equally, the Cyber-scanner doesn't show clips from either *Attack of the Cybermen* or *Silver*

suffer - for - the - defeats - he - inflicted - on - the - Cybermen. When - the - freighter - was - underway - the - Cyberleader - ordered - the - capture - of - the - bridge. When - the - bridge - was - secure - the - human - technology - was - overridden. The - Cyber-Plan - was - changed. Now - the - freighter - would - explode - its - anti-matter - engines - in - Earth's - atmosphere. The - occupation - of - the - planet - would - then - proceed - as - planned. The - human - technology - was - so - primitive - that - the - warp - engines - misphased - causing - a - time-jump. The - freighter - was - lost. The - Main - Fleet - survives.

---

'MILITARY LOG – Scott reporting. My squad were sent to investigate the disappearance of a party of palaeontologists. They had entered a newly discovered cave system four weeks beforehand, and had been attacked. There was only one survivor, the team leader Kyle. Our scanners failed to register the murderers, advanced androids, but did detect an alien space-traveller – known as the Doctor – who had arrived in the caves with his companions. The androids were protecting an armoured hatch. Behind it was an armed explosive device. Both the androids and the device were sending ultrasonic transmissions into deep space (Sector 16) and it became clear that the bomb was being controlled remotely from that point. We were able to jam the signal and defuse the device. We travelled to the source of the transmissions in the Doctor's craft, and discovered an army of Cybermen in control of an Earth freighter. The Cybermen took control of the ship, but the freighter went into timewarp. We managed to inflict casualties on the Cybermen, and evacuated the freighter. The ship exploded with no significant loss of life. The Doctor recovered our party, and returned us to our native time, where the Cyber-fleet was dispersed.' [12]

The Cybermen were unafraid of contravening galactic law or arms treaties, and were prepared to destroy entire planets using Cyber-bombs. But the war against the Cybermen united many planets, and humanity's position was not as weak as it could have been. Earth was aware of the Cybermen's vulnerability to gold and **INITEC** developed the "glittergun", a weapon that exploited this weakness. There was more gold on Voga than in the rest of the known galaxy, and when those vast reserves were used against the Cybermen, humanity inflicted massive defeats. [13]

## ? 2530 – ATTACK OF THE CYBERMEN [14]

[CYBER - HISTORY - COMPUTER]--------------------------

**Background** – As - predicted - the - human - race - has - defeated - the - Cyber-Race. We - had - thought - the - Cryons - extinct - but - now - Cryon - guerilla - forces - have - made - recent - gains - on - Telos. Our - hibernation - equipment - is - failing. We - face - total - defeat. A - three-man - time-machine - built - by - an - unknown - humanoid - alien - race - recently - landed - on - Telos.

**Controller** – The - Cyber-Controller - has - decided - that - the - time-vessel - will - travel - back - to - 1985 - to - avert - the - destruction - of - Mondas. Comet - 9/1-2/4-4 - will - be - converted - into - a - bomb - and - detonated - in - the - atmosphere - of - Earth. We - shall - evacuate - Telos. For - two - weeks - the - slave-workers - have - been - planting - explosives - on - the - surface - of - Telos. When - detonated - this - will - eradicate - the - Cryons - as - well - as - providing - scientific - data - on - atmospheric - disturbances. The - TARDIS - has - been - captured. Cyber-control - intercepted - a - signal - sent - to - the - Time - Lords - by - the - Doctor.

**Supplemental** – Once - again - the - Doctor - has - interfered - in - our - plans. The - mercenary - Lytton - allied - himself - with - the - Cryon - guerilla - movement. Explosives - were - planted - in - Cyber-control. The - Controller - was - destroyed. We - face - total - defeat.

--------------------------------------------------------

Realising that they were beaten, the Cybermen launched an

*Nemesis,* the latter of which at least should appear. 'The History of the Cybermen' in *DWM* Issue 83 suggested that the scope tunes into the TARDIS telepathic circuits, which seems a little implausible. One fan, Michael Evans, has suggested that as there is no indication how long before *Attack of the Cybermen* the time machine crashed on Telos, it is perfectly possible that the Cybermen have had it since before *Earthshock* and used it to research their future before using it to alter history. This would certainly be a logical course of action. For other possible explanations see *Cybermen* (p72 and p79–80).

10 [see also THE CYBER WAR page 186]. *Earthshock.* Scott's suspicion of aliens perhaps suggests that there is little peaceful contact with aliens in this period, and that the conference concerns only the human colonies. The Cyberleader in *Revenge of the Cybermen* says that they were defeated by "humans". That planets are so prepared to go to war indicates that the Cyber-race is a major threat to galactic security. The words of those of Lytton in *Attack of the Cybermen.*

11 *Earthshock.* The Cyberleader says "We meet again" when he meets the Doctor in *Earthshock.* He may be referring to the Cyber-race as a whole, rather than to himself as an individual.

12 The Doctor notes that he

has returned Scott's group to their native time in *Time-Flight*, and Nyssa adds that the Cyber-fleet has been dispersed.

13 *Revenge of the Cybermen* [see also THE CYBER WAR page 186]. In *Battlefield*, UNIT are aware of the Cybermen's vulnerability to gold. In *Original Sin*, Vaughn hints that his company designed the glittergun (p287).

14 Dating *Attack of the Cybermen* – No date is given on-screen, but the story takes place after *The Tomb of the Cybermen* as the Controller remembers surviving that story. *Attack of the Cybermen* takes place at a time when the Cybermen face imminent total defeat on a number of fronts. Although the Cybermen know of Lytton's people, and he is fully aware of the situation on Telos, I don't think this is the period that *Resurrection of the Daleks* is set in. In *Resurrection of the Daleks* Stien says that the Daleks captured people from many different periods, so this could well be Lytton's native time (Lytton talks of humans as his "ancestors", so his home planet, Vita 15, is a human colony). Lytton seems to flatter the Cybermen by declaring them "undisputed masters of space" – *Attack of the Cybermen* shows them to be in an extremely weak position, but only a decade or so beforehand the Cybermen were in the strong position he describes.

15 *Revenge of the Cybermen*.

attack on Voga, detonating Cyber-bombs that blew the planet out of orbit. The Vogans were forced into underground survival chambers. After this time, the Cybermen disappeared, and it was believed that they had died out. [15]

> 'After the Cyber War, and the virtual extinction of the Cyber-race, *Earth had begun to consolidate its position. War-time supply lines became peace-time trading routes, and it was now clear that in the face of an over-whelming threat on the scale of the Cybermen or the Draconians, human colonies would have to rely on Earth – and its military – for their security*. Relations with colony planets were often strained, but both Earth and the colonies needed each other for mutual defence.'
>
> [From Breakout to Empire: Essays on the Third Millenium, Federation Archivist Ven Kalik]

## 2540 – FRONTIER IN SPACE [16]

At this point, Earth's "Empire" was still democratic, ruled by an elected President and Senate, although the Earth Security forces also had political influence. Ironically, although millions had died in the colonies, neither the Draconian War *nor the Cyber War* had affected Earth directly, and the planet still faced a massive population crisis. The Bureau of Population Control strictly enforced the rule that couples could only have one child. The Arctic areas were reclaimed. New Glasgow and New Montreal were the first of the sealed cities to be opened, and the Family Allowance was increased to two children for those who moved there. The Historical Monuments Preservation Society existed to protect Earth's heritage. Although there was a healthy political opposition, any opposition to the principles of government by either anti-colonialists or pacifists was ruthlessly suppressed. Under the Special Security Act, a penal colony was set up on the Moon to house thousands of political prisoners, each of whom served a life sentence with no possibility of parole or escape. In 2539, Professor Dale, one of the most prominent members of the Peace Party was arrested and sent to the penal colony on Luna.

Larger colonies such as those in the Sirius System were given Dominion Status, and allowed regional autonomy, including powers of taxation and extradition. The smaller worlds were ruled by Governors appointed directly by Earth.

In 2540, interplanetary tension mounted as human and Draconian spacecraft were subjected to mysterious attacks. Cargos were stolen and ships were destroyed. Each planet blamed the other, and eyewitnesses on both sides claimed to have seen their enemy. On Earth, war with the "Dragons" appeared to be inevitable. A member of the Peace Party, Patel, sabotaged a spacedock and was arrested.

On 12 March, Earth cargo ship *C-982* was attacked only minutes from Earth at co-ordinates 8972-6483. The News Services monitored and broadcast their distress calls. Anti-Draconian riots flared up in Peking, Belgrade and Tokio. The Draconian Consulate in Helsinki was burnt down, and in Los Angeles the President was burnt in effigy. When the *C-982* docked at Spaceport Ten, Security discovered a mysterious traveller, the Doctor, on board. He resisted the mind probe, even on level twelve, and was sent to the Lunar Penal Colony. He was convinced that a third party was trying to provoke war, a possibility that no one else had considered. A small ship under the command of General Williams was sent to the Ogron home planet at co-ordinates 3349-6784, where the true masterminds, the Daleks, were revealed. [17]

The Daleks at this time were one of the greatest powers in the universe. [18]

'It was typical Dalek strategy: divide and conquer. By using a sonic device operating on the fear centres of the brain that also caused amnesia, the Daleks convinced the crews that they saw their enemies. Ogron mercenaries were employed to spread fear throughout the galaxy. If war had started, millions would have died, there would have been mutual destruction, and the Daleks could have conquered both Empires. So...'

[*The Children of Davros*, Njeri Ngugi]

Stevenson claims that "the Cybermen died out centuries ago"; the Doctor replies that "they disappeared after their attack on Voga at the end of the Cyber War".

16 Dating *Frontier in Space* – The story takes place "somewhere in the twenty-sixth century" according to the Doctor. In the first scene the freighter enters hyperspace at "22.09.72.2540 EST". This is probably nine minutes past ten at night on the seventy-second day of 2540, although the President is later seen cancelling a meeting on "the tenth of January". The novelisation (also by Malcolm Hulke) gives the year as "2540", which *The Terrestrial Index* concurred with, although it misunderstood the relationship between Earth and Draconia at this time, suggesting that they are part of "the Alliance" [see also THE ALLIANCE page 163]. It isn't made clear whether the human military know of the Daleks before this story.

17 *Frontier in Space*. The co-ordinates of the Ogron planet change: the Doctor thinks they are 3349-6784, Jo prefers 2349-6784.

18 According to the Doctor in *Death to the Daleks*.

19 Dating *Planet of the Daleks* –
The story is set at the same
time as *Frontier in Space*.
Nevertheless, the American
*Doctor Who* comic dated this
story as 1300 AD.

20 BENNY'S BIRTHDAY – It is
stated in *Love and War* (p46), in
many later books and in the
writers' guide that Benny
comes from "the twenty-fifth
century". For a while, the
writers worked on the
assumption that she was from
2450 (e.g.: *The Highest Science*
p34, and *The Pit* p9). In *Falls the
Shadow* we learn that Benny
was born in '2422' (p148).
However, Paul Cornell's initial
character guide had specified
that she was born in '2472',
which, as *Love and War* is set
the day after Benny's thirtieth
birthday, would makes it 2502
(in the twenty-*sixth* century).
Causing further complications,
*Love and War* is definitely set
after *Frontier in Space* (2540). In
subsequent books there was
confusion, with some novels
claiming that Benny does
indeed come from the
"twenty-sixth century" (e.g.
*Transit* p186, and *Blood Heat*
p3).

 Latterly, so as not to
contradict the television series,
it has been decided that Benny
is definitely from the
twenty-sixth century. Benny
has since explained that there
are a number of calendars in
use in the cosmopolitan galaxy
of her time and in our terms
she is "from the late
twenty-sixth century" (*Just War*
p136) – this is intended to

# & 2540 – PLANET OF THE DALEKS [19]

'Space travel was developed after we studied captured Dalek
spaceships. We intercepted Dalek military transmissions to
the planet Spiridon in the ninth system, many systems from
Skaro. It was the standard Dalek tactic: rule by terror. Bacteria was released, killing the intelligent natives of the planet.
The Daleks landed and there were mass exterminations followed by total subjugation. A group of twelve Dalek scientists was experimenting with an anti-reflective lightwave that
made them invisible, although the power needed was such
that invisible Daleks soon exhausted themselves through
lightwave sickness. It was vital that we stopped them. We
needed volunteers to go further than any Thal mission had
gone before: and all six hundred men and women in the
Division volunteered. Commander Miro and six colleagues
were sent to Spiridon. Although they were not warlike people, they managed to freeze the entire Dalek army by setting off an ice volcano.'

[Thal Oral Records]

'... a massive Dalek army was moved to Spiridon in the
ninth galactic system. A force of ten thousand Daleks was
assembled, the largest in the whole of Dalek history. They
were kept in suspended animation, frozen by a
neutron-powered refrigeration unit. The core of Spiridon
was made of "molten ice", which is why the Daleks had
selected the planet. When the mission to set Earth to war
with Draconia stalled, plans to invade the entire galaxy were
shelved; instead they would concentrate on the Solar Planets. The Dalek Supreme, a member of the Supreme Council, arrived to oversee the operation, but the entire army
was neutralised by an icecano eruption. Supreme Command
sent a rescue ship, and preparations were made to mobilise
the army, but it was a mammoth undertaking.'

[*The Children of Davros*, Njeri Ngugi]

**Bernice Surprise Summerfield was born on 21 June 2540 on the
human colony of Beta Caprisis, to Isaac Summerfield, a starship**

commander in the Space Fleet, and his wife Claire. [20]

The Draconian Ambassador Ishkavaarr and the Earth President agreed that the planet Heaven should become an open world where both races would bury their dead. Years later, several interplanetary agreements were signed there by the President and the Draconian Emperor. Before he died, Ishkavaarr wrote:

"If I may be allowed to be a prophet, I believe that Heaven was given to both our peoples deliberately. There is a purpose in the giving, and a purpose that we may not discover for many years. I believe that purpose is a good and just one." [21]

'Losing ten thousand Daleks on Spiridon was a major setback. *When the humans and Draconians became allies, the situation became disastrous.* A series of Dalek Wars were fought across the galaxy for decades, in which billions of people died and the front continually changed. The Daleks were driven further and further back.' [22]

[The Children of Davros', Njeri Ngugi] [23]

Life on the front was harsh: tens of thousands were killed by Dalek Plague on Yalmur alone. Other planets on the front line included Capella, Antonius, Procyon and Garaman (the location of a Space Fleet station). On the other hand the Core Worlds – the heavily populated and fashionable heart of the Earth Empire – were safe and prosperous. The planet Ellanon was a popular holiday planet; Bacchanalia Two was the home of the Club Outrageous. There were shipyards on Harato, and thriving colonies on Thrapos 3 and Zantir. The Spinward Corporation's financial and administrative centre on Belmos was a space station the size of a planet. Humanity had also discovered Lubellin, "the Mud Planet", and the spotless Tarian Asteroids.

The best whiskey from this time was made in South America, but some people preferred Eridanian Brandy. [24]

The *Dalekbuster* commanded by Isaac Summerfield was reported to have broken formation and fled during a space battle, and its captain was branded a coward. In late 2547, at the height of the Second Dalek War, the Daleks attacked the human colony on Vandor Prime in the Gamma Delphinus system, and Claire

explain away some of the contradictions in the past. Paul Cornell and Jim Sangster have astrologically determined Benny's birthday as 21 June, a date that first appeared in *Just War* (p135).

21 *Love and War* (p10-11).

22 THE DALEK WARS – In *Death to the Daleks*, Hamilton states that "My father was killed in the last Dalek War" which implies that there was more than one. We know from other Dalek stories that humanity and the Daleks came into conflict throughout history. However, there are almost certainly no Dalek Wars between *The Dalek Invasion of Earth* and *The Rescue* (2167-2493), as Vicki has only heard of the Daleks from history books discussing the Invasion (she doesn't even know what they look like). According to Cory in *Mission to the Unknown*, the Daleks have been inactive in Earth's sphere of influence for a millennium before *The Daleks' Master Plan* (between 3000 and 4000 AD).

In the New Adventures, Dalek Wars take place in Benny's native time – her father fights in them, and her mother is killed in a Dalek attack. What is more, Ace spends three years fighting Daleks in this time period between *Love and War* and *Deceit*. As such, there is a mass of information about the Wars in many of the novels.

According to *The Terrestrial Index* there are a string of Human–Dalek conflicts, the First to Fourth Dalek Wars – a numbering system that is never used on television (in *Planet of the Daleks*, the Doctor uses the term "Dalek War" to describe the events of *The Daleks*, which did not involve humanity). "The Second Dalek War" in Lofficier's terms is fought in the twenty-fifth century when 'the Alliance' [see also THE ALLIANCE page 163] (Draconians, Thals and Humans) ally against the Daleks. Not only is there no evidence for this on-screen, it explicitly contradicts what we are told: the Thals don't have space travel at this time and think that humans are mythical (*Planet of the Daleks*), and the first contact between humanity and the Draconians was in 2520, leading to a short war, followed by twenty years of hostility and mutual mistrust (*Frontier in Space*).

So, I prefer to reserve the term "Dalek Wars" for the group of conflicts that presumably took place after *Frontier in Space* when the Human and Dalek Empires first come into contact. In terms of the New Adventures, Benny's father fought in the Second Dalek War (*Lucifer Rising* p65), whereas Ace fought in the Third (*Lucifer Rising* p309).

23 *Love and War* (p14, p29–9).

24 *Deceit.*

25 A number of contradictory accounts of Benny Summerfield's early life have appeared in the New Adventures. In *Love and War*, Benny's birthplace is identified

Summerfield was killed. Bernice Summerfield was sent to military boarding school. [25]

Hardened criminals on Earth were given the choice of facing the death penalty or becoming Dalek Killers. The most notorious of the DKs was Abslom Daak. In 2555 Benny Summerfield visited Earth for the last time. On this, or a previous trip, she went to Stuttgart. [26]

The corporations, such as Ellerycorp, Peggcorp, Spinward, and IMC, maintained battlefleets of their own. During the Battle of Alpha Centauri a small squadron of Silurian vessels beat back the main Dalek force, which fled into hyperspace. Daleks also managed to infiltrate human Puterspace. By the late 2560s, it became clear that Earth was going to win the wars with the Daleks. [27]

As often happens in wartime, the Dalek War saw a leap in human technological progress. A variety of intelligent weapons systems was developed: dart guns, data corrupting missiles, spikes, clusters and forceshells, random field devices, self-locating mines and drones.

Earth's Space Fleet included 1000-man troopships armed with torpedoes that could destroy a Dalek Battlesaucer. A fleet of X-Ships, warp vessels, was used to ferry communications, personnel and supplies. Most troopers were placed in Deep Sleep while travelling to the warzones: this was done to conserve supplies, not because the ships were particularly slow – it now only took a matter of weeks to cross human space. Ships still used warp engines, but now they used ion drive to travel in real space.

Computer technology was now extremely advanced. The Space Fleet Datanet was a vast information resource, and data was stored on logic crystals. Nanotechnology was beginning to have medical applications: a nanosurgical virus was given to most troopers to protect against various alien infections, and cosmetic nanosurgery beautified the richest civilians. Holograms were now in widespread use for communications, display, entertainment, combat and public relations. Holosynths, simulations of people, acted as receptionists and could answer simple enquiries. HKI Industries, based on Phobos, specialised in the manufacture of transmats. These had a range of only a couple of thousand kilometres, but they were installed on all large ships and linked major cities on most colony worlds. Hoverspeeders were still in use.

By the end of the Dalek Wars, the fastline, a state of the art, almost real-time, interstellar communication system had been developed. [28]

In 2566, Bernice Summerfield published *Down Among the Dead Men*, her study of archaeology, particularly that of the Martians. [29]

In 2568, the Spinward Corporation's computer, the Net, predicted that when the Dalek Wars ended, Earth's authorities would begin to show an interest in their activities on Arcadia. [30]

## ? 2570 (Late June) – LOVE AND WAR [31]

Bernice Summerfield and her group arrived on Heaven to survey the artefacts of the extinct Heavenite civilisation on behalf of Ellerycorp.

'The Vacuum Church of Heaven was a death-worshipping religion, and so it was fitting that it had established itself on the graveyard-planet of the galaxy. It thought that "the universe is an accident and that life is meaningless". While the more fanatical members of the religion supported terrorism, and the group practised human sacrifice (on volunteers), the Church also supported the mourners that visited Heaven and contributed a vast amount to the Imperial budget. The Church provided a focus for the Hoothi attack on Heaven in the twenty-sixth century, with many of its members being Hoothi hosts or agents.'

[*Religions of the Galaxy*]

Billions of the dead were reanimated by the Hoothi, and when they had been defeated the ecology of Heaven had been devastated. The planet was evacuated shortly afterwards.

Following this time, Ace spent three years in the twenty-sixth century during the time of the Third Dalek War. After a series of adventures, including a spell working for IMC, she ended up with the Special Weapons Division of Space Fleet, fighting alongside the Irregular Auxiliaries, reputed to be the most dangerous arm of the military. [32]

Hamilton's father died during the last Dalek War. [33]

## ? 2573 – DECEIT [34]

'One of the most bizarre cases of a corporation out of control was exposed by Agent Defries at the end of the Dalek

as Beta Caprisis (p75), but in *Sanctuary* Benny recalls that her mother was killed on a raid on Vandor Prime (p185). We might speculate that she was born on the former and moved to the latter. As pointed out in *Set Piece* (p132) there is some confusion about the exact sequence of events during the raid that killed Benny's mother. Accounts also vary as to whether Benny's father disappeared before or after her mother's death. Benny was only seven when all this happened, so she is almost certainly misremembering some details or blocking out some of her unpleasant memories. We learn about her visit to Stuttgart in *Just War* (p137), and that she hasn't been to Earth in the fifteen years before *Deceit* (p102). This contradicts *Lucifer Rising* (p171).

26 Abslom Daak first appeared in Marvel's *Doctor Who Weekly* Issue 17, and has returned a number of times since. He was mentioned in *Love and War* (p46–7 – we also meet Maire, another DK in the novel), before he appeared in the (cloned) flesh in *Deceit*.

27 *Love and War* (p5, p64). *Deceit* (p4).

28 *Deceit*.

29 *Theatre of War*. The date of publication is given as both "2566" (p36), and "2466" (p135), I prefer the first date [see also BENNY'S BIRTHDAY page 192]. Appendix II of *Sky Pirates!* is "A Benny Bibliography", and contains further details of the

volume.

30 *Deceit* (Prologue).

31 Dating *Love and War* – The dating of this novel causes a number of problems as it features the debut of Bernice Summerfield [see also BENNY'S BIRTHDAY page 192]. It is the "twenty-fifth century" (p46), and it is "five centuries" since Ace's time (p26). The novel clearly takes place after *Frontier in Space*, (see p10–11 of *Love and War* or p252 of *The Programme Guide*, fourth edition), as it refers events of that story: (e.g.: the peace established between humanity and the Draconians, the female president, and the lunar penal colony). Heaven is established "three decades" before the events of the novel (p92), and *Frontier in Space* is set in 2540 so the novel can't take place before about 2570. Latterly, the decision has been made that Benny is from the twenty-sixth century, so this is the date that has been adopted for this story. It is late June, as Benny celebrates her birthday just before the book starts, although it is autumn on Heaven.

32 *Deceit*. Many of the subsequent New Adventures contain references to Ace's exploits in Space Fleet.

33 *Death to the Daleks*.

34 Dating *Deceit* –The novel is set "two, probably three Earth years" after *Love and War* (p85), and as such the dating of the story is problematic [see also BENNY'S BIRTHDAY page 192].

Wars. She requested a troopship to investigate the Arcadia system, base of the Spinward Corporation. The nearest troopers were on Hurgal, although some were taking part in a pirate hunt in the Hai Dow system. Instead, Defries was assigned the troopship *Admiral Raistruck* and a squad of Irregular Auxiliaries. She was also given a "secret weapon", the Dalek Killer Abslom Daak, who was kept in cryosleep. The ship's crew were told that they were going on a Dalek hunt.

The *Admiral Raistruck* arrived in the Arcadia system and encountered an asteroid field carved to resemble terrified human faces. It was clear that Arcadia was subject to SYSDYDS (System Defence in Strength). The *Admiral Raistruck* was attacked by fighters, but this was only a feint. The real attack came from behind: an energy-being that was not affected by the ship's torpedoes. The ship was destroyed. Out of over a thousand people, there were only four survivors: Defries, Daak, and Troopers Ace and Johannsen. They discovered that Arcadia had been kept at a medieval level of technology. The population had been kept in ignorance, and company law was enforced by android Humble Counsellors. All offworlders were killed as plague-carriers. The power behind Spinward was the Pool, "the collective brains of the Corporation", vats of brainmatter, culled from generations of colonists, housed in a space station in orbit around Arcadia. Pool intended to manufacture a universe of pure thought, making itself omnipotent. The troopers destroyed Pool.'

[*Greed Incorporated: The Rise of the Space Corporations*, M. Ashe]

The Dalek Wars were all but over, and although Dalek nests survived on a number of worlds, the army and Space Fleet were gradually demobilised.

'The aftermath of the Dalek Wars saw, paradoxically, both a centralising and broadening of political power. Although at this time the colonised worlds were still numbered only in hundreds, the Government of Earth exercised only nominal authority over them. As the power of the interstellar corporations waned, Earth found itself increasingly able to enforce its rule'

[*From Breakout to Empire: Essays on the third Millenium*, Federation Archivist Ven Kalik]

During the Dalek Wars, the Colonial Office had been superseded by Earth Central, while Spacefleet had been expanded and modernised. The Office of External Operations, "the Earth's surveyors, official couriers, intelligence gatherers, customs officers and diplomats" now had a staff of five thousand. While the corporations remained powerful, the Earth government was now able to reign in some of their power and break some of their monopolies.

> 'There appears to have been a revolution among the Daleks at this time. One Dalek declared itself Emperor, and asserted its authority over the Supreme Council. The Expansionist Daleks reoccupied Skaro, driving the Thals from the planet and maybe even exterminating the entire race.'
>
> [The Children of Davros, Njeri Ngugi] [35]

Around the year 2590, radiation levels on the surface of Argolis had dropped to such a level that the planet became habitable again. [36]

## ? 2600 – DEATH TO THE DALEKS [37]

'By the twenty-seventh century, the Daleks had resorted to germ warfare in an attempt to weaken the human race. The Daleks fired plague missiles into the atmospheres of many of the Outer Planets. Thousands died, and ten million people were threatened. Earth scientists quickly discovered an antidote to the plague: parrinium, a chemical that acted as both a cure and an immunity. It only existed in minute quantities on Earth, and it was so rare that it was one of the most valuable known substances. A chemical-detecting satellite surveying the planet Exxilon discovered that parrinium was almost as common there as salt was on Earth. A Marine Space Corps mission was despatched to Exxilon. The Daleks wanted to secure the supplies for themselves so that they could force the Space Powers to accede to their demands.'

[The Children of Davros, Njeri Ngugi]

Both the blurb and the history section in the Appendix of the novel state that Deceit is set in "the middle of the twenty-fifth century", just after what The Terrestrial Index calls the Second Dalek War (p62–3). This is restated at various other points in the book (e.g. p69, and p216). It is contradicted, though, by other evidence in the book: Arcadia was colonised 379 years before Deceit (p115), but not before the EB Corporation's first warship was operational in 2112 (p27), so the book must be set after 2491 AD. The book also refers to the Cyber Wars [see also THE CYBER WAR page 186] In the Marvel strips Abslom Daak comes from the mid-twenty-sixth century.

35 Before the return of Davros, the Daleks are ruled by the Supreme Dalek, except in The Evil of the Daleks where they have an Emperor. Skaro is not mentioned in The Dalek Invasion of Earth (except by Ian and the Doctor when they refer to their adventure there), The Power of the Daleks, Frontier in Space or Death to the Daleks. In Planet of the Daleks the Thals seem to dominate the planet. I suggest that the Daleks are not based on Skaro in these stories, these Daleks are the Expansionists who left their homeworld early in their history and only returned after The Planet of the Daleks.

36 "Three centuries" after The Leisure Hive.

37 Dating Death to the Daleks –

There is no date given on-screen, but it takes place after the Dalek Wars [see also THE DALEK WARS page 193]. *The Programme Guide* placed it in 'c 3700' (first edition), 'c 2800' (second edition), and *The Terrestrial Index* in 'the twenty fifth century'. 'The TARDIS Logs' offered a date of '3767 AD' (the same year as *The Monster of Peladon*). *The Official Doctor Who and the Daleks Book* claimed that the Dalek Plague used in this story is the Movellan Virus, and so set the story between *Resurrection of the Daleks* and *Revelation of the Daleks*, around 3000 AD. This is nonsense, though, as that plague would have no effect on humans – as the Doctor says in *Resurrection of the Daleks*, "it is only partial to Dalek". The gas that disfigures humans seen in *Resurrection of the Daleks* is not the Movellan Virus, but a weapon that the Daleks themselves are immune to. The Daleks routinely use germ warfare throughout their history (we see it in *The Dalek Invasion of Earth, Planet of The Daleks, Death to the Daleks* and *Resurrection of The Daleks*).

38 In *Love and War* the Doctor says that after they lost the Wars, the Daleks "started coming up with other schemes", which is presumably a reference to their use of blackmail and germ warfare in this story.

39 *Original Sin* (p204).

40 Dating *Shadowmind* – The

## SPECIAL REPORT: MARINE SPACE CORPS

As soon as we arrived within range of the planet, we suffered total power failure. Our ship landed without damage, but we were unable to take off again. We managed to get a message off to Earth before total power loss, but it didn't reach Earth. We explored the area and discovered a fantastic city that was thousands of years old. The Exxilon natives guarded this City fanatically, and the priests ensured that anyone caught there faced certain death. Wilkins was killed by the Exxilons, and Commander Stewart was seriously injured, only surviving on a diet of sulphagen tablets.

After a month a ship landed on Exxilon. As we watched its descent spiral, we assumed it must be the relief ship, possibly a Z-47. Daleks emerged and attempted to exterminate us, but they were also affected by the power-drain. (Their travel machines were powered by psychokinetic energy and still functioned, but their weapon circuits were useless.). They told us that their own colonies were affected by the plague, and millions were dying. Reluctantly we agreed to help each other to mine parrinium and try to discover a way to leave Exxilon. Shortly after this Commander Stewart died from his injuries and Railton was killed by the Exxilons. The Daleks recruited the majority of the Exxilons by offering to wipe out a minority faction. This horrified us, but the parrinium mining began almost immediately. With our help, the Daleks managed to destroy the device that was causing the energy-drain. We had tricked the Daleks into loading bags of sand into their ships, rather than the parrinium. Galloway sacrificed himself to destroy the ship. We loaded the parrinium aboard our own ship and left Exxilon, watching the alien city destroy itself.' [38]

During the twenty-seventh century, oxygen factories were built in London. [39]

## 2673 – SHADOWMIND [40]

This was the time of Xaxil, the twenty-fourth Draconian Emperor.

Thousands of years before, the Shenn of Arden had discovered "hypergems" that boosted their telepathic ability. Around 2640 one group of Shenn began to hear a mysterious voice from the sky that ordered them to construct kilns. This voice was the "Umbra", a sentience that had evolved from carbon structures on a nearby asteroid.

By this time, the planet Tairngaire was heavily populated and a member of a local alliance of planets, the Concordance, with its own space fleet that had recently seen action in the Sidril War. In 2670, colonists from Tairngaire set up camp on the planet Arden. The Colonial Office decreed that the natural features of the planet should be named after characters from the works of Shakespeare. Accordingly, the main settlement was called Touchstone Base, and there was a Lake Lysander, a Titania River and a Phebe Range of mountains.

> 'Captain's Log, Captain Kausama, C.S.S. *Broadsword* reporting.
>
> After completing wargame trials in the Delta Epsilon system, the *Broadsword* was recalled to Tairngaire by Admiral Vego. We were to investigate the situation at the Arden: all contact had been lost with the settlers, and five ships sent to investigate had also vanished. Alien duplicates of humans were found to be operating in New Byzantium: alien creatures occupying artificially constructed human bodies. The plan was to proceed to the Arden skystation, then assess the situation. We discovered that the "Umbra" – a carbon structure based on an asteroid in the Arden system that had somehow become sentient, had taken control of a group of Shenn, the natives of Arden. Umbra was building "shadowforms", extensions of its power. We located Umbra, and blocked off the Sun's rays, effectively rendering it "unconscious".'

During the twenty-seventh century, a Haitian deciphered the Rihanssu language, allowing a peace treaty to be drawn up that ended the war between Earth and that race. [41]

As the expanding Earth Empire became more established and powerful it became more corrupt. There had been examples of humanity oppressing native species for centuries. The Swampies of Delta Magna and the Alphidae of Terra Alpha, for example, had been displaced and oppressed. Slavery was formally reintroduced on many worlds. The time-sensitive Tharils had once been the owners of a mighty empire themselves, with

Doctor tells Ace that "by your calendar the year is twenty-six seventy-three" (p29). The events of *Frontier in Space* in "twenty-five forty" (p74) were "one hundred and thirty years ago" (p61).

41 STAR TREK – In the Pocket Books' range of *Star Trek* novels, particularly those by Diane Duane, the Romulans call themselves 'Rihanssu', and the race is referred to in *White Darkness* (p129). A few of the other New and Missing Adventures have included such *Star Trek* in-jokes: there are many, for example, in *Sanctuary*, another of David McIntee's books, and Turlough refers to the Klingon homeworld in *The Crystal Bucephalus* (p104). *Star Trek* and *Doctor Who* have radically differing versions of the future, and *The Left-Handed Hummingbird* establishes that *Star Trek* is merely fiction in the *Doctor Who* universe. Maybe, just as Trekkies in the seventies managed to get NASA to name a prototype space shuttle after the USS *Enterprise*, the *Star Trek* fans of the future managed to name a lot of planets after ones from their favourite series – Vulcan, as seen in *The Power of the Daleks*, being one of the first.

42 The Swampies and Alphidae appear in *The Power of Kroll* and *The Happiness Patrol* respectively. Slavery exists at the time of *Warriors' Gate* and *Terminus*, and the work camps referred to in *The Caves of Androzani* are also near-slavery. Stephen Gallagher has stated in interviews (see, for example, *In-Vision* Issue 50) that Rorvik's crew come from N-Space, and their familiarity with English (such as the graffiti), "sardines" and "custard" suggest they come from Earth. The coin flipped is a "100 Imperial" piece, and they use warp drive, both suggesting an Earth Empire setting, although the date is arbitrary.

43 Dating *The Highest Science* – Sheldukher's ship arrives at Sakkrat in "2680" (p17). It is "two hundred and thirty years" in Benny's future (p35) [see also BENNY'S BIRTHDAY page 192].

44 *The Crystal Bucephalus* (p40).

45 Dating *The Sensorites* – Maitland says "this is the twenty-eighth century". *The Programme Guide* set the story in 'c 2600' in its first two editions, *The Terrestrial Index* settled on 'about 2750'. 'The TARDIS Logs' gave the date as '2765'.

territory stretching across several universes, including N-Space and E-Space. Now they were captured by slavers. The Tharils were a valuable commodity: they alone could navigate the ships using warp drive based on 'Implicate Theory', and so were extremely valuable. Many humans became rich trading in Tharils. One privateer, a veteran of Tharil hunts on Shapia commanded by Captain Rorvik, vanished without trace following a warp drive malfunction. [42]

## 2680 – THE HIGHEST SCIENCE [43]

In 2680, the authorities reported that Sheldukher had died while resisting arrest on the planet Hogsumm.

During the twenty-eighth century, the Legions attempted to undermine the business consortia of the galaxy, but their plot was uncovered by the Time Lords and temporal inhibitors were placed around their homeworld, imprisoning them. [44]

## c 2764 – THE SENSORITES [45]

During the twenty-eighth century, spacecraft from INNER (Interstellar Navigation, Exploration and Research) ploughed deeper and deeper into space, searching for minerals and other natural resources. On Earth, air traffic was becoming congested.

'SENSE-SPHERE - A planet rich in molybdenum, inhabited by the shy, telepathic Sensorites. A five-man Earth ship discovered the planet Sense-Sphere in the twenty-eighth century, but the Sensorites refused to trade with Earth, fearing exploitation. The Earth mission left, and shortly afterwards, the Sensorites began dying from a mysterious new disease. Within a decade, two out of ten Sensorites had died. By the time a second Earth mission arrived, the Sensorites were terrified of outsiders. They used their psychic powers to place the crew of the ship in suspended animation, a process that drove one human, John, mad. It became clear that the Sensorites were suffering from nightshade poisoning, introduced to the city water supply by the previous Earth expedition. The second expedition left, promising not to return to the planet.'

[*Bartholomew's Planetary Gazetteer*, Volume XIX]

By 2765, INITEC had built the first of a chain of Vigilant laser defence space stations in orbit around Earth. The station proved vital in preventing the Zygons from melting the icecaps and flooding the world. [46]

## ? 2782 – KINDA [47]

The homeworld was overcrowded, and teams were sent to many worlds to assess them for possible colonisation.

'S14 – Primeval forest world, local name Deva Loka ("The land of the Kinda"). The natives are humanoid telepaths and live in harmony with nature. Trees come into fruit all year round, and the climate hardly varies throughout the year. Despite this, the planet was classified unsuitable for colonisation by the mission sent to investigate it.'

[*Bartholomew's Planetary Gazetteer*, Volume XIX]

## ? 2875 (Day Three, Week Forty-seven, Mid-November) – REVENGE OF THE CYBERMEN [48]

A mysterious planetoid was detected entering the solar system, and it eventually became the thirteenth moon of Jupiter. It was named Neophobus by humans, and the Nerva Beacon was set up to warn shipping of this new navigational hazard. Nerva was one of a chain of navigational beacons, which also included Ganymede Beacon at vector 1906702.

Fifty years later the civilian exographer Kellman began his survey of Neophobus, setting up a transmat link with the Nerva Beacon and renaming the planetoid Voga. Fifteen weeks later, an extraterrestrial disease swept through Nerva. Once the infection began, the victim died within minutes. The medical team on board the station were among the first people to perish, and Earth Centre immediately rerouted all flights through Ganymede Beacon. As loyal members of the Space Service, the Nerva crew remained on board. Ten weeks after the plague first struck,

46 *Original Sin* (p287).

47 Dating *Kinda* – An arbitrary date. I assume that the colonists are from Earth, as they have recognisably English names, although they only refer to a "homeworld", which Todd says is overcrowded. The attitudes of Sanders perhaps suggest an early colonial period, and the story would seem to be set after *Colony in Space* in which colonists are seen as "eccentric". The colonists are from Earth in Terrance Dicks' novelisation, where the Doctor suggests they are from the time of the 'Empire'. 'The TARDIS Logs' set the story in the '25th Century'.

48 Dating *Revenge of the Cybermen* – In *The Ark in Space*, the Doctor is unsure at first when the Ark was built ("I can't quite place the period"), but he quickly concludes that "Judging by the macro slave drive and that modified version of the Bennet Oscillator, I'd say this was built in the early thirtieth century... late twenty-ninth, early thirtieth I feel sure". The panel he looks at appears to be a feature of the Ark, not the original Nerva Beacon. However, in this story when Harry asks whether this is "the time of the solar flares and Earth is evacuated", the Doctor informs him that it is "thousands of years" before [see also THE SOLAR FLARES page 226]. Mankind has been a spacefaring race for "centuries" before this story, when they fought the Cyber War [see also

THE CYBER WAR page 186],
according to both Stevenson
and Vorus. It is clearly
established in other stories that
Earth is not abandoned in the
twenty-ninth century. This then,
would seem to be the story set
in the "late twenty-ninth, early
thirtieth century". The
Cybermen are apparently
without a permanent base of
operations, so the story is
presumably set after the
destruction of their base on
Telos in *Attack of the
Cybermen.*

*The Programme Guide* set
the story in 'c 2400' and 'c
2900', while *The Terrestrial
Index* preferred 'the tail end of
the 25th Century'. 'The History
of the Cybermen' in *DWM* Issue
83 suggested a date of '25,514'.
*Cybermen* placed the story in
'2496', but admitted the
difficulty in doing so (p71–2).
The Discontinuity Guide offered
'c 2875'.

49 Dating *The Robots of Death*
– An arbitrary date, but one that
takes into account the
development of humanoid
androids (although Tara has
them centuries before). In the
New Adventure *Legacy* we are
told that this story is set on the
second moon of Saturn. *The
Programme Guide* set the story
'c 30,000', but *The Terrestrial
Index* preferred 'the 51st
Century'.

50 *The Robots of Death.* In the
script, it was originally
'Gimwold's Syndrome' but Tom
Baker ad-libbed, renaming the
condition after Peter Grimwade,

all but four people on the station were dead.

[CYBER - HISTORY - COMPUTER]-----------------------------
**Background** – We - are - the - last - of - the - Cybermen.
Our - ship - contains - the - components - that - will - allow
- us - to - build - a - new - Cyber-army. First - we - must -
destroy - the - Planet - of - Gold. We - have - been - contacted - by - a - human - traitor - Kellman. He - has - located
- Voga.

**Cyberleader** – Kellman - will - use - a - Cybermat - to -
spread - Neurotrope - X. The - poison - will - kill - all - but
- four - crewmen. When - the - plague - has - run - its -
course - we - shall - dock - with - Nerva. Cyber-bombs - will
- be - attached - to - the - four - crewmen. They - shall - be
- sent - to - Voga - and - once - they - are - in - place - the -
Bombs - will - be - detonated. When - Voga - is - destroyed
- the - galaxy - will - be - ours.

[Last Entry]

-----------------------------------------------------------------------------

## ? 2877 - THE ROBOTS OF DEATH [49]

By the late twenty-ninth century, robots had become so advanced that many people found themselves unnerved by their
inhuman body language. Psychologists christened this
"Grimwade's Syndrome", or "robophobia". [50]

'The Stormminers of Japetus venture out on two-year missions into the hundred-million-mile expanse of desert. Sand
blown up in storms is sucked into scoops, where the zelanite,
keefan and lucanol are sifted out. The water supplies for the
eight-man crew is totally recycled once a month, but the
crew live in relative luxury. Most of the work is done for
them by the robots: around a hundred Dums, capable of
only the simplest task; a couple of dozen Vocs, more sophisticated; and one Super-Voc co-ordinating them. With such

help, how could anything possibly go wrong?'

[*A Tourist Guide to the Galaxy*, second edition]

## ? 2878 – THE POWER OF KROLL [51]

The Sons of Earth Movement claimed that colonising planets was a mistake and demanded a return to Earth, but most of its members had never been to the homeworld, which now suffered major famines. The Sons of Earth supplied gas-operated projectile weapons to a number of native species, including the Swampies from the third moon of Delta Magna, employing the services of the notorious gun-runner Rohm-Dutt.

A classified project, a methane catalysing refinery, was set up on the third moon. Two hundred tons of compressed protein were produced every day by extracting material from the marshlands, and sent to Magna by unmanned rocket.

## ? 2884 – THE CAVES OF ANDROZANI [52]

'SPECTROX – "The most valuable substance in the universe". In small doses (the recommended dose is 0.3 of a centilitre a day) spectrox can halt the ageing process and double human lifespans; there is some evidence that with a sufficient quantity of the substance a human might live forever. Spectrox is refined from the nests of the bats of Androzani Minor, a dangerous process carried out by androids. Supplies of spectrox were halted when the scientist Sharaz Jek and his androids rebelled against Androzani Major. The Praesidium sent a taskforce to capture Jek, and they captured the refinery, but Jek removed the supplies of spectrox. After six months, the supplies were destroyed in a mudburst, a tidal flood of primeval mud.'

[*The Sirius Apocathery* Third Edition]

By the beginning of the thirtieth century, the Empire had become utterly corrupt. Planetary Governors, such as that of Solos, would routinely oppress the native races of the planet. Natives were often little more than 'work units', fit only for manning factories or mines where it was uneconomic to use humanoid

the production assistant on the story. In *The Universal Databank* the two names were erroneously conflated to become 'Grimwold's Syndrome'.

51 Dating *The Power of Kroll* – Kroll manifests "every couple of centuries" according to the Doctor, and this is his fourth manifestation, suggesting that it is at least eight hundred years since Delta Magna was colonised. *The Terrestrial Index* set the story in the '52nd Century', 'The TARDIS Logs' 'c 3000 AD'.

52 Dating *The Caves of Androzani* – There is no indication of dating on-screen. Sharaz Jek seems worried when it appears that the Doctor and Peri are from Earth, suggesting it has political influence. The supplies of Spectrox must be so limited that they have little long-term effect on the human race, explaining why it is not referred to in any other story.

**53** The Solonians appear in *The Mutants*, the Mogarians in *The Trial of a Time Lord* Parts Nine to Twelve.

**54 THE THIRTIETH CENTURY** – While I don't think that the Earth was ravaged by solar flares at this time [see also Dating *Revenge of the Cybermen* page 201, THE SOLAR FLARES page 226 and Dating *The Ark in Space* page 231], the Doctor's description of a "highly compartmentalised" Earth society of the thirtieth century in *The Ark in Space* matches similar descriptions of Earth in stories set at this time: Earth society is "efficient" and run by the Great World Computer in *The Ice Warriors*, "grey" in 'The Mutants' and "highly organised" in *The Trial of a Time Lord* Part Ten. We learn of the world famine, the extinction of plant life and the artificial food in *The Ice Warriors* (and food shortages are also referred to in *The Trial of a Time Lord* Parts Nine to Twelve). In terms of the New Adventures, this is the native time of Cwej and Forrester, and we meet them there in *Original Sin*, a story that ties in quite closely with *The Mutants* (Solos is even mentioned on page 318).

We first learn of the decline of the Earth Empire and the Overcities in *The Mutants* although in that story Ky calls them "sky cities" and claims that they were built because "the air is too poisonous", not because of the wars. We learn of a "Great World Computer"

robots. Alien races across the galaxy, such as the Mogarians, resented Earth's exploitation of their planets, but could do little. Humanity was "going through the universe like a plague of interplanetary locusts". Mogar, in the Perseus Arm of the galaxy, was a rich source of rare metals such as vionesium. Although Earth assured the Mogarians that they only required limited mining concessions, they were soon strip-mining the planet, and the shipments to Earth received Grade One security. [53]

Human civilisation was more efficiently run than ever, under the auspices of the Great World Computer. But at the beginning of the thirtieth century, the hub of the Empire regularly suffered massive famines. Around 2900 AD, an artificial food was created on Earth that solved the problem. On the land once used to grow food, up-to-date living units were built to house the ever-increasing population. The amount of growing plants on the planet was reduced to an absolute minimum. All plant life on the planet became extinct, and every native animal species died out except humanity and the rat. [54]

In 2905, Chris Cwej's father graduated from the Academy. He served in the Adjudication service until 2971, as his ancestors had for centuries. [55]

The Nerva Beacon completed its mission at Voga. The space station remained operational for many centuries afterwards. [56]

Roslyn Sarah Forrester was born in 2935. [57]

Around 2945, the Wars of Acquisition reached Earth. The Pollution levels on the surface of the planet reached such a point that the population of Earth was forced to live in vast sky cities. The Overcities were built over the battle-torn Earth using a new form of cheap and effective null-gravity. They floated around a kilometre from the Earth's surface, supported on stilts and by null-grav beams. Half Earth's population, everyone that could afford it, lived in the Overcities and Seacities. The wealthier you were, the higher the levels that you were allowed to access. The surface of Earth became the Undertown, a flooded, ruined landscape. The Vigilant belt of defence space stations proved invaluable at repelling alien attacks, and within ten years the front had shifted so far away from Earth that humanity had almost forgotten that they were taking place. After a few years of austerity, Earth benefited from a technological and economic upsurge. It was "a time of peace and prosperity: well, for the peaceful and prosperous, at least". Earth was a cosmopolitan place, with races such as Alpha Centauri, Arcturans, Foamasi and Thrillip living in the lower areas of the Overcities, although aliens were treated as second-class citizens. Earth at this time had a human population of thirty billion, with almost as many robot workers. The Data Protection Act was modified in 2945 to reflect the changes in technology and society.

Over the generations a semi-feudal system had developed:

'A Baron is responsible for sections of an Overcity, typically controlling a few hundred levels. The whole city (an area the size of an old nation state) is run by a Viscount, while a Count or Countess is responsible for ten cities (equivalent to a continent). Earth, and each of the other planets, is ruled by a Marquis or Marquessa. The solar system and its environs are under the authority of its Lord Protector, the Duke Marmion. The Divine Empress rules with grace and magnificence over the whole of the Earth Empire, on which thousands of suns never set, and which stretches across half the galaxy. Few on Earth now realise that She is Centcomp, the computer network that runs the solar system, setting judicial sentences, running navigational and library databases, and co-ordinating virtually every aspect of life.'
[*Terra Genealogica*, 2970 edition] [58]

Christopher Rodamonte Cwej was born in 2954 in Spaceport Nine Overcity. [59]

During the 2950s, anti-magnetic cohesion was developed. [60]

In 2957, Roz Forrester was squired to Fenn Martle. She would be his partner for fifteen years; he would save her live on five occasions. [61]

The Black Dalek and the Renegade Dalek Faction used the Time Controller to hide from Davros a trillion miles from Skaro, on Earth in the mid-1960s. [62]

## ? 2966 - THE EVIL OF THE DALEKS [63]

'By the mid-thirtieth century, the Emperor had realised that the Daleks were doomed, unless they could capitalise on the difference between themselves and humanity. The Daleks were unable to make this distinction on their own, and so the Emperor hatched an elaborate trap in three timezones

that regulates society in *The Ice Warriors*. This sounds like "centcomp" in *Original Sin*, so we might presume that the Empress is a biological component of the Great World Computer.

The animal extinctions in Cwej and Forrester's time are mentioned in *Just War* (p143), although we see bears and wolves in *The Ice Warriors*, and hear of a variety of animal specimens in *The Ark in Space*. Pigs and dogs survive until at least the year 5000 AD (*The Talons of Weng-Chiang*, and *The Invisible Enemy*), there are sheep and spiders on the colony ship sent to Metebelis III in *Planet of the Spiders*, Europa is well stocked with animal life in *Managra*, and *The Ark* contains a thriving jungle environment complete with an elephant and tropical birds. Presumably animal species survive offworld, or Earth is eventually restocked via cloning or zoos.

55 Original Sin (p160–1).

56 Nerva Beacon has a "thirty year assignment" according to Stevenson in *Revenge of the Cybermen*, so it ought to be decommissioned around 2915. We see the Beacon again in *The Ark in Space*.

57 According to a discussion document about Roz and Cwej prepared by Andy Lane for the New Adventures authors. She is in her early forties when she joins the Doctor (*Original Sin*).

58 *Original Sin*, and *The Mutants*.

**59** According to a discussion document prepared by Andy Lane, and confirmed in *Head Games* (p205).

**60** *The Carnival of Monsters*. It was discovered "a thousand years" after Jo' was born.

**61** *Original Sin* (p32 and p219).

**62** [see also THE THIRTIETH CENTURY page 204, THE DAVROS ERA page 223]. This takes the Doctor's remark to the Black Dalek in *Remembrance of the Daleks* that the Daleks are "a thousand years" from home literally. The statement is clearly rhetorical: *Remembrance of the Daleks* itself can't be set at this date, as Skaro still exists in 4000 AD, which is a shame as Davros develops a revolutionary new foodstuff in *Revelation of the Daleks* which might have tied in with the artificial food developed a century before *The Ice Warriors*.

**63** Dating *The Evil of the Daleks* – There is no date given for the Skaro sequences in the scripts. The Doctor murmurs that this is "the final end" of the Daleks, and most fans have taken this statement at face value when they come to date the story, although a line cut from the camera script of *Day of the Daleks* stated that the Daleks survived the civil war and that the Human Daleks were defeated. *The Terrestrial Index* set *The Evil of the Daleks* 'a century or so' after *The Daleks' Master Plan*. John Peel

for their old enemy, the Doctor. The Daleks tricked the Doctor into believing that they wished to become more human. He was all too willing to educate the Daleks about the "Human Factor", highlighting the difference between the two races: humans are not blindly obedient and show mercy to their enemies. However, this merely enabled the "Dalek Factor" to be distilled, and once this was done, the Emperor planned to instil it into all humans throughout the galaxy, forcing them to become Daleks. Instead, the Doctor managed to "humanise" a number of Daleks. Civil war broke out between the "Human" and "Dalek" factions. Every Dalek in the galaxy had been recalled to Skaro in preparation for the conquest of humanity, and in the ensuing battle they were all wiped out. The Emperor was exterminated by his own kind and the Daleks disappeared from the Milky Way for over five hundred years.'

[*The Children of Davros*, Njeri Ngugi]

## 2975 – ORIGINAL SIN [64]

In the early 2970s, mankind fought a short but brutal war with the Hith, a sluglike race. Hithis was annexed by the Empire and terraformed. The Hith were displaced, becoming servants and menial workers on hundreds of worlds. The last Wars of Acquisition ended shortly afterwards, when Sense-Sphere finally capitulated. The Earth Empire now stretched across half the galaxy.

Soon after the Hith Pacification, Roz Forrester saw a man kill a Ditz. When he denied it, she ate his ident and arrested him for perjury and not having valid ID. The incident entered Adjudicator folklore. A year later, Forrester killed her partner Fenn Martle when she discovered he had betrayed the Adjudication Service and that he was on the payroll of Tobias Vaughn. She attended Martle's funeral, and shortly afterwards her memories of his death were wiped by the Birastrop Doc Dantalion and replaced with false memories that Martle had been killed by the Falardi.

Christopher Cwej graduated from the Academy in 2974. During his training on Ponten IV he had achieved some of the highest marksmanship and piloting scores ever recorded. Cwej's first assignment was a traffic detail, and a year later he was squired to Roslyn Forrester.

The very same day, serious riots started throughout the Empire, particularly on Earth itself. Insurance claims were estimated at five hundred trillion Imperial schillings, a total that would bankrupt the First Galactic Bank. Worst of all, it was revealed that the Adjudication Service was rife with corruption. The riots had been sparked by the release of icaron particles from a Hith battleship captured by INITEC and kept in hyperspace in Overcity Five.

When the source of the radiation was removed, it was clear that the Empire was collapsing. At the time of the rioting on Earth, the Rim World Alliance had applied to leave the Empire. Over the years, all the major corporations had moved from Earth to the outer-rim planets. A Landsknecht flotilla was sent to pacify them. Rioting also began on Allis Five, Heaven, Murtaugh and Riggs Alpha. Colony worlds took the opportunity to rebel, stretching the resources of the Landsknecht to their limit.

By the end of the thirtieth century most planets in the Earth Empire had achieved some form of independence from the homeworld. [65]

At this time, Armstrong Transolar Aerospace was building Starhopper craft on Empire City, Tycho, Luna. [66]

In 2983, Kimber met Investigator Hallett while he was investigating granary shortages on Stella Stora. The Doctor visited this timezone a number of times. On one occasion, before Mel joined him, he involved Captain Travers in a "web of mayhem and intrigue", but the Doctor did save his ship. On other visits, the Doctor met Investigator Hallett and visited Mogar. [67]

## 2986 (16 April) – THE TRIAL OF A TIME LORD Parts Nine to Twelve [68]

'DEMETER SEEDS – Large silver seeds created by the thrematologist Professor Sarah Lasky. They would grow even in desert conditions, and had a three-fold yield compared with normal crops.'

[Flora and Fauna of the Universe, Professor Thripstead]

'VERVOIDS – Humanoid plants created by the thrematologist Professor Sarah Lasky. Lasky planned that the Vervoids would

and Terry Nation 'agreed that *The Evil of the Daleks* was the final story' (*The Frame* Issue 7), but did so before *Remembrance of the Daleks* was written. Peel's novelisation of *The Evil of the Daleks* is set around the year 5000. 'A History of the Daleks' in *DWM* Issue 77 claimed that *The Evil of the Daleks* is set around '7500 AD'. In *Matrix* Issue 45 Mark Jones suggested that the Hand of Omega is sent into Davros's future, thousands of years after Dalek history ends. This story has to be set before the destruction of Skaro in *Remembrance of the Daleks* (and by implication before the rest of 'The Davros Era' [see also THE DAVROS ERA page 223]). In *Mission to the Unknown* Cory states that the Daleks have not been active in the galaxy "for a thousand years", although later it transpires that they did in fact begin conquering territory five hundred years before. I suggest that the civil war in *The Evil of the Daleks* is not the "final end" of the Daleks, but it does represent a severe defeat for them, one that removes them from the Milky Way for five hundred years.

64 Dating *Original Sin* – The Doctor tells us that this is the "thirtieth century" (p23). Although we are told at one point that "2955" was "four years" ago (p86), the year appears to be 2975 – this ties in with the birthdates established for Cwej and Forrester in the discussion document, and the

fact that Cwej's father graduated "seventy years" before, in "oh-five".

65 *The Mutants.*

66 *The Sorceror's Apprentice* (p17).

67 *The Trial of a Time Lord.* We can perhaps infer that all of these unrecorded adventures took place in the Doctor's future, between the end of his trial and his adventure with the Vervoids.

68 Dating *The Trial of a Time Lord* Parts Nine to Twelve – The Doctor tells the court that this is "Earth year 2986". A monitor readout suggests it is "April 16".

69 Dating *The Mutants* – The Doctor tells Jo that they have been sent to "the thirtieth century". The story must take place "many years" after *Original Sin*, where events are set into motion that will eventually mean the collapse of the Empire. *The Programme Guide* set the story slightly later ('c 3100').

70 *The Mutants.* The words are those of the Doctor, Ky, Jaeger and the Administrator. The last quote is the Doctor in *Frontier in Space.* In *Original Sin,* Viscount Farlander says that "nobody leaves the Empire" (p125), but by the time of *The Mutants* the Doctor says that Solos is "one of the last" planets to gain independence.

71 THE SECOND ICE AGE – When Clent explains the historical background to *The*

make robots obsolete:Vervoids bred and grew rapidly, were quick to learn and cheap to maintain. For an undisclosed reason, the Vervoids also had a poisonous spike. A consortium was ready to exploit them, but as they were being transported back to Earth in the intergalactic liner *Hyperion III,* the Vervoids went on the rampage, killing a number of the passengers and crew, including Lasky. Every example of the species was wiped out using the mineral vionesium, that accelerated their growth.'

[*Flora and Fauna of the Universe,* Professor Thripstead]

## c 2990 – THE MUTANTS [69]

The ruling Council *that succeeded the Divine Empress on her death,* came to realise that "Earth is exhausted… politically, economically, biologically finished ", and "fighting for its survival". It was "grey and misty" with "grey cities linked by grey highways across grey deserts… slag, ash, clinker". Earth's air was so polluted by this point that the entire population now had to live in the vast sky cities if they wanted to breathe. Earth "cannot afford an Empire any longer". These were "the declining years of Earth's planetary empire".[70]

One of the last planets to gain independence from Earth was Solos. For many years, the Marshal of the planet had deliberately resisted reform, despite organised resistance from the native Solonians themselves. When the Solonians began mutating into insect-like creatures, the Marshal ordered the "Mutts" destroyed, believing them to be diseased. From his Skybase in orbit above the planet, he had been conducting experiments on the atmosphere of Solos, attempting to render it more suitable for humans.

An independence conference was arranged between the Solonian leaders and the "Overlords" from Earth, in which Solos was to be declared independent. The Administrator was assassinated at the meeting, and martial law was declared instead. An Investigator sent from Earth met Professor Sondergaard, a scientist who for many years had been investigating the history of Solos. He had discovered that every five hundred years the Solonians underwent a radioactive metamorphosis – the process that was transforming the population into Mutts and altering the atmosphere was seasonal. Earth helped Solos to discover the true form of the mutation, before leaving the planet alone.

## ? 3000 – THE ICE WARRIORS [71] [72]

"And then suddenly, one year, there was no spring. What happened was not understood until the icecaps began to advance."

On Earth, the Second Ice Age had begun. Glaciers rapidly spread across every continent, displacing tens of billions of people to the equatorial regions. Scientists attempted to come up with a theory that might account for the iceflow. They quickly ruled out a number of the possibilities: a reversal of Earth's magnetic field, interstellar clouds obscuring the Sun's rays, an excessive burst of sunspot activity and a severe shift of the Earth's angle of rotation. They came to realise that the extinction of Earth's plant life had dramatically reduced the carbon dioxide levels in the lower atmosphere, leading to severe heat loss across the world. Scientists frantically tried to reverse the flow of ice, installing Ioniser Bases at strategic points across the globe: Britannicus Base in Europe, and complexes in America, Australasia, South Africa and Asia. These were all co-ordinated by the Great World Computer.

Many refused to leave their homelands and became scavengers. Before long, everywhere on Earth apart from the equatorial areas was an arctic wasteland, home to wolves and bears. When captured, scavengers were registered and sent to the African Rehabilitation Centres. Scientists remained behind to measure the flow of the ice with movement probes.

'During the Second Ice Age, humanity uncovered Varga's expedition. The Martians threatened Britannicus Base with sonicweaponry. *The staff at the base did not take time to explain about New Mars or that the Martians were now responsible members of the galactic community.* They didn't feel that the ship was of sufficient archaeological importance. Instead they ionised it.'

[*Down Among the Dead Men Again*, Professor B S Summerfield (unpublished)] [73]

*Ice Warriors* he implies that the ice age began a century ago, but people are still being evacuated from England during the story, suggesting that glaciation is a more recent phenomenon. It would seem that although the global temperature drop is a direct result of the destruction of plant life, its consequences weren't felt immediately. This would also explain why the Ice Age isn't mentioned in any other story set between 2900 and 3000.

The scientific consensus, of course, is that destroying the forests would cause global *warming* because of the resulting rise in carbon dioxide levels. *The Terrestrial Index* and *Legacy* (p90) both suggest that the Ice Age began as a result of "solar flares" (presumably in an attempt to link it with Earth's evacuation in *The Ark in Space*), but in *The Ice Warriors* Clent supplies the true reason.

72 Dating *The Ice Warriors* - The date of this story is never given on screen. Clent says that if the glaciers advance then "five thousand years of history" will be wiped out. If he is referring to Brittanicus Base, a Georgian house, this would make the date about 6800 AD. If he is referring to human or European history, the date becomes more vague. It has to be set well over a century in the future, because the world has been run by the Great World Computer for that long. In *The Talons of Weng-Chiang*, the Doctor talks of "the Ice Age about the year

five thousand". One peculiarity is that the Martians have only been buried for "centuries", although it is also made clear that they have been buried since the First Ice Age, when mastadons roamed Earth. An article in *Radio Times* at the time of broadcast stated that the year is "3000 AD". The first edition of *The Making of Doctor Who* said that the Doctor travels "3000 years" into the future after *The Abominable Snowmen*, making the date 4935 AD. Every fan chronology I have encountered that gives a date for this story claims it is set in or around 3000 AD.

73 Benny discovers about the events of *The Ice Warriors* in *Legacy* (p89). It is a mystery why no one recognises the Martians in this story, as they have been part of the galactic community for centuries – they appear, for example, in *Original Sin* (p37).

*Humanity had spread throughout the galaxy, and had crushed all opposition in its path, even the Dalek Empire. Now, though, the Earth economy lay in ruins. Unable to support the military and bureaucratic machinery needed to rule over the colonies and dominions, unable even to evacuate their home planet, the once-mighty Earth Empire finally fell. The collapse of the Empire formed a political and military vacuum across the galaxy.*

## Section Seven
## The Far Future

# TIMELINE: 3001 to The End of the Universe

*continued overleaf*

| | | |
|---|---|---|
| 2,000,000 | c | DRAGONFIRE |
| 4,000,000 | ? | THE SUN MAKERS |
| 10,000,000 | c | THE ARK |
| 10,000,000 | c | FRONTIOS |
| 10,000,700 | c | THE ARK |
| | ? | THE SAVAGES |
| | ? | **THE ALSO PEOPLE** |
| | ? | **TIMEWYRM: APOCALYPSE** |

*Although Earth's political power quickly collapsed, humanity had colonised the galaxy. Towards the end of the Third millennium, forms of feudalism were reintroduced. There are a number of reasons why this apparently backwards step was taken: humanity saw that a number of advanced alien races had a feudal system, such as the Martians; the Arab states now controlled Earth, and their strict authoritarianism was attractive; under the Imperial system of government, factory workers on colony worlds were often little more than serfs or slaves, with little representation in government anyway, and feudalism at least guaranteed them some protection under the law; the collapse of central authority led to individuals staking claims to planets, or whole systems; a series of wars were fought early in the Fourth Millennium, and army commanders were often given, or simply took, planets as rewards.*

*Feudalism saw many forms and many planets were now ruled by hereditary monarchs. Princes and warlords provided tribute to the monarchy in return for protection and land rights. At the same time, new ultraspace ships were developed that could travel the incredible distances between galaxies. Limited exploration and colonisation outside the Milky Way took place. Not everything changed: vast and ruthless corporations still existed. The Magellanic Mining Conglomerate, for example, exploited planets in the Magellanic Clouds in just the same way IMC had done over five hundred years before.* [1]

## c 3025 – THE SORCEROR'S APPRENTICE [2]

Although many remained patriotic, and a new Empress was crowned, it was clear that the Empire was collapsing. The Landsknechte Corps had fallen, and the newly-independent human worlds were now building vessels of their own.

Over the years, a number of ships had been lost near Avalon, and the military suspected that the planet housed an advanced weapons system that might prove useful in restoring order and despatched a fleet. The technology could not be removed from Avalon, and it attacked all electronic equipment. The people of Avalon, lost human colonists, had become superstitious peo-

1 FEUDALISM – A number of stories set in the far future hint at an almost medieval political system: *The Curse of Peladon*, *The Ribos Operation*, *Terminus*, and *Revelation of the Daleks*, as well as the New and Missing Adventures *Original Sin* and *Managra*. I speculate that this marks a specific era in the political history of humanity and have placed these stories together.

2 Dating *The Sorceror's Apprentice* – The TARDIS crew discover a spaceship built in '2976' (p17), and this leads the Doctor to suggest that this is the "end of the thirtieth century" (p33 and p48). We learn that the colony was founded in 2145 (p203), 846 (Avalonian?) years ago (p33), making it the year 2991. Later, though, we learn that the "city riots" seen in *Original Sin* were "*fifty years ago*" (p156), so it must be nearer 3025. Perhaps the Avalonian year is slightly longer than that of Earth or they have miscalculated the legendary year of Landfall.

3 Dating *The Ribos Operation* –
A date for the story is not given
on-screen. While my date is
arbitrary, Ribos is close to the
Magellanic Clouds, suggesting
that humans have developed at
least some level of intergalactic
travel. *The Terrestrial Index*
placed the story in 'the late 26th
century', apparently confusing
the Cyrrhenic Alliance with the
force established to fight the
Cybermen in *Earthshock*.

ple who believed in dragons, elves and magic – beliefs that the advanced alien machinery had made into reality.

> 'Human space broke up into local alliances, confedera-
> tions, unions and affiliations such as the Cyrrhenic Alli-
> ance. These groups often had the same sort of size and
> influence as alien space powers, such as the Alpha
> Centauri, Draconians and Martians, typically only con-
> trolling a single star system. Ironically, although it was
> now possible to travel between galaxies, travel within
> the Milky Way had become more difficult - many of
> these space powers guarded their territory fiercely (a
> network of hyperspace Tollports was established) and
> new forms of warp drive were reliant on rare resources
> such as the mineral Jethrik.'
>
> [Federation History, Grith Robtts]

## ? 3078 – THE RIBOS OPERATION [3]

Ships, such as Pontense-built battleships, were powered by the rare mineral jethrik. Communication across the galaxy was via hypercable, and highly trained mercenaries, the Schlangi, were available for hire.

Three light centuries from the Magellanic Clouds, the Cyrrhenic Alliance included the planets Cyrrhenis Minima (co-ordinates 4180), Levithia and Stapros, as well as the protectorate of Ribos (co-ordinates 4940) in the Constellation of Skythra, 116 parsecs from Cyrrhenis Minima. The Alliance fought a series of Frontier Wars.

> 'The Graff Vynda-K fought campaigns in the Frontier Wars,
> including a battle in which he led two legions of his men for a
> year in the Freytus Labyrinth. He also fought on Skaar and
> Crestus Minor. He was an unstable, temperamental man, though,
> and when he returned home he discovered that his people had
> allowed his half-brother to take the throne. The High Court of
> the Cyrrhenic Empire rejected the Graff's claim for restitution,
> and he spent eighteen years plotting his revenge...'
>
> [Nasty Great Rotters of the Galaxy, R K Cossin]

'Garron was a con-man from Hackney Wick, forced to leave Earth after an attempt to sell Sydney Opera House to the Arabs backfired. Among his exploits was a successive scheme to sell the planet Mirabilis Minor to three different, unsuspecting clients. Aware of the Graff Vynda-K's thirst for revenge, and need for a powerbase, Garron sent him a letter proposing to sell him the planet of Ribos for the sum of ten million Opeks, forging a survey suggesting that the planet was rich in Jethrik…'

[*Nasty Great Rotters of the Galaxy*, R K Cossin]

In the late thirty-first century, people from the Overcities began to recolonise the surface of Earth. One group, later known as the Concocters, created Europa, a bizarre and eclectic fusion of historical periods built on the site of Europe: there were three Switzias, four Rhines, six Danubes and dozens of black forests. Each Dominion represented a different period between the fourteenth and early twentieth century history: so, for example, there were five Britannias – Gloriana, Regency, Victoriana, Edwardiana and Perfidia. The undead, descendants of Jake and Madeline, dwelt in Transylvania. Fictional and historical characters, Reprises, were cloned, and the people from the Overcities jostled with the likes of Byron, Casanova, Crowley, Emily Bronte, and the Four Musketeers. The Vatican, a vast floating city equipt with psychotronic technology, was built to impose order on Europa (the true papal seat having moved to Betelgeuse by this time). The Concoction was masterminded by Persona, a being formed from the merging of the Jacobean dramatist Pearson and the ancient Mimic. [4]

The seeds of the Galactic Federation were sown during the first third of the thirty-second century, as the space powers of the Milky Way began forging links and alliances. Over the course of the first half of the millennium, the various Alliances began to forge links with one another, and with alien races. These groups drifted closer and closer together, until the Galactic Federation was formed. Virtually the entire civilised galaxy was involved to some degree or another. *From the limited exploration outside the Milky Way,* it was clear that some of the other nearby galaxies were united political entities, and the Federation both preserved peace in the Milky Way and defended it from any external threat. [5]

4 *Managra.*

5 *Legacy* (p164).

6 Dating *Managra* – The Doctor
sets the co-ordinates for
"Shalonar – AD 3278"; the
TARDIS lands in the same
timezone, but the wrong
location (p26). Later Byron
states that he was created "in
the middle of the thirty-third
century" (p113).

7 These are the Doctor's words
from *Lucifer Rising* (p51). An
excommunicated Knight of
Oberon, Orcini, appears in
*Revelation of the Daleks*. One
of the moons of Uranus is
called Oberon, and I speculate
that this is the location of the
Order's base. The forthcoming
New Adventure *GodEngine* will
confirm this.

8 *The Curse of Peladon* and its
two sequels *The Monster of
Peladon* and the New
Adventure *Legacy* are set at the
time of a Galactic Federation.
The date of its foundation is
given in *Legacy* (p164). The
words are those of Alpha
Centauri and the Doctor from
*The Curse of Peladon*. The
Megara also follow "The
Galactic Charter" in *The Stones
of Blood*, and they are from
2000 BC. Many other stories
refer to "Intergalactic Law",
"Intergalactic Distress
Signals", and so on – there are
clearly certain established
standards and conventions that
apply across the galaxy,
although who sets and
enforces them is unclear.

9 Dating *The Menagerie* – It is
"centuries" (p67) after Project
Mecrim was initiated in 2416.
The Doctor suggests that it

## 3278 – MANAGRA [6]

For centuries, the Nicodemus Principle had prevented a Reprise from becoming the Pope of Europa. In 3278, Cardinal Richelieu assassinated Pope Lucian and attempted to succeed him. He faced opposition from the Dominoes, a secret organisation stretching across the Dominions. Behind the scenes, the Persona attempted to seize control of Europa. Persona was destroyed, but Richelieu succeeded in becoming Pope Designate.

> "As Earth went through Empire and Federation, the fortunes
> of the Guild of Adjudicators waxed and waned. Eventually,
> they became unnecessary. A thousand forms of local jus-
> tice had sprung up. Every planet had its own laws, and its
> own police. The universe had passed them by. The Guild had
> nothing to adjudicate. They degenerated into a reclusive or-
> der of assassins known as the Knights of the Grand Order of
> Oberon, dreaming of past glories and crusades for truth." [7]

Around the turn of the thirty-fifth century, nearly three hundred years after the first steps towards confederation, the Headquarters of the Galactic Federation on Io were officially opened and the Federation (or Galactic) Charter was signed. Founder members included Earth, Alpha Centauri, Draconia, New Mars and Arcturus. At this point in history, Earth was regarded as "remote and unattractive" and it was ruled by an aristocracy, "in a democratic sort of way". The Federation prevented armed conflicts, and even the Martians renounced violence (except in self-defence). Under the terms of the Galactic Articles of Peace (paragraph fifty-nine, subsection two), the Federation couldn't override local laws or interfere in local affairs (except in exceptional circumstances), and was hampered by a need for unanimity between members when taking action. [8]

## ? 3417 – THE MENAGERIE [9]

The Doctor discovered the truth behind Project Mecrim and ended the reign of the Knights of Kuabris, who were led by the android Zaitabor. Over the centuries, they had prevented scientific discovery on the planet, and discouraged historical research.

## ? 3483 - "TERMINUS" [10] ->

Passenger liners travelled the universe, often falling victim to raiders, such as those combat-trained by Colonel Periera.

Lazars' Disease swept the universe, spreading fear and superstition, even among those in the rich sectors. Sufferers were sent secretly to Terminus, a vast structure in the exact centre of the known universe. The station was run by Terminus Incorporated, who extracted massive profits by using obsolete passenger liners to transport the victims to Terminus. The facility was manned by slave workers, the Vanir, kept loyal to the company by their dependency on the drug Hydromel. The Lazars were either killed or cured by a massive burst of radiation from Terminus's engines.

Nyssa of Traken and the Garm, one of the original crew of Terminus, planned to reform the station by introducing proper diagnoses and controlled treatment.

### REPORT: SPACE SPECIAL SECURITY SERVICE [11]

After a thousand years, the Daleks have returned to our galaxy. We have uncovered evidence that over the last five hundred years they have gained control of more than seventy planets in the ninth galactic system and forty in the constellation of Miros. They have reoccupied their home planet of Skaro.

We also believe that the Daleks have resumed their experiments with Time Travel. Of all the races in the universe, only the Daleks are known to have broken the time barrier, although we know that Trantis has tried in the past, without success. Dalek technology is the most advanced in the universe.

## & 3885 – THE CURSE OF PELADON [12]

'For countless centuries, the people of the primitive planet Peladon had worshipped the creature Aggedor. Centuries before, under the beneficent rule of King Sherak, Peladon turned away from the ways of war and violence. In 3864, a Federation shuttlecraft crashed on Peladon, after falling foul of an ion storm

happened "a millennium or three" (p126) and "hundreds, perhaps thousands of years ago" (p102).

10 Dating *Terminus* – Once again, an arbitrary date, although the system of government seems aristocratic. Intergalactic travel is suggested. *The Terrestrial Index* saw Terminus Inc. as one of the 'various corporations' fought by the Doctor in the late '25th century'. The FASA role-playing game gave the date as '4637 AD'.

11 *Mission to the Unknown*, and *The Daleks' Master Plan*. The Daleks occupy Skaro at this time, and according to Marc Cory they haven't been heard from for five hundred years before this point.

12 Dating *The Curse of Peladon* – There is absolutely no dating evidence on-screen. The story takes place at a time when Earth is "remote", has interstellar travel and an aristocratic government. Although the Federation seems to be capable of intergalactic travel at the time of *The Monster of Peladon*, Gary Russell suggested in the New Adventure *Legacy* that Galaxy Five was a mere "terrorist organisation" (p27). Remarkably, given the lack of on-screen information, there has been fan consensus about the dating of this story and its sequel: *The Programme Guide* set the story in 'c 3500', and made the fair assumption that the Federation succeeded the

collapsed Earth Empire. *The Terrestrial Index* revised this slightly to 'about 3700'. 'The TARDIS Logs' suggested '3716'. *Legacy* is set "a century" after *The Curse of Peladon*.

13  The history of Peladon is recounted in *Legacy* (Chapter One), which weaves together information from the television stories, the novelisations and new material.

14  *The Invisible Enemy*. Clones are seen before this date in the Missing Adventure *Managra*. Marius distinguishes between the Kilbracken Technique, which instantly creates a "sort of three-dimensional photocopy", and a true clone that would take "years" to produce.

en route to the base at Analyas VII. One of the survivors, Princess Ellua of Europa, was rescued by the Pels, and within a year the human princess married the King, Kellian. Six months after that, she had persuaded him to apply for Federation membership. Their son, Peladon, was born a year later.

The Preliminary Assessment Team arrived when Peladon was King. As they landed, the spirit of Aggedor was abroad, killing Chancellor Torbis, one of the chief advocates of Federation membership. This was revealed as a plot brewed between the High Priest of Aggedor, Hepesh, and the delegate from Arcturus. If the planet was kept from Federation membership, then Arcturus would be granted the mineral rights to the planet. Arcturus was killed while attempting to assassinate one of the delegates, and Hepesh was killed by Aggedor himself. Peladon was granted membership of the Federation.' [13]

[*Federation History*, Grith Robtts]

The first human clone was created in 3922 using the Kilbracken holograph-cloning technique. The process was unreliable and the longest a clone ever lived was ten minutes fifty-five seconds. Most serious scientists thought of it as "a circus trick of no practical value". [14]

## & 3935 – THE MONSTER OF PELADON [15]

'When scientists from the Federation surveyed Peladon, they discovered that the planet was rich in trisilicate, a mineral previously only found on Mars that was the basis of Federation technology: electronic circuitry, heat shields, inert microcell fibres and radionic crystals all used the mineral. Duralinium was still used as armour-plating.

King Peladon died, and was replaced by his daughter, the child Thalira. As she grew up, Federation mining engineers came to her world, and although her people were resistant to change, gradually advanced technology such as the sonic lance was introduced to Peladon.

The Federation was subject to a vicious and unprovoked attack from Galaxy Five, who refused to negotiate. The Federation armed for war, with Martian shock troops being mobilised.

Peladon's trisilicate supplies would prove crucial in this struggle. The planet was still prone to superstition, however, and when the spirit of Aggedor began to walk once more, killing miners that used the advanced technology, many saw it as a sign to leave the Federation. For a time, production in the mines halted. It was the work of a breakaway faction of Martians, led by Azaxyr and working for Galaxy Five. When the plot was uncovered, Galaxy Five quickly sued for peace.'

[*Federation History*, Grith Robtts]

In the mid-fortieth century a 'Cyber-fad' swept the Federation. The Martian archaeologist Rhukk proved that both Telos and New Mondas had been destroyed, so the Cyber-race had been eradicated. Briefly the public were fascinated by the Cybermen, and documentary holovid crews went to the dead worlds of Voga and Telos. [16]

Zephon became all-powerful in his own galaxy, the Fifth, when he defeated Fisar and the Embodiment of Gris who had tried to depose him. The Daleks recruited Zephon to their Master Plan, and he secured the support of the rulers of two further galaxies, Celation and Beaus. The conspiracy also included Trantis, Master of the Tenth Galaxy (the largest of the outer galaxies), Gearon, Malpha, Sentreal and Warrien.

Around 3950, Mavic Chen became the Guardian of the Solar System, ruling over the forty billion people living on Earth, Venus, Mars, Jupiter and the Moon colonies from his complex in Central City. At this time, the prison planet Desperus was set up to house the most dangerous criminals in the solar system.

Shortly afterwards, the Daleks contacted Chen. They needed Taranium, "the rarest mineral in the universe", found only on Uranus, and if Chen supplied it the Daleks would make him ruler of the entire galaxy. He agreed, and set up a secret mining operation shortly afterwards. The population of the solar system knew nothing of this, and many showed an almost religious devotion to Chen. His reputation was enhanced in 3975, when all the planets of the solar system signed a non-aggression pact. For the next twenty-five years they lived in peace under the Guardianship, and the solar system, though "only part of one

15 Dating *The Monster of Peladon* – Sarah guesses that it is "fifty years" after the Doctor's first visit, and this is later confirmed by other people, including the Doctor, Thalira and Alpha Centauri.

16 *Legacy*. We learn that the Vogans were "ultimately self-destructive" and that the Cybermen eventually managed to settle on a "New Mondas", as they wished to do in *Silver Nemesis*, although this second homeworld has also been destroyed by the time of *Legacy*. Cybermen appear again in *The Crystal Bucephalus*.

17 In *The Daleks' Master Plan*, Mavic Chen seems to have been Guardian for a very long time: he says, when accused of stealing the taranium, "Why should I arrange that fifty years be spent secretly mining to acquire this mineral..." (implying that he has been actively involved with the plot for half a century). Then again, he is the newest member of the conspiracy, the "most recent ally". John Peel's novelisation, loosely based on the original scripts, claims that the crime rate on Earth soared fifty or sixty years before *The Daleks' Master Plan* (3940–3950) as the population increased. Mavic Chen was elected and set up the prison colony on Desperus. This scene does not appear in the broadcast version (it is replaced by a line that William Hartnell delivers as "The Daleks will stop at anything to stop us."). The non-aggression pact is referred to in *The Daleks' Master Plan*. This perhaps suggests that planets in the solar system were in conflict before this time, and Chen's hope that peace will spread throughout the universe implies that much of known space is at war. A short scene in the New Adventure *Legacy* suggests that Chen did not become Guardian until much later.

18 Dating *Legacy* – The dating of this book is problematic. It has to be set after "3948", when a couple of the reference texts were written (p37). The Doctor says that it is "the thirty-ninth century" (p55) and later

galaxy", now had a status that was "exceptional... it has influences far outside its own sphere", and it was hoped that by following Chen's example peace would spread throughout the universe. [17]

## c 3985 – LEGACY [18]

The Federation fought a number of wars to secure its position and to protect democratic regimes. GFTV-3 covered the main news stories of this era: atrocities on the Nematodian Border, the android warriors of Orion, slavery on Rigellon, Operation Galactic Storm. The Martian Deep Space Cruiser, *Bruk*, one of the largest vessels the galaxy had ever seen, was built by the Martian Star Fleet at this time, and it helped to enforce law throughout the galaxy.

> 'With the trisilicate mines exhausted, Peladon faced a choice between becoming a tourist resort or leaving the Federation altogether. While Queen Thalira ruled, the question remained unaddressed, but within four years of her death her successor King Tarrol applied to leave the Federation, suggesting that Peladon ought to try and find its own solutions to its problems. His choice had perhaps been made easier by the carnage caused when an ancient weapon, the Pakhar Diadem, had been tracked to his world. This decision probably saved the planet – had they remained in the Federation the planet would almost certainly have been targeted by the Daleks thirty years later, during the Dalek War.'
>
> [*Federation History*, Grith Robtts]

## 3985 – THEATRE OF WAR [19]

> 'HELETIA – A colony founded by a group of actors wanting to stage the greatest dramas of the universe. Although confined to one small area of their own planet, Heletia became an expansionist power, fighting a war with the Rippeareans. They believed that only races with a sophisticated theatre were really truly civilised. Following the death of their Exec, the Heletians sued for peace.'
>
> [*Bartholomew's Planetary Gazetteer*, Volume VIII]

## c 4000 – MISSION TO THE UNKNOWN [20]

"This is Marc Cory, Special Security Agent, reporting from the planet Kembel. The Daleks are planning the complete destruction of our galaxy together with powers of the Outer Galaxies. A war party is being assemb–"

In the year 4000, there was an Intergalactic Conference in Andromeda attended by Chen. The Outer Galaxies and the Daleks held a council at the same time, sending Trantis to Andromeda to allay suspicion. In 3990, Bret Vyon joined the Space Security Service. Within five years he had gained the First Rank, and he reached the Second Rank three years after that. The SSS and the UN Deep Space Force had been monitoring Dalek activity for five hundred years, and they were to prove vital in discovering the Daleks' scheme.

## 4000 – THE DALEKS' MASTER PLAN [21]

'Shortly after concluding a mineral agreement with the Fourth Galaxy, Mavic Chen left Earth for a short holiday, or so he told Channel 403, the news channel. In reality his *Spar* headed through ultraspace to Kembel, the Daleks' secret base. There he met the delegates from the Outer Galaxies for the first time, and presented the Daleks with a full emm of taranium. The mineral was stolen by Space Security Agents who had been sent to the planet to investigate the disappearance of Marc Cory. They stole Chen's ship, which was pursued by the Daleks, who forced it down on to the surface of Desperus. The ship broke free from Dalek control and reached Central City on Earth. Pursued by Chen's own security forces and other Space Security Agents, the group with the taranium broke into a research facility and found themselves transported across the galaxy by an experimental teleportation system to the planet Mira, home of the Visians, invisible monsters. Mira was close to Kembel and the group returned to the Daleks' base, somehow appropriating a time machine. They fled through time and space with the Daleks in pursuit. Eventually the Daleks captured the taranium, and they exterminated their allies in readiness for universal domination. However, when they activated the Time Destructor they destroyed their own army, transforming the surface of Kembel from lush jungle to barren desert in seconds. The universe was safe once more.'

[*The Children of Davros*, Njeri Ngugi]

narrows this down to the "mid-thirty-ninth century give or take a decade" (p84) (c 3850). The novel is set "one hundred years" after *The Curse of Peladon* (p106) (date uncertain), at a time when "young" Mavic Chen is still a minor official, and Amazonia, who first appeared in *The Curse of Peladon*, is the Guardian of the Solar System (p237) (before 3950). It is "thirty years" before a Dalek War that might well be *The Daleks' Master Plan* (p299) (therefore 3970) and "six hundred years" after *The Ice Warriors* (p89) (therefore 3600). The book takes place a couple of months before *Theatre of War*, and as this book is definitely set in 3985, I have adopted this last date.

19 Dating *Theatre of War* – The book is set soon after *Legacy*, in "3985" (p1), a fact confirmed by Benny's Diary "Date: 3985, or something close" (p21), and the TARDIS's Time Path Indicator (p81).

20 Dating *Mission to the Unknown* – *Mission to the Unknown* is set shortly before *The Daleks' Master Plan*.

21 Dating *The Daleks' Master Plan* – The date "4000" is established by Chen. The draft script for *Twelve-Part Dalek Story* set the story in '1,000,000 AD'.

22 "Thirty years after" *Legacy* (p299). *The Crystal Bucephalus*.

23 Dating *Delta and the Bannermen* – An arbitrary date. Murray says that "the fifties on Navaro were never like this", which might just suggest that he was there to witness them for himself. However, Nostalgia Trips are notorious throughout the "five galaxies", suggesting that the story is set in a period of intergalactic travel. In *Dragonfire*, Svartos serves "the twelve galaxies", so perhaps it is set later than this story. While only the Daleks had broken the time barrier by 4000 AD (*The Daleks' Master Plan*), the human ship in *Planet of the Spiders* and the Movellan ship in *Destiny of the Daleks* have "time warp capability", and we see a couple of races developing rudimentary time travel around now (Magnus Greel in 5000 AD, and the Metebelis Spiders a little later). Though, in the Twelfth century, the Sontaran Lynx used his ship's osmic projector to travel forward in time. Such secrets are limited, and are lost by the time of *The Ark*. *The Terrestrial Index* set this story 'c 15,000'.

24 THE DAVROS ERA – The last four televised Dalek stories (*Destiny of the Daleks*, *Resurrection of the Daleks*, *Revelation of the Daleks* and *Remembrance of the Daleks*) form a linked series in which the creator of the Daleks, Davros (first seen in *Genesis of the Daleks*), is revived, then

Around 4015, a massive Dalek War split the Federation. When it was over the organisation was forced to re-evaluate itself. Mavic Chen's descendants eventually ended democracy in the Federation. The Chen Dynasty of Federation Emperors ruled for thousands of years. [22]

## ? 4287 – DELTA AND THE BANNERMEN [23]

'Tonight, once again, we'll be presenting evidence of negligence on the part of Nostalgia Trips, the time travel holiday company. You may remember we reported on Nostalgia Trips following the notorious incident with the Glass Eaters of Traal. Now it appears that a Hellstrom II star cruiser has been lost on 1950s Earth. What happened to the passengers, a party of Navarino holidaymakers from the tri-polar moon of Navaro, is still unclear.

And on a brighter note we'll be reporting from Tollport G715, where they are expecting their 10,000,000,000th customer later today. We hope to talk live to the Tollmaster, just as soon as we get the remote cameras working.

But first, more on the Bannerman invasion of the home planet of the Chimerons. Reports just in claim that the Chimeron Queen has escaped her home planet in a stolen Bannerman craft...'

[The Channel 403 News Headlines]

Around this time Arcturus won the Galactic Olympic Games, with Betelgeuse coming a close second, while the economy of Algol was subject to irreversible inflation. The galaxy was now ruled by a human President and was becoming overpopulated, with famine a problem on worlds across known space. Tranquil Repose on Necros had been established for some time as a resting place for the dead of the galaxy – literally, as they were kept in suspended animation there until whatever had killed them was cured by medical science. The "rock and roll years" of twentieth century Earth were extremely popular. The DJ's grandfather managed to purchase some genuine records from Earth on a visit there. [24]

# ? 4500 - DESTINY OF THE DALEKS [25] [26]

'The Daleks encountered a new threat: the Movellans, a race of humanoid androids from system 4X-Alpha-4. The origin of this race is unknown. Were they robot slaves who had rebelled against their masters? Old enemies from another galaxy? Whatever the case may be, the Daleks were forced to abandon all operations elsewhere in the galaxy, including Skaro, and mobilise a huge battlefleet. The two mighty fleets faced each other in space, their battlecomputers calculating the moment of optimum advantage. There was instant stalemate, and not a shot was fired for centuries. The vast Dalek Fleet was kept completely occupied, except for the occasional raiding mission for slave workers on outer planets such as Kantra or on starships of Earth's Deep Space Fleet. The Daleks came to realise that they were too dependent on logic to win a war fought by another logical machine race. Their battlecomputers offered the suggestion that they should turn to their creator, Davros. The Dalek Supreme ordered that a force should be sent to Skaro to recover Davros from the ruins of the Kaled Bunker. Mining operations started up, and the Daleks discovered their creator, who had survived in suspended animation for centuries. A Movellan party was sent to Skaro to investigate Dalek operations. As they arrived, the Daleks' slaves managed to break free. Before a Dalek ship could arrive from Supreme Command, the slaves had overpowered the Movellans, and defeated the small Dalek force. Davros was captured by the human force, who returned to Earth in the Movellan ship.'

# & 4590 - RESURRECTION OF THE DALEKS [27]

'Davros was put on trial by the human authorities. Humanity had abandoned the death penalty, so instead Davros was placed in suspended animation aboard a prison station in deep space. While Davros slept, humanity discovered a cure for Becks Syndrome.

Without Davros's assistance, the Daleks were helpless. The Daleks lost the war when the Movellans released a virus that only affected Dalek tissue. Weakened, the Daleks

captured and imprisoned by Earth, before re-engineering the Daleks and gradually taking control over his creations. The series ends with the ultimate destruction of the Daleks' home planet of Skaro. Here, for convenience sake, I refer to the events of these four stories as 'the Davros Era', a term that is never used on-screen.

It is never stated exactly when the Davros Era is set, although it is clearly far in Earth's future and must be after any other story featuring Skaro. (Some fans have speculated that there may be a 'New Skaro' that the Daleks move to after this, but there is no evidence for this on-screen, and on the occasions when we see Skaro it is clearly the same world.) This would mean that the Davros Era is after the events of *The Daleks' Master Plan* (4000).

The first two editions of *The Programme Guide* set *Destiny of the Daleks* at 'c 4500'. *The Terrestrial Index* took the Doctor's speech to the Black Dalek in *Remembrance of the Daleks* that the Daleks are "a thousand years" from home literally, and set the stories in, respectively, 'as the 27th century began', 'towards the end of the 27th century', 'as the 28th century began' and 'about 2960'. 'The TARDIS Logs' chose "8740 AD" for *Destiny of the Daleks*. Ben Aaronovitch's novelisation of *Remembrance of the Daleks* and his introduction to the *Abslom Daak – Dalek Killer* graphic album had extracts from a history book, *The Children of Davros*, published in '4065', apparently well after *Remembrance of the Daleks*.

In *Lucifer Rising* by Andy Lane we discover that the Guild of Adjudicators eventually becomes the Grand Order of Oberon referred to in *Revelation of the Daleks*, yet the Adjudicators are still active in Lane's *Original Sin*, so in terms of the novels *Revelation of the Daleks* must take place well after 2975.

25 This is what we know of Earth and its neighbours at the time of the Davros Era.

26 Dating *Destiny of the Daleks* – [see also THE DAVROS ERA page 222]. The Daleks and Movellans have been locked in stalemate for "centuries". Earth has a Deep Space Fleet. In *Resurrection of the Daleks*, it is made clear that there is deadlock between the Movellans and the Daleks' *computers*, not the Daleks themselves.

27 Dating *Resurrection of the Daleks* – [see also THE DAVROS ERA page 222]. This is the sequel to *Destiny of the Daleks*. Davros says he has been imprisoned for "ninety years". According to some reports, the rehearsal script set the story in 4590, which would follow the date established in *The Terrestrial Index*. This date also appears in *The Encyclopaedia of the Worlds of Doctor Who*.

28 Dating *Revelation of the*

were forced to rely on hired mercenaries and Duplicates – conditioned clones produced by their experiments in genetic engineering performed on humans snatched from many timezones. *The Dalek chain of command had been shattered, and the various surviving Black Daleks vied for supreme command of the Dalek race.* One Supreme Dalek came up with an audacious plan that would strengthen the Daleks' position *and unite the Dalek factions behind him.* Davros would be released from his prison, and would use his scientific genius and understanding of the Daleks to find an antidote for the Movellan virus. Dalek Duplicate technology would be used to strike on two further fronts: one group infiltrated twentieth century Earth, while a second group – duplicate versions of the Doctor and his companions – would assassinate the High Council of Gallifrey. The plan totally failed. Once Davros was released, he attempted to usurp control of the Dalek army, planning to completely re-engineer the race. This met with resistance from those loyal to the Supreme Dalek and the two factions began fighting. The Duplicates rebelled, destroying the prison station. The resulting explosion destroyed the Dalek battlecruiser.'

## ? 4615 – REVELATION OF THE DALEKS [28]

'Although affected by the Movellan virus, Davros reached an escape craft that he had prepared. He was picked up by a freighter en route to the planet Necros. Once there, he formed an alliance with local businesswoman Kara. Davros took control of Tranquil Repose, and secretly began to break down the corpses into a foodstuff. This ended famine across the galaxy, and Davros gained a reputation as "the Great Healer".

Meanwhile, the Daleks reoccupied Skaro, and a new Supreme Dalek came to power. The Daleks had developed biomechanoid computers that interfaced with human brains to provide the Daleks with the creativity that they had lost, and they began to reassert their power. [29]

When Kara discovered that Davros was also growing a new army of genetically re-engineered Daleks from the corpses, and planned to use them to take effective control of her company, she hired the services of the assassin Orcini, an excommunicated member of the Grand Order of Oberon. Davros, like the Daleks before him, had been keeping track of the Doctor's movements. When one of the Doctor's friends, the agronomist Arthur Stengos, died, Davros prepared for the Doctor to attend the funeral. Orcini and the Doctor thwarted Davros's plans, and the Daleks were summoned from Skaro to capture their creator.'

## ? 4663 – REMEMBRANCE OF THE DALEKS [30]

'On his return to Skaro, Davros managed to usurp control from the Supreme Dalek and declared himself Dalek Emperor. With his body now wasted, Davros was reduced to little more than a disembodied head. He fashioned a new casing for himself. Most Daleks supported Davros, who genetically re-engineered the race and oversaw a complete revamp of Dalek technology. These "Imperial Daleks" were given new cream and gold livery, improved weapons, sensor plates and eyestalks. As always, some Daleks dissented: this "Renegade Dalek" faction followed the Black Dalek and fled Skaro using the Time Controller. Both factions had discovered the existence of the Hand of Omega, a powerful Gallifreyan device capable of manipulating stars. They converged on Earth in 1963...

...Davros was unable to control the device, however, and it travelled to Skaro in his native time and made its sun go supernova, obliterating the planet. Although Davros escaped, his flagship was destroyed and the Dalek homeworld was destroyed forever.'

[The Children of Davros, Njeri Ngugi]

## 5000 – THE INVISIBLE ENEMY [31]

5000 AD was "the Year of the Great Breakout", when humanity "went leapfrogging across the galaxy like a tidal wave" *once again*. To prepare the way, the Space Exploration Programme was instigated in the late fiftieth century, and a huge methane/oxygen refinery was set up on Titan. On asteroid K4067 the

Daleks – [see also THE DAVROS ERA page 222]. This story is set an unspecified amount of time after *Resurrection of the Daleks*. It has been long enough for Davros to gain a galaxy-wide reputation and build a new army of Daleks. The galaxy is ruled by a human President and faces famine.

29 Skaro has been abandoned for "centuries" before *Destiny of the Daleks*, but the Supreme Dalek seems to be based there in *Revelation of the Daleks*. We seen the biomechanoid in *Remembrance of the Daleks* – presumably the Daleks haven't developed it when they lose the war with the Movellans.

30 Dating *Remembrance of the Daleks* - [see also THE DAVROS ERA page 222]. This story is the sequel to *Revelation of the Daleks* and again there is no indication of how long it has been since the previous story. Davros has completely revamped the Daleks and their technology, presumably a fairly lengthy process.

31 Dating *The Invisible Enemy* – The Doctor states that it is 5000 AD, "the Year of the Great Breakout" and implies that the human race has not yet left the solar system, which contradicts virtually every other story set in the future – indeed, this story would fit very neatly into this timeline about the year 2100. 'The TARDIS Logs' offered the date '4778'.

**32** *The Talons of Weng-Chiang.* This happened "about the year 5000" according to the Doctor, "the fifty-first" century according to Greel. Presumably it is after 'The Invisible Enemy' - it is a little odd that just two televised stories after the Doctor and Leela met Greel there is no mention of him in his native time. The Doctor says that he was with the Filipino army during their final advance.

**33 THE SOLAR FLARES** – The Solar Flares ravage Earth "thousands of years" after the thirtieth century [see also Dating *Revenge of the Cybermen* page 201]. The last recorded human activity on Earth for millions of years is in the fifty-first century (*The Talons of Weng-Chiang*, and *The Invisible Enemy*). I speculate that the Solar Flares occur relatively soon after this time.

The first edition of *The Programme Guide* claimed that Earth was only evacuated between 'c 2800' and 'c 2900', while the second suggested dates between 'c 2900' and 'c 4300'. *The Terrestrial Index* attempted to rationalise the statement that the Ark was built in the "thirtieth century", by stating that Nerva was built, but then the Solar Flares "abated", Nerva was not informed, and the population of Nerva went on to recolonise Ravolox 'between 15,000 and 20,000' (as seen in *The Mysterious Planet*). This contradicts the date for *The Mysterious Planet* established on-screen and

centre for Alien Biomorphology (the Bi-Al Foundation) treated extraterrestrial diseases, as well as tending those who were injured in space. Regular shuttle runs were set up between the planets of the solar system and "good-for-nothing" spaceniks also travelled the cosmos.

Photon beam weapons were in common use, as were visiphones. Sophisticated robots and computers were built. The native language of the time was Finglish, a form of phonetic English.

In the Ice Age around the year five thousand, Findecker's discovery of the double-nexus particle had sent human technology into a cul-de-sac, but humans nonetheless developed limited psychic techniques such as the ability to read and influence the weak-minded. The Ice Age affected Earth once more, and the world was governed by various Alliances. The Peking Homunculus, an automaton with the cerebral cortex of a pig, assassinated the commissioner of the Icelandic Alliance, almost precipitating World War Six. The Supreme Alliance came to power, and horrific war crimes were committed. The Supreme Alliance was finally defeated by the Filipino Army at the Battle of Reykjavik. The Alliance's Minister of Justice, Magnus Greel, the infamous Butcher of Brisbane, had performed terrible scientific experiments on one hundred thousand prisoners in an attempt to discover time travel and immortality. He escaped the collapse of the Alliance to the nineteenth century using a beam of zygma energy. He feared that Time Agents would pursue him. [32]

Even farther in the future, the Earth was ruled by the World Executive. Earth at this time was technically advanced, with advanced suspended animation techniques, fission guns and power supplied via solar stacks and granavox turbines. Scientists monitoring the Sun predicted a series of massive solar flares: within only a matter of years the surface of Earth would be ravaged and virtually all life would be wiped out. It would be five thousand years before the planet would be habitable again. [33]

The High Minister and the Earth Council began working on humanity's salvation. Carefully screened humans, the Star Pioneers, were sent out in vast colony ships to places such as Colony 9 and Andromeda. Nerva was converted into an Ark housing the cream of humanity, some one hundred thousand people, who were placed in suspended animation along with samples of animal and plant life. The Ark also contained the sum of human knowledge stored on microfilm.

The rest of humanity took to thermic shelters, knowing that they would probably not survive. When the solar flares came, every living thing on the Earth perished.

One group of Star Pioneers reached Andromeda and encountered the Wirrn, a race of parasitic insects who lived in the depths of space, visiting worlds only to breed. [34]

## ? 5433 – PLANET OF THE SPIDERS [35]

"Our ancestors were colonists and explorers. Four hundred and forty-three Earth years ago, their starship came out of its time-jump with no power left and crashed on Metebelis III."

[Oral Tradition of Metebelis III]

A few sheep survived the crash, as did a handful of spiders. The spiders found their way to the cave of the Blue Crystals, and the energies there mutated them, making them grow and boosting their intelligence and psychic ability. The "Eight-Legs" came to dominate the planet, harvesting the human population. The Eight-Legs were ruthless – they wiped out 269 villagers, the entire population of Skorda, when they tried to resist. After forming a psychic bridge with a Tibetan monastery on twentieth-century Earth, they plotted to travel back in time to conquer their homeworld, but they were defeated. Their Queen, the Great One, who had planned to complete the crystal lattice of the cave and use it to dominate the universe, was killed.

While those in Nerva slept, human colonies such as Gal Sec carved out a new Empire, with bases across half the galaxy. They retained legends of Nerva, "The Lost Colony", from the time of the Expansion, but most didn't believe that such a place really existed. In time, the colonies grew to distrust talk of

would represent a rather implausible oversight on behalf of the Earth's authorities. The book's supposition that the Solar Flares caused the Ice Age we see in *The Ice Warriors* (a theory repeated in *Legacy*) is specifically ruled out by dialogue in *The Ice Warriors*.

**34 ANDROMEDA** – According to the TARDIS Information File entry faked by the Master, *Castrovalva* was a planet in the Phylox series in Andromeda. There is some evidence that Zanak raided worlds there: the ground is littered with Andromedan bloodstones (*The Pirate Planet*). In the *The Daleks' Master Plan*, an intergalactic conference was held in the Andromeda galaxy. In *The Ark in Space*, we learn that Star Pioneers from Earth reached Andromeda and discovered that it was infested with the Wirrn. For a thousand years the two races fought each other, until humanity succeeded in destroying the Wirrn's breeding grounds. Mankind went on to colonise the galaxy, and by the time of *The Trial of a Time Lord* Parts One to Four, the civilisation was established on planets such as Sabalom Glitz's homeworld, Salostopus. At that time, Andromedans capable of building advanced robots and harnessing black light stole Matrix secrets and fled the wrath of the Time Lords. The Doctor considers visiting "the constellation of Andromeda" in *Timelash*.

35 Dating *Planet of the Spiders* – The colony ship that crashes on Metebelis III has intergalactic capability, as Metebelis is in the Acteon Galaxy. *The Terrestrial Index* claimed that the colony ship was 'lost during the early days of the 22nd century', dating *Planet of the Spiders* itself as 'c 2530'. 'The TARDIS Logs' suggested '4256'.

36 *The Sontaran Experiment.*

37 *Zamper.*

38 *The Highest Science.*

39 Dating *Tragedy Day* – There is no indication of the date in the book, although "Pantorus" is mentioned here (p83) and in *Zamper* (p57), perhaps suggesting they are set around the same time. It is "597" years since the planet was colonised (p597).

40 "Five thousand years" before *The Crystal Bucephalus* (p114).

41 Dating *Zamper* – It is "the sixtieth century" (p77). Earth appears to be populated at this time [see also THE ABANDONMENT OF EARTH page 231].

"Mother Earth". [36]

Along the Eastern edge of the galaxy there was political upheaval for a thousand years. Many human colony worlds such as Pyka, Marlex, Dalverius, Pantorus and Shaggra were at war with each other, and the galaxy's monetary system was in almost permanent crisis. In the fifty-fourth century, a consortium of industrialists attempted to solve the problem. Eventually they built Zamper, a planet within its own mini-universe that would be neutral and would supply state-of-the-art battleships to all sides. The only way to the planet was through a hyperspace gate controlled by Zamper itself, and the planet was completely self-contained, in order to keep its designs secret. In 473 years of operation, Zamper became rich, and maintained a balance of power in East Galaxy. The operation was completely smooth – averaging one minor technical failure every two hundred years. [37]

In 5665, the Chelonians launched an attack on the human colony of Vaagon, but their tanks vanished mysteriously before they could complete their conquest. Believing themselves to be blessed by divine intervention, the colonists were quite unprepared when the Chelonians reinvaded several generations later, and the colony was wiped out. [38]

## ? 5597 – TRAGEDY DAY [39]

On the Earth colony Olleril (a planet governed by the principles laid down in the ancient records *The Collins Guide to the Twentieth Century*, *One of Us* by Hugo Young, *The Manufacture of Consent* and *The Smash Hits Yearbook*, and as such having an eccentric, unworkable political and economic system that was an almost exact copy of the United Kingdom in the twentieth century) the Doctor defeated the plans of precocious boy genius Crispin, leader of the secret society of Luminus, something that not even the arachnid mutant Ernie "Eight Legs" McCartney, the most feared assassin in the Seventh Quadrant, could achieve.

Around 5764, there was a Dalek Civil War so serious that the Time Lords intervened. [40]

## c 5995 – ZAMPER [41]

There was revolution on Chelonia, and the peaceful forces of Little Sister overthrew Big Mother and initiated a cultural reformation that saw the warlike race transformed into the galaxy's foremost flower-arrangers. Forty years later, many Chelonians hankered for the old blood-and-glory days, and Big Mother's fleet headed for Zamper to purchase a powerful Series 336c Delta-Spiral Sun Blaster – a ship whose effectiveness had been demonstrated in the Sprox civil war and the skirmishes of Pancoza, capable of withstanding neutronic ray blasts of up to an intensity of sixty blarks. With this, power could have been wrested back from Little Sister, but the Chelonians discovered that the Zamps, sluglike creatures used to build the ships on the planet, had their own dreams of conquest and were building their own battleship. In a variation of the Diemlisch manoeuvre (first used in the Third Wobesq-Majjina War), the Chelonian fleet destroyed itself in order to seal the gate between Zamper and the rest of the universe.

After a thousand years, the Star Pioneers had destroyed all the Wirrn breeding grounds, making Andromeda suitable for colonisation. One Wirrn Queen survived, and travelled through space towards Earth. After thousands of years she reached the Nerva Beacon, and although she was killed by the automatic defences on the station she managed to damage the systems that would have revived the humans, and to lay her eggs. [42]

After travelling for around seven thousand years in the Time Corridor created by the Doctor, Sutekh finally perished at the beginning of the ninetieth century. [43]

In 6198, the Federation Scientific Executive funded a research project into genetic experimentation. Geneticist Maximillian Arrestis hired a team of consultants to develop the Lazarus Intent, a religion that he hoped would become a moneymaking venture and allow him to survive his own death. His 'miracles' were publicised for three years, and his predictions of disasters all came to pass. The Codex of Lazarus was published early in the sixty-third century, and for nearly a decade he reaped the financial rewards of being the 'Messiah'.

Not content with this, Arrestis began to sell defence secrets to the Cybermen, Sontarans and Rutans. The Federation was fighting a war with the Sontarans at the time. In 6211, a stealth attack by the Sontarans wiped much of the Federation DataCore on Io. Three weeks later Tersurus was destroyed by an earthshock bomb, sold to the Sontarans by the Cybermen. This didn't stop the Federation from winning the war. When the

42 *The Ark in Space.* As the colonists are scheduled to be revived after "five thousand years" (c 10,000 AD), the Wirrn Queen must arrive on Nerva before that time.

43 *Pyramids of Mars.*

44 *The Crystal Bucephalus.*

45 In *The Ark in Space* Vira notes that scientists calculated that after the solar flares on Earth it would be "five thousand years before the biosphere was viable". In *The Sontaran Experiment* we learn that humanity has spread across the galaxy, that Earth has been habitable for "thousands of years" but that it has remained abandoned.

46 Dating *The Crystal Bucephalus* – The Doctor says that they are "six or seven centuries into the tenth millennium" (p27), but he also says that it is the "108th century", which is in the *eleventh* millennium (p40). This latter date is the correct one – elsewhere we learn that "10,663" was in the recent past (p69). Although the exact date is not specified in the novel, Craig Hinton worked from the assumption that it was set in the year 10,764 and I have adopted that date.

Sontaran Emperor suspected that Arrestis had double-crossed him, the traitor was brought to the Sontaran Throneworld and executed. 'Lazarus' became a martyr, the saviour of the galaxy, and, as he had always intended, it was the Intent of his followers to resurrect him.

After the great cybernetic massacres of the eighty-fifth century, sentient androids fell out of favour. From this point most robot servants were connected to a central webwork rather than being autonomous.

Eventually civil war broke out in the galaxy, splitting the Federation into the Confederation, democratic rebels, and the Humanic Empire ruled over by the Chen dynasty. Early in the war, Mirabilis had sided with the rebel forces, those opposed to the Emperor. The final battle of the war took place in the Mirabilis system. The democratic forces won, but the Imperial Fleet devastated Mirabilis itself with an atmospheric plasma burst that killed ninety percent of the population. Chen was captured and executed, ending the Chen dynasty.

The galaxy entered a new dark age, in which scientific progress all but ceased. During the ninetieth century, the remnants of the Federation became the Union. There were two other forces for unity, the Elective, a massive criminal organisation that controlled all criminal activity between New Alexandria and the Perseus Rift, and the Lazarus Intent, a religious organisation that now commanded eight quadrillion people.

The Antonine rescue raid on Scultiis in 9381 failed when their weapons were disrupted by the natives' electric fields.

Around the end of the one hundredth century, two Silurian scientists, Ethra and Teelis, worked on time travel experiments. The results were published in the March 9978 edition of *Abstract Meanderings in Theoretical Physics.* [44]

The Earth became habitable again around 10,000 AD. Humanity did not recolonise their homeworld. [45]

## 10,764 – THE CRYSTAL BUCEPHALUS [46]

In 10,753, Alexhendri Lassiter stabilised a time gate and rescued Lazarus from the Sontaran Throneworld, fulfilling the Lazarus Intent. But the truth about the false Messiah quickly became clear, and Arrestis seized control of the criminal Elective. Meanwhile, Lassiter and his brother Sebastian built the Crystal Bucephalus, a time travel restaurant on the planet New Alexandria that aimed to send the galaxy's elite to the finest eating establishments in time and space.

Eleven years later, the Crystal Bucephalus was destroyed,

and Arrestis was revealed as Lazarus. Over the next century the Union collapsed. It was replaced by the Junta, a military dictatorship that had developed from the Elective. For a millennium there was barbarism, until the Junta was overthrown by the Confederation.

## c 15,000 – THE ARK IN SPACE [47]

The colonists on Nerva were reawoken, to discover that the Wirrn had infested the Ark. They were defeated, and humanity prepared to reoccupy their homeworld. It was planned that they would restock the planet with plant and animal life and rebuild human civilisation. [48]

## & 15,000 – THE SONTARAN EXPERIMENT [49]

'[REPORT TO SONTARAN GRAND STRATEGIC COUNCIL]

Field Major Styre of G3 Intelligence has been killed while conducting a Military Assessment Survey on the planet Earth. The planet had acquired strategic value in our war with the accursed Rutans, and it was believed to be devoid of intelligent life. Styre was sent to confirm our initial findings, and to capture Earthlings for assessment. Our fleet stood ready to invade the galaxy, awaiting Styre's findings. A mission from Gal Sec colony answered a fake distress signal, and their ship was vaporised. Styre proceeded to experiment on the nine survivors, including a group that was allowed to roam loose, which was monitored by a survey robot. These were members of the slave caste, though, and in a duel with a human of the warrior caste, Styre was killed, his robot immobilised and his spacecraft destroyed.'

"The Dalek War against Venus in Space Year 17,000 was halted by the intervention of a fleet of War Rockets from the planet Hyperon. The rockets were made of a metal completely resistant to Dalek firepower. The Dalek taskforce was completely destroyed." [50]

*We know little about the future of humanity following this*

47 Dating *The Ark in Space* – In this story, Harry twice suggests that they are "ten thousand years" after the time of the Solar Flares [see also THE SOLAR FLARES page 226], and the Doctor confirms this in *The Sontaran Experiment*, which takes place immediately afterwards.

*The Terrestrial Index* set the stories between '15,000 and 20,000'. 'The TARDIS Logs' suggested a date of '28,537'. *Cybermen* offered the year '? 14714'. 'The TARDIS Special' gave the date 'c 131st Century'.

48 THE ABANDONMENT OF EARTH – Earth is abandoned for "ten thousand years" between the time of the Solar Flares and *The Sontaran Experiment* (c 5000–c 15,000 AD), and for at least three thousand five hundred years before (and an unknown amount of time after) *Birthright* (c 18,500 AD–?). A line cut from the rehearsal script but retained in the novelisation of *Planet of Evil* reveals that 'The Tellurian planet [Earth] has been uninhabited since the Third Era' (significantly before 37,166 AD).

49 Dating *The Sontaran Experiment* – The story immediately follows 'The Ark in Space'.

50 *Genesis of the Daleks.*

51 [see also ANDROMEDA Page 227]. Inter Minor is in the Acteon Group, as is Metebelis III (*Carnival of Monsters*), although it is later referred to as the Acteon Galaxy (*The Green Death* and *Planet of the Spiders*). The Isop Galaxy is the location of Vortis (*The Web Planet*), and Artoro and the Anterides are referred to in *Planet of Evil.*

52 Dating *The Web Planet* – The story seems to take place in the future, as the Animus craves "Earth's mastery of Space". Bill Strutton's novelisation places it in '20,000', although the Doctor suggests that the TARDIS's 'time pointer' might not be working. The New Adventure *Birthright* suggests that Earth is abandoned at this time, but it is established in *The Ark in Space* and *The Sontaran Experiment* that man has spread through the universe.

53 Dating *Birthright* – Ace says she was born "Oh, probably about twenty thousand years ago" (p134), although quite how she reaches this figure is unclear. It is "year 2959" of the Charrl occupation of Earth (p1) when they start their scheme, which will take "almost five hundred years" (p60), but curiously it is "year 2497" (p109) when they finish! This is presumably a misprint, and ought to read '3497'.

54 *Shada.* Chris Parsons's dating of the book gives a figure of "minus twenty

*point, and what information we do have is fragmentary.* Humanity's influence was now felt in other galaxies, such as Andromeda, Acteon and Isop, Artoro and the Anterides.[51]

## ? 20,000 – THE WEB PLANET [52]

'VORTIS – Planet in the Isop Galaxy, home of the mothlike Menoptra, who worshipped in glorious temples of light and lived in the flower forests. They kept an antlike race, the Zarbi, as cattle. The planet was invaded by the Animus, an entity that could absorb all forms of energy, and which pulled three planetoids into orbit around Vortis, including the planet Pictos. Most of the Menoptra fled to Pictos, and the descendants of those that remained slowly devolved into sightless dwarfs, the Optera. The Animus used the Zarbi as soldiers, and had dreams of galactic conquest until it was destroyed by the Isop-tope, a Menoptra weapon.'

[*Bartholomew's Planetary Gazetteer*, Volume XXII]

## c 22,000 – BIRTHRIGHT [53]

For 3497 years, the insectlike Charrl occupied the planet Anthykhon, far from the major spacelanes. Their vast hive pumped ammonia into the already-depleted atmosphere; the planet's ozone layer had been depleted; the seas had dried up; the soil was barren. The native life, the Hairies, survived by adapting to this environment. The Charrl were not savages, indeed they had created over three hundred of the seven hundred wonders of the universe, before coming to this world to escape solar flares on their own planet. The Charrls made contact with Muldwych, a mysterious time-traveller exiled to Anthykhon at this time, and together they attempted to traverse the Great Divide back into the verdant past of their world. Anthykhon was Earth during one of the several periods far in the future when the planet was isolated and forgotten.

Carbon-dating suggests that 'The Worshipful and Ancient Law of Gallifrey' was written around 22,000 AD.[54]

## ? 25,000 – THE FACE OF EVIL [55]

A Mordee colony ship landed on an unnamed world and developed a computer failure. The Doctor helped them by linking the computer to his own mind, but he neglected to remove his personality print from the data core. The computer became schizophrenic. Many centuries later, it was worshipped by the colonists as Xoanon, and it had split them into two groups, the "Sevateem", the descendants of Survey Team Six, and the Tesh, formerly the technicians, to whom Xoanon granted psychic powers. Xoanon was attempting to breed superhumans, but the Doctor returned and made a reverse transfer, curing the computer. Leela, a warrior of the Sevateem, left with the Doctor.

## 37,166 – PLANET OF EVIL [56]

'ZETA MINOR – A planet on the edge of the universe, beyond Cygnus A, as distant from the Artoro Galaxy as that is from the Anterides. A Morestran survey team was sent to the planet to locate a new energy source, as their home planet faced disaster. They discovered that at night Zeta Minor passed into an incomprehensible universe of "anti matter", and that as a result it was impossible to remove anything from the planet without incurring the wrath of powerful creatures. When Professor Sorenson, the only surviving member of the survey team, returned to Morestra, he tried to generate energy from planetary motion.'

[Bartholomew's Planetary Gazetteer, Volume XXVI]

In forty-two thousand years time, a new breed of Zamps should be ready to conquer the universe. [57]

## ? 100,000 – INFINITE REQUIEM [58]

Far in the future, representatives of over seven hundred cultures, including the Monoids, Morestrans, Rakkhins and Rills, used the Pridka Dream Centre. The Pridka were a race of blue-skinned, crested telepaths, and the Centre used their healing skills. At any one time, fifteen thousand individuals would be booked into the Centre, making it a tempting resource for the Sensopaths, a psychic communal mind intent on dominating the physical world.

thousand years", with time running backwards over the book. This might be a property of the book, rather than an indication it comes from the future.

55 Dating *The Face of Evil* – The date is arbitrary, the story could take place at any point in the far future. The Doctor states in *The Invisible Enemy* that the year 5000 is the time of Leela's ancestors. Humans evolve limited psychic powers around the fifty-first century (*The Talons of Weng-Chiang*) and the Tesh have psychic powers, so they might originate after that time, although they probably receive their powers from Xoanon. In *The Sun Makers*, the Usurian computer correctly guesses that "Sevateem" is a corruption of "Survey Team", and that Leela comes from a "degenerate, unsupported Tellurian colony", perhaps suggesting that there are many such planets. *The Terrestrial Index* set the story 'several centuries' after the '52nd Century'. 'The TARDIS Logs' offered the date '4931'.

56 Dating *Planet of Evil* – While it could be argued that the date '37,166' that appears on the grave marker might use some Morestran scale of dating, the Doctor does state that the TARDIS has overshot contemporary London by "thirty thousand years". The New Adventures *The Dimension Riders* and *Infinite Requiem* both suggest that the Morestrans are not human.

57  *Zamper* (p249).

58  Dating *Infinite Requiem* –
Events at the Pridka Dream
Centre occur "Beyond Common
Era of Earth Calendar" (p83),
and the presence of Morestrans
and Monoids emphasises this.
This date is arbitrary.

59  Dating *The War Games* – It is
stated that humanity has been
killing itself for "half a million
years" before this story takes
place, which (coincidentally)
ties up with the date 309,906
established for the Doctor's
first Trial (or "Malfeasance
Tribunal") in *The Deadly
Assassin*. 'The TARDIS Logs'
suggested a date of '48,063' for
this story, *Apocrypha* offered
'5950 AD'.

60  In *The War Games* it is
established that the War Lords
have "ten" zones under their
control (this is emphasised by
the map we see), including the
Control Zone. However,
fourteen distinct war zones are
referred to: W.W.I ("1917"), the
Roman Zone ("2000 years"
before 1917), the Franco–
Prussian War (1870–1), the
Thirty Years War (1618-48), the
Jacobite Rebellion ("1745"), the
English Civil War (1642–6), the
Boer War (1899-1902), the
American Civil War ("1862"),
Napoleon's advance into
Russia ("1812"), the Russo–
Japanese War ("1905"), the
Boxer Rising (1900), the
Crimean War (1853–6), the
Mexican Uprising (1867) and
the Greek Zone (c 500 BC).

61  "Half a million years" after

## 309,906 – THE WAR GAMES [59]

A race of alien warlords attempted to raise an army of galactic
conquest by programming human soldiers kidnapped from various points in history with stolen Time Lord technology, supplied by the renegade War Chief. When the plan was uncovered, the Time Lords confined them to their planet by erecting
a forcefield and dematerialised their leader, the War Lord. [60]

After "half a million years of industrial progress", the Ancient One, a Haemovore, was the last living creature to in-
habit an Earth the surface of which was "just a chemical
slime".
This timeline was erased by the Ancient Haemovore itself,
when it killed Fenric and prevented him from releasing the
poison that would start the destruction of life on Earth. [61]

## ? 802,701 – TIMELASH [62]

The third Doctor and Jo visited Karfel, preventing a great famine. The Doctor also reported the scientist Magellan to the
praesidium for unethical experimentation on the reptilian
Morlox. Over the next century, Magellan accidentally merged
himself with a Morlox in an accident with Mustakozene 80 and
became the Borad. He took control of Karfel, enforcing discipline with an army of androids and the threat of exile into a
time corridor, the Timelash. The Borad planned to provoke a
war with the neighbouring planet Bandril and then to populate
Karfel with mutated clones of himself. He was thrown into the
Timelash, ending up in Loch Ness in the twelfth century.

Man fought the Primal Wars in the Tenth Segment of Time. During this period much scientific knowledge was lost, including
the cure for the common cold. [63]

Millions of years in the future, Earth's mineral wealth was
finally exhausted, and its people were dying. In return for their
labour, the Usurians moved mankind to Mars, which they
terraformed, and then on to Pluto, where six megropolises were
built, each with its own artificial sun. [64]

# c 2,000,000 – THE TRIAL OF A TIME LORD
## Parts One to Four [65]

Five centuries prior to this time, a group of Andromedans based on Earth stole scientific secrets contained in the Matrix of the Time Lords. By order of the High Council, the Magnotron was used to move Earth and its entire constellation two light years. The Andromedans, though, knew that the Time Lords had discovered them and had built a survival chamber. They entered suspended animation, awaiting their rescue. The Robot Recovery mission sent to recover the Andromedans missed Earth in its new location and sped on into the depths of space.

'The planet Ravolox in the Stellian Galaxy is fascinating, and not only because it has the same mass, angle of tilt and period of rotation as Earth. Five hundred years ago, it was devastated by a fireball. Everyone on the planet died with the exception of "The Tribe of the Free". They worship the god Haldron, and slay any space traveller trying to steal his totem, a black-light converter made from pure siligtone. They believe that their ancestors' space travel brought down the wrath of their god, and caused the solar fireball.

Beneath the surface lies Marb station, a completely self-contained system, regulated by the station guards that maintains strict water rationing and population control. They worship "the Immortal", a being they claim lives in a citadel within their complex.'

[*Extinct Civilisations*, Woris Bossard]

'Sabalom Glitz came from Salostopus in Andromeda. Glitz was an habitual jailbird and thief, always on the lookout for a fast grotzit. He formed a business partnership with the renegade Time Lord the Master, who knew that Earth had been moved and renamed Ravolox by the High Council. His accomplice at this time was a young man, Dibber. After this time, he acquired a ship, the *Nosferatu*, which raided space freighters and ended up on Svartos with a rotten cargo and a mutinous crew. Glitz tried to sell both to Kane, the ruthless leader of Iceworld.'

*The Curse of Fenric*. When Wainwright asks the Doctor how he knows about the Haemovores' future, the Doctor says "I've seen it".

**62** Dating *Timelash* – No date is given on-screen. I have arbitrarily set it in the same year that the Time Traveller met the Eloi and the Morlocks in H.G. Wells's *The Time Machine*. There is no indication on-screen exactly when the third Doctor visited Karfel; the novelisation suggests that it was 'at least one hundred years' before this story, during the time of Katz's grandfather.

**63** *The Ark*.

**64** *The Sun Makers*.

**65** Dating *The Trial of a Time Lord* Parts One to Four – The Doctor consults his pocket watch and suggests that it is "two million years" after Peri's time, and this date is confirmed in both the camera script and novelisation. Although never stated on-screen, the Time Lords might erase the Ravolox Incident from the timestream after *The Trial of a Time Lord*. *The Terrestrial Index* attempted to rationalise the various 'ends of the Earth' seen in *Doctor Who*, but in doing so it ignored virtually every date given on-screen. It is claimed, for example, that this story was set 'c 14,500'. 'The TARDIS Special' gave the date as 'two billion' AD, an understandable mishearing of the Doctor's line.

**66** Dating *Dragonfire* – No date is given on-screen, although this is the native time of Sabalom Glitz, and so the story takes place after *The Trial of a Time Lord* Parts One to Four. Iceworld services "twelve galaxies", and Glitz comes from Andromeda [see also ANDROMEDA page 227], suggesting that intergalactic travel is now routine. According to the novelisation, Svartos is in the "Ninth Galaxy".

67 *Head Games* and *Goth Opera*.

68 Dating *The Sun Makers* – Set unspecified "millions of years in the future" according to contemporary publicity material, but this is never stated explicitly on-screen. Earth has had time to regenerate its mineral wealth, which would suggest that the story is set a long way into the future. *The Programme Guide* failed to reconcile *The Sun Makers* with other stories, claiming that the Company dominated humanity only from 'c 2100' to 'c 2200' (first edition), or 'c 2200' to 'c 2300' (second edition). *The Terrestrial Index* suggested that the Earth was abandoned some centuries after the '52nd Century', and was recolonised '5000 years' later. 'The TARDIS Logs' suggested that the story was set 'c 40,000'.

[*Nasty Great Rotters of the Galaxy*, R K Cossin]

## c 2,000,000 – DRAGONFIRE [66]

On the space trading colony of Iceworld, on the dark side of the planet Svartos, Kane was assembling an army of soldiers in cryosleep. This deep cryogenic technique ensured that when revived they would have no memories of their former life, and would serve him without question. Many chose to serve Kane willingly. They would have the Mark of the Sovereign burnt on to the palm of their right hand by Kane, whose natural body temperature was minus 193 Celsius. One of his officers, Belazs, joined Kane when she was sixteen, and served him for twenty years.

Kane earned many crowns trading supplies to space travellers, many of whom were drawn to Iceworld by the legends of a fire-breathing dragon in the ice tunnels beneath the colony. No one knew of Kane's past, as revealed in Proammon Planetary Archive Criminal History Segment 93-12-03: Kane was an exile from the planet Proammon, guilty of systematic acts of violence and extortion with his lover Sana, who killed herself rather than face trial. He was sent to the barren planet Svartos and remained there for three thousand years, slowly building his powerbase and dreaming of a return to Proammon. The key to his plans was the Dragonfire, a source of energy contained within the head of the Dragon, a biomechanoid sent to Svartos to prevent Kane from escaping the planet.

The Doctor uncovered the truth, and showed Kane that Proammon had been destroyed a thousand years after Kane's exile. The Doctor's companion, Melanie Bush, elected to stay behind and help run Iceworld, now renamed the *Nosferatu II*, with Sabalom Glitz.

After a year, Glitz abandoned Mel on the planet Avalone following a failed banking scam he had tried, using software designed by Mel for more innocent purposes. He teamed up with Dibber once again, found a Miniscope and briefly met Romana. [67]

## ? 4,000,000 – THE SUN MAKERS [68]

'Usurius Company Report. Zero-Zero-Five. The Tellurian Solar System is no longer economically viable. There was a history of resistance on Pluto, particularly among the Ajacks, the miners of Megropolis Three. Executive Grade Kandor from Megropolis Four survived for three years in the correction centre, but apart from that, the suppressants in the atmosphere and food worked perfectly and the Company raised many talmars from the three hundred million workers. However, a rebellion was started by the Doctor, a Gallifreyan with a long history of violence and economic subversion. He imposed a growth tax and rendered the Pluto operation uneconomic.'

During the Twenty-Seventh Segment of Time, humanity attempted time travel experiments, but they proved to be a total failure. [69]

"Fleeing from the imminence of a catastrophic collision with the Sun, a group of refugees from the doomed planet Earth…"
[TARDIS Information File]

## c 10,000,000 – THE ARK [70]

In the Fifty-Seventh Segment of Time, ten million years hence, scientists realised that Earth was falling towards the Sun. With the help of the Monoids, a mysterious race whose own planet had been destroyed in a supernova many years before, humanity constructed a great space vessel that contained the entire human, Monoid, animal and plant population of Earth held on microcells in miniaturised form. Audio space research had revealed a world that would be suitable for colonisation: Refusis II. It would take seven hundred years to reach the new world, and to symbolise the journey and the survival of man, a vast statue of a human carved from gregarian rock was begun.

The ship set out, and the few humans and Monoid servants remaining active, the Guardians, watched Earth's final destruction. Very soon afterwards the common cold swept through the vessel, brought by a space traveller. One of her companions cured the disease using animal membranes.

## c 10,000,000 – FRONTIOS [71]

A vast colony ship containing thousands of people and the technology and material capable of rebuilding the whole of human civilisation was sent to the Veruna system on the distant edge of

69 *The Ark*. Earth, and a number of races known to Earth, most notably the Daleks, achieved limited success with time travel experiments, but these have presumably been forgotten by now.

70 Dating *The Ark* – The Commander states that this is "the fifty-seventh segment" of time, which the Doctor instantly calculates to be "ten million years" after Steven and Dodo's time.

71 Dating *Frontios* – According to the Doctor, the story happens "on the outer limits. The TARDIS has drifted too far into the future". The inhabitants of Frontios are among the very last humans, and they have evacuated Earth in circumstances that sound very similar to those of *The Ark* – although their colony ship is of a very different design and there is no sign of the Monoids. It is difficult to judge their level of technology, as virtually everything is lost in the crash, but it does not seem as advanced as that of *The Ark*.

72 Dating *The Ark* – The last
two episodes of the story take
place at the end of *The Ark*'s
journey, "seven hundred years"
after the first two episodes.

the universe. Every system on the colony ship was failure proof, but they failed anyway, and the ship crashed on Frontios. Most of the crew died in the crash, and many more from the diseases that spread through the colony immediately afterwards, but eventually Captain Revere restored order. For ten years, the survivors planted and harvested crops, stocking up with food. And then the meteorite bombardments began, striking the colony with such accuracy that it was clear that it was being deliberately targeted. For thirty years the bombardment continued, but that wasn't the worst of it: the dead were swallowed up by the earth. Over the years the number of people deserting the colony, Retrogrades, swelled.

And then Captain Revere was swallowed by the earth while he investigated the mineral wealth of the planet, leaving his son, Plantagenet, in command. The colony was in danger of falling apart. It was being targeted by the Tractators, insect creatures with the power to harness gravity. Under the command of their leader, the Gravis, they had pulled down the colony ship, and then pelted it with asteroids. The Gravis had arrived five hundred years before and planned to channel the gravity fields and pilot Frontios throughout the cosmos, but he was isolated and transported to the planet Kolkokron. Without their leader, the Tractators were mindless drones, and the survival of the human colony was assured.

## c 10,000,700 – THE ARK [72]

Seven hundred years after leaving the solar system, the Monoids now controlled the ship bound for Refusis II, and the statue commemorating the voyage was now of a Monoid. The humans now called the ship *The Ark* after an old Earth legend, but the Monoids kept the descendants of the Guardians in check with heat prods. The fever that had swept *The Ark* seven hundred years before had never fully abated, and it had weakened the humans.

*The Ark* arrived at Refusis II, and Launcher 14 was sent to the surface. At first there was no sign of life, but it quickly transpired that the native Refusians were invisible giants. Nevertheless, I, the leader of the Monoids planned to take his race's microcells to the planet, and to destroy *The Ark* with a bomb planted in the head of the statue. With the Refusians help, the statue was thrown overboard, exploding harmlessly in space. The Refusians allowed the humans and Monoids to live on their world, if they promised to live in peace.

So, humanity survived the final destruction of its homeworld by travelling across the universe and rebuilding human civilisation on distant planets. What happened in the untold billions of years after that is a mystery – any TARDIS attempting to travel further into the future than this exceeds its time parameters, and the Time Lords themselves are unaware of anything beyond this time. "Knowledge has its limits; ours reaches this far and no further". [73]

Scientists can speculate on the distant future. They think, for example, that Earth's sun will finally become a supernova in ten billion years time. [74]

*Elsewhere, eventually, the universe settles into a golden age of scientific, evolutionary and social perfection. Utopian societies with incomprehensibly advanced technology trade and live in peace with one another.*

## ? – THE SAVAGES [75]

"A distant point of time, an age of great advancement, peace and prosperity". On one planet in this period, the Elders maintained a utopian civilisation free from material needs, with unlimited energy. They survived by draining life energy from the savages who lived in the wastelands outside their beautiful city. "The Traveller from Beyond Time", the Doctor, ended this injustice, and his companion Steven Taylor remained behind to rule the civilisation as it renounced barbarism.

## ? – THE ALSO PEOPLE [76]

In the galaxy known as Home Galaxy, a number of races achieved starflight at around the same time. They encountered each other in a star system with a white dwarf star. Over thousands of years, a Worldsphere was built enclosing the star: a Dyson Sphere with a surface area of $2.77 \times 10^{17}$ km². The People of the Worldsphere developed into perhaps the most advanced and peaceful race the universe has ever seen. Their technology was such that they

73 In *Frontios* a message flashes up on a TARDIS console screen – "Boundary Error – Time Parameters Exceeded". Likewise, in *The Sun Makers* the Doctor is worried that the TARDIS might have "gone right through the time spiral". This limitation doesn't seem to affect the TARDIS in *The Ark* or *The Savages*, or the New Adventure *Timewyrm: Apocalypse*, which are also set in the distant future. The words are those of the Doctor in *Frontios*, and the novelisation of that story makes it clear that "ours" refers to the Time Lords, and that the story is set at the 'edge of the Gallifreyan noosphere'. Perhaps it is significant that the Time Lords are unable to travel beyond the time of Earth's destruction.

74 *Colony in Space*.

75 Dating *The Savages* – At the end of *The Gunfighters* the Doctor claims that they have now landed at "a distant point in time" (see the quote below). The Elders have the technology to track the TARDIS, but are not capable of time travel themselves. They declare themselves to be "human".

76 Dating *The Also People* – The remains of "A sub-gas giant that had broken up sixty-two billion years previously" are referred to (p168). As the universe is only fifteen billion years old at time of going to press, the novel must be set many tens of billions of years in the future. This is perhaps confirmed by the Doctor's

observation that "the diary's pretty much clear" until "the heat death of the universe" (p186).

77 Dating *Timewyrm: Apocalypse* – The novel is set "several billion years" in the future (p3), "ten billion years" before the end of the universe (p178).

78 *Timewyrm: Revelation* (p197).

79 *Millennial Rites.*

signed a non-aggression pact with the Time Lords of Gallifrey. They had military capability – thirty years before the Doctor visited them, twenty-six billion individuals died in a war against an insectoid race, a war in which they used weapons with a thirty-light-year range. The two trillion being population, the people and the also people – sentient machines – of the Worldsphere was managed by God, a computer the size of a planet with almost infinite processing power.

On a holiday to the Worldsphere the Doctor solved the murder of viCari, the first drone to be killed for over three hundred years.

## ? – TIMEWYRM: APOCALYPSE [77]

Billions of years in the future, the guardians of the universe, even the Time Lords, were long extinct. The people of Kirith (the only planet orbiting a red giant in Galaxy QSO 0046 at the edge of the universe) never grew old or unhappy. For 3833 years, the Kirithons had been ruled by the eighty-four Panjistri who gave them food and technology. For nearly a thousand years the Panjistri performed genetic experiments, forcing the evolution of the Kirithons and attempting to create a being that had reached the Omega Point: an omniscient, omnipotent entity capable of halting the destruction of the universe. They succeeded in creating a golden sphere of expanding light, but the machine destroyed itself and the Panjistri, knowing that the universe must end.

And ten billion years later, its purpose achieved, our universe was destroyed in the Big Crunch. All matter imploded to a central point, returning to the state from which it was created "a bright blazing pinprick of sheer energy".

"One mad prophet martyr journeyed too far and saw the Timewyrm. He saw it in a timeline that he could not be sure of, devouring Rassilon or his shade, during the Blue Shift, that time of final conflict when Fenric shall slip his chains and the evil of the worlds shall rebound back on them in war." [78]

Just as there was a universe before ours, so another universe will be formed from the ashes of ours, and the physical laws there will be very different. This will be the domain of Saraquazel. [79]

**Section Eight**
**Gallifrey**

## TIMELINE: Gallifrey [1]

*The history of the Time Lords and their home planet of Gallifrey is shrouded in mystery. The Time Lords came to know little of their own past, and much that we have learnt is shrouded in mystery and self-contradiction. It is extremely difficult to reconcile the various accounts of the origins of the Time Lords. [Where such information was suppressed by the authorities, it appears in square brackets.]* [2]

Gallifreyan history can be divided into two periods: "the Old Time", the semi-legendary foundation of Time Lord society, aeons ago, and "recent history", that which has happened within living memory (with Time Lords, of course, living a long time). [3]

We have only a few scraps of knowledge about the history of Gallifrey before the discovery of time travel. Gallifrey was the home of "the oldest civilisation in the universe", and had had "ten million years of absolute power" by the time of the Doctor's second Trial. Gallifreyans mastered the use of transmats when the universe was less than half its present size. Time Lords used to speak and write Old High Gallifreyan, which eventually became a dead language. **Gallifrey meant, literally, "they that walk in shadows"**. Gallifreyans were naturally telepathic and could build "living" machinery that was also telepathic. They possessed a "reflex link", superganglions in their brains that allowed the Time Lord intelligentsia to commune. The Time Lords discovered that they had a "dark side" of their minds. Masonry from the Old Time survived deep beneath the Capitol. **Gallifrey had a moon, Pazithi Gallifreya.** [4]

At the very dawn of Time Lord history were "the Dark Days", "the time of Chaos". [One of the Doctor's most closely guarded secrets was that he was somehow involved with this period.] [5]

"In the days before Rassilon, my ancestors had tremendous powers which they misused disgracefully. They set up this place, the Death Zone, and walled it around with an impenetrable force field. Then they kidnapped other beings and set them down here...Even in our most corrupt period, our ancestors never allowed the Cybermen to play the game – like the Daleks they played too well...Old Rassilon put a stop to it in the end. He sealed off the entire zone and

1 GALLIFREYAN TIME – The Doctor says on a number of occasions that time is relative, but his home planet of Gallifrey seems to exist in a special relationship with time that makes it impossible to place it within a consistent timeframe relative to the rest of the universe. Some stories suggest that the Time Lords existed in the ancient past (*Genesis of The Daleks, Image of The Fendahl*), some are clearly contemporary (*The Three Doctors, Arc of Infinity*), some suggest a future setting (*Nightmare of Eden, Shada*). We learn that Time Lord civilisation is at least twelve million (*Image of The Fendahl*), over ten million (*The Trial of A Time Lord*), two million (*The Deadly Assassin*), one hundred thousand (*Underworld*) or mere "many thousands" (*The Three Doctors*) of years old. In the unbroadcast version of the first episode, Susan claimed to be from 'the forty-ninth century'. In the New and Missing Adventures it has been established that Gallifrey existed in the ancient past, billions of years ago (page 196 of *Goth Opera*).

As we might perhaps might expect, the Time Lord system of dating is incomprehensible to humans: in *The Invasion of Time* Kelner suggests that Doctor might like his office decorated in the style of Earth in relative date 034143989; the Doctor expressed a preference for 4370119 (could this be the twentieth century?), and claimed that both were in the

073 period.

2 In *The Deadly Assassin* the Time Lords don't know that their power comes from the Eye of Harmony, and in both that story and *The Trial of a Time Lord*, they haven't heard of the Master. In *The Deadly Assassin*, even the Doctor seems unaware of the APC Net, and knows little about Rassilon.

3 The phrase "the Old Time" is first used in *The Deadly Assassin*. Not all Gallifreyans are Time Lords, the Time Lords are the ruling elite of Gallifrey – the Doctor seems to say in *The Invisible Enemy* that there are only "one thousand" Time Lords. However, the terms "Time Lord" and "Gallifreyan" seem to be interchangeable for most practical purposes. Likewise, "Time Lord" is used to refer to the Doctor's race even before they master Time Travel (e.g.: *Remembrance of the Daleks* where the "Time Lords" have trouble with the prototype of the Hand of Omega). Gallifrey is first named in *The Time Warrior*. The home planet of the Time Lords was called Jewel in the *TV Comic* story 'Return of the Daleks'.

4 *The Trial of a Time Lord. Genesis of the Daleks. The Five Doctors. The Pit.* We learn that Susan is telepathic in *The Sensorites*, and it has been stated on a number of occasions that the Doctor (e.g. *The Three Doctors*), the TARDIS (e.g. *The Time Monster*) and all Time Lords (e.g. *The Deadly Assassin*) are telepathic. The

forbade the use of the Time Scoop…[There are rumours and legends to the contrary. Some say his fellow Time Lords rebelled against his cruelty and locked him in the Tower in eternal sleep.]"

[The Doctor] [6]

Gallifreyans were naturally "time sensitive", with a unique understanding of time. Ancient Gallifreyans discovered dematerialisation theory and transdimensional engineering. They built the Time Vortex, a vast transdimensional spiral encompassing all points in space and time. As noted, the Time Lords' ancestors built the Time Scoop. [7]

## CAT'S CRADLE: TIME'S CRUCIBLE

Gallifrey was ruled by the Pythias, a line of prophetesses who, since the 254th Pythia, rejected technology in favour of magic and superstition. Time travel was achieved by psychic prophecy, not physical means. The Pythias were guided by the prophesies in *The Book of Future Legends*, and saw their heritage as the Bright Past. Five thousand years before Rassilon, the great philosopher Pelatov lived.

At the time of the Intuitive Revelation, the age of Rassilon, the barbaric Gallifreyan Empire spread across the universe, encompassing the Pen-Shoza, Jagdagian, Oshakarm, the Star Grellades, Mirphak 2 and the rebellious Aubert Cluster. For aeons, Gallifreyan Heroes such as Ao had fought campaigns against foes such as the Gryffnae, Lacustrine Sattisar and the Batworms of the Asteroid Archipelago. The Winter Star was besieged for a century. The great Hero Haclav Agusti Prydonius, commander of the *Apollaten*, defeated the marauding Sphinx of Thule, and was sent to observe a dispute brewing between Ruta III and the Sontara Warburg.

Across the cosmos, the ruling seers were dying: the Sphinx of Thule; the Logistomancer of A32K, foreseer of a cold empire of logic; the Core Sybilline of Klanti; the Sosostris in the West Spiral; and The Nameless-that-Sees-All in the North Constellations. The 508th Pythia was the last of her line. After a visit from a Master Trader of the South, she finally recognised that the Veil of Time would soon only be traversed physically, not mentally. She instigated the Time Programme. The first time vessel, the Time Scaphe, powered by the mental energy of its crew, was launched, but it vanished. The Pythia was overthrown by

Rassilon and his neo-technologists. As her followers fled to Karn, the Pythia cursed Gallifrey with her dying words: its people became infertile, the colonies began to demand their independence, and Ice Age commenced. The only good omen was the return of the Time Scaphe.

Two Gallifreyans ensured that their people became the Lords of Time: Rassilon and Omega. Rassilon was the "greatest single figure in Time Lord history", yet "no one really knows how extensive his powers were" and he "had powers and secrets that even we don't understand". The Time Lords came to revere Omega as their "greatest Hero", "one of the greatest of all our race". [8]

Omega, Rassilon, and another Time Lord **known as 'the Other' to modern Time Lords,** together developed validium, a "living metal" designed to be the last line of defence for Gallifrey. [9]

> "Today we tend to think of Rassilon as the founder of our modern civilisation, but in his own time he was regarded mainly as an engineer and an architect. And, of course, it was long before we turned away from the barren road of technology."
>
> [Co-ordinator Engin] [10]

> "Long, long ago we learnt the secret of time travel, but in order to make it a reality we had to have a colossal source of energy. Omega provided that energy by a fantastic feat of solar engineering."
>
> [The Doctor]

Omega was a member of the High Council; the solar engineer who found and created the power source needed for time travel – the energy released by a supernova. He was lost in the explosion, and the Time Lords believed that he had been killed. [11]

> "A long time ago on my home planet of Gallifrey there lived a stellar engineer called Omega. It was Omega who created the supernova that was the initial power source for Gallifreyan time travel experiments. He left behind him the basis on which Rassilon founded Time Lord society, and he

Doctor has also stated on a number of occasions that the TARDIS is alive (e.g. *The Five Doctors*), and so is the Nemesis. *The Invisible Enemy*. Omega has a "dark side" to his mind in *The Three Doctors* and the Valeyard [see also THE VALEYARD page 259] represents the Doctor's dark side (*The Trial of a Time Lord*). In *Falls the Shadow*, the Doctor refers to this as the "Dark Design". *The Deadly Assassin* – Engin says that deep beneath the Capitol there are "vaults and foundations dating from the Old Time". *Cat's Cradle: Time's Crucible*.

5  *The Five Doctors. Silver Nemesis*.

6  *The Five Doctors*.

7  *City of Death, Warriors' Gate*, and *Time and the Rani. The Claws of Axos* and *The Robots of Death. Just War. The Five Doctors*.

8  Omega first appears in *The Three Doctors*, and reappears in *Arc of Infinity*. The Hand of Omega appears in *Remembrance of the Daleks*. The first reference to Rassilon is in *The Deadly Assassin*, and after that he becomes the central figure of Gallifreyan history, and is referred to in many subsequent stories (the quotes are from the Doctor, in *The Five Doctors* and *Shada* respectively). Both are the legendary founders of Time Lord society, both are "the greatest" of the Doctor's race and supply the energy

necessary for time travel. The first time that it is explicitly stated that they were contemporaries is in *Silver Nemesis*, although earlier in the same series *Remembrance of the Daleks* attempted to rationalise the two accounts of Time Lord origins.

9 *Silver Nemesis*. The Other has been mentioned in countless New and Missing Adventures, his first appearance being in the novelisation of *Remembrance of the Daleks*.

10 *The Deadly Assassin*.

11 *The Three Doctors*.

12 *Remembrance of the Daleks*.

13 *The Three Doctors, The Deadly Assassin*, and *Remembrance of the Daleks*.

14 *The Deadly Assassin*.

15 *The Two Doctors. The Five Doctors*.

left behind the Hand of Omega. The Hand of Omega is the mythical name for Omega's remote stellar manipulator – the device used to customise stars. And didn't we have trouble with the prototype…"

[The Doctor] [12]

The Gallifreyans successfully concluded the experiments, becoming the Time Lords. Mastery of time required an unimaginably vast energy supply, which Rassilon set about acquiring. [13]

"And Rassilon journeyed into the black void with a great fleet. Within the void no light would shine. And nothing of that outer nature continue in being except that which existed within the Sash of Rassilon. Now Rassilon found the Eye of Harmony, which balances all things that they may neither flux, whither nor change their state in any measure, and he caused the Eye to be brought to the world of Gallifrey wherein he sealed this munificence with the Great Key. Then the people rejoiced."

[*The Book of the Old Time*]

Through the millenia, the Time Lords came to believe that the Eye of Harmony was a myth, and that the Sash of Rassilon was of merely symbolic importance. In reality, the Sash prevented the wearer from being sucked into a parallel universe, and the Eye of Harmony was the nucleus of a black hole, from which all the power of the Time Lords devolved. "Rassilon stabilised all the elements of the black hole and set them in an eternally dynamic equation against the mass of the planet". [14]

Rassilon introduced the symbiotic nuclei the "Rassilon Imprimatur" into the genetic make-up of Time Lords, allowing them to fully travel through time. He also discovered the secret of temporal fission. [15]

[The holes that were created in the fabric of space/time as a result of Rassilon's experiments unleashed monsters from another universe.] "The myths of Gallifrey talk about nameless horrors infesting our universe that were only defeated through the might of the Time Lords". [For over a thousand years, across the cosmos, the Ancient Gallifreyans fought the Eternal Wars against monsters from another universe, including the Vampires and the Yssgaroth, during which the great general Liall a Mahajetsu died. The Matrix contains no record of this war.] When Rassilon overthrew the Pythia, Gallifrey was cursed with a plague that only a few survived. [Some suggest that Rassilon himself released the virus to wipe out all that knew of his mistake – they claim that Omega was deliberately sealed in his black hole by Rassilon. One Gallifreyan, Kopyion, escaped the purges.] [16]

When Rassilon was young, a Vampire Army swarmed across the universe. Each vampire could suck the life out of an entire planet.

> "Energy weapons were useless, because the monsters absorbed and transmuted the energy, using it to become stronger. Therefore Rassilon ordered the construction of bowships, swift vessels that fired a mighty bolt of steel that transfixed the monsters through the heart – for only if his heart be utterly destroyed will the Vampire die... The Vampire Army: so powerful were the bodies of these great creatures, and so fiercely did they cling to life, that they were impossible to kill, save by the use of bowships. Yet slain they all were, and to the last one, by the Lords of Time - the Lords of Time destroying them utterly. However, when the bodies were counted, the King Vampire, mightiest and most malevolent of all, had vanished, even to his shadow, from time and space. Hence it is the directive of Rassilon that any Time Lord who comes upon this enemy of our people and of all living things, shall use all his efforts to destroy him, even at the cost of his own life..."
>
> [*The Record of Rassilon*]

This war was so long and bloody that afterwards the Time Lords renounced violence forever. [17]

[A marginal illustration in one book of legends showed an owl being overcome by a bat. The owl was a traditional symbol of Rassilon, and the bat a symbol of the Vampires. Throughout Gallifreyan history, some heretics worshipped Rassilon the Vampire, believing that Rassilon was bitten by the Great Vampire,

16  *The Pit.*

17  *State of Decay.*

18 *Goth Opera*.

19 *Underworld*.

20 *Shada*. *Four to Doomsday*.

21 *The Deadly Assassin* and *The Invasion of Time*.

22 *The Invasion of Time* – the Doctor becomes "the first President since Rassilon to hold the Great Key", implying that Rassilon was President. *Shada*. *Four to Doomsday*.

23 THE KEY – In *The Deadly Assassin*, the Great Key is "an ebonite rod" that seals the Eye of Harmony within its monolith. By *The Invasion of Time*, that artefact is called "the Rod", and the Great Key is an ordinary-looking mortise key that is capable of powering the Demat Gun and has been hidden from the President by successive Chancellors since the time of Rassilon. We might presume that the Chancellor tells the President that the Rod *is* the Key, which led to the confusion of the two. However, as two Chancellors we know about, Goth and Borusa, are both in line to be President, while knowing the whereabouts of the real Great Key, it seems we haven't been told the whole truth. In *The Trial of a Time Lord*, "The Key of Rassilon" allows access to the Matrix through portals such as the Seventh Door, and the Keeper of the Matrix wears it on his robes – this is presumably an entirely different artefact.

24 *Shada*. *The Deadly Assassin* and *The Five Doctors*. *State of*

and that Rassilon became a vampire towards the end of his life. [18]

When the Gallifreyans were new to space/time exploration, they discovered the inhabited world of Minyos, and were worshipped by the population. In return they gave technology to the Minyans. The Minyans eventually used nuclear technology to destroy their planet. The Time Lords subsequently renounced intervention in the affairs of other planets. [19]

As President of the Time Lords, Rassilon ushered in an age of technological and political progress. The phrase "the Great days of Rassilon" appeared in the Gallifreyan book *Our Planet's Story* read by every Time Tot. Even races such as the Urbankans that knew nothing of the Time Lords heard the legends of Rassilon. [20]

Rassilon gained credit for many scientific achievements: He created the Transduction Barriers surrounding Gallifrey to prevent the unauthorised landing of a TARDIS or similar vehicle. A Quantum Forcefield also exists as a barrier against more conventional threats. [21]

Rassilon also invented the Demat Gun, a weapon that used the Great Key. The weapon fired a beam that could erase a being totally from the timeline. [This weapon was so powerful that the Great Key was hidden from all future Presidents by successive Chancellors – **the Presidents were given the Rod of Rassilon instead.**] The Time Lord Tribunal could impose dematerialisation on other races or individuals, such as the War Lord. [22] [23]

Rassilon became associated with the following relics or concepts, all of which had "stupendous power". Many were either lost or their true purpose became unknown, but all were imbued with great powers: the Sash of Rassilon; the Great Key of Rassilon; Rassilon's Star (the Eye of Harmony); the Rod of Rassilon, *which most Time Lords believe to be the Great Key* ("Rassilon's Rod!" is also a mild Gallifreyan expletive); the Wisdom of Rassilon; The Record of Rassilon; the Directive of Rassilon; The Tomb/Tower of Rassilon; the Game of Rassilon; the Seal of Rassilon; the Black Scrolls of Rassilon; the Harp of Rassilon; the Coronet of Rassilon; the Ring of Rassilon; the Rassilon Imprimatur; the Key of Rassilon (*not the Great Key, but one which allows access to the Matrix*); and the Legacy of Rassilon. **The Horns of Rassilon, also known as the Sign of Rassilon, is a magical warding sign.** [24]

Rassilon was also a legislator. In his time, five principles were laid down and the Constitution was drafted: Article Seventeen guaranteed the freedom of political candidates and another clause allowed a unanimous vote of the High Council to over-rule the President. Thanks to Rassilon, TARDIS databanks contained 18,348 coded emergency instructions. Older TARDISes (Type 40 and older) had a magnetic card system, the Record of Rassilon, containing emergency instructions regarding the Vampires. The "Rules Governing Time Lords" were probably drafted at this time. Article Seven of Gallifreyan Law forbade Time Lords to commit genocide. The death penalty was abolished, except in extreme circumstances that threatened Gallifrey, such as genocide or the unauthorised use of a TARDIS. The prison planet Shada was set up to house the most dangerous criminals in the universe; the only key was encoded in the pages of Rassilon's book *The Worshipful and Ancient Law of Gallifrey*, housed in the Panopticon Archive. [25]

Apparently dead, Rassilon was entombed in the Dark Tower, where he remained ever since in eternal sleep. Legends stated that anyone reaching the Tower and taking the Ring of Rassilon would gain immortality. Gallifreyan children are familiar with the story and learnt a nursery rhyme: "Who unto Rassilon's Tower Would Go Must choose: Above, Between, Below".

Rassilon had discovered the secret of Perpetual Regeneration: "timeless, perpetual bodily regeneration – true immortality". Only the power-mad would attempt such a thing. Since his entombment, Rassilon prevented four such Time Lords from discovering the secret of true immortality. [26]

**There are many "R.O.O." texts: those dealing with legends of Rassilon, Omega, and the Other.** [27]

[*The Red Book of Gallifrey* concerns the Dark Time and talks of Rassilon the Ravager, Omega the Fallen, and the Other. It also contains magical incantations. [28]]

**The Green and Black Books of Gallifrey discuss legends of the future, including the Timewyrm.** [29]

*The Book of the Old Time* is the official version of Rassilon's

*Decay. The Five Doctors. The Two Doctors. The Trial of a Time Lord. Remembrance of the Daleks. Timewyrm: Revelation* (p54), and *No Future* (p203).

25 *Shada. The Deadly Assassin, and The Five Doctors. State of Decay. The Androids of Tara. The Trial of a Time Lord.*

26 *The Five Doctors.*

27 *Goth Opera* (p119).

28 *No Future* (p203).

29 *Timewyrm: Revelation* (p65).

30 We hear a female voice read an extract from the modern translation of *The Book of the Old Time* in *The Deadly Assassin*. The last extant copy of *The Black Scrolls of Rassilon* is destroyed in *The Five Doctors*.

31 *The Mutants. The Deadly Assassin. The Leisure Hive. The Trial of the Time Lord. Shada. The Deadly Assassin. The Trial of a Time Lord.*

32 Many of the alien races encountered by the Doctor on his travels know of the Time Lords.

33 *Earthshock. The Hand of Fear. The Two Doctors. The Time Warrior. The Deadly Assassin. The Invasion of Time.*

achievements, and a modern transgram has been made of it. [*The Black Scrolls of Rassilon* contain a forbidden account of the same period, including the secrets of Rassilon's power, but the only known copy was destroyed by Borusa. [30]]

Over the next ten million years, the Time Lords discovered an indestructible material and learnt to engineer micro-universes. They abandoned tachyonics for warp matrix engineering, invented the Magnotron and developed Gallifreyan Morse. Eventually, they abandoned the barren road of technology. Over time, the Primitive Phases One and Two of the Matrix were relegated to the Archives. Phases Three to Six remained in use. [31]

Alien races from all periods of recorded time had dealings with the Time Lords, from those in the ancient past, such as the Kastrians and Sutekh, to those in the far future, such as the Usurians. Other races and individuals who knew something of the Time Lords and Gallifrey (without having heard just of the Doctor or another individual) included the Andromedans, the Bandrils, the Cybermen, the Daleks, the Fendahl, Fenric, the Guardians, Mawdryn's race, the Mentors, the Minyans, the Sisterhood, the Sontarans, the Third Zone, the Keeper of Traken, Vampires and the Vardans. Clearly the Time Lords have visited many worlds in many time periods, even in an official capacity. [32]

However, although the Time Lords are "forbidden to interfere", they were also committed to protecting weaker species and preventing aggression against indigenous populations. They also authorised (or prevented) other races' time travel experiments and defended the Laws of Time. As such, they did intervene in the affairs of other races and can almost be thought of as "galactic ticket inspectors". This work was *apparently* carried out by the Celestial Intervention Agency, and the vast majority of Time Lords did not concern themselves with the universe outside the Capitol, and were more concerned with internal politics. [33]

More Presidents came from the Prydonian Chapter than from all the other Chapters combined. Prydonians were seen as cunning, but claimed that they "merely see farther ahead than most"; they wore scarlet and orange robes. Other Chapters included the Arcalians (who wore green) and Patrexes (who wore heliotrope). [34]

The Time Lords timelooped the Fifth Planet, home of the Fendahl, twelve million years ago. [35]

At some point, the Time Lords Rungar and Sabjatric were sent to Shada, where they remain. [36]

The Type 40 TT-Capsule was introduced when Salyavin was young, but was withdrawn centuries before the Doctor "borrowed" one, being by then a "Veteran and Vintage Vehicle". [37]

When young, Salyavin learnt how to project his mind into others' and was sentenced to imprisonment in Shada as a result. He escaped, using his powers to erase all knowledge of the prison planet. A schism in the College of Cardinals led to a rival President setting himself up on Drornid. [38]

Three thousand years ago, Mawdryn and his followers stole a Metamorphic Symbiosis Regenerator. Two thousand years ago, the Time Lords abandoned interspacial geometry. In the lifetime of some contemporary Time Lords, President Pandak III ruled for nine hundred years. [39]

The Doctor was born under the sign of "Crossed Computers" – the same year as the Rani, and probably the Master and Drax – perhaps around 2116 AD. He was also a contemporary of the Monk, the War Chief and Runcible. The War Chief recognised the Doctor, but not vice versa. The Doctor knew Hedin and Damon, and the unnamed Time Lord who warned him about the Master. **He was one of forty-five Cousins from the House of Lungbarrow.** [40] [41] [42]

The Doctor's mentor lived up a mountain near his home. He taught the Doctor to see the beauty in a simple daisy and to look into his own mind, and told him ghost stories about the Vampires. The Doctor was interested enough in Gallifreyan history to learn the dead language Old High Gallifreyan. He admired Salyavin and was frightened by stories of the Fendahl. [43]

The Doctor attended University with the Rani, where his speciality was thermodynamics. He studied at Prydon Academy (where he was taught by Borusa), the Time Academy and "the Academy" (with the Master). He was taught by Azmael. He used to build time jammers to disrupt other students' experiments.

34 *The Deadly Assassin.*

35 *Image of the Fendahl.*

36 *Shada.*

37 The Doctor's TARDIS is first referred to as a "Type 40" in *The Deadly Assassin. Shada. The Pirate Planet.*

38 *Shada.*

39 *Mawdryn Undead. The Stones of Blood. The Deadly Assassin.*

40 THE DOCTOR'S AGE – The Doctor was 236 years old when he left Gallifrey (he is 759 in *The Ribos Operation*, and has been operating his TARDIS for 523 years by the next story *The Pirate Planet*). He was 309 when he attended his tech course with Drax ("450 years" before *The Armageddon Factor*). The Doctor tells Victoria that he is "450" in *The Tomb of the Cybermen*; the Master of the Land of Fiction says the Doctor is "ageless" in *The Mind Robber*. The Doctor claims to have been a scientist for "thousands of years" in both *Doctor Who and the Silurians* and *The Mind of Evil*. The Doctor says he is "749" in *Planet of Evil, The Brain of Morbius* and *The Seeds of Doom*, and "nearly 750" in *Pyramids of Mars*. He is "750" by *The Robots of Death*, 756 or (more probably) 759 in *The Ribos Operation*, nearly 760 in *Nightmare of Eden*, 750 again in *The Creature from the Pit* and *The Leisure Hive*, 900 in *Revelation of the Daleks* and *The Trial of a Time Lord* Part One, but "over 900" in Part

Nine. In *Time and the Rani*, both he and the Rani are "953", and the Doctor had gained "900 years experience" by *Remembrance of the Daleks*. In the draft scripts of *The Power of the Daleks* and *The Underwater Menace* he was '750', and he was due to celebrate his 751st birthday in *The Stones of Blood*. In the New Adventures he is around a thousand years old – according to *Sleepy* he celebrated his 1000th birthday during *Set Piece*.

41 PAST LIVES – The orthodox view accepted wholesale by most fans is: that the Doctor is a Time Lord who can regenerate his body twelve times when it is seriously injured; that William Hartnell played the first Doctor; and that by *Survival* the Doctor has regenerated six times, so Sylvester McCoy played the seventh incarnation of the Time Lord. This version of events is actually established very late in the show's history. The term "regeneration", for example, is not even used until *Planet of the Spiders* (at the end of the eleventh series); the word "incarnation" is not used until *The Trial of a Time Lord* (the twenty-third series); and on-screen the different Doctors have never been referred to as the first Doctor, second Doctor, and so on.

The orthodox view is only referred to in half a dozen stories: In *The Three Doctors* the Time Lords claim that the Hartnell Doctor is the "earliest". We learn that the Time Lords

The Doctor at this time was called Theta Sigma, his nickname. He eventually scraped through the Academy with fifty-one per cent on the second attempt. The Master got a higher grade at cosmic science than the Doctor. The Doctor claimed that he was a late developer who always wanted to be a train-driver. The Doctor attended a tech course with the Class of '92, which included Drax, after which he gained his doctorate. [44]

The Doctor had a family, which perhaps included an uncle. The Doctor's family owned a home in South Gallifrey. Susan is his granddaughter "and always will be", *so he must have children of his own.* Susan describes her home planet as "quite like Earth, but at night the sky is a burned orange, and the leaves on the trees are bright silver". She learnt about the Dark Tower. [45]

The Doctor was a member of the Prydonian Chapter but forsook his birthright. Like all Time Lords he swore an oath to protect the Law of Gallifrey. He claimed he was a pioneer among his people. The Doctor also claimed to have built the TARDIS, and Susan claimed that she coined the acronym, but later events contradict this. His reflex link connected him to the Time Lord intelligentsia. Before leaving Gallifrey the Doctor was used on a diplomatic mission on at least one occasion, when he visited the inauguration of Station Camera in the Third Zone. Following a campaign by the Doctor, the Time Lords banned Miniscopes. [46]

*The exact circumstances of the Doctor's departure are still a mystery.* The Doctor claimed at various times that he left his home planet because he was either "exiled", "bored" or "kicked out". He took a Type 40 TARDIS Mark I, the Hand of Omega, the validium statue, and his granddaughter Susan. The Doctor and Susan left Gallifrey "ages" before, possibly fifty years before the Monk. [47]

The following image appeared early in the Doctor's memory: "Here was a cowled figure shaking a fist at a dark castle, and in the next picture he was cowering from something huge and fearful. Then he was running." [48]

Many other Time Lords are known to have left Gallifrey in the Doctor's lifetime. Azmael left Gallifrey to become Master of Jaconda. The Rani was exiled following illegal experiments on animals: genetically re-engineered mice she had created ate the

President's cat and attacked the President himself. She became ruler of Miasimia Goria. The Doctor's mentor left Gallifrey for Earth and became known as K'Anpo. The Doctor left before the Monk, the War Chief and probably before the Master. [49]

Morbius, leader of the High Council, proposed that the Time Lords should end their policy of non-interference. When the High Council rejected this, he left Gallifrey and raised an army of conquest, promising them immortality. Devastating several planets on the way, the Cult of Morbius arrived on Karn, home of the Sisterhood. The Time Lords attacked them on Karn, destroying his army. Following a trial, Morbius was vaporised. Solon had removed Morbius's brain before his execution and preserved it. [50]

## THE TWO DOCTORS

Although the Doctor was now travelling through space and time, the Time Lords still occasionally used him as an agent or messenger, and the Doctor's second incarnation was also sent to Camera to call a halt to the time travel experiments of Kartz and Reimer.

## THE WAR GAMES
## SPEARHEAD FROM SPACE

In 309,906 the Doctor faced a Malfeasance Tribunal, and the Time Lords found the Doctor guilty of interfering in history. They exiled him to Earth in the twentieth-century timezone, changing his appearance. The Tribunal continue to monitor the Doctor. [51]

## TERROR OF THE AUTONS

Around this time, the Master removed Time Lord files containing information about the Doomsday Weapon and the Sea Devils, *and many other races.* The Time Lords sent a messenger to warn the Doctor about the Master's imminent arrival on Earth. [52]

## COLONY IN SPACE
## THE CURSE OF PELADON

are limited to twelve regenerations in *The Deadly Assassin*, and this is reinforced in *The Keeper of Traken*, *Logopolis*, *The Five Doctors* and *The Twin Dilemma* (although in the first three of these we learn that it is indeed possible for a Time Lord to regenerate more than twelve times, and in the fourth Azmael initiates a thirteenth regeneration, the strain of which kills him). It is *Mawdryn Undead* (in the twentieth series) before the Doctor explicitly states that he has regenerated four times and has eight regenerations remaining. In *The Five Doctors* the Hurndall Doctor sees the Davison Doctor and concludes "so there are five of me now" and refers to himself as "the original, you might say". Finally, in *Time and the Rani*, the Doctor talks of his "seventh persona".

More often the evidence about the Doctor's past is ambiguous or inconclusive: he seems vague about his age throughout his life, the details varying wildly from story to story and likewise his name, his doctorate and why he left Gallifrey. In *The Deadly Assassin* Runcible remarks that the Doctor has had a facelift and the Doctor replies that he has had "several so far" (in the original script he had done so a more specific 'three times'). In *The Trial of a Time Lord*, the Valeyard comes from somewhere between the Doctor's "twelfth and final incarnation" (not 'twelfth and thirteenth'). No unfamiliar

Doctors come to light in *The Three Doctors* or *The Five Doctors*. On two occasions (*Day of the Daleks*, *Resurrection of the Daleks*) an attempt to probe the Doctor's mind is abruptly halted just as the William Hartnell incarnation appears on the monitor.

There have been a number of hints that the incarnation of the Doctor played by William Hartnell was not the first. In the script for *The Destiny of Doctor Who*, the new Doctor confides to his astonished companions that he has 'renewed himself' before. In the transmitted version of the story, *The Power of the Daleks*, the line does not appear, but neither is it contradicted. In *The Brain of Morbius*, Morbius succeeds in mentally regressing the Doctor back from his Tom Baker incarnation, through Jon Pertwee, Patrick Troughton and William Hartnell, but this time no-one interrupts and we go on to see a further eight incarnations of the Doctor prior to Hartnell. This is indisputable: however much we might want to fit this scene into the continuity of the series as established elsewhere or rationalise it away, here, as the sequence of mysterious faces appears on the scanner, Morbius shouts "How far Doctor? How long have you lived? Your puny mind is powerless against the strength of Morbius! Back! Back to your beginning! Back!". These are certainly not the faces of Morbius, as has occasionally been suggested, or the

## THE MUTANTS

The Time Lords sent the Doctor on various missions to other planets and times. These were always at crucial points of galactic history, with implications for the entire universe. The Doctor was sent to Uxarieus to prevent the Doomsday Weapon from falling into the hands of the Master; to Peladon to ease the passage of that planet into the Galactic Federation and prevent galactic war; and to Solos, where the Doctor delivered a message to Ky, the leader of the Solonian independence movement, that allowed him to fulfil his race's evolutionary potential.

## THE THREE DOCTORS

The cosmic energy of the Time Lords was suddenly drained by a black hole. Unable to power their machinery, the Time Lords called on the Doctor to help them. They brought two previous incarnations of the Doctor into his present to try and counteract whatever was draining the power.

Two incarnations of the Doctor travelled into the black hole and arrived in a universe of anti-matter. They discovered that Omega lived, maintaining an entire world with his mental control of a singularity. Omega resented the Time Lords, feeling that he had been abandoned. He couldn't leave his domain – if he tried it would have ceased to exist before he left it. He needed the Doctors' help to leave. But the Doctor learnt that Omega's body had long been destroyed, and only his will remained. It would be impossible for him to return to the universe of matter. The Doctors tricked their way back to their TARDIS, apparently destroying Omega in a matter/anti-matter explosion.

The power drain ended, and the Time Lords had a new source of energy. In gratitude, the Doctor's exile was lifted.

## PLANET OF THE DALEKS
## GENESIS OF THE DALEKS
## THE BRAIN OF MORBIUS

After his exile, the Doctor's services were still called on from time to time. At the Doctor's request, the Time Lords piloted the TARDIS to Spiridon, the location of a Dalek army. The Time

Lords predicted a time when the Daleks would dominate the universe. They sent the Doctor to prevent the creation of the Daleks. The Time Lords also apparently sent the TARDIS to Karn, to prevent the resurrection of Morbius.

## THE DEADLY ASSASSIN

"Through the millennia, the Time Lords of Gallifrey led a life of peace and ordered calm, protected against all threats from lesser civilisations by their great power. But this was to change. Suddenly and terribly, the Time Lords faced the most dangerous crisis in their long history…"

The Doctor received a telepathic message, warning him that the President was going to be assassinated. He returned to his home planet immediately, only to find himself implicated in the assassination. The President had been due to resign anyway, after centuries in office, and the attack appeared motiveless. The Doctor's old enemy the Master had lured him back to frame him for the murder. The Master had exhausted his regenerations, and had been found by Chancellor Goth on the planet Tersurus. Although Goth had been the favourite to succeed, he had learnt that another was to be nominated by the outgoing President. In return for his help, the Master had killed the incumbent. The Master wanted full access to the Matrix, as he needed to find a way to prolong his life. He discovered that he might regenerate again if he had a powerful enough source of energy – the Master selected the Eye of Harmony. The Doctor prevented the Master from destroying Gallifrey, but the Master escaped.

It was a chance encounter with *The Book of the Old Time* that had first nudged the Doctor's own thoughts back towards his world's archao-barbaric past. A suspicion had been born in his mind that before regeneration there had been reincarnation. Some memories might be more than racial inheritance. Nothing lasts that does not change. [53]

Borusa regenerated at some point between this and the Doctor's next visit to Gallifrey. [54]

Doctor's ancestors, or his family. Morbius is not deluding himself. The Doctor does not go on to win the fight, he almost dies, only surviving because of the Elixir, it just happens that Morbius's brain casing can't withstand the pressures either. The production team at the time (who bear a remarkable resemblance to the earlier Doctors, probably because eight of them – Christopher Barry, George Gallacio, Robert Banks Stewart, Phillip Hinchcliffe, Douglas Camfield, Graeme Harper, Robert Holmes and Chris Baker – posed for the photographs used in the sequence), definitely intended the faces to be those of earlier Doctors. Producer Philip Hinchcliffe said 'We tried to get famous actors for the faces of the Doctor. But because no one would volunteer, we had to use backroom boys. And it is true to say that I attempted to imply that William Hartnell was not the first Doctor'. Two stories later, in *The Masque of Mandragora*, the Doctor and Sarah Jane discover "the old control room", and one of the Doctor's old costumes. As we have never seen the room or the costume before, the implication is that an unseen incarnation (presumably prior to Hartnell) used it.

42 *The Creature from the Pit. Time and the Rani. Terror of the Autons. The Armageddon Factor. Nightmare of Eden. The Time Meddler. The War Games. The Deadly Assassin. Arc of Infinity. Terror of the Autons.*

# IMAGE OF THE FENDAHL
# UNDERWORLD

~~Whether a coincidence or not,~~ soon after learning of his plan-et's past, the Doctor began to encounter survivors from his race's ancient history, the Fendahl and the Minyans.

## THE INVASION OF TIME

The Doctor was contacted by the Vardans, a race capable of travelling down energy waves, including thought. The Vardans had infiltrated the Matrix, and now wanted to commence the physical invasion of Gallifrey. The Doctor tricked the Vardans, returning the invasion force to their home planet, then timelooping it.

**While in the Matrix, the Doctor became aware of the Timewyrm. He sent his future self a warning. [55]**

Leela and K9 elected to stay behind on Gallifrey. Leela and Andred married soon afterwards, but the Doctor was unable to attend the ceremony. Borusa became President, and regen-erated once again. [56]

Romana was selected by the White Guardian to work with the Doctor to recover the six segments of the Key to Time. [57]

Romana was born 384 years after the Doctor left Gallifrey. Romana read *Our Planet's Story* as a Time Tot. For her seventieth birthday, she was given an air-car. As part of her studies, Romana studied the lifecycle of the Gallifreyan Flutterwing, and she even-tually graduated from Prydon Academy with a Triple First. Romana was an historian and worked in the Bureau of Ancient Records. [58]

## SHADA

The Doctor prevented Skagra of Drornid from imposing his mind as the "universal mind" by using the powers of the Time Lord mind-criminal Salyavin.

With the quest for the Key to Time long completed, Romana was recalled by the Time Lords. Before she could return, the

TARDIS fell through a CVE into E-Space. [59]

## STATE OF DECAY

The Doctor destroyed the Great Vampire, who had survived the war with the Time Lords and fled to E-Space.

## ARC OF INFINITY

Omega had survived, and convinced a member of the High Council, Hedin, that he had been wronged by Gallifrey. With access to a bio-data extract, Omega would be able to bond with a Time Lord, re-entering our universe; Hedin chose the Doctor. When the High Council discovered this, they recalled the Doctor's TARDIS to Gallifrey (only the third time this had been done in the planet's history), and lifted the ban on the death penalty. Killing the Doctor would break the renegade's link with our universe. The Doctor survived vaporisation by entering the Matrix, where he discovered Omega's plan. He tracked Omega to Amsterdam, where the renegade's new body proved unstable and disintegrated.

The TARDIS was fitted with the latest surveillance equipment, increasing the range of information that could be recorded by the Matrix. [60]

## THE FIVE DOCTORS

Borusa regenerated once more. He had become dissatisfied with ruling Gallifrey. Now he wanted "perpetual regeneration", a secret discovered by Rassilon that allowed true immortality, not simply the vast lifespans granted to other Time Lords. He discovered the ancient Time Scoop machinery and restarted the Game of Rassilon, pitting four incarnations of the Doctor and his old friends against a selection of old enemies. The High Council discovered the energy drain and searched for the Doctor. Discovering that he no longer existed, in any of his incarnations, they recruited the Master.

Rassilon gave Borusa the immortality he sought, transforming him into a living statue. The Doctor was declared President

lifetime. In his novelisation of the story Terrance Dicks states that Morbius came to power after the Doctor left Gallifrey, and that the Doctor heard of Morbius on his travels.

51 *The War Games* – the event is recalled and dated in *The Deadly Assassin*, the Doctor's exile begins in *Spearhead from Space* (continuing until *The Three Doctors*, and we learn the Tribunal is still monitoring the Doctor in *Terror of the Autons*.

52 *Terror of the Autons* – The files are referred to in *Colony in Space* and *The Sea Devils*. Presumably, although this is never stated, the Master also finds out about many of his other future allies and accomplices from these files.

53 *Cat's Cradle: Time's Crucible* (p210–11).

54 A different actor plays Borusa in each of his televised appearances (Angus MacKay in *The Deadly Assassin*, John Arnatt in *The Invasion of Time*, Leonard Sachs in *Arc of Infinity*, and Philip Latham in *The Five Doctors*).

55 *Timewyrm: Genesys*.

56 We learn of Leela and Andred's marriage in *Arc of Infinity*. In *The Ribos Operation*, the Doctor wishes that he'd thrown the President to the Sontarans, suggesting that Borusa has become President (although the treacherous Kelner apparently survived *The Invasion of Time* and he'd have a strong constitutional case, as

the Doctor named him Vice-President...). By *Arc of Infinity* Borusa is President.

57 *The Ribos Operation*.

58 The Doctor has been operating the TARDIS for "523" years before *The Pirate Planet*, Romana claimed to be "148" in the previous story *The Ribos Operation*. *Shada*. *The Pirate Planet*. *The Ribos Operation*. She is first named as a Prydonian in *The Romance of Crime*. *The Ribos Operation*. *Shada* and *State of Decay*.

59 *Meglos* and *Full Circle*.

60 *The Trial of a Time Lord*. The Inquisitor tells the Doctor that this happened "on your last visit". That was technically *The Five Doctors*, but the TARDIS landed in the Death Zone on that occasion, not the Capitol. Either there was an unrecorded visit to Gallifrey between *The Five Doctors* and *The Trial of a Time Lord* or the device was fitted during *Arc of Infinity* (and in this story we do see Time Lord technicians working on the vehicle).

61 According to the Doctor in *Warriors of the Deep*.

by Chancellor Flavia, but left Gallifrey before he could take up office.

The most advanced TARDIS model at this time was a Type 57. [61]

## RESURRECTION OF THE DALEKS

The Daleks planned to assassinate the High Council of the Time Lords using Duplicates of the Doctor and his companions, but the Doctor prevented this before they had programmed the Duplicates.

## ATTACK OF THE CYBERMEN

At the Doctor's request for help, the Time Lords piloted the TARDIS to Telos.

## THE TRIAL OF A TIME LORD

The Doctor discovered that the planet Ravolox was in fact Earth in the far future, but didn't know what had moved the planet two light years or, more importantly, why. Despite this, the High Council were worried that he knew too much, and they brought the Doctor to a vast space station. At first, the Doctor was told that this was to be an impartial enquiry into the Doctor's activities. The Doctor also learnt that as he had neglected his duties, he had been deposed from the Presidency.

The Valeyard, the prosecuting council, successfully argued that the Doctor was guilty of interference on a grand scale, and the enquiry became a trial. It was revealed that the Doctor's actions on Thoros Beta had led to a threat to the course of universal evolution. The Time Lords had been forced to intervene directly, killing the scientist Crozier, the Mentor Kiv and possibly the Doctor's companion Peri. When the Doctor's own evidence proved beyond all doubt that on another occasion he had committed genocide, wiping out the Vervoids to save Earth, the Doctor faced a death sentence.

They Doctor had claimed all along that the Matrix was being tampered with. The Keeper of the Matrix was brought in as an expert witness, but as he spoke, the Master appeared on the

Matrix screen, demonstrating that it was indeed possible to breach the security of the Time Lords' computer.

The Master explained that Andromedans had also managed to enter the Matrix from their base on Earth and had stolen valuable scientific secrets. To protect their position, the High Council had covertly ordered the destruction of Earth. Perhaps the Master's greatest bombshell was the identity of the prosecuting council: the Valeyard was an amalgamation of all that was evil in the Doctor, somewhere between his twelfth and final incarnation. [62] The Master had encountered the Valeyard before, and knew that the High Council had brought him in to frame the Doctor, in return for which the Valeyard would gain the Doctor's remaining regenerations.

When the truth about Ravolox was revealed, popular unrest deposed the High Council. Both the Master and Valeyard moved to take advantage of the situation: the Master planned to take control of the planet, the Valeyard attempted to assassinate senior members of the Time Lord hierarchy. Both failed: the Master was trapped by the Limbo Atrophier, a booby trap placed on the Matrix files. The Valeyard was believed destroyed by his own particle disseminator, but somehow he survived and when last seen he had assumed the guise of the Keeper of the Matrix.

The Doctor suggested that once order was restored, the Inquisitor should run for President.

## REMEMBRANCE OF THE DALEKS

Addressing Davros, the Doctor claimed to be "President-Elect of the High Council of Time Lords... Keeper of the Legacy of Rassilon". Its work done, the Hand of Omega returned to Gallifrey.

## BLOOD HARVEST
## GOTH OPERA

Three Time Lords, Rath (younger brother of Goth), Elar and Morin, took responsibility for matters of security. Most Time Lords considered this a rather lowly position, but the Committee of Three, as they styled themselves, used their office to build

**62 THE VALEYARD** – It is unclear exactly what the Valeyard is. The Master, who knows a great deal about him, says "There is some evil in all of us, Doctor, even you. The Valeyard is an amalgamation of the darker sides of your nature, somewhere between your twelfth and final incarnation, and I must say you do not improve with age". This is rather vague, and it seems that the Valeyard might be a potential future for the Doctor (like those presented to him in *The War Games* or those of Romana in *Destiny of the Daleks*), a projection (like Cho-je in *Planet of the Spiders* or the Watcher in *Logopolis*) or an actual fully-fledged future incarnation (as he was in the original script). The Master seems to have met the Valeyard before, and sees him as a rival (he also says "... as I've always known him, the Doctor" – suggesting that he would normally refer to himself as 'the Doctor' not 'the Valeyard'). Whatever the Valeyard is, he doesn't have any qualms about killing his past self – perhaps if the sixth Doctor died, the Valeyard would gain his remaining regenerations by default. His survival at the end of the Trial, when we had seen him disseminated (and the Doctor has promised to mend his ways), perhaps suggests that he is something more than just a mere Time Lord.

Note also that the Master says "twelfth and final", not 'twelfth and thirteenth', leaving open the possibility that the

Doctor will survive the end of his regenerative cycle.

The New and Missing Adventures have tended to steer clear of the Valeyard; indeed the Writers' Guide states 'anything featuring the Valeyard is out – he's a continuity nightmare, and a rather dull villain'. Despite this, a number of the novels (particularly *Time of Your Life*, *Head Games* and *Millennial Rites*) have developed the idea first aired in *Love and War* that the Doctor sacrificed his sixth incarnation ("the colourful jester") to create a stronger, more ruthless seventh persona ("Time's Champion") who is better equipped to change his destiny. Ironically, later books have suggested that this action might well have been the catalyst that brought the Valeyard into being.

their own powerbase. Using their expertise, they planned to kill Rassilon in his Tower, and take control of the galaxy. At the time of President Flavia's inauguration, they were defeated by the Doctor, Ace, Benny and Romana.

The three traitors were sentenced to vaporisation. Romana settled back on Gallifrey, and was greeted by Ruathadvorophrenaltid, a Time Lady acquaintance of the Doctor. Ruath planned to be the consort of the Vampire Messiah, and targeted the fifth Doctor. Romana alerted Gallifrey and the Doctor to the threat, and was rewarded with a seat on the High Council.

Appendices

# UNIT Dating

The UNIT stories are set in an undefined 'end of the twentieth century' era: perhaps wisely the production teams didn't specify exactly in which years the stories took place, and they could comfortably fit at any time between the mid-sixties and the mid-nineties. *Doctor Who* fans have attempted to pin down the dates more precisely on a number of occasions over the years, but the results have always been hotly contested. As successive production teams came and went, a mass of contradictory and ambiguous evidence had built up. In the entries for each story I have tried to list every clue to the dating of the UNIT era, but to come up with a consistent timeframe, this evidence has to be prioritised. It is a matter of individual judgement as to which clues are important and which can be ignored.

A number of firm dates are given in dialogue during the course of the series, but unfortunately they all contradict each other:

**1.** In *The Web of Fear* (broadcast in 1968) Anne Travers establishes that *The Abominable Snowmen* was set in "1935". Earlier, Professor Travers had said that this was "over forty years ago". Some fans have suggested that Travers is senile or confused, but his demolition of Harold Chorley in the story shows that although he is crotchety, he remains sharp-witted. From this, we can only conclude that *The Web of Fear* is set in 1975 or quite soon afterwards. *The Invasion* is "nearly four years" after that according to the Brigadier in that story. So, *The Invasion*, the first story to feature UNIT, was broadcast in 1968 but was set around 1979.

**2.** In *Pyramids of Mars* (first broadcast in 1975) Sarah Jane says that she is "from 1980". I take this to mean that *The Time Warrior*, her first story, is set in 1980. There is, I suppose, a case to be made that she might be referring to the date of *Terror of the Zygons*, her last visit to 'contemporary' Earth, but either way it refers to a story featuring UNIT. Anyone trying to contradict Sarah's statement is suggesting that she doesn't know which *year* she comes from. It is difficult to believe that Sarah is rounding up – the year is specified so precisely, and it jarred in 1975. The statement isn't 'vague' or 'ambiguous', she doesn't say 'I'm from around then', she specifies a year, and not the easy option 'I'm from 1975' which would have been a conveniently rounded-up figure that would have brought the threat to history closer to home for the viewing audience. So we have to conclude that Sarah does indeed come from 1980.

**3.** *K9 & Company* is set in late December 1981, the year it was broadcast. K9 has been crated up waiting for Sarah since 1978. The format document for the proposed spin-off series stated that Sarah was born in '1949' and that 'she spent three years travelling in space and time (15.12.73–23.10.76)'. The story has to be considered canonical, as Sarah and K9 appeared together in *The Five Doctors*.

**4.** *Mawdryn Undead* states that the Brigadier retired in 1976, presumably after the thirteenth series. A host of references pin down the dating for *Mawdryn Undead* more precisely than just about any other story. There are two timezones, and these are unambiguously "1977" and "1983". The dating of this story splits fans: how can any serious chronology ignore such clear dating, yet how can such clear dating ignore the show's previous continuity? *DWM*'s 'UNIT Special' cleverly redated the story to 1981/1983, claiming that the royal occasion being celebrated was the marriage of the Prince and Princess of Wales. But this has the disadvantages that **(a)** it doesn't explain why everyone is running around in "1977–the Queen's Jubilee" T-shirts, and **(b)** it reduces the period Lethbridge-Stewart was a teacher by four years. A way to correct this would be to move the story to 1983/1989, keeping the six-year gap and the later timezone in 1983, and in effect budging everything up six years. However, this would interfere with the dating for *Planet of Fire* (which is definitely set in either 1984 or 1985), or else Turlough would return to his people while he is still exiled to Earth. So, the Brigadier retires in 1976.

**5.** *Battlefield* is set "a few years" in Ace's future – apparently in the mid-to-late 1990s. According to Ben Aaronovitch, the story's author, it takes place in '1997'. Whatever the case, it is established once again that the UNIT stories are "a few years" in the future.

As noted in the entries for the individual stories, there are a wealth of non-dialogue clues that might be used to pin down the dates. Here are a few of the more telling:

**1. Calendars:** *The Dæmons* apparently takes place in a year when 29 April is a Saturday, or perhaps a Sunday 1972 or 1978. Two calendars appear in *The Green Death*: one suggests that the story is set in February 1972, but the other says it is April of an unspecified year. *The Android Invasion* would seem to be set in a year when 6 July falls on a Friday (1973, 1979, 1984 or 1990).

**2. Historical and Political Details:** Here the evidence overwhelming suggests that either the political history of the early 1970s is very different to reality, or the UNIT stories aren't set in the early 1970s. The Prime Minister is called "Jeremy" in *The Green Death*, and is a woman by the time of *Terror of the Zygons*. The United Nations is more powerful than its seventies equivalent. The Cold War has been over for "years" before *Robot*. Two pieces of information perhaps suggest it is the early seventies: in *Doctor Who and the Silurians*, a taxi driver wants his fare paying in pre-decimal currency and Mao Tse Tung seems to be alive at the time of *The Mind of Evil* (he died in 1976).

**3. Fashions:** Except for *The Invasion* and *Battlefield*, the fashions and cars all resemble those of the year the programme was made. There was no attempt to mock-up car number plates or predict future fashions. The UNIT soldiers sport haircuts that would have been distinctly non-regulation in the 1970s, but this is just as true today. The UNIT era looks and feels like the 1970s.

**4. Technology:** On the other hand, the technology is far in advance of the 1970s. IE sells highly advanced computers and electronic components; UNIT carry very compact walkie talkies and have access to experimental laser guns in a couple of the later stories. Colour televisions and even colour videophones are commonplace. Man has landed on Mars; there are space freighters and advanced artificial intelligences. Comprehensive space and energy programmes are underway, and they are projections of then-current research (in *The Ambassadors of Death*, for example, we are told that preparation for space travel is a lot faster than the old days of the moonshots). This is the near future.

We might also want to refer to interviews with the production team, to find out what they intended.

Derrick Sherwin, the producer at the time the UNIT format was introduced, said in the *Radio Times* of 19 June 1969 that the seventh series would be set in 'a time not many years distant from now, when such things as space stations will be actuality'. In an interview with the *Daily Mail* two days later, Jon Pertwee stated that his Doctor would be exiled to Earth 'in the 1980s'. *The Making of Doctor Who*, written by Malcolm Hulke and Terrance Dicks, and published in 1972, placed *Spearhead from Space* in '1970'. *Doctor Who and the Sea-Devils*, also by Hulke, and published in 1974, said that 'North Sea oil had started gushing in 1977'. When asked in *DWB* Issue 58 why the dates for *Mawdryn Undead* contradicted what was established in the Pertwee era, Eric Saward, the script editor for the story admitted that the 1977/1983 dates were 'a mistake'.

The editors of the early New and Missing Adventures consciously chose to set the UNIT stories on or about the year they were broadcast. In practice, when a date is specified it is left pretty much to the discretion of an individual author, and there have been a number of discrepancies – see the entries for each story. In *No Future* (which unambiguously follows the *Mawdryn Undead* version of events, and is set in 1976), we learn that the Monk was tampering with time in the 1970s, which might have interfered with or confused the established UNIT timeline. *Who Killed Kennedy* establishes definite dates for the early UNIT stories.

There isn't a right answer. Even if we limit ourselves solely to dates specifically and unambiguously given in on-screen dialogue,

then the Brigadier retires three years before his first appearance as the commanding officer of UNIT. It is utterly impossible
to try to incorporate every calendar, E-reg car and videophone
into a consistent timeframe. However, none of the dates given
on-screen place the 'UNIT era' earlier than the late sixties or
later than the early eighties. Because of this, for the purposes of
this book, I prefer to keep the dates vague: all the UNIT stories
took place in 'the seventies', give or take a year or so. Whether
this means 1966–1973 as *The Discontinuity Guide* suggests, or
the late seventies/early eighties as the production team of the
Seventh series clearly intended, I leave to personal preference.

# Gallifrey — Notes on the Planet's Background [1]

The planet Gallifrey, world of the Time Lords in the constellation of Kasterborous, is one of the oldest and most powerful oligarchies in the universe. Its political and scientific influence is prevalent throughout the cosmos. But it is a world apart. Its power is substantially used for observation rather than involvement. Over the millennia, its self-imposed isolation has made it a staid and decaying society, obsessed with its own self-importance and tradition. It was not always so...

Ancient Gallifrey in The Old Time or The Dark Time, the Time of Chaos, was a world of both questing endeavour and dark superstition. It was the heart of a space-faring Empire, the hub of trade and commerce between other worlds. But the Gallifreyans were a race cursed with communal telepathy. The majority of the populous shared each others' minds and thoughts. No mind was alone. The superstitious people worshipped the Menti Celesti — literally, heavenly minds — who were the free-thinking Gods.

By training or natural ability, some Gallifreyans could achieve private thoughts: an individuality above the mass mind of the general populous. They became revered Heroes: great philosophers, scientists and explorers, much in the style of the Greek Heroes, renowned for their deeds and derring-do.

Ancient Gallifrey was governed by the line of Pythias, wise seer women, who saw the future. The Empire prospered under their rule, but for all its enlightened education and scientific advancement, their reign also encompassed barbarism.

Amongst the ideas and goods traded through the Empire, there were also slaves. A primitive Time Scoop was employed to import alien servants and gladiators for the Games enacted in the Death Zone. Such popular "entertainment" provided an outlet for the extremes of emotion that telepathic crowd behaviour could engender. Thus through a skilful mix of manipulation and superstition, the ruling Pythia was able to control Gallifrey and its

1 This is virtually the whole of the text of a document 'Gallifrey - Notes on the Planet's Background (from ideas prepared for the *Doctor Who* TV series)' by Andrew Cartmel, Ben Aaronovitch and Marc Platt. The document was written for Virgin, is dated 9.11.90, and comes to six and a half sides of A4 paper, including the coversheet. It outlines what fans have called 'The Cartmel Master Plan' – an attempt during the twenty-fifth and twenty-sixth series on television to redefine the origins of the Doctor and that of the planet Gallifrey, to reintroduce mystery to the series' basic set-up, and to suggest that much of what we had been told about the Time Lords and the Doctor had been deliberately fabricated (as such, it doesn't answer all the questions it raises). On-screen the 'Master Plan' was mainly confined to a handful of obscure references (and a handful more that were cut before broadcast).

The document embraces concepts from *The Deadly Assassin, Silver Nemesis, The Five Doctors, State of Decay, The Brain of Morbius, The Invasion of Time, Arc to Infinity, Trial of a Time Lord, Remembrance of the Daleks* (and Ben Aaronovitch's novelisation of his story), *The Three Doctors, Underworld, The Time Monster* and *Planet of the Spiders*, as well as two unmade Marc Platt stories, *Cat's Cradle* and *Lungbarrow*. A number of the New Adventures have adopted ideas from the document, including the first two novels by Platt and Aaronovitch, *Cat's Cradle: Time's Crucible* and *Transit*.

The last half-page of the document outlines the Doctor's link to his planet's ancient history and explains the origins of his granddaughter, Susan. It must remain a secret – for the moment at least. Anyone speculating about the contents of this last page ought to bear in mind that the Virgin Writers' Guide categorically states that 'The Other is not the Doctor'.

Empire.

Rassilon, a high ranking Hero, saw that the stifling authority of the Pythias threatened Gallifrey's true destiny as a supreme galactic power. He stood for the influence of Reason against the Pythian reign of superstition. His skills as a tactician had defeated an invasion of Vampires that threatened the whole galaxy. He knew that Gallifrey could not progress until the aimless telepathic abilities of the people were given purpose. With a group of supporters, he deposed the Pythia and set about the restructuring of all Gallifreyan society. This period of cultural renaissance became known as the Intuitive Revelation.

The followers of the Pythia fled to Karn and set up a quasireligious cult as guardians of a flame fountain that distilled an Elixir of eternal life.

Rassilon undertook to reform Gallifreyan society and thus consolidate the planet's supremacy. Aware of the corrupting influence of absolute power, he repeatedly rejected the offers of a coronation, announcing that he could not rule the planet alone.

The suicidal end of the line of the Pythias had one immediate and deadly effect on Gallifrey. The Pythia embodied the fertility of the planet, she was Gallifrey itself. As she took her own life, the last of the line cursed the planet in revenge for her overthrow. Gallifrey became a sterile world. There were no more children. Unborn babies died in their mothers' wombs. Rassilon was forced to find an immediate answer, before the Gallifreyans became extinct.

Eager to hold Gallifrey to ransom, the Sisterhood of Karn offered the salvation of their elixir. But in the face of disaster, Rassilon was able to forge a fresh solution.

From the existing hierarchy of Gallifrey, a new social design was evolved. Power was shared through a High Council whose members represented the Chapterhouses of Gallifrey. Each Chapter comprised groups of the ancient Families of Gallifrey, of whom Rassilon saw the need for legislative control to stabilise dwindling population numbers.

It was decreed that each Family would have a genetic bank known as a Loom, from which a set quota of Family members would be generated. Bio-genetic engineering would allow the

Gallifreyans to regenerate their bodies at the moment of death through a sequence of thirteen lives. At the end of the final life, when a Family member died, a new replacement member was generated on the Family Loom. Parents have not existed on Gallifrey since this time; all family members are Cousins to one another. (This makes the business of Susan being the Doctor's granddaughter all the more intriguing...)

The Looms were installed in all Family Houses across Gallifrey. Each House was adapted as bio-architecture, programmed to serve and look after its incumbent family. These were living buildings invested with a low degree of sentient awareness, even encompassed in their furniture and fittings.

Families were headed by the most senior Cousin. One other was selected as a Housekeeper, an interactive medium between the Cousins and the living House itself. The House would become as much a part of a Family as its Loom or its Cousins; occasionally with frighteningly possessive results!

The Chapters had their own Academies whose leaders were appointed as Cardinals to serve on the High Council in the newly constructed Vatican-like Capitol. The "Civil Service" members supporting the Council were known as Ordinals. Below them came the plebeian classes, trained as skilled technicians and artisans.

As a symbol of power, Rassilon had the Matrix developed: a vast extra-dimensional panotropic computer net containing all the information amassed by Gallifreyan culture. It stored all research and postulation, and the mind of every dying Gallifreyan passed into its capacity. Thus it could predict the future and give judgement on the past. As such, the Matrix is Gallifrey, the essence of that planet and its culture. In many ways, the Matrix replaced the Pythia, if not in wilful delegation, at least as a living repository of all knowledge.

To achieve his reforms, Rassilon needed vast resources of energy. He found an ally in Omega, the chief of the scientific fraternity and also a Cousin of Rassilon. But while Rassilon was the practical strategist laying foundations for a new society, and Omega was the provider, there was a third, darker figure; an "Eminence Grise", with whom power was shared in an inner sanctum before plans were laid for the judgement of the High Council.

His origins, birthplace, even appearance are an unrecorded mystery. He never served on the High Council. Some legends hint that he may not have been born on Gallifrey, others that he was endowed with powers far greater than either Rassilon or Omega, but he kept these veiled beneath the Gallifreyan shape he wore. How influential his role really was is uncertain. His presence as part of the Triumvirate has always been overshadowed by the myriad achievements of Rassilon and the martyrdom of Omega; he was known simply as "the Other." Nevertheless, a minor festival known as Otherstide is annually celebrated in his honour.

Under the rule of the Pythia, experiments had started into time travel. Rassilon deemed their use of telepathy as a travel source to be dangerous, but still rationalised their basic concepts for his own experiments.

To develop time travel as a completely viable facility, Omega estimated that a preliminary energy source equal to a supernova was required. He developed a remote stellar manipulator device which would induce the controlled detonation of a star and channel the energy released back to Gallifrey. This device was known as the "Hand of Omega".

The device succeeded in its task and Gallifrey acquired the energy source it needed, but Omega, who had gone to oversee the project himself, was lost in the supernova explosion. His sacrifice offered unlimited power to the Gallifreyans. They truly became Time Lords.

In their early days as Time Lords, the catastrophic destruction of the planet Minyos, whose inhabitants sought to emulate their "gods" the Gallifreyans, emphasised the need for radical change in Gallifrey's role in galactic politics.

After Omega's death, the remaining two-thirds of the Triumvirate set about consolidating Gallifrey's position. Two courses were open to the Time Lords: to control the universe as supreme rulers; or to act as guardians, overseeing the natural development of time and space. Either way their own position had to be unassailable. Gallifrey itself had to be protected.

In an astonishing feat of engineering, Rassilon entered the

black hole left by Omega's supernova and sealed its vast singularity energy in an icon of power known as the "Eye of Harmony". He brought the Eye back to Gallifrey and so balanced the existence of the planet against the colossal energy source of the black star. Gallifrey was now unassailable.

Ironically, the stabilising influence of the Eye of Harmony has surely affected Time Lord society as well. Over millennia, development has steadily ground slower and slower; Gallifreyan culture has become less adventurous, and more complacently staid. The people's telepathic abilities have also dwindled. Rassilon's legacy and laws still guide the Time Lords, but the meanings of many of his icons of power are now lost. (The line of Pythias also survives, not only on Karn, but in other offshoot manifestations – witness Lady Peinforte.)

Another product of the Intuitive Revelation was validium, a living metal, created as an ultimate defence for Gallifrey. The metal could think for itself, but in the wrong hands might act as a generator of destruction. It eventually proved itself too dangerous to be employed. Too many enemy forces were gaining access to the element and so the largest section was secreted away from Gallifrey in an asteroid where, it was hoped, it would be safe from interference

While both Rassilon and Omega were virtually canonised, if not deified, there were no further records of the Other in any of the histories. Speculation says that he left Gallifrey altogether; legend says that he grew weary of being an all-powerful player at the chess game of the universe. Instead he longed to be a pawn on the board in the thick of the action. Common sense says that he retired quietly.

# THE SANDS OF TIME
## Justin Richards

As part of this month's celebrations, the Missing Adventure is a sequel to the classic television story *The Pyramids of Mars*.

Arriving in Victorian London, the fifth Doctor, Nyssa and Tegan run straight into trouble: Nyssa is kidnapped in the British Museum by Egyptian religious fanatics; the Doctor and Tegan are greeted by a stranger who knows more about them than he should and invited to a very strange party.

Why are rooms already booked for the Doctor at the Savoy? How can Lord Kenilworth's butler Atkins be in Egypt and London at the same time? What is the history of the ancient mummy to be unwrapped at Kenilworth's house? And what has all this got to do with Nyssa?

The Doctor's quest for answers leads him across continents and time as an ancient Egyptian prophecy threatens 1990s England. While the Doctor attempts to unravel the plans of the mysterious Sadan Rassul, mummies stalk the night and the sands of time begin to slip through his fingers.

ISBN 0 426 20472 7
£4.99

# The 50th New Adventure
## and
# The Wedding of the
# Twenty-First Century

*Virgin*

### Publishing

cordially invites you to the wedding

of

## Mr. Jason Kane

and

## Professor Bernice Summerfield

in the village of Cheldon Bonniface in the year 2010

---

*This month sees the publication of the 50th New Adventure,* Happy Endings *by Paul Cornell.*

*The book features a number of celebratory innovations:*
- *A new cover design for New Adventures*
- *A specially commissioned painting of the bride, groom and guests, made available to the public in the form of a poster*
- *A chapter written by 25 authors of previous New Adventures*
- *A complicated story featuring an old enemy and many old friends*
- *A wedding song (with sheet music)*
- *Many merry quips and some dreadful puns*

*Guests have been invited from all over the past and future of the galaxy – don't miss the wedding of the twenty-first century.*